American Cinematographers in the Great War, 1914–1918

To Kevin Brownlow: as film historians we all stand on his shoulders.

American Cinematographers in the Great War, 1914–1918

James W. Castellan
Ron van Dopperen
Cooper C. Graham

British Library Cataloguing in Publication Data

American Cinematographers in the Great War, 1914–1918

A catalogue entry for this book is available from the British Library

ISBN: 9780 86196 717 9 (Paperback)

Front Cover: Newsreel cameraman Nelson E. Edwards with German army chaplain. Western front, 1916. [Courtesy Wiegman family.]

Published by
John Libbey Publishing Ltd, 3 Leicester Road, New Barnet, Herts EN5 5EW, United Kingdom
e-mail: john.libbey@orange.fr; web site: www.johnlibbey.com

Direct orders: **Marston Book Services Ltd:** direct.orders@marston.co.uk

Distributed in Asia and North America by **Indiana University Press**, Herman B Wells Library – 350, 1320 E. 10th St., Bloomington, IN 47405, USA. www.iupress.indiana.edu

Printed and bound in China by 1010 Printing International Ltd.

Contents

List of Abbreviations

AA	Auswärtige Amt (German Foreign Office)
AAPA	Auswärtige Amt Politisches Archiv (German Foreign Office Political Archive)
ACC	American Cinema Corporation
A.C. Film Company	American Correspondent Film Company
CPI	Committee on Public Information
DDM	Durborough Draft Manuscript
INS	International News Service
KPQ	kaiserliche und königliche Pressequartier (Austro-Hungarian Military Press Headquarters), also known as k.u.k. Kriegspressequartier
NAMPI	National Association of Motion Picture Industry
NARA	National Archives and Records Administration
NEA	Newspaper Enterprise Association
OHL	Oberste Heeresleitung (German Military High Command)
WHD	Wilbur Henry Durborough
ZfA	Zentralstelle für Auslandsdienst (German Foreign Propaganda Agency)

The Authors

COOPER C. GRAHAM is retired from the Library of Congress where he was a curator in the Motion Picture, Broadcasting and Recorded Sound Division. He is the author of numerous articles, as well as *Leni Riefenstahl's "Olympia"* and (in collaboration) *D.W. Griffith and the Biograph Company*.
Email: c.graham2@att.net

RON VAN DOPPEREN studied history at the University of Utrecht, Holland, where he wrote his Master of Arts Thesis on the American World War I documentary films (1988). He now works as a communication advisor for the Dutch government.
Email: rjvan@telfort.nl

JAMES W. CASTELLAN is an independent scholar researching a biography of Oswald F. Schuette and articles about some historically significant individuals with whom Schuette associated including photojournalist and cinematographer Wilbur H. Durborough. Castellan, a graduate of Brown University with an M.S. from the University of Pennsylvania, retired from the pharmaceutical industry in 2001.
Email: james.castellan@gmail.com

For more information, visit the authors' weblog on
http://www.shootingthegreatwar.blogspot.nl

Chapter 1

Over There

This book is a book on film. However, it starts as primarily a newspaper story. There are several reasons. In 1914 newsreels were still very young. While some major studios such as Pathé and Universal were already in the newsreel business, newspapers were entering into an intense period of competition and were seeking new ways to improve profits. It was a cutthroat war between vigorous and expanding entities, imitating what was happening among nations overseas. So there was a rush to send the journalists to the war. As the appeal of newsreels became ever more apparent to the newspapers, there was also a great need for cinematographers, who in many cases had been press photographers until very recently. It is a credit to them how quickly they adapted to lugging and working with 150 pounds of cumbersome film equipment after having worked for years with a Kodak or Graflex.

Since many of them were newspaper people, it was very difficult in many cases to distinguish much difference between the journalists and the cameramen, although there may have been a type of caste system giving deference to the writers. Once overseas they suffered the same problems and shared the same successes. They were in bed together, literally. In October 1914 in Antwerp as it was being shelled by the Germans, Edwin F. Weigle, cinematographer for the *Chicago Tribune*, Donald C. Thompson, photographer for the *New York World*, Arthur Ruhl of *Colliers* and Edward Eyre Hunt, who wrote *War Bread*, were cowering under the same roof at 74 rue du Péage. Later Horace Green wrote about the same shelling, and James H. Hare, another famous war photographer, photographed the battered facade of the building, American flag still flying, for *Leslie's Weekly*. It was a new kind of war, and the journalists and photographers were in it together.

There was another aspect about the newspapers' evolving relationship with the cinematographers. At least since the Civil War, the Americans had learned that having an accredited war correspondent at the scene of battles was a terrific way to sell newspapers. Perhaps the epitome of the war correspondent in America was Richard Harding Davis, whose dispatches from Cuba during the Spanish-American War had electrified the public and sold millions of newspapers for Hearst, *Scribners* and the *New York World*. Everyone wanted to emulate Davis so most newspapers called their reporters in Germany correspondents, and most at least simulated possessing expert knowledge of the country, military matters and so on, as well as having special

1

Fig. 1. Albert Dawson on the eastern front, winter 1915–1916. World War I gave birth to a new type of war journalist, the camera correspondent. [Reproduced from Motography, *8 April 1916.]*

relationships with government leaders and military experts. This became the model for cinematographers, who were then called film correspondents. David Mould and Gerry Veeder called them "photographer-adventurers" but it is really the same idea.[1] They therefore made their films in a certain way: instead of just pointing a camera at the scene and shooting, as a newsreel cameraman would do, they would generally have an assistant, who was the real working cameraman, while they were in the picture themselves, interviewing a general or a statesman, or in some cases, in the actual battle. Some cameramen did this more than others. Two cinematographers who were very much in their own films were Albert K. Dawson and Wilbur H. Durborough. Perhaps it was significant that they both wrote extensively about their film adventures, true correspondents in the literary sense. Both Dawson and Durborough had assistant cameramen who actually shot their films. Other cameramen were not comfortable in this role; and Edwin F. Weigle and Nelson Edwards were not in their own films much. Nevertheless Weigle and Edwards were publicized by their papers as newspaper cameramen, with extensive articles about them in the *Chicago Tribune* and Hearst papers respectively.

In the period after World War I had been declared in 1914 and before America entered it almost three years later, there was a complex struggle among the combatants to influence public opinion in America. Some of this struggle was carried on by the combatants themselves through well-funded propaganda committees, foreign offices and other government agencies. Other parties involved, such as owners of newspapers and film companies, were influenced by a combination of ambition, ideology, patriotism and not least, greed.

When World War I started, while many of the powers involved believed they were prepared, they were wrong. None of them envisioned a long war; all expected the conflict to be over in six months. So there had been very little thought about propaganda, as correspondent William G. Shepherd pointed out:

> The great machinery of that cyclonic blast that hit the civilized world of 1914 left newspaper correspondents entirely out of its operations. It ignored them, and therefore had no way of dealing with them. We puzzled the generals. The rules said no newspaper correspondents allowed. But there were always American newspaper correspondents around somewhere.[2]

And there had been even less thought about motion pictures. Even if there had been some comprehensive plan trying to reconcile the needs of the military and necessity for public relations, there would have been major problems. In most countries there was a division between the military, who felt that the war was their business, and the civilian governments, who for better or worse, had to concern themselves with civilian morale and public opinion abroad.

Germany

Most of this book will deal with the Central Powers. This is not because the authors are pro-German, but because of all the warring nations, Germany allowed correspondents a certain leeway, especially when things were going well on the battlefield and less well on the propaganda front.

Nevertheless Germany was a prime example of this rift between the military and the civil government. Although it is usually considered an authoritarian nation, Wilhelmine Germany suffered from deep conflict between the armed forces and the government. This was exacerbated by the deep fear of the conservative government and the army toward the Social Democratic party. It has been suggested that the war was a welcome way out of the upcoming elections which it was presumed would have resulted in a big win by the Social Democrats. But the declaration of war did not result in any serious thought about propaganda. And if there had been, the same rift between the liberals, social democrats and the nationalists would have resulted in the same stalemate.

Fig. 2. Baron Mumm von Schwarzenstein, head of the German foreign propaganda agency (Zentralstelle für Auslandsdienst). [Courtesy Library of Congress.]

At the outbreak of the war in Germany, propaganda matters for neutral countries abroad were a complete muddle. Matthias Erzberger, the prominent politician and specialist in propaganda who was well connected to the Reich Chancellor Bethmann-Hollweg, counted at least 27 different bureaus or departments inside the *Reich* involved with propaganda in foreign countries, none of whom had any idea of what the others were doing.

Erzberger was a prominent politician of the Center Catholic parties. This was an advantage for him because he was not particularly affiliated either to the right wing nationalist parties nor the Social Democrats or Communists on the left. His affiliations with the Catholics also helped him forge a good relationship with the Vatican. Later he unsuccessfully tried to keep Italy from entering the war. He was an opponent of unrestricted submarine warfare and by 1917 was a voice in trying to end the war. After the war, Erzberger was assassinated by nationalists in Germany for negotiating and signing the armistice with the Entente.

To deal with the propaganda problem, Erzberger had established the *Zentralstelle für Auslandsdienst* (ZfA) in October 1914. It was a very loose organization and was bound to have problems since it included conflicting representatives from the Reich Naval Section, the Army General Staff, the Auswärtiges Amt, (Foreign Office, hereafter called the AA) as well as Erzberger's organizations.

Baron Mumm von Schwarzenstein (AKA Freiherr von Mumm), who handled propaganda matters for the AA, was the nominal head of the ZfA for its first two years. Although it was originally established only to deal with printed matter abroad, soon it also was funding propaganda films. The ZfA might have had the advantage of keeping the mutually hostile lions in one cage, but relations were bound to be tense. On the one hand, the AA, which was trying to placate German ambassadors like Count Graf von Bernstorff, Ambassador to the United States, to maintain good relations with neutrals abroad and also looking favorably on pro- German enterprises like that of Hearst who wanted to produce friendly propaganda, were almost forced to cooperate with the foreign press and neutral governments. On the other hand the Army, typical of most armies, made no bones about finding the foreign press, professional war correspondents and other observers in general nuisances at best and at worst probably spies. In answer to a telegram of 8 August 1914 asking the official position of the government with regard to the flood of requests from American journalists who wanted to come to Germany, Gottlieb von Jagow, the Secretary of Foreign Affairs, replied bluntly, "General Staff refuses in principle the entry of foreign journalists".[3] With a few exceptions forced upon it, this remained the General Staff position throughout the war. The army also ran censorship in general, including that of film, through its *Reichspresseamt*, part of Department IIIb, and had virtually unlimited powers to impede or stop any propaganda enterprise that it did not like.

In addition, the army, conservative to the core, was fundamentally hostile to film and photography in general, and felt that the only suitable method to communicate information to the public was through print. The Army High Command (*Oberste Heeresleitung*) issued the following directive, on 6 October 1914, entitled 'Conditions for the Permission of Photography at the Front'. The Germans allowed only the following firms or their representatives:

> The firms should be purely German and under patriotic-minded German leadership, have ample capital and work with German funds.
>
> (1) Only German film cameras, German products and German film material may be used.
>
> (2) The firms themselves not only are recognized in this regard as responsible for themselves, but also for representatives at their disposal sent to the theatres of operations.
>
> (3) The photography at the theatres of operations and in the areas occupied by German troops is permitted only with the approval of the General Staff of the Army.[4]

In addition, even after the army released the films, they would have to undergo a further police censorship. For instance, it was even forbidden to photograph the streets of Berlin without permission from the Berlin police. Since it devolved on the General Staff to arrange trips to the front, grant interviews and so forth, the General Staff could cause problems simply by doing nothing. This would cause real problems for most journalists, and even more so for the cinematographers since they were held in contempt by the military. Truly, as Edward Lyell Fox said, "… photographers in warring Germany can have nothing but easy consciences; they see so little".[5]

A member of the ZfA was Major Erhard Eduard Deutelmoser. In 1912, Deutelmoser was made Press Officer and head of the Press Section in the Prussian Ministry of War, which had been founded in the wake of the Balkan War of 1912. After the outbreak of World War I, he was put in charge of press policy and censorship in the previously-mentioned *Reichpresseamt*, which was one of the sections in Department IIIB of the General Staff. However, in October 1915, Deutelmoser was made head of the War Press Section, which meant that he no longer dealt with the AA. Major (later Lieutenant Colonel) Karl Brose had been head of Department IIIb from 1900–1910 and was temporarily retired, but when war broke out, he was placed in charge of Department IIIb, partly to beef up the department. He was a significant choice because Brose had not worked primarily in the press section; he was trained for military intelligence.

Section IIIb had four major tasks: overall supervision of all press releases regarding the war effort; transmission of all press releases; military intelligence, and military counter-intelligence.[6] It seems quite clear that Section IIIb would not consider the free and open transfer of information to neutrals as its major concern or even a minor one.[7] Mumm von Schwarzenstein wrote:

> And where a question of a trip to the front is concerned, there is a standing war between us [AA] and the Representatives of the General Staff. Their press section is accommodating enough but Counterintelligence (Colonel Brose!) and the tactical section mostly defy all our efforts. For all that, this part of our operation is quite well incorporated, and I am only sorry that Major Deutelmoser, who has always had understanding for our wishes, is now giving up this part of the work so that it will then come under the General Staff, under the direct leadership of the completely blind Colonel Brose … .[8]

This resulted in many journalists and cinematographers sitting in Berlin waiting for clearance from the authorities so that they could get their stories.

Aside from all this, even if the cinematographer was accredited by the Army, there were still the major problems of shooting at the front. An Austrian cinematographer reported in the *Wiener Abendzeitung* that after getting all credentials deemed necessary, he got to the front and began to film. He was almost immediately arrested, and was told at staff headquarters that the enemy had spotted his lens and thought it was an observation telescope and directed all fire on that spot. So getting shots at the front was not really possible, and the film people limited themselves to shots of engineers, field bakeries, airfields and so forth.[9]

There were of course Americans on the scene.

One of the most prominent was Lewis Hart Marks. He was born in New Orleans on 14 July 1883. His father Ferdinand Marks was born in Germany and naturalized in Louisiana on 16 May 1867. Marks' father worked in the insurance business and apparently did quite well in the new world. Lewis studied medicine at Tulane and graduated in 1906, and then worked as a post-graduate at Johns Hopkins and Harvard University. Around 1907 he traveled to Frankfurt am Main where he became an assistant to the famous Dr. Paul Ehrlich, who discovered salvarsan, the cure for syphilis, in 1909. How good a research chemist Dr. Marks was is unclear with some commenting that his work was marginal and others that he was quite a good chemist and researcher. He has quite a few medical articles to his credit, especially between 1900 and 1910. In addition to his work at Dr. Ehrlich's clinic, he was also being paid by the German army for work on vaccines. Some of Marks' financing came from the United States. According to a Bureau of Investigation report a very prominent group of German-American Jews, including Congressman Herman A. Metz, whom we will encounter again, Albert Lorsch, Virginia L. Stern, Benjamin Stern, Ernest Thalmann and Adolph Lewisohn were each to pay $10,000 a year to Marks to support his research. In addition, Benjamin Guggenheim who died on the *Titanic*, included among his numerous bequests one for $125,000.00 to Marks. In Frankfurt am Main Marks also performed research for the Mulford Chemical Company that produced serums and other medicinals back in the States.

The war ended Marks' research work when the German Army took over his

Fig. 3. Dr. Lewis H. Marks: research chemist, business man and secret agent for the German government. This portrait was taken in the 1930s. [Courtesy Chemical Heritage Foundation.]

building for anti-aircraft purposes and he moved to Berlin where he took up residence at the Adlon Hotel. By now Marks was an authorized Mulford Chemical Company commercial agent for Germany and Austria while still in the pay of the German War Ministry. This arrangement appears to have benefited both parties because there is a statement by the Mulford Company that Marks was paid over $53,000 for the sale of tetanus, antidysenteric and antimeningitis serums to the German government, probably for their army. Marks' U. S. passport application issued 13 February 1916 also mentions trips to Holland, Romania and Scandinavia noting his occupation as commercial advisor which suggests that he was trying to peddle these various serums in these countries as well but sold none based on the statement's silence.[10]

Back at the Adlon Hotel he became familiar with the American contingent of correspondents, offering them advice and lending small sums of money, putting them in contact with Germans who could be of service in getting them to the front and securing interviews with government officials, work that appears to have been undertaken for continued support by the German War Ministry. Another interesting item in Marks' file is an AA letter to the Polizeipräsident of 13 December 1914 cited in full below from Freiherr von Mumm that mentions Marks was also a member of a propaganda committee in Frankfurt am Main. Marks' services to the German

7

government may have extended far beyond serving on propaganda committees and reporting on the activities of journalists. In the files of the AA there is a memorandum dated 6 June 1915 from Arthur Zimmerman, then German Undersecretary of State for Foreign Affairs, but who was already acting as Secretary of State for his chief Gottlieb von Jagow. Zimmermann was later notorious for the Zimmermann telegram, which was so instrumental in finally deciding America to enter the war on the Entente side, as well as his attempts to foment revolts both in Ireland and India. The memorandum on AA stationery informed all concerned that Lewis Marks was taking a trip abroad from 18 to 28 June 1915 in the service of German interests, and that all military and civil authorities should give him all assistance.

Why he was an agent working with American journalists is not clear. His ancestry was German, and like many German-American Jews, he was probably inclined to be pro-German, at least partly because of the Jewish dislike of Tsarist Russia and its anti-Semitism. He also may have desperately needed a more reliable source of income to support his high lifestyle once he lost his past research income and made no future serum sales. As we shall see, he will associate with most of the figures mentioned here, not least the man below.

Ambassador James W. Gerard

Ambassador James W. Gerard, like everyone else in this tale, is a colorful figure. He was born in 1867, graduated from Columbia University, was chairman of the Democratic campaign committee of New York County, served in the Spanish American War, appointed justice of the New York Supreme Court in 1908 and appointed ambassador to Germany in 1913. He was certainly pro-British, receiving a medal from King George V after America entered the war. He has been described as a Tammany hack, appointed ambassador to pay off some of President Wilson's political debts as well as a courageous statesman with a terribly difficult job in Berlin. Wilson did not much like him. Be that as it may, he apparently did an effective job in repatriating American citizens stranded in Germany after the outbreak of the war and was a highly effective voice in describing what he felt to be substandard conditions in German POW camps.

He apparently loathed the Germans. In a speech that he gave to the Ladies Aid Society on 25 November 1917:

> We must disappoint the Germans who have always believed that the German-Americans here would risk their property, their children's future and their own neck, and take up arms for the Kaiser. The foreign Minister of Germany once said to me 'your country does not dare do anything against Germany, because we have in your country 500,000 German reservists who will rise in arms against your government if you dare to make a move against Germany'.

> Well, I told him that might be so, but that we had 500,001 lamp posts in this country, and that was where the reservists would be hanging the day after they tried to rise. And if there are any German-Americans here who are so ungrateful for all the benefits they have received that they are still for the Kaiser, there is only one thing to do with them. And that is to hog-tie

Fig. 4. American Ambassador Gerard in his office in Berlin, photographed by Albert K. Dawson around April 1915. [Courtesy Library of Congress.]

them, give them back the wooden shoes and the rags they landed in, and ship them back to the fatherland.

… there is no animal that bites and kicks and squeals and scratches, that would bite and squeal and scratch equal to a fat German-American, if you commenced to tie him up and told him that he was on his way back to the Kaiser.[11]

It is a remarkable speech. Granted that it was made after America entered the war and feelings were running high; it was bound to offend a large number of German-Americans whether they were pro-Entente or not. And if Gerard did make the remark about lampposts to Bethmann-Hollweg, Foreign Minister of Germany, it was bound to make his career in Germany far more difficult.

One of Gerard's major problems was with the American correspondents in Berlin. If the German Foreign Office was the correspondents' Scylla, the Ambassador was their Charybdis.

Gerard felt that most of the correspondents in Berlin were pro-German, and he was outspoken about it. Banes of his existence were Oswald F. Schuette and Raymond Gram Swing:

Referring to report of September 24, 1915, made by Agent B. D. Adait of the Chicago office, I this day proceeded to the Ritz Carlton Hotel [New York] where I held a lengthy interview with former Ambassador James G. Gerard. Mr. Gerard stated that there is no question regarding the violent pro-Germanism as shown by Schutte while representing the Chicago

Daily News in Germany; that it [is] still possible that Schutte still favors the enemy; that while at Berlin he was a close friend of one Swing, a fellow newspaper man and a young all around worthless character.[12]

Gerard also identified Walter Niebuhr, whom Durborough had photographed along with the other correspondents and was now employed by the Committee on Public Information, as pro-German. It is not surprising that after Schuette returned to Washington, DC, in July 1918 he wrote H. L. Mencken that his letter to Schuette had been opened by the War Department revealing his mail was still being watched.[13]

There was an encounter between the correspondents and Gerard in Berlin. The American journalists covering the Central Powers had been furious because their dispatches bound for the United States would reach London and then be cut to shreds by the British censors or never be sent on at all. It reached a point where *The Daily News* filed a story that was sent via Nauen to Saybrook, Long Island, by radio and thus never passed through British censors at all:

BLAME BRITISH CENSORS

Newspaper Men with German Army Say News Is Suppressed

Ask Gerard to Obtain Relief – Restrictions Are Tighter

BY RAYMOND E. SWING

American newspaper correspondents in Berlin have united in the following declaration:

"We, the undersigned American citizens, representing American newspapers in Berlin and with the armies of the central powers, finding that many of our dispatches concerning both political and military events are suppressed, mutilated or delayed by the London censors, call the attention of American publishers to this situation. We emphasize that in these circumstances we are unable to present to the American public a vital half of a true and fair statement of the most important events of the war."

British Have Changed Policy

"The London censorship, which for a time treated our dispatches in a spirit of fair play, has gradually changed its policy until to-day its restrictions from an American standpoint are impossible. We have asked Ambassador Gerard to inquire if the American government can secure to the American press the facilities for getting legitimate cable news unhampered by the handicap of the British censorship."

Signed by *The Daily News* Men

The declaration is signed by Ackermann of the United Press, Bennett of the Chicago Tribune, Brown of the New York Times, Conger of The Associated Press, Enderis of the International News Service, Hale of the New York American, Oswald F. Schuette and Raymond E. Swing of The Chicago Daily News and Wiegand of the New York World.

[Recently Mr. Schuette, while with the German armies in France, filed three dispatches for *The Daily News*, a total of over 3,000 words. One badly mutilated dispatch of about 600 words was all that was permitted to pass by the British censor.][14]

Gerard had done nothing about censorship over the past year since the day Schuette had helped organize the correspondents and filed this early censorship dispatch:

The Chicago Daily News/ September 6, 1915

Wireless from Berlin, September 6 (via Sayville)

WIRELESS CENSORSHIP ROILS

Germans Resent U. S. Ban on Messages of Railroad Stockholders

American censorship of wireless dispatches interfered seriously with the efforts of German stockholders to be represented properly at the reorganization of the Wabash and Missouri Pacific systems, according to complaints made by leading German bankers with American connections. They say that dispatches with reference to those reorganizations were turned back by the United States naval censor at Sayville, L. I., apparently because of the fear that the messages contained military advices in violation of American neutrality.

There is considerable resentment here because of the fact that the American government exercises censorship over German wireless messages and none over the English cable service.[15]

The correspondents asked Gerard to protest to London. The pro-British Gerard stalled, then agreed to send their protest but said he would not endorse it. In fact, he sent it but said he disagreed with it, which was not part of the deal since he had said he would forward their protest with no comment at all. There was a huge altercation in Ambassador Gerard's office in which Oswald F. Schuette, reporter for the *Chicago Daily News*, said that Gerard had violated their agreement, and Swing said that he was not frightened by any ambassador, adding, sotto voce, even if the ambassador was in the habit of taking up the passports of Americans who did not kowtow to him. Gerard then accused all the correspondents present of being German agents, and in the pay of the German government. (Of course, in the case of William Bayard Hale, Gerard was right.) The reporters went public with their accusations. Gerard agreed to some sort of retraction, but evidently he was still angry about Schuette's pro-Germanism.

In response to Gerard's perfidy, Schuette worked to organize the American correspondents in Berlin to address important common issues such as this British censorship matter as well as for fellowship. As a very young journalist, Schuette found great benefit, both professional and social, in being active in the local press club and retained life membership in the three clubs where he worked for various newspapers: Chicago, Milwaukee and the National Press Club in Washington, DC. He had served as a club officer at a very young age in Milwaukee and in 1913 had been appointed President by the National Press Club board on which he was serving to fill a vacancy due to a resignation.

Marks learned of this effort and offered to provide the refreshments, assuring his welcomed presence and immediate access to developments and intelligence that would be of great interest to his German contacts.

Memorandum of the first meeting of the A. C. A.

The American Correspondents Association (A. C. A.) was founded Sept. 6, 1915 at an evening meeting at the Hotel Adlon Berlin, with Dr. Marks as host.

Of some possible 18 members of such an association as was organized an hour later, the following eleven gentlemen were present and contributed their views to the discussion of plans:

Messrs: [Carl W.] Ackerman, [James O'Donnell] Bennett, [Cyril] Brown, [Harry] Carr, [Wilbur H.] Durborough, [Edward Lyell] Fox, Jacobs, [Walter] Niebuhr, [?] Powers, [Oswald

Fig. 5. The Adlon Hotel lobby, circa 1914. Described by the New York Times as the "undoubted news center of the German Empire", the Adlon was the place to be in Berlin for most American war correspondents.

F.] Schuette, [Karl H.] von Wiegand. [Jacobs was probably the correspondent for the *Brooklyn Eagle*.]

The company was called to order at 10 o'clock by Mr. Oswald Schuette, Chicago Daily News, who informally outlined the purposes of the meeting and the possible benefits to be derived from the organization of American correspondents resident in Berlin. This outline met with favor and there was informal discussion by all present. The best of feeling characterized these preliminaries and this was precisely the spirit which the project of an association was intended to foster.

It having been spontaneously agreed that the founding of an association was desirable both for reasons of professional efficiency and of fellowship, a vote was called and it was unanimous to that effect. The name "American Correspondents Association" was then unanimously adopted.

The Association proceeded to the election of officers. For President Mr. Conger, who was absent, was proposed by Mr. Bennett, Mr. Schuette by Mr. von Wiegand and Mr. Bennett by Mr. Powers. Mr. Conger received 6 votes, Mr. Schuette 3 and Mr. Bennett 2. Mr. Fox was teller. Mr. Conger's election was promptly made unanimous.

Other officers were elected as follows:

Vice-president: Mr. von Wiegand; second vice-president Mr. Bennett [;] secretary: Mr. Schuette[;] Treasurer: Mr. Ackerman; Chairman Board of Directors, Dr. Jacobs.

In the absence of President Conger, Vice-president von Wiegand took the chair.

The matter [of] censorship, of relations with the imperial government, and of receiving

American correspondents temporarily stopping in Berlin was discussed at length but no measures were settled upon.

As a slight recognition of his untiring and kindly service to the American correspondents assigned to Berlin, Dr. Marks was made the first honorary member of the A. C. A.

It was urged that every effort be made to insure at the next meeting the presence of Messrs. Albrecht, Bouton, Dreher, Schweppendick, Spanith, and Swing who had been unable to attend the organization meeting.

Vice[-]president von Wiegand appointed the following committee on organization, with instructions to report at a meeting of the association called for Thursday evening, Sept. 9 at the Adlon – Messrs. Schuette, Jacobs and Bennett.

After further informal discussion and the signing of their names by the eleven charter members, the meeting adjourned at midnight.[16]

The Adlon

One of the major landmarks in World War I, the Hotel Adlon, was an oasis and home away from home to foreigners in Berlin and certainly to the Americans. It certainly deserves a section of its own.

The Hotel Adlon was opened in 1907 by Lorenz Adlon. Right next to the Branden-burg Gate on the *Unter den Linden*, it quickly became a center for Berlin culture and night life. The Kaiser was fond of the hotel, stayed there often, and often recom-mended it to his royal guests instead of staying in one of his drafty palaces. Many of the journalists stayed there including Cyril Brown of the *New York Times*, Philip M. Powers of the Associated Press, Karl H. Wiegand of the *New York World*, Walter Niebuhr of *Harpers Weekly* and the United Press.[17] Among the cinematographers was Wilbur F. Durborough, Edwin F. Weigle, Irving Guy Ries and Nelson Edwards. H. L. Mencken, who visited the hotel somewhat later in 1917, thought that most of the American correspondents who frequented the Adlon were an indifferent lot, and Mencken, as was his custom, described them frankly, if not brutally:

> They were, in the main, an indifferent lot, and I was somewhat upset by my first contact with the unhappy fact that American newspapers are sometimes represented abroad by men who would hardly qualify as competent police reporters at home. Of those that I recall, the best was James O'Donnell Bennett, of the *Chicago Tribune*. He held himself aloof from the rest, and seldom joined in their continuous boozing in the bar of the Adlon Hotel. Others were Oswald F. Schütte, of the *Chicago Daily News*; Raymond Swing, who was also with *the Daily News*; William Bayard Hale, who represented Hearst; Seymour Conger, head of the Associated Press Bureau; Carl W. Ackerman, head of the United Press Bureau; Guido Enderes [Enderis] and Philip Powers, both of the Associated Press; Oscar King Davis, and Cyril Brown, both of the *New York Times*. There were yet others, but I forget them.[18]

Mencken was also right in saying that Bennett was head and shoulders better than the other correspondents. His coverage of the First World War is so good that it is a pity it has not been collected in book form, probably because Bennett was pro-Ger-man and, as George Orwell said, history is written by the winners.

Hayden Talbot described the Americans at the Adlon in late 1915, but he wrote the story from the point of view of an anonymous reporter confiding his story to Talbot, probably to avoid libel laws:

> When he [the anonymous reporter confiding to Talbot] landed in Berlin, he found the American correspondents at the Adlon Hotel were a law unto themselves. As intense as is the German dislike of all speakers of English, this favored little group of a dozen flamboyantly American newspaper men ruled the roost – so far as Berlin's principle hostelry is concerned. For these 'boys' Herr Adlon himself is willing, eager, to break any rule. 'Verboten' and the 'boys' are strangers – at the Adlon. Do three or four of them come in in the wee sma' hours of the morning – still unsatisfied as regards thirst – Herr Adlon's orders permit a discreet porter to find a bottle from some mysterious corner.

> So much for the purely social, personal side of life as it is lived by the American newspaper men in Berlin. My friend tells me on occasions the bartender at the Adlon has gone so far as to produce a large American flag on a standard and place it in a prominent place when the 'boys' congregate there for afternoon cocktails.

> The fact that the bartender and most of the servants are in the employ of the Secret Service – that every night a carefully written record is made by these servants of all conversations in English they have overheard – does not seem to dim the joy of living in Berlin, insofar as the newspaper men are concerned.[19]

Because of the difficulty in getting out of Berlin, the correspondents were to spend much time at the Adlon. Even the ones who did not stay there put in their time in the Adlon bar, the great meeting place for gossip and intrigue. And for the first part of the war, there they stayed, waiting for hell to freeze over.

Britain

Like the Germans, the British took the position during the war that the military was going to run it and civilians were to keep out. Unlike the Germans, there were no attempts – and no need – to find neutral journalists to listen to their side of the story. There would be a total ban on correspondents at the fronts, either journalists or photographers, unless they had been approved by the War Office. And there would be no foreigners. This essentially meant that the British took somewhat the same attitude as the Germans when it came to the kind of British they wanted to cover the war. They wanted only correspondents from conservative newspapers who had gained a reputation as sound, good chaps who could be called upon to play the game the way the British military wanted the war reported. And as Phillip Knightley pointed out they would be placed in particular units, very much as the Americans would do with correspondents in the Gulf War.[20]

The official attitude to war correspondents at the time was neatly summarized by Kitchener's casual remark, "Out of my way, you drunken swabs".[21] This is rather surprising since of all nations, the British had a fine and honorable tradition of war correspondents. William Russell of the *Times* covered the Crimean War brilliantly. Russell also covered the Confederate side of the American Civil War for the *Times* in great detail, while Frank Vizetelly, the *London Illustrated's* best artist and war correspondent provided superb illustrations.[22] Winston Churchill himself covered the war in the Sudan as a sub-altern and also as a war correspondent, writing two books in the process, and also a third on the Boer War.[23]

Perhaps this is the trouble. Russell's coverage of the Crimean War showed that the military was incompetent and riddled with nepotism. He also made a heroine of Florence Nightingale, but mostly by exposing the deplorable conditions in the military hospitals. Lord Ragland accused Russell of being a traitor, mostly because of Russell's reports, and his exposure of the generals' incompetence caused Lord Aberdeen's government to topple.[24] Kitchener had hated correspondents since the Su-

Fig. 6. The British feelings on war correspondents can best be described by quoting Field Marshall Kitchener's famous dictum: "Out of my way, you drunken swabs".

dan. The British also had been badly burned in the Boer War, again being accused by the press of incompetence and then also accused of barbarity against the Boers. The British knew that war correspondents could be dangerous, not so much because they might betray military secrets to the enemy, but because they exposed the ineptness of the military. The military might reply, perhaps with some accuracy, that displaying the deficiencies of the armed forces is doing as great a service to the enemy as publishing the details of a new model artillery weapon. On the other hand, if there are faults, they need to be pointed out, not only to the general public, but to the armed forces themselves as well.

Some British who should have known better cursed the correspondents. While the American correspondent E. Alexander Powell was in Antwerp before its fall in October of 1914, Winston Churchill arrived in the city with an *ad hoc* group of marines and naval reservists that he had picked up in his capacity as First Sea Lord, to "save the city" against the oncoming Germans. It was a silly and unauthorized thing to do, and far outside his responsibilities. One day, Churchill was lunching with Sir Francis Villiers and the Staff of the British Legation at the Hotel Saint Antoine. Powell heard two British correspondents approach Churchill's table and ask for an interview.

"I will not talk to you", he almost shouted, bringing his fist down upon the table. "You have no business to be in Belgium at this time. Get out of the country at once."

It happened that my table was so close that I could not help but overhear the request and the response, and I remember remarking to the friends who were dining at the table with me: "Had Mr. Churchill said that to me, I should have answered him, 'I have as much business in Belgium at this time, sir, as you had in Cuba during the Spanish American War'".[25]

Because of the lengths to which British censorship extended, the British embarrassed themselves several times. For example, on 27 October 1914, the battleship HMS *Audacious* was sunk by a mine off the coast of Ireland. The SS *Olympic* was nearby and tried to tow the damaged vessel before it went down, but its efforts were unsuccessful. The British refused to allow the sinking to be announced, and included the *Audacious* on all public lists of ship movements for the rest of the war. Many passengers were of course aware of the attack, and of course the Americans talked about it. There were in addition many photos of the sinking, and even a motion picture. The Germans knew that the ship had been lost by 22 November 1914.[26] The British finally got around to announcing that the *Audacious* had been lost only after Armistice Day.

George Allison was chief of International News Service (INS) operations in London, and bought thousands of newsreels and photographs, virtually everything he could get his hands on, for William Randolph Hearst. While having a drink at the London Press Club, Allison ran into a man who had photographs taken from the *Olympic* of the foundering of the vessel and was looking for a buyer. Alison jumped at this unbelievable opportunity and bought the photographs. At the same day his photos arrived in the New York office of INS another passenger from the *Olympic* came into Hearst's New York office. "He rushed, strangely enough to one of our newspaper offices, burning to tell his story. The paper was skeptical. It appeared that it might be a phoney yarn. While the doubts were being expressed, my pictures arrived."[27] The photographs were a major scoop, and to make it worse, they ran in the Hearst press, since Hearst was an anathema to the British. The moving picture film even ran in *Hearst-Vitagraph News Pictorial* in 1916. Finally, fed up with Hearst, the British Home Office banned Hearst from the use of cables or any other facilities in Britain, because of "… Garbling of messages and breach of faith".[28] The ban remained fixed, and the only Americans who covered any British campaign in World War I did so without any help from the British Government.

Italy

Italy did not enter the war on the Entente side until 22 May 1915. However it had been recently blooded in the War of 1912 against Turkey and had produced motion pictures of the war, so measures were in place for an eventual war, even though it did not know until the last moment which side it would join. General Luigi Cadorna, Supreme Commander in Italy who possessed near dictatorial powers, wanted to ban all journalists from the front. On 23 May 1915, the leading Italian newspapers petitioned the government and general staff for permission to file stories after the Supreme Command had approved them, but only they would be allowed to do so. And similar to Germany's system, the correspondents, only under close military escort, were allowed to visit the front in large groups. The favorite government paper was the *Corriere della Sera* which got many special favors and preferential treatment. It can be doubted that Hearst or anyone else was able to call in many favors from the Italian government. If this was not a sufficient deterrent to war correspondents, the War Powers Act of 22 May 1915 allowed the government to examine and seize any publication as well as postal, telegram or telephone communication that might be 'prejudicial to the supreme national interests'. And worst of all, the publication of any information not from official sources was forbidden.[29] In the spring of 1915, when William G. Shepherd went to General Cadorna's headquarters at Udine in hopes of getting a story, an "Italian Count, disguised as a soldier" told him, "Well, you may remain in Udine if you wish to; but if you do, we will be forced to shoot you".[30]

France and Russia

Neither country wanted foreign correspondents and would arrest them on sight. In the first part of the war, the French forbade any film correspondents, even their own, at the front.[31] Donald Thompson complained of numerous arrests by the French, and Robert R. McCormick, co-editor of the *Chicago Tribune*, was only allowed to be a journalist in Russia because he was a personage known to the entourage of the Tsar. His father had been ambassador to Russia. It was made very clear to him that he was not a war correspondent, and not to advertise himself as a war correspondent.[32]

Austria-Hungary

Whatever the shortcomings of the Austro-Hungarian mobilization and staff work (and at the beginning of the war, they were considerable), in the film propaganda war, the Austro-Hungarians were far smarter and more capable than any of the other powers in World War I. This was made possible because of the Austrians' flexible and receptive approach to journalists. As early as March 1915, the Austrian Military Museum under the direction of Colonel Wilhelm John had opened a film archive which was made available to war correspondents. Photographers who returned from the front were required to have their footage screened by the censors at this archive in Vienna. They also had to deposit a duplicate negative of these films at the museum. Compared to other belligerents, the Austro-Hungarian military press office was remarkably well advanced, even to the point of admitting women to the front as official war artists. In fact, the Great War started off with a wave of war correspondents coming into the Dual Monarchy. One hundred and eighteen correspondents were accredited to the Austro-Hungarian army, including some reporters from neutral countries. Arthur Ruhl, correspondent for *Collier's Weekly,* has given a vivid descrip-

Fig. 7. The village square of Nagybiesce, where the Austro-Hungarian military press headquarters was located. Compared to other belligerent countries, the Austro-Hungarians were remarkably well advanced in public relations and knew how to handle foreign correspondents. Reproduced from Collier's Weekly, 5 February 1916.

tion of the operations of the *k.u.k Kriegspressequartier*, the military press office in Teschen and Nagybiesce:

> At the beginning of the war England permitted no correspondents at all at the front. France was less rigid, yet it was months before a few favored individuals visited the trenches. Germany took correspondents to the front from the first, but these excursions came at irregular intervals, and admission to them involved a good deal of competitive wire-pulling between the correspondents themselves. The Austro-Hungarians, on the other hand, prepared from the first for a large number of civilian observers, including news and special writers, photographers, illustrators, and painters, and, to handle them satisfactorily, organized a special department of the army, this Presse-Quartier, once admitted to which – the fakirs and fly-by-nights were supposed to be weeded out by the preliminary red tape – they were assumed to be serious workmen and treated as the army's guests.

> For the time being they were part of the army – fed, lodged and transported at the army's expense and unable to leave without formal military permission. They were supposed to "enlist for the whole war", so to speak, and most of the Austro-Hungarian and German correspondents had so remained, but a good deal of freedom was allowed observers from neutral countries and permission given to go when they felt they had seen enough. Isolated thus in the country – the only mail the military field post, the only telegrams those that passed the military censor – correspondents were as 'safe' as in Siberia.[33]

As we will see, the Austro-Hungarians extended hospitality to film correspondents Edwin F. Weigle, Albert K. Dawson and Frank E. Kleinschmidt and gave them a chance to get into the field and shoot film. The only correspondent found who took a dim view of the Austrians was William Gunn Shepherd:

One hundred and eighteen writers were accredited to the [Austro-Hungarian] army. They included Germans, Austrians, Swiss, Swedes, Danes and Americans.

…They were established in a Kriegspresse-Quartier in a little town some ninety miles behind the front, under Colonel John, Curator of the War Museum in Vienna. They lived like lords and officers in those days…. Their food was given to them, free – splendid Hungarian wines included – in a great mess hall; and every man got tobacco and cigarettes as part of his rations.

In fact, these men got everything they wanted – except news.

…They passed miserable hours in waiting for promised trips to the front which did not materialize. When I reached the Austrian press headquarters in October of 1914, after the fall of Antwerp, I found the writers there a discontented and altogether miserable lot.[34]

In defense of the Austro-Hungarians, in October 1914 the news on the Austrian front was as equably miserable as the writers may have been. As we shall see, the cinematographers were there at a later, happier time for the Germans and Austro-Hungarians.

So, the situation was bleak for any coverage by the neutral cameramen. But as William G. Shepherd said, there were always American war correspondents around somewhere. One could not get away from them (Colour Plate 1). We shall see what they did in spite of major obstacles.

Notes

1. David H. Mould and Gerry Veeder, "'The Photographer-Adventurers': Forgotten Heroes of the Silent Screen", *Journal of Popular Film and Television* 3 (1988): 118–129.

2. William G. Shepherd, *Confessions of a War Correspondent* (New York: Harpers and Brothers, Publishers, [c 1917]), 107.

3. Gottlieb von Jagow to AA, 3 September 1914, AAPA, WK Nr. 3, Bd. 1, 205551-000036.

4. Hans Barkhausen, *Filmpropaganda für Deutschland* (Hildesheim, Zurich, New York: Olms Presse, 1982), 22; Ulrika Oppelt, *Film und Propaganda im Ersten Weltkrieg* (Stuttgart: Steiner Verlag 2002), 103.

5. Edward Lyell Fox, *Behind the Scenes in Warring Germany* (New York: McBride, Nast and Company, 1915), 42.

6. Jürgen W. Schmidt, "Against Russia – Department IIIb of the Deputy General Staff, Berlin, and Intelligence, Counter Intelligence and Newspaper Research, 1914–1918", *Journal of Intelligence History*, 5, 2 Hamburg, LIT Verlag (2005): 73–89.

7. It says a lot about the Army attitude towards the dissemination of information that after the war, Brose and Cavalry Captain Tornau burned most of the documents of Section IIIb, since they dealt with sensitive domestic issues. Ibid.

8. Telegram from Freiherr v. Mumm to Carl W. Ackerman,1 September 1915. It says a lot that Mumm would complain in writing about an officer in the German army to a neutral American journalist.

9. Fritz Terveen "Die Anfänge der deutschen Kriegsberichterstattung in den Jahren 1914–1916" in *Wehrwissenschaftl. Rundschau* Vol. 6 (June 1956): 318, cited in Hans Barkhausen, 22. AAPA, R121616, Mai 1915 – 31 Dezember 1915.

10. In Re Lewis Hart Marks: German Activities. Agent Ed. L. Newman, 6 October 1917, Bureau of Investigation File 27865, MID file 9140-734.

11. James W. Gerard, "Loyalty and German-Americans", Speech to the Ladies Aid Society. This website has an audio recording of the speech. http://www.firstworldwar.com/audio/loyalty.htm

12. C.F. Scully, "In Re: Oswald F. Schuette (Dr. Marks)(German Activities)", Department of Justice, 19 October 1918, case no. 314677, FBI Files, National Archives , College Park, MD. Swing was Raymond Gram Swing, who later became a notable radio news announcer for Voice of America.

13. H. L. Mencken, *35 Years of Newspaper Work: A Memoir by H. L. Mencken* (Baltimore: Johns Hopkins University Press, 1994), 71.

14. Raymond Swing, "Blame British Censors" (Wireless from Berlin via Sayville), *Chicago Daily News* (1 August 1916).

15. Oswald F. Schuette, (Wireless from Berlin via Sayville), *Chicago Daily News* (6 September 1915).

16. Bureau of investigation Files, MID 9140-734; see also M1194 File 9140-363 (Walter F. Niebuhr), National Archives, College Park, MD.

17. Alphabetisches Verzeichnis der z. Zeit hier wohnhaften Berichterstatter der Staaten. AAPA, R121616 Mai 1915 – 31 Dezember 1915.

18. Mencken, *35 Years of Newspaper Work*, 65.

19. Hayden Talbot, 'Says German Patience Is Bound to Win', *New Castle News* (12 November 1915): 9. For more on spies at the Adlon, see Carl W. Ackerman, 'Gerard Weeds out Spies in American Embassy', *Binghamton Press* (21 April 1917): 9.

20. Phillip Knightley *The First Casualty: The War Correspondent as Hero and Myth-Maker from the Crimea to Iraq*. Revised Edition (London and Baltimore: John Hopkins University Press, 2004), 483–500.

21. *The First Casualty*, p. 89.

22. Amanda Foreman, *A World on Fire. Britain's Crucial Role in the American Civil War* (New York: Random House, 2010)

23. William Manchester, *The Last Lion: Visions of Glory*, I (New York: Delta Paperback, 1983) pp. 297, 311.

24. Orlando Figes, *The Crimean War: a History* (New York: Metropolitan Books., Henry Holt and Company, 2010) 308–311.

25. E. Alexander Powell, *Fighting in Flanders* (New York: Charles Scribner's Sons, 1914), 182–183. Churchill was in Cuba in 1895, on leave from his regiment just before the Spanish American War, and while there wrote articles for the *Daily Graphic*.

26. James Goldrick, *The King's Ships Were at Sea: the War in the North Sea, August 1914 – February 1915* (Annapolis, Maryland: Naval Institute Press, c1984), 141–142.

27. George F. Allison, *Allison Calling*, (London: Staples Press, Ltd. 1948), cited in Louis Pizzitola, *Hearst over Hollywood: Power, Passion and Propaganda in the Movies* (New York: Columbia University Press, 2002), 135–136.

28. *Prescott* (Arizona) *Daily Miner* (12 October 1916), citing the London *Daily Messenger* and the *Times*, 1, 6.

29. Mark Thompson, *The White War* (London: Faber and Sons Ltd.; New York: Perseus Books, 2008), 211–212.

30. Shepherd, *Confessions of a War Correspondent*, 117–118.

31. Laurent Véray, 1914–1918: the First Media War of the 20th Century, *Film History* 22.4 (2010): 410, citing generally Laurent Véray, *Les films d'actualité français*.

32. Lloyd Wendt, *Chicago Tribune: the Rise of an American Newspaper* (Chicago, New York, San Francisco: Rand McNally Company, 1979), 409; Robert R. McCormick, *With the Russian Army: Being the Experiences of a National Guardsman* (New York: Macmillan Company, 1915), viii.

33. Arthur Ruhl, "A War Correspondents' Village", *Collier's* (5 February 1916): 10. Much of Ruhl's article was reprinted in Arthur Ruhl, "The War Correspondent", Francis J. Reynolds, Allen L. Churchill, Francis Trevelyan Miller, eds., *The Story of the Great War: History of the European War from Official Sources*. Vol. 1 (New York P. F. Collier and Son, 1916), 113–123. The Germans thought the situation in Teschen was far too cushy. Not only the war correspondents were there, but also the Austrian ArmeeOberKommando (AOK) including chief of staff Conrad von Hötzendorff and his mistress, and the Germans complained that it was too comfortable and too far from actual military operations. Richard L. DiNardo, *Breakthrough: The Gorlice – Tarnow Campaign*, 1915, (Santa Barbara, California, Denver Colorado, Oxford, England: Praeger, 2010), 20.

34. Shepherd, *Confessions of a War Correspondent*, 113–114.

Chapter 2

Over Here

On 28 July 1914 World War I officially began in Europe. However, just as there are often preliminary geological disturbances before the major explosion of a volcano, there had been flash points involving the United States and especially Germany for quite some time. In addition, the United States, like Germany and the other major powers in Europe, was expansionist in mood and had been since the Spanish American War. There were bound to be collisions. This had led to numerous incidents both with Germany and England.

In 1898 naval units of Kaiser Wilhelm II suddenly appeared in Manila Bay looking for anchorages in the Philippines. Admiral Dewey, who was busy blockading the Spanish fleet, heatedly told the Envoy, Captain Lieutenant Paul Hintze, that if the Germans wanted war with the United States, they could have it. In 1902–03 there was an English, German and Italian blockade of Venezuela when it could not pay its international debts, challenging the Monroe Doctrine. This led to President Roosevelt's corollary: America could intervene in situations like this when countries in this hemisphere could not pay their international debts. In 1909 there were rumors that the Kaiser, also known as "Wilhelm the Sudden", was planning to buy a port on the Pacific coast of Mexico at Baja California, much to the horror of his own foreign office. Again, the Americans expressed their displeasure. In 1911 there was the Second Moroccan Crisis in which France and England forced Germany into a humiliating withdrawal of its claims in Morocco. It is conjectured that this debacle was responsible for the Kaiser's subsequent hatred for England and the ultimate decision to enter World War I. The Americans were alarmed. Even in the first Moroccan crisis of 1905, President Theodore Roosevelt told a British diplomat: "[The Kaiser] is altogether too jumpy, too volatile in his policies … I would never count on his friendship for this country". Meanwhile the Hearst press had been exacerbating relations with England, especially on the Irish question, the payment of duties by the British at the newly-opened Panama Canal, and overall with its pro-German stance.

Then the Kaiser had another inspiration: that the Japanese were in league with the Mexicans to overthrow the white European nations. Hence was born the expression "The Yellow Peril". The Kaiser first decided that the Russians should fight the Japanese. The result was the Russo-Japanese war of 1904–1905 in which Russia was trounced. The Kaiser finally decided that it was up to America to stop the Japanese.

This fantasy would perhaps not have been so important if publisher William Randolph Hearst, the largest controller of American public opinion and a rabid pro-German, had not swallowed it hook, line and sinker.

The Kaiser and the Germans were also deeply involved in Mexico. German agents were sent into Mexico to stir up trouble, on the theory that the more the Americans were up to their neck in problems with Mexico, the less time they would have for European affairs. In addition the Germans had extensive holdings in Mexico, which Germany wanted to protect. Mexico was in the throes of a revolution in 1913 and 1914, and was already a hot spot. Porfirio Diaz, the conservative, pro-business dictator of Mexico, who had always backed foreign commercial and mining interests and had been supported (and bribed) by them in turn, had been ousted by the revolutionaries. The revolution soon involved the colossal and controversial William Randolph Hearst.

It is difficult to decide where to introduce Hearst in this saga. Hearst controlled hundreds of newspapers and magazines in the United States, so his editorials and choice of articles influenced thousands of Americans. But there was far more to Hearst than this. He had hired or made deals with almost everyone in the public media. While he could be extremely mercenary, he was also capable of investing in enterprises involving his rivals. He had influence in the government and, as we will soon see, the State Department. He has been the subject of many books and magazine articles both then and now by people who both loved and hated him. He dominated the entire period described in this book and everything that happened in it. He was the founder of an empire, a newspaper magnate, a yellow journalist, one of the richest and most influential men in America, and soon to have major moving picture interests.

Hearst was in favor of full-scale American intervention in Mexico, both because it was in line with his general ideology (he was after all the man who almost single-handedly instigated the American war with Spain in 1898) and because he had large financial interests in Mexico which were threatened by the revolutionaries. He had supported Porfirio Diaz, who had always been scrupulously careful to rule in Hearst's favor in Mexican affairs before he was overthrown. President Wilson after his inauguration had adopted a hands-off Mexico policy, which Hearst loathed. In Mexico in 1913 after the revolution had deposed the dictator Porfirio Diaz, the dreamy, idealistic Francisco Madero assumed the presidency and was acclaimed by huge crowds in Mexico City. It appeared that the revolution was over. But General Victoriano Huerta assumed dictatorial powers shortly afterward and apparently had Madero killed on 22 February 1913. Huerta was a brutal, often drunken, but not incompetent officer whom President Woodrow Wilson loathed. The British government as well as most American business interests along with Ambassador Henry Lane Wilson and the American State Department supported Porfirio Diaz and later Huerta, the latter on the basis that whatever his faults, he could at least restore order in Mexico.

The newly elected President Woodrow Wilson refused to recognize Huerta and recalled Henry Lane Wilson, the pro-Huerta American ambassador, which brought things to a head. As Kevin Brownlow put it: "Now began 'Carranza's rebellion', the struggle between isolated rebel commanders – Carranza, Villa, Zapata, Obregon – and Huerta's Federal Army. And it was during this period that Pancho Villa began his unlikely connection with motion pictures."[1]

Fig. 8. Wilbur H. "Bill" Durborough (1882–1946). [Courtesy Mrs. Robert M. (Bea) Durborough.]

The American public, greatly interested in the Mexican troubles, was infatuated with Villa. A flood of newspaper men, photographers and movie people flowed to Mexico. And this brings us to our first film and newspaper correspondent, Wilbur Henry Durborough.

Wilbur H. Durborough was born on 11 October 1882 in Rising Sun, Kent County, Delaware.[2] After trying a number of different occupations, he assembled a small photo portfolio and sought employment as a newspaper photographer. His work probably demonstrated more ability than the average amateur because he started at the *Philadelphia Inquirer* late in 1909.[3] In little more than a year his growing photographic skill, professional experience and personal initiative was recognized by Hearst's *Chicago Examiner* when it hired him away in early 1911. Although he, like most newspaper photographers of the time, didn't get bylines for his photos, his initiative for the *Examiner* made the news that spring when an individual involved in a political election bribery scandal threatened him with a gun for attempting to snap his photo on a public sidewalk.[4]

His work and gift for self-promotion must have continued to build his confidence as a professional news photographer. In 1912 he left the security of the *Examiner* to seek work as a more lucratively compensated independent photojournalist with his own Chicago office.[5] That year was a presidential election year and he possibly started as an independent in time to cover the three conventions, the Republican Convention mid-June held at the Chicago Coliseum, the Democratic Convention in Baltimore in early July and the Bull Moose Convention in early August back at the Chicago Coliseum. The earliest published newspaper photos with the simple attribution to W. H. Durborough were taken at the Bull Moose Convention in August.[6] It began what would soon develop into a long relationship between Durborough and the Newspaper Enterprise Association (NEA) based in Chicago. Sam Hughes, managing editor for the NEA, probably noticed this enterprising photographer not long after his arrival at the Windy City and Durborough may have approached him seeking a contract when first setting out on his own. Although it appears he quickly established an exclusive arrangement with the NEA, he started out peddling photos to other newspapers.

The Newspaper Enterprise Association was founded in 1902 by E. W. Scripps of the Scripps Newspapers. Unlike United Press or Associated Press, which covered hard news stories, the NEA provided sports, editorials, photographs, light stories, cartoons and human interest material to a couple of hundred newspapers, usually in small or medium sized towns, that could not afford to hire a traveling photojournalist. Hughes astutely assessed the potential of this young photojournalist with only two years' experience. He recognized the physical energy to travel anywhere on short notice, the willingness to endure long separations from his family, the self-confidence to work independently, the personality to approach anyone and, not least, the initiative and competitive zeal to obtain good photos under difficult time constraints and circumstances. Sam Hughes hired him as a traveling photographer assigned to provide feature photos with informative captions, often accompanied by additional correspondence, of major national events. Occasionally he would accompany another NEA specialist correspondent as the photographer. It was a good match.

It was at the NEA that Durborough really hit his stride. It appears he soon ceased any speculative work and contracted exclusively with the NEA which gave him steady assignments. They obtained exclusive rights to his submitted photos which the NEA copyrighted and credited with his byline when published. Durborough enjoyed the travel and high pay with expenses, meeting major news personalities, witnessing important news events of the day and, not least, the personal satisfaction of knowing he was among the best in his profession.

Soon after he started with them he demonstrated his initiative and creative promotional approach by partnering with another Chicago press photographer, Frederick H. Wagner of the *Chicago Tribune*, to form Wagner & Durborough. It was an ad hoc aerial photography company formed to provide unique photo coverage of major auto races for NEA subscribers.[7] It was the first of his professional extracurricular efforts that editor Sam Hughes appears to have appreciated for the benefit accruing to the NEA.

Durborough traveled widely and his photographs which were often prominent in NEA features cover an extensive range of subjects reflecting the progressive era in

America. During 1913 he covered the Great Dayton Flood and drove around southern Wisconsin chasing Gypsies who had allegedly kidnapped a young Indiana girl. In June he covered the West Virginia coal miners' strike where the governor had declared martial law and sent in the state militia to occupy the area and force the miners out of their company homes. Later in September he was in Calumet, Michigan, for the 1913 copper mine strike where unarmed daughters of the striking fathers were arrested for "intimidation" when picketing the mines in sympathy with their fathers in the presence of armed guards, soldiers and strikebreakers, and made several stunning portraits of the strike's queen, Big Annie Clemens, also known as Annie Klobuchar Clemenc, who has since become an icon of the feminist and labor movements. In late October he was at the Pine Ridge Reservation in South Dakota with the NEA movie correspondent Gertrude M. Price to photograph some of the participants re-enacting the Wounded Knee massacre of 1890 for *Indian Wars* being made by Chicago's Essanay Film Company. Two participants, a Sioux warrior and an army scout who had both survived the original event, were in the cast that featured Buffalo Bill. It was here Durborough likely had his first close experience with cinematography.[8]

When the Mexican Revolution and Villa hit the headlines, the NEA was eager to satisfy American's public demand for coverage and gave Wilbur H. Durborough his first major international assignment. In November 1913 Durborough left Chicago to photograph the Revolution. He stationed himself in El Paso, Texas, just across the border from the state of Chihuahua in northern Mexico and became friendly with Pancho Villa, whom he photographed often. He obtained some excellent photographs of Villa's troops in action during the Second Battle of Ciudad Juarez, which was one of Villa's most famous fights.

Newspapers using his photos now generally noted Durborough as their "staff photographer" but with this Mexican assignment Durborough regularly filed accompanying correspondence which at least one Scripps publication used and officially credited him as "staff photographer and correspondent".[9] Some of his early photographs sent to the NEA of the Mexican rebels included not only a photo of General Villa with General Rodriguez ready to charge into the battle of La Mesa[10] but also one featuring General Villa shaking his hand. That rebel victory cleared the Federal Army from the Juarez area and forced their retreat to what would be the Federal Army's last outpost in northern Mexico at Ojinaga.[11] Durborough traveled to Texas to avoid the physical hardship of the desert route taken by the Mexicans and rejoined the rebel army as it approached their objective.[12] He returned to Presidio, Texas, to file his story and waited with many other journalists including Charles A. Pryor, an independent photographer and cinematographer, along the river just west of Ojinaga. A little before midnight, they witnessed the initial assault by Villa's cavalry which was repelled by the Federal forces. The next morning Durborough and Pryor rode across the river to Villa's camp and spent a couple of hours administering first aid. They returned to Presidio around noon "too sick to even look at lunch".[13]

each other without an interpreter. Villa is a far greater man than most people think. He is deep, very modest, always on the alert, and is respected by all who know him. He is a born general and never gives an order to any of his men that he could not carry out himself. He can ride better than any man in his army, rope a steer quicker, and is conceded to be the best shot in Mexico. His men, cowboys, rough peons and even outlaws, have seen him do all these things, and he has won their unanimous admiration.

We were lying around camp one morning after breakfast, just before the battle of Tierra Blanca, when Villa noticed three of his troopers trying to rope a steer. The steer was a bad actor and the men missed him several times.

EDITOR'S NOTE.—W. H. Durborough, staff photographer and correspondent of The Star, who has been sending splendid pictures and vivid stories from the scene of fighting in Mexico to this newspaper, spent nearly all his time with Gen. Villa's army. He early fell into the good graces of the rebel general, who helped him in his work and befriended him in tight pinches in the war-ravished land. At the suggestion of the editor, Durborough will write from Mexico a series of articles on "Campaigning With Villa," the accompanying story being the first.)

Our Staff Photographer, Durborough, Shaking Hands With Gen. Villa

Fig. 9. Pancho Villa and Durborough realize that they can do each other some good. Seattle [Washington] Star, 23 February 1914.
[Courtesy University of Washington Libraries.]

Later that day Durborough claims Pryor suggested they sneak away, ride farther down the Rio Grande and cross over to the Mexican Federal forces. Leaving all Villa credentials in a Presidio post office safe and taking only still cameras, they rode to within two miles of Ojinaga and were escorted by sentries to meet General Jose Ynez Salazar eating his dinner of beans. Durborough explained he represented "several hundred American newspapers" and that Pryor "was making movie pictures". He took a photo of the general and then had Pryor take one of him and the general eating beans together.[14] Salazar had the two men shown around their Ojinaga defenses with permission to take any pictures they wanted. When General Salazar released them, Durborough claims the general presented him with his sword as a souvenir to take back to Texas.[15] After several more skirmishes, the final stage of the battle was forced on 10 January when General Villa arrived to lead his men. The Federal Army collapsed with many participants escaping across the Rio Grande and taken into custody by the US Army.[16] It was at the Battle of Ojinaga that Durborough would suffer the only documented war wound of his career, a slight bit of shrapnel in his knee from a rebel shell that exploded about 30 feet away.[17]

Back in Chihuahua, Villa turned to civil matters and raising desperately needed money. He confiscated some very large ranches and took cattle from others. In February an angry British owner of one of the ranches, William Benton, went directly to Villa to protest. Villa had him arrested and executed on 17 February 1914, ignoring diplomatic pleas otherwise. Durborough, who was again back in Mexico, witnessed Villa's performance on 22 February at the ceremony commemorating the lives of the three revolutionary martyrs: Francisco Madero, Jose Maria Pino Suarez and Abraham Gonzalez. That day Villa had met the train bringing back the exhumed body of former Chihuahua Governor Gonzalez who had been executed in the desert and unceremoniously buried by Huerta forces on the night of 6 March 1913. A few days later Durborough's NEA editor Sam Hughes recalled him back home to Chicago.[18]

After the many hardships he had undergone in covering the Mexican troubles, Durborough surely enjoyed his next NEA assignment given his enthusiasm and success playing baseball as a young man. He accompanied sportswriter Hugh S. Fullerton as photographer on a swing through the south visiting baseball spring training camps in the second half of March.[19] But this was only a very brief interlude before he was again rushing back to Mexico.

In the meantime, Hearst, the man who had instigated the war with Spain in 1898, was certainly not going to be left at the post when it came to publicizing the events in Mexico. Two of Hearst's best cameramen were A. E. Wallace and Ariel Varges. Hearst sent them both to cover the events in Mexico that were beginning to assume much greater importance, especially at Tampico and Vera Cruz (infra) in April of 1914.

Ansel Earle Wallace was born on 30 October 1884 in South Bend, Indiana, to John M. and Virginia E. Wallace. He, his brother Harry, and his father were all photographers. Wallace's rise to prominence as a photographer was rapid. When he was twenty, he was listed as one of the photographers working for William H. Raw at the St. Louis World's Fair.[20] Wallace started with the Hearst newspapers as a photographer as early as 1910, and moved to New York in that year. He and Ariel Varges were favorites of Edward Hatrick, the editor of the International News Service (INS), and Wallace sent back some notable pictures and newsreels before World War I.

Wallace appears to have been a ladies man. He is also indirectly responsible for having originated the term "cheesecake" to describe an attractive woman showing a lot of leg in a photograph. In 1948, Charles L. Mathieu, then editor of MGM's *News of the Day*, related:

> Back around 1912–1913 the present International News Photos was being created. Mr. Hearst had ordered all Hearst newspaper photographic departments under the control of E. B. Hatrick …. The man in charge of the photographic department was A. E. Wallace. Our office was in the old Rhinelander building in downtown New York and Wallace had a secretary or office worker in a wholesale cheese company somewhere in the neighborhood. The girl was very attractive, would come over and meet Wallace in the office. She had extremely attractive gams and as this was the day when long skirts were worn, any excuse to make pictures for the newspapers revealing pretty legs was welcome. When an opportunity to stage one of these

27

Fig. 10. Ansel E. Wallace, one of Hearst's favorite newsreel cameramen. If he was attractive to women, his soulful looks may have helped. [Private collection Cooper C. Graham.]

photographs came up, Wallace's girl was always used as a model and she became well known to all photographers in the office, many of whom practiced exposure and focusing their cameras on her pretty legs. On account of her association with the cheese business she was nicknamed 'Cheese' and everybody called her by that name … I think it was Bill Hearfield of the *New York Journal* Staff at that time who remarked while covering and posing some pretty girls, 'Well, let's have a little cheesecake'. Most of the boys covering knew of 'Cheese' – Wallace's girl – and immediately got the significance of the remark … Thus was born the word 'cheesecake'.[21]

If Wallace was attractive to women, his dapper clothes and soulful looks may have helped. In the photographs of Wallace, there is a certain style about him. He always appears elegant, even when he is wearing a Cossack hat sitting in a droshky in Poland or perched on a handcar in shirtsleeves in Vera Cruz. This, as well as his undoubted competence both as a photographer and also as a writer, is probably one of the reasons that he often covered occasions which seemed to call for a certain social flair, such as the coronation of George V in London in June 1911 as a still photographer.[22]

In 1912 he was in the news several times. On 6 February he filed a patent for a flash apparatus for cameras that automatically triggered the flash powder when the shutter button was depressed. Whether his particular device was ever widely accepted is not known, but clearly something very like it was used widely in news photography before the invention of the flash bulb.[23]

On 1 May 1912 he accompanied aviator Frank T. Coffyn on a trip with his seaplane from New York harbor over the Upper Bay to the Italian liner *Ancona*, out of New York Harbor about a quarter of a mile beyond the Statue of Liberty, to deliver a message to one of the passengers. It was partially a stunt story, but it was still a first in aviation to deliver a message to an ocean liner at sea by seaplane. It is also worth noting that this flight occurred only eight years after Kitty Hawk. The story was covered by a number of newspapers, including the *New York Times* and a number of aviation journals. Wallace got a by-line and wrote a short statement for the *New York American*. Frank Coffyn gave a longer statement, presciently commenting that aerial photography would be useful in a war, and also complemented Wallace's bravery as a photographer and a novice flyer:

> Just as we were passing Castle Williams – it was between Wallace and the shore – he half rose against the footrest, and leaned away out of the machine and across my lap, resting his camera on my knees. It was about the coolest, nerviest, perhaps the most foolhardy piece of business I ever saw.

> The picture he got from that crazy maneuver may repay Wallace for the danger he ran. Certainly it is the finest aerial photograph I ever saw for detail and perspective. It is also the first aeroplane picture which shows the wing of the aeroplane as all other camera men that have been taken up have been satisfied to point their cameras earthward between their knees and let it go at that.[24]

Later that year, Wallace was with President William Howard Taft's party as a photographer when Taft visited the Panama Canal in December 1912.[25] Wallace's photographs got a complete page in the *New York Times* of 12 January 1913.

Later in 1914, after Hearst's International News Service (INS) was incorporated, Wallace became a newsreel cinematographer. His first assignment in Mexico was to be a juicy one. Shortly after his inauguration, President Wilson had sent Nelson O'Shaughnessy as Chargé d'Affaires on a fact-finding mission to the dictator Victoriano Huerta, to see if he was as villainous as he had been portrayed. O'Shaughnessy and his wife were close to Huerta and, while aware of his faults, were not unsympathetic to him. Evidently with the help of John Bassett Moore, then counselor of the State Department, Hearst sent Wallace to Mexico. In January 1914 he filmed Huerta's Mexican Army, and on 10 January 1914 he filmed Nelson O'Shaughnessy and his wife Edith on board the USS *Michigan* at Vera Cruz.[26] O'Shaughnessy was not simply an onlooker. On 12 January O'Shaughnessy discussed with Victoriano Huerta the arrangements for Wallace to film fighting between Huerta's Federals and the Insurgents. It says quite a lot about the cozy relationship between the State Department, Hearst and Huerta that, in spite of Wilson, they were willing to establish a presumably pro-Huerta camera shoot for Huerta.

Huerta had a reputation both for brutality and for alcoholism, and Wallace went too far in his filming of the dictator. According to Edith O'Shaughnessy:

> … while we were talking N[elson] was rung up to hear that an English woman reporter and Wallace, the cine man, sent us from the State Department, had been put in prison for trying to take a photograph of Huerta at the Café Colon, while he was taking his copita. They were both released at a late, or rather an early hour, and I think they richly deserved their experience. Huerta's reputation for drinking is very much exaggerated.[27]

The all-powerful *Chicago Tribune* and its co-editor Joseph Patterson took a very

Fig. 11. Co-editor of the Chicago Tribune, *Joseph Patterson. Films were one of his key instruments in promoting his newspaper. Studio portrait, circa 1912.*
[Courtesy Library of Congress.]

similar stance to Mexico as did Hearst, so while Patterson may have been a neutral as far as World War I was concerned, he was very much of an interventionist when it came to Mexico. The *Tribune* would make Edwin F. Weigle its principal cinematographer in Mexico. But in any discussion of Weigle it is crucial at the outset to introduce Joseph Medill Patterson, because Weigle's cinema career is very much due to the backing, both morally and fiscally, of Patterson and the *Chicago Tribune*.

Joseph Medill Patterson was the grandson of Joseph Medill, founder of the *Chicago Tribune*, and the brother of the more famous Elinor "Cissy" Patterson. Joseph was also the cousin of Medill and Robert R. "Bertie" McCormick, sons of his aunt Katherine. At this time, before World War I, a complicated arrangement had been worked out in which Bertie McCormick and Patterson shared responsibility for managing the paper. They even took turns being totally in charge during alternate months, a plan that sounds unworkable, but in fact worked out quite well.

Joseph Patterson could be considered to be an extreme case of what one used to call a trust-fund baby. He had been born into a very socially prominent Chicago family possessing a fortune from the *Tribune*, although he hated the inherited wealth and social prominence without being able to wean himself from it. Joseph's father Robert W. Patterson had been much prized by Joseph Medill as an excellent newspaperman, while his mother Elinor, Joseph Medill's second daughter, was by all reports a social climber. As a youth, Joseph Medill Patterson attended Groton, then went to Yale, where he was a member of the Scroll and Key. He worked sporadically for the *Tribune*, sometimes as a police reporter, and wrote several plays and novels, in some of which he described, as faintly disguised autobiography, the life of a pampered drone. He joined the Socialist Party but became disillusioned. He was a member of the Illinois state legislature, where he attacked the traction trust and won. He tried farming, but this caused a rift between him and his first wife, because he wanted to farm seriously and she wanted to make the estate an English deer park. As part of his persona, when he and his cousin Robert took over the *Tribune* as co-editors, he wore old clothes and battered hats and insisted that his employees call him Joe. His major interests at the paper were the features and the Sunday Magazine section. He turned the weekend paper into a popular magazine with subjects such as sports, fashion, comics and the like. He was extremely interested in the comic pages, which he made the best in any newspaper of the time. And, many years before it became acceptable let alone fashionable, he liked motion pictures. He wrote a long, affectionate article about nickelodeons that ran in the *Saturday Evening Post* on 23 November 1907. By 1912 he ordered the paper to start reviewing films, naming the critic Mae Tinee. He attained his greatest success in furthering the collaboration of the newspaper with the film industry when he introduced the famous film serial *The Adventures of Kathlyn* with producer William Selig. According to Terry Ramsaye, this serial generated such a wide popular following that the *Tribune*'s circulation grew by 35,000 copies. Said Ramsaye: "The *Tribune* had grown to dignity and glory on appeal to the upper classes, now it was out to take the volume off the bottom where the volume always is".[28]

All of which may make Patterson sound like a lightweight. He was not. After America entered World War I, he resigned his commission in the Illinois National Guard, enlisted in the army as a private in the Rainbow Division, and was in five major battles including one in which he was gassed. He left the army as captain. After Patterson's death in 1946, General Douglas MacArthur, his former commanding officer, called Patterson the finest natural soldier that he had ever known.[29] Patterson and the *Tribune* were shrewd enough to see what a draw "war pictures" could be. And Patterson did not strengthen the comics, pictorial sections, features and women's pages simply because he liked the light side of the news. They sold papers, and at the time, the *Tribune* was in the middle of a vicious circulation battle in Chicago with the Hearst papers that descended to hiring gangsters to keep rival newspapers off the streets. The *Tribune* was determined not to lose this fight and if films would help, then so be it.

Patterson had two additional characteristics that were to influence Weigle's film coverage. First, by 1914, he was already an isolationist. He denied being pro-German, but the *Tribune* was always ready to publish the German side of a question, and he later admitted that he was not pro-British, which was an understatement. Patterson's stance was very much typical of the prevailing mood in the Midwest, which was much less pro-Entente than on the East Coast. In his book *The Notebook of a Neutral* he attacked England's hypocrisy and repeated the arguments of the most sword-rattling German of them all, Friedrich von Bernhardi. He argued that war was ennobling, a form of social Darwinism to cull out the weak nations, that treaties were indeed mere scraps of paper, that whatever Germany did, including sinking the *Lusitania,* was none of America's business, and went so far as to say that any American who did not put his country's best interests before all other considerations was a traitor.

Second, Patterson craved adventure. All his life he wanted to be a war correspondent. He convinced William Randolph Hearst to send him to China to cover the Boxer Rebellion when he was still in college, only to arrive in China after the Rebellion was over. When he met Weigle, an ambitious young man hungry for adventure, Patterson must have felt that he had found a kindred soul.

Edwin Frederick Weigle was born in Chicago on 13 March 1889. His parents, Adolph H. Weigle and Sophie Weigle, emigrated from Württemberg in 1879. Edwin was the product of Chicago high schools and spoke German. In 1908 he was already listed as a photographer for Hearst's *Examiner* and went to work for the *Chicago Tribune* in 1909.[30] Weigle had some lurid assignments for the *Tribune* before World War I. Jack Johnson, the champion prize fighter, hit him with a cane, which got Johnson arrested. Later on, Weigle was one of the photographers chosen for a raid organized by Max Annenberg on a notorious gambling den. He and Norman Alley shot photographs of the gamblers, which resulted in a car chase through the streets of Chicago complete with gunfire.[31] This was all presumably fascinating for Patterson. The two men became close friends, and Weigle said that Patterson was "later more than a brother to me – a man whose true friendship and excellent companionship I shall never forget".[32]

The Vera Cruz incident in April 1914 had already involved the United States, Mexico and Germany in a sort of preliminary round. If Spain and China were prologues and military training grounds to World War II in 1936, Mexico and Vera Cruz fulfilled the same role for the Americans before World War I. Most cinematographers, still photographers and many of the journalists who will be mentioned later showed up in Vera Cruz. For most of them, it would be their first taste of anything like war and the experience of covering a military conflict. It started off with what was called the "Tampico Incident".

On 9 April 1914, United States sailors, picking up supplies with the gunboat *Dolphin* in Tampico, had mistakenly entered a restricted area. They were arrested by the Mexicans and paraded through the streets of Tampico. The sailors had been picking up supplies at the usual area on the Tampico docks for doing so and had no idea that the area had been restricted. When the Mexican officials in Vera Cruz realized what had happened, they let the sailors go and made a verbal apology to the United States Navy. This was not sufficient for the admiral in charge of the naval unit, Henry Mayo, who insisted on a written apology from the Mexicans and further demanded that General Victoriano Huerta salute the American flag on Mexican soil. Huerta refused, partially on the logical grounds that since the United States did not recognize his regime, he saw no reason why he should salute its flag. To complicate the issue, there had been news that the German steamer *Ypiranga* from Hamburg was delivering a shipment of arms amounting to fifteen million cartridges and two hundred machine guns to General Huerta in Vera Cruz. These arms shipments were one reason why the usual area where the American Navy landed in Tampico had been restricted. Germany at the time was trying with some success to stir up trouble between Mexico and the United States, and the events in Vera Cruz and Tampico added fuel to the fire. President Wilson ordered the United States to intervene in Mexico at Vera Cruz.

It was Vera Cruz that sparked the *Chicago Tribune*'s entry into the film business. Edwin F. Weigle had hounded the editors to be allowed to go to Mexico as a correspondent, but they had not taken him seriously. He then hocked a diamond ring that he owned and borrowed a camera from a friend, Harold Brown of the *Chicago Herald*.[33] Patterson, perhaps impressed by this dedication, promoted Weigle to special correspondent for the *Tribune* in 1914 and sent him to Vera Cruz for the *Chicago Tribune*. Victor Milner shot newsreels for Pathé and Wilbur H. Durborough traveled to Vera Cruz for the NEA and also assisted Edwin F. Weigle. In his report on Vera Cruz for the *Tribune*, Weigle called Durborough "my associate" and claimed to have been the first man to film Americans in actual warfare.[34]

Patterson accompanied Weigle, first to Vera Cruz and then later to Belgium, France and Germany. Weigle's films and photographs first achieved prominence during the American invasion of Vera Cruz in the wake of the incident. Probably because Patterson was tipped off that something was going to happen in Vera Cruz, Weigle, accompanied by Durborough, had already arrived there ready to film – with his borrowed camera – several weeks before the marines and navy landed on 21 April 1914. When Admiral Charles J. Badger ordered the marines to land, Weigle was on the dock in Vera Cruz filming them:

> On Wednesday morning I was in the train [station], had watched a company of Mexicans embark and tried to get them to come out and pose for a picture. [Wilbur H.] Durborough rushed up breathlessly.
>
> 'For God's sake get out of here before they get you', he gasped.
>
> 'Why so?' I wanted to know.
>
> 'Seven boatloads from the Prairie have just landed.' He answered, and we beat it towards the wharf.
>
> There Mexicans were scurrying in all directions, officials and laborers running for cover. When the marines disembarked, Durborough, [Burge?] McFall, a reporter for the Associated Press, and I were the only men left on the dock.
>
> Ten minutes after the Americans landed I saw one of our men killed. The bullet missed me by six inches. I had been taking moving pictures – the first ever taken of Americans in actual warfare – and wanted to get a snapshot of the street in the direction of the firing. Leaving the machine with Durborough I went over to a crowd of our men who were lying face downward, shooting up the street. Two of the men made room for me, and just as I crouched the man on my right reached around for a cartridge from his belt.
>
> The next second a bullet passed through his head.[35]

Fig. 12. American sailors fire at snipers. One of the photographs taken by Weigle and Durborough. The same scene also appeared in the film trade press publicity on Weigle's The Battle of Vera Cruz. *[Courtesy Library of Congress.]*

It is unclear whether Weigle or Durborough took the stunning still photographs and the films of the US marines and navy landing at Vera Cruz. Weigle may have handled the filming while Durborough did more still photography. In any case, they filmed at the Post Office, the Hotel Terminal and the railroad yards, the shelling of the hotel and the Naval Academy by the USS *Prairie*, as well as Americans rounding up snipers and protecting refugees. To get the films back to the *Tribune* offices, Weigle placed them on one of the first rescue ships that reached Galveston on 25 April. There they were held up by quarantine regulations, but by 27 April, Monday, they were in the mail as special delivery matter. There were seven dozen films, and seventy four photographs.

By 18 May, Weigle's films were being shown at the Colonial and La Salle theaters in Chicago. Privately, Patterson commented that there was too little action in the films for them to be a total success, but maintained that they had promotional value, and that Weigle had gained valuable experience.

In the meantime, two INS cameramen, both A. E. Wallace who had previously been sent to Mexico by Hearst and his colleague Ariel Varges, came to Tampico and Vera Cruz. They hitched a tug called the *Senator Bailey* from Galveston, and apparently as they sailed by thumbed their noses at Victor Milner, the Pathé photographer, still sitting on the dock in Galveston, also trying to get to Vera Cruz.[36] Milner eventually got a ride on a navy ship and beat the Hearst reporters. He cheerfully reported scooping Wallace and Varges, especially as they had earlier left him stranded in Galveston:

> But we arrived in Vera Cruz and arrived there in good time – time enough, in fact for me to have set up and been photographing my International News rivals as they came into port on their chartered tug. There were no two more surprised men in Mexico than Varges and Wallace of the News [sic] when they saw that it was I who was taking pictures of their arrival at the Mexican port.[37]

Based on contemporary descriptions in newspapers and trade journals of the Hearst-Selig newsreels, Wallace and Varges photographed views of the following: the temporarily disabled transport USS *Meade*; scenes in Galveston incident to the arrival in that city of refugees from the adjoining republic; the boat crew of the USS *Dolphin*, who figured in the Tampico incident that brought about the landing of American troops in Mexico and the Yankee soldiers at Vera Cruz; the occupation of the port by U.S. troops as they sailed by; the sailors and marines who seized the city; damage caused by fire from USS *Prairie*, as well as the arrival of regulars from Galveston and graphic shots of caring for the wounded. According to the *Reading Eagle* on 3 May 1914:

> The improved weekly, Hearst-Selig News, depicting a special war edition, since the outbreak in Mexico, will contain the following interesting scenes: Battleship fleet on the way to Vera Cruz, arrival at Vera Cruz, landing of Uncle Sam's marines and bluejackets, marines killed and wounded, with a heavy loss on the Federal side, Nelson O'Shaughnessy being deported, Admiral Badger on the U. S. battleship *Arkansas*…. These pictures were taken by the four [sic] expert camera men of the Hearst-Selig news who were aboard the various battleships and who landed with the marines at Vera Cruz.[38]

The stories from Vera Cruz dried up quickly after the landings. One area that looked like a potential hot spot was El Tejar, ten miles southwest of Vera Cruz, which had been occupied by the marines because it was the location of the waterworks for Vera Cruz. It was the most remote outpost from Vera Cruz and quite cut off from the rest of the American forces. On 30 April, the army took over occupation of Vera Cruz and relieved the bluejackets. At El Tejar, the Mexicans gave an ultimatum to the marines there to surrender the waterworks. The marines refused, and Army General Frederick Funston reinforced the garrison at El Tejar with another 600 men. The Alvarado Railroad ran between Vera Cruz and El Tejar, so Wallace, Durborough, Arthur Ruhl of the *New York Tribune*, Adrian C. Duff of the American Press Association, Jimmy Hare of *Colliers* and Joseph Rucker of *Universal Animated Weekly*, sniffing a story there, stole a handcar and went to El Tejar, Wallace holding a flag of truce made from a bath towel.[39] As it turned out, plans for a negotiated settlement of the Mexican-American controversy were already under way, and in addition Huerta had enough troubles without a full scale war against the Americans. The Federales apparently had no intention of attacking and were simply bluffing so they could turn the Veracruzano water supply off. In his diary on 2 May 1914, Richard

Fig. 13. On the handcar to or from El Tejar. Seated, left to right: Arthur Ruhl, Adrian Duff, A. E. Wallace,
Wilbur H. Durborough. Standing, left to right: Jimmy Hare, Joseph Rucker.
[Photo from International Photographer, *April 1938.]*

Harding Davis, who was also covering the "incident" in Vera Cruz, noted: "The Selig moving picture folks took moving pictures and several 'stills' in which the war correspondent was shown giving cigarettes to the brigands".[40]

Wallace apparently stayed in Mexico even after Vera Cruz stopped being news. Later in July 1914, the State Department reported Wallace trying to persuade Pancho Villa to pose for the Hearst-Selig movie camera, but Villa supposedly refused, possibly because Hearst's anti-Mexican Revolution sentiments were already becoming well-known.[41] In any case footage of Pancho Villa at Torreón is included in *Hearst Selig News Pictorial* No. 42 on 23 July 1914. The incident also suggests that Wallace or Hearst-Selig was willing to pay up front to get the hot stories.

As Vera Cruz wound down, Durborough could count the experience as a success. His many excellent Vera Cruz photos sent to the NEA appeared widely among their subscribers. His close relationship with Weigle during his filming of *The Battle of Vera Cruz* was an experience that made tangible and realistic Durborough's own film project to be organized later in 1914. Moreover, some of the Vera Cruz film itself would be used by Durborough in his special 1916 fall film tour.

After Mexico, Wallace was once again at the Panama Canal on the SS *Ancon* for the canal's official opening in August 1914. He sailed back to New York from Cristobal. His film appeared in *Hearst Selig News Pictorial* No. 54, 3 September 1914: "The formal opening of the Panama Canal by the U. S. ship Ancona [sic] is the other subject of the reel, and a very entertaining one as it is supplemented by various scenes in the Canal Zone". [42] He was soon to be sent to a very different location.

Another Hearst newspaperman who was in Mexico, if not Vera Cruz, was Nelson Edwards, but at a slightly later time. Because Nelson Edwards was mentioned by name in the Senate Hearings on Brewing and Liquor Interests and German and Bolshevik Propaganda, he will always go down in the history books as the man whom William Randolph Hearst sent to Germany in 1916 to cover the German side of the war.[43] This is a great disservice to Edwards, one of the great newsreel cameramen of the twentieth century, and to the members of his family. Many of them followed in his footsteps as cameramen, and the Edwards family recorded many of the film images that are part of our history.

Nelson Elisha Edwards was born in Point Pleasant, Mason County, West Virginia on 25 November 1887 to Jake C. and Margaret Edwards. The Edwards had been farmers in West Virginia, but when Nelson was only six months old, the Edwards pulled up stakes and moved to Plevna, Reno County, Kansas by covered wagon, a journey that took between two and three and a half months, depending on different versions. Edwards later reported, "They tell me they let me fall out of the wagon once on the way. They say the wheels missed me by only an inch." They settled into what Edwards called "a hole in the ground".[44] The original Edwards home was a classic Kansas dugout built right into the sod. Farming in Kansas could be tough, and it broke a lot of families, but because of the recent introduction of Turkey Red wheat from Russia by the Mennonites, Kansas was already being celebrated as the "Wheat State". Perhaps Jake Edwards had been persuaded to move to Kansas by the reports of the money to be made in wheat. In any case, the family appears to have done well. By 1915, photographs of the Edwards property show a solid, prosperous house and farm. Jake Edwards served twice as a member of the Kansas State House of Representatives, in 1915 and 1917. He also was appointed county chairman. The Edwards had nine sons and one daughter.

Nelson was a tall, muscular man with prominent cheekbones, a hawk nose, lighthouse eyes peering out at the world from under heavy eyebrows, and thick, dark hair which photographed jet black. He tended to look short in his photographs because he was so stocky, but he was quite large. He was athletic, enjoyed sports including boxing, wrestling and hunting, and was, as his son-in-law put it, a 'man's man'. Even a hundred years later his face, staring up from old photographs, is compelling. He was never without a sense of humor, but he also looked like he could make things go his way, and Edwards did exactly that.

As an anonymous reporter for the *Hutchinson Kansas News* put it in a story about

Fig. 14. Nelson Edwards (1925) with his new movie-camera invention. The spring motor in the side bag with the flexible drive shaft cranks the camera which can be held in any position.
[Courtesy Corbis Images.]

Edwards: "There are no figures to show how many Reno county farm youths have paused behind a plow under a hot Kansas sun, gazed into the sky and wished they might go out and see the world". Farming for subsistence in the early part of the twentieth century seems to have impelled a lot of young men to get as far away as possible. As an escape route, Edwards first tried business school at Iola, Kansas, in 1907 but it did not take. As he later said, "I had a strong desire to become one of those long-haired artists and starve to death in a French garret. Instead, I only starved, so, when I found a photographer who was eating, I left school and went to work with him."[45] The photographer with whom he worked was apparently Richard E. Gleave, in Kansas City. Unfortunately there was reluctance among photographers to teach others their craft, and evidently Edwards did not learn much.[46] Edwards left Kansas and went to New Orleans to learn photography in 1908.[47] With whom he apprenticed is not known, but he evidently did learn retouching, either in Kansas City or New Orleans. In a brief autobiographical sketch that he later wrote for The Henry Ford Peace Ship List of Members, he noted that it was a chance retouching job that led him into photography.[48] From New Orleans, Edwards took a tramp steamer to New York, and by 1910, Edwards was in Newark, New Jersey. According to his family, he worked for a man known as 'Bucky Walter', who was probably the celebrated photographer Floyd A. Walter. Walter's photography studio was located at 607 Broad Street in Newark in 1911, and for a while, Edwards was getting his mail at the same address.[49] Edwards also had charge of the studio at Hahne & Co.

In 1912 Edwards was working as a still photographer in New York for Edward B. Hatrick, chief of photo syndication for INS, and so Edwards was now indirectly part of the Hearst Empire. INS was originally the wire and syndication service that Hearst had established to control and to sell his feature and syndicated material. It also included the photographs and later the newsreels that Hearst produced. Hatrick at this point was in charge only of photography since Hearst had not yet moved into newsreels, but Hatrick and Edwards were already experimenting with a moving picture camera and selling the results to Pathé News.[50] Hatrick also had moving pictures shot at Wilson's first inauguration and sold the results to Harry Warner, one of the future Warner Brothers, who got the pictures into theaters the day after the inauguration. Since Edwards mentions having filmed the inauguration, it is likely he at least had a hand in the filming.[51] Warner paid INS $2,000.00 for the newsreel. Thus Hatrick was able to demonstrate to Hearst that money could be made in the newsreel business. Hearst authorized Hatrick to negotiate with Colonel William Selig in Chicago to produce a Hearst-Selig newsreel. The *Hearst-Selig News Pictorial* came into being on 28 February 1914.[52]

This is the moment when Edwards started filming in Mexico, at a slightly later period than A. E. Wallace and Ariel Varges. While Hearst, after his Mexican ranch was seized and five employees were murdered, later became strongly anti-revolutionary and wanted American intervention in Mexico, he was relatively non-bellicose in 1914. The newsreel coverage appears to have been even-handed. On 18 July 1914, *Motion Picture News* noted in *Hearst-Selig News Pictorial* No. 35, "Mexican news has started to come to the front again". In No. 42 (23 July), "General Villa receives the greatest honor among celebrities through the camera-man in this week's pictorial. He is caught before Torreon while his followers accord him the acclaim of a hero. Other scenes with the rebel army in Mexico give this issue more than ordinary timeliness." A safe conduct dated 2 August 1914 by Carranza's Constitutional Party gave Edwards permission to travel to Saltillo in the state of Coahuila.[53] On 15 September 1914, *Motion Picture News* resumed its comments on the Hearst-Selig films from Mexico. In No. 50 (20 August), "We have almost forgotten poor little Mexico and her troubles in the absorption of the great European war. This review reminds us that important events in the history of that country are still going on by showing us General Carranza's entrance into the capitol, and the assumption of the government by the Constitutionalists." In No. 54 (3 September), "Mexico, although she has been chased from the front page of the newspapers, is still alive in this week's films. The transfer of the government to the Constitutionalists in Mexico City forms the news from that section of the world." In No. 56 (10 September), "General Carranza, now provisional president of Mexico, enters the capitol".

It will be noted that while Hearst himself was pro-Huerta, he did not interfere with newsreels of Carranza's apparent triumph. INS had previously sent Wallace and photographer Ariel Varges to Mexico, and some of these features could have been shot by Wallace or Varges, but there seems little doubt that many of them were shot by Edwards. Edwards claimed to have filmed Villa, and there are pictures of Carranza's entry into Mexico City in Edwards' scrap book. In addition, Varges was probably not on the scene by then, since Hearst recalled Varges and sent him to Europe shortly after the outbreak of war. Wallace appears to have left even earlier and was shooting the opening of the Panama Canal on the SS *Ancon*.[54]

Fig. 15. Edwards, with heavy police protection, filming a riot, circa 1915.
[Courtesy Wiegman family.]

After the war started in 1914, Edwards was sent to Canada to photograph the Canadian troops leaving for the war. Edwards shot the story of Thomas Edison's sixty-eighth birthday in Orange, New Jersey, that appeared in *Hearst-Selig News Pictorial* No. 15, 22 February 1915. Edwards was assigned to cover the Standard Oil strike at Bayonne, New Jersey, in 1915, producing footage that eventually appeared in *Hearst-Selig News Pictorial* No. 60, July 1915:

> When I went to Mexico to cover the operations of Pancho Villa, I expected to be shot at on more than one occasion. But there didn't a bullet come near me. I was never safer in my life.
>
> When I went to Bayonne, N. J. to cover a strike at the works of the Standard Oil Co., I expected to find plenty of husky cops on the job and no danger at all. But there weren't any cops, or, if there were, they remained discreetly out of sight, and I was shot at not once but several score of times, stopped several bricks, was missed by some few hundred other bricks, was chased four blocks by an enraged mob bent on murder and was punched in the right eye by an extremely powerful person – oh, extremely powerful person!
>
> This just goes to show that you never can tell what you are going up against when you start forth with the old camera and tripod.
>
> I approached the works of the Standard Oil Co. with due caution. I had been warned by other photographers that it was dangerous work. Guards and deputy sheriffs armed with Winchester rifles were posted behind a barricade at the end of a short street which led to the main entrance to the grounds surrounding the plant. Every once in a while the mob would rush down this street until some of the more daring got close to the barricades, where the deputies could not hit them, and then would fire over the rail with revolvers and also hurl bricks.
>
> Such a battle was in progress, and I sought an elevation from which to work. I was just setting up my camera when I heard a roar of hundreds of angry voices, and a man circled the corner.

He was hatless, gasping for breath, terror-stricken and breaking all track records. In one hand he clutched tightly a still camera. He saw me, and without stopping, shouted:

'Beat it! They're after me. They want to lynch me!'

He kept right on going. Also, I got into action myself. I knew I couldn't run with my heavy camera and tripod, so I took a chance on hiding in a doorway. And I ducked out sight just in time. The next second the mob passed. Many of them had armfuls of bricks, which they hurled at the fleeing photographer.

I gathered that photographers were unpopular around there. And I was right. The rioters feared that the authorities would use the photographs as evidence on which to prosecute. Consequently the mob sought to drive photographers away. Nevertheless, I think I got some remarkable moving pictures of rioting and shooting. It was the real thing in the way of excitement. I'm afraid the pictures may be a little unsteady. I know my hand was when I cranked.[55]

Edwards did not stay in New Jersey long. There was a tie-in between the Selig studio and the Panama-Pacific Exposition which was taking place in the summer of 1915 in San Francisco. Hearst-Selig News Pictorials featured exhaustive coverage of the Exposition, and Edwards was needed to help cover it. He left for California, probably in August 1915. So, in the summer and fall of 1915 Edwards was still acting as a still photographer for the *San Francisco Call* and *Post*. And it was here that Hearst called him to war.

* * *

In the misty dawn of 5 August 1914, when World War I was just three hours old, the General Post Office ship CS *Alert* arrived at its final destination, the Varne Bank. Slowly but without any interference, the steamer dragged from the bottom of the North Sea five German cables leading to the United States. By cutting these muddy cables all major German communication channels were severed instantly. Meanwhile, with the outbreak of war in Europe, events there started to displace Mexico in the headlines. Even though the United States was neutral, it was far from disinterested in the events taking place there.

In the American Midwest a vein of anti-war sentiment ran deep, partially because of the pacifism of leaders of the Progressive movement, such as Senators Robert La Follette and George Norris, as well as the traditional dislike of the Progressives toward the autocratic government of the Tsar.

In addition, there were many German and Irish immigrants in the cities of the Midwest, especially Chicago. In some cases, German-Americans were pro-German even to the point of being willing to fight on the German side. Most were not interested in fighting for Germany but were not willing for America to enter the war on the side of Britain, Russia and France. The Irish in Chicago were strongly anti-British. The Irish Mayor of Chicago, Big Bill Thompson, wanted to "punch King George in the snoot", and had at first refused to greet French Prime Minister Viviani and General Joffre when they visited Chicago in 1917.[56] Many of the

Scandinavians in the central and upper mid-west were also lukewarm about involvement in a European war.

There is another subgroup that should be mentioned. It seems almost grotesque in light of Nazi activity twenty years later, but Germany was also interested in recruiting German-American Jews for their cause. They reasoned that German Jews had been well assimilated in Wilhelmine culture, and were also relying on the Jews' dislike of the Tsar's murderous pogroms in Russia and Poland. In general, the Jewish response to German propaganda was tepid. While some had done well in Germany, they also remembered the deep pockets of anti-Semitism in Germany. Nevertheless, some Americans of German Jewish heritage, such as Jacob Henry Schiff and Samuel Untermyer, showed interest, and to some degree the Germans felt that their propaganda was off to a good start.

So it seemed almost inevitable that Chicago would become a center of pro-German sentiment. The *Chicago Tribune* was pro-German. The *Chicago Daily News* prided itself on being totally neutral. However, it had very strong ties with Germany.

Victor F. Lawson, the editor and owner of the *Chicago Daily News* and a self-taught newspaper businessman, was personally as well as financially sensitive to addressing the needs of Chicago's large hyphenated American communities which included those of German, Irish, Polish, and Scandinavian descent. Being a first generation American and son of Norwegian immigrants placed him among the large Midwest segment of the population tending toward neutrality and wishing to avoid involvement in any European war. His approach to the war coverage was to present both sides of the conflict by journalists of integrity with the expectation they would report sympathetically from the perspectives of their particular German or Entente beats, occasionally reminding his correspondents on both sides of the conflict to avoid including their opinions in dispatches. He felt that by presenting both sides equally his paper could provide a balanced view of the war. One very personal Lawson idiosyncrasy was the great value he placed on his early Sunday school experience which led him to never support an activity that would draw people from religious instruction on Sunday; thus sponsoring movies on Christmas was fine but not on Sundays. Lawson sent Edward Price Bell, his first permanent foreign correspondent, to London where he would serve for more than 20 years. During the war he was on the Ypres Salient when the Germans first used mustard gas and "asphyxiating shells", flew over the western front through German shrapnel and witnessed scores of British and German planes in a full-dress air battle. Besides covering England for the *Daily News* he was Lawson's closest sounding board for all major new appointments in Europe and for managing his foreign bureaus. After America entered the war he considered volunteering for service even though 48 years of age. Bell would later be nominated for the Nobel Peace Prize for his initiative promoting a meeting between British Premier Ramsey MacDonald and President Herbert Hoover that resulted in the 1930 Naval Conference in London.[57] On the other hand, to balance Bell in

IF AN INVADING FLEET SHOULD COME—THE MEETING OF THE DREADNOUGHTS

Fig. 16. War was good for business. From Caricature: the Wit and Humor of a Nation in Picture, Song and Story *(New York: Leslie-Judge Co., 1915).*

London for Germany Lawson hired Raymond E. Swing (later Raymond Gram Swing of radio fame), Oswald F. Schuette, both of whom were introduced in Chapter 1, and Harry Hansen, all of whom were pro-German, so there is no doubt that Lawson's readers would get the German side as well as the Entente side of the war. We will meet these people again.

The American public was hungry for pictures, especially moving pictures of the war. The streets on the Lower East Side of New York City were brightly lit by spotlights that focused on colorful billboards advertising the latest films. Walking alongside these cinemas, film director Lawrence Marston reported with a feeling of astonishment on the numerous war movies that were being shown. "Long range notions", he said, "are not in favor of the artists and the favorite themes seem to be close views of Uhlan charges and executions of prisoners tied to the cannon's mouth".[58]

The European war offered the American entertainment industry some enticing new business opportunities. According to the trade paper *Variety*, the outbreak of war would mean more wealthy customers coming in from Europe. *Billboard* in an editorial stated it would be better for the industry if East-European immigrants like Poles and Serbs left the country as soon as possible to fight for their Fatherland, as they didn't spend any substantial money on theatres anyway, and new American customers from countries like Great Britain or France and Germany would make for a much better substitute.[59]

The movie trade papers also had high hopes for the future. Surprisingly, *Motion Picture News* in August 1914 accurately predicted a long war that would last for several years, which would stimulate exports of American films abroad and bring about a major boost to the film business. Eastman Kodak in September stated the country had enough unexposed film to last for another year, and despite the fact that prices for developing footage rose substantially, the American film industry entered World War I with an a self-confidence that bordered on callousness. From the West Coast, reports came that most of the studios were producing films as if nothing had happened. As producer Louis J. Selznick told *Moving Picture World*: "… As far as his company was concerned, the turmoil in Europe would not be at all for the worse".[60]

From the moment war broke out in Europe, there was a great demand in the American theatres to see motion pictures of what was actually happening on the battlefields. Such scenes were however very scarce, particularly in the opening months of the war. The general expectation was the war would be over by Christmas, and to prevent competitors from releasing their films, producers forged ahead. For instance, in October 1914, Sawyer Inc. presented what was advertised as "The Only Authentic Films of the War in Europe". The footage, the company explained, had been shot by official cameramen from Serbia, Russia and Turkey. *Variety*, reviewing the movie, identified the film as a revamp of scenes that had been taken during the recent Balkan wars. Apart from producers, exhibitors also concocted some very clever publicity schemes to promote their war films (Colour Plate 4). In Cincinnati, A.G. Bauman, who ran the Dreamland Theatre, presented *The Fall of France*. Among his customers, there were many German-Americans who must have been intrigued to see a movie with such a promising title. In the lobby of his theatre, Bauman had set up a display with specially selected war bulletins. As a result of this presentation, Bauman's receipts doubled within a week. The actual contents of the film were completely unrelated to the recent war in Europe. *The Fall of France* had been released in January 1914 and was a pictorial drama on the war between France and Prussia in 1871.

Despite the heat wave in many parts of the country, customers flocked to the cinema in order to watch all of these war films. Moviegoers with different ethnic and family backgrounds from Europe made a potentially dangerous concoction. For the trade paper *Billboard* a reporter in New York City wrote: "In the lobbies of the theatres where the films were billed in German, Italian, French and Yiddish I overheard discussions in broken English which, in several instances, nearly ended in blows".[61] These war movies are nowadays characterized as "silent", but the audience at the time often was particularly vocal and noisy. While watching these films, customers frequently cheered, sang songs or applauded. In order to maintain order, the National Board of Censorship decided to send a letter to all film producers, asking them to start all war films with an introduction on screen, urging the audience to be neutral while watching the exhibition. The censors also advised all producers not to exhibit any gruesome or horrific scenes.

This kind of voluntary censorship apparently did not please some of the local authorities, and within a short time stronger measures were implemented. In August 1914, police commissioner David A. White in San Francisco – fearing disturbances – banned all war films, either drama or documentary. Local exhibitors strongly protested against his decision, and as a result the banning of these movies was restricted to films dealing with any military conflicts – past or present – in Europe. Exhibitor Stillwell however had no wish to comply with that restriction and showed *Faithful until Death*, a film on the Franco-Prussian war. The final legal decision on this case clearly showed how ineffective local censorship on war films had become. Because films could only be censored on moral grounds, documentary war films were considered a genre that could not be banned or shown in any restricted form. As a result, the judge decided to revoke White's restrictions and within a short time war films of many sorts could be shown again in and around San Francisco. Similarly, in Los Angeles exhibitors themselves organized their own censorship guidelines and decided that actual war films should be free from any censorship because such movies had an educational value. On the East Coast, war films from Europe were closely screened. In New York City for instance, the trade press reported that a large group of fifty inspectors visited the cinemas. If any war film showed a partiality to a belligerent country, the permit for the theatre would be revoked. Judging from contemporary reports, some clever exhibitors found a way to deal with this situation. *Called to the Front* was exhibited just outside of the city limits, where the inspectors had no jurisdiction. According to *Variety*, the movie was a box office success.

The censors in New York were particularly concerned with a war film entitled *The Ordeal*. This film soon became an important case for the national film industry. The story centers around a young Frenchman who refuses to join the colors. In his sleep, he sees himself as a soldier at the front, while his hometown is being occupied by the German army. He is arrested by the Germans and taken from prison to be interrogated by a brute General who shows a striking similarity to Kaiser Wilhelm II. When asked where his comrades are hidden, the Frenchman refuses to give any answer. Putting more pressure on him, the Germans execute his parents and girlfriend. The movie was such a clear case of a pro-Entente film that the trade papers *Variety* and *Moving Picture World* declared it should be banned from the American theatres immediately. Notice had also been given by the German-American Chamber of Commerce to the National Board of Review that this film was a clear-cut example of an outspoken film that was anything but impartial to the European war.

In response to this, the film producer of *The Ordeal* stated the film had been approved by the Secretary of State. He had discussed this subject personally with counselor Robert Lansing, he said. In reality, the film company had received a letter from the State Department saying it had no authority whatsoever on this subject, but the

The general decides on a new plan in Life Photo's "The Ordeal"

Fig. 17. Scene from The Ordeal. *Despite its pro-Entente character attempts to ban this film proved ineffective. [Reproduced from* Motography, *7 November 1914.]*

purported endorsement by the State Department gave the production company just enough time to arrange a premiere exhibition in New York City. The show ran for about a week before the local censors revoked the permit for exhibition. After consultation with the National Board of Review, the movie was adjudged a potential danger to law and order because of its pro-Entente character. In November 1914, this decision was backed up by the legal authorities of the State of New York. *Moving Picture World* reported: "This establishes the claim that the police powers of the city extend not alone to pictures or plays that are obscene or immoral ... but include also pictures or plays which are believed to be against public policy".[62]

However, the influence of censorship on war films, if any, didn't last long. On 26 May 1915, the Federal Court put a stop to the ban that had been placed on *The Ordeal*. Judge Whitaker's decision to allow this film to be shown, he said in an interview, was in no way influenced by the recent sinking of the *Lusitania* by the Germans. According to the judge, people who had been critical about this film were mostly foreigners, and there was no reason why American citizens shouldn't see this film. For the American film industry, this decision on *The Ordeal* opened the door to the showing of war films, without any substantial hindrance from censorship. A movie may have been shot from the Entente or the German side, and as far as documentaries were concerned they could usually be shown in the theatres without any adjustments. From 1915, when in Europe the armies had become accustomed to the daily routine of trench warfare, censorship of war films in the United States played a marginal role. The National Board of Review also appears to have adjusted itself to this new situation. As an advisor of the board said in an interview with the *New York Times*: "What, pray, is war if it is not terrible! The faithful presentation of some details of close fighting should be shown to Americans to satisfy them that is far from a game of ping-pong".[63]

As *The Ordeal* decision may have shown, while Germany may have been doing reasonably well militarily in 1915, it was losing the propaganda war in the United States. The Germans felt, not without reason, that French and British propaganda dominated the media, especially on the Anglophile East Coast (*The Ordeal* being an example), and the cosmopolitan West Coast as well. The only route to get news from Germany to the United States was via London and, especially early in the war, the British censored all news out of Germany. So America tended to hear only the Entente side of the story. Germany had not helped itself much in the propaganda war, either. The Germans' propaganda in the United States had been amateurish – either far too pedantic, or with little concept of the kind of message to deliver to the American public.

Meanwhile in America, the cutting of the communication cables from Germany to the United States was a harsh blow from which the German government never fully recovered. From then on, the Entente controlled practically all news going by cable to America. Against an avalanche of strictly censored news reports from press agencies in London and Paris, the Germans could only use their radio stations at Sayville, Long Island, and Tuckerton, New Jersey, to broadcast their side of the story to the American media. These wireless messages were expensive and mostly reserved for diplomatic dispatches. To complicate matters even further, the United States government in 1915 seized control of the two stations when it was found out that secret messages were sent to direct the German submarines to their next prey out in the Atlantic.

The outbreak of war caught Germany at an enormous disadvantage, as far as any possibilities to influence public opinion in America were concerned. Since 1917, when the United States entered the war, a legend has risen – fuelled by Entente propaganda – that plans for a carefully prepared publicity campaign, financed with millions of dollars from the German Foreign Office, were executed systematically in America. The truth of the matter is less exciting. There was no blue print, no grand design, no "fifth column". German propaganda in the United States tried to work undercover but it was most of all a makeshift operation, put together by a relatively small group of men.

But their basic problem went further than this. The Germans had an expression for a certain kind of propaganda: *Propaganda der Tat*, or "propaganda of the deed". The idea being that what a country does is as important as what it says. Although it may have had an expression for it, Germany's deeds in the first part of the war often put the lie to their words. Germany's violation of the neutrality of Belgium had been a propaganda disaster from which it never totally recovered. Germany tried to make an issue of the supposed use by the English and French of dum-dum bullets, specifically outlawed by the Hague Convention, only to invent and then employ on the battlefield chlorine gas, phosgene gas, mustard gas and inventing the flamethrower, which made dum-dum bullets seem like rather small beer. The Germans had suffered bad experiences in the Franco-Prussian War with *francs-tireurs* (French for civilian or guerrilla snipers), and had developed a policy of mass reprisals against civilian populations for any acts against German soldiers by irregulars. They shot numerous civilians in Belgium on little or no evidence of hostile acts to the Germans. Unrestricted submarine warfare had also become an issue between Germany and America by January of 1915, although the *Lusitania* would not be sunk until May. Whatever their words, German deeds were menacing. There had already been German sabotage attempts against American industry, and they had been caught at it, and Germany was clearly stirring up discord among America, Japan and Mexico. Even their early successes in the war tended to work against them because their battlefield victories suggested anything but an unprepared, peace-loving nation trying to defend itself against encirclement.

But there was another group in America which was decidedly in favor of intervention in Europe. They are generally described as the Easterners, who are considered far more cosmopolitan in their view of international affairs than their mid-western neighbors. This may be true, but as Marxists love to point out, from the moment that J. P. Morgan Jr. and other Eastern bankers put up $12,000,000 to Russia, $50,000,000 to France and $500,000,000 to the British government, it is hard to see how the United States was ever going to be pro-German.[64] There was more than this, of course. Theodore Roosevelt, no longer in office but very much in the fray, said he could never forgive what the Germans had done in Belgium.

Ambassador von Bernstorff and propaganda chief Bernhard Dernburg decided that it would be a good idea to send Americans to cover the war from the German side of the fronts. This was also true of motion pictures. The Germans distributed *Messter-Woche*, the German newsreel, as well as some military documentary films, but Dernburg felt that the films were so heavy-handed that they would never appeal to the American audience, and so saw advantages to sending American filmmakers to Germany to cover the war. James O'Donnell Bennett, of the *Chicago Tribune*, previously mentioned in Chapter I and the *Tribune's* major correspondent, admitted to being pro-German and was an early voice decrying British propaganda about German atrocities. He was joined in his denial of German atrocities by John McCutcheon, also of the *Tribune*, and by Hansen of the *Chicago Daily News*. The *Irish Voice* reported on 4 March 1915 that virtually all Irish American leaders in

Fig. 18. German Ambassador von Bernstorff during an interview, circa 1915.
[Courtesy Library of Congress.]

Chicago endorsed the refusal of aid to Britain, even though they might sympathize with France and Belgium.

As the German army swept across Belgium and took Brussels in a relentless grey wave, on 23 August 1914 the Dutch steamer SS *Noordam* arrived in New York harbor. On board was the German Ambassador to the United States, Count von Bernstorff, back from his summer vacation in Europe. He had been instructed by the Foreign Office in Berlin to bring along the former Secretary of State to the Colonial Office, Dr. Bernhard Dernburg, and Privy Councillor Heinrich Friedrich Albert of the Ministry of the Interior.

Dernburg had been one of the chief colonial administrators for Germany in Africa, but came to America as a delegate of the Red Cross. Dr. Albert's background was chiefly financial. His duty initially was to float German loans for the war effort. It will be noted that neither man had had any experience with press matters or propaganda. Neither man was attached to the German embassy and had a semi-of-ficial function, which was most convenient for von Bernstorff. As he said in his memoirs, this way he couldn't be compromised in his relations with the American administration, by giving out any controversial statements to the American press: "I considered it my duty to give up, as far as I personally was concerned, all propaganda in favour of the German cause".[65]

In reality the German Ambassador kept in close touch with his two associates on propaganda matters, including the use of films, and communicated directly on these affairs with Berlin. Shortly after their arrival in September 1914, Dernburg took his cue from von Bernstorff and launched a press office in New York City, the German Information Service, with offices at 1123 Broadway. He also became the first, semi-official spokesman for the German government in America.

The press office was set up by Matthew B. Claussen, publicity manager for the Hamburg-America Line, who, like many of his colleagues from the Hamburg-America Line, had gone on a leave of absence because numerous German ships were held up indefinitely in American ports. Dernburg picked Claussen for this job presumably as a result of the extensive amount of advertising that he handled. It was expected that he could influence the American media to print the free weekly news sheet that was given out by the German Information Service. Claussen accepted the offer and set up a bureau that translated German articles from various sources which were edited into a news sheet. He also became a trusted advisor for Dernburg's propaganda committee, together with the American journalists William Bayard Hale and George Sylvester Viereck.

Hale was an Episcopal minister who turned towards journalism. He became the managing editor of *Cosmopolitan* magazine, then wrote for various newspapers and became a foreign correspondent for the *New York Times*. Hale had written President Wilson's campaign biography in 1912. Impressed by his talents and interested in learning the true political situation in Mexico, Wilson sent him there in 1913–1915 as a confidential agent reporting directly to the President. As Barbara Tuchman memorably described this episode in his life: "His qualifications for the mission consisted in knowing nothing whatever about Mexico, but a good deal about Wilson".[66] He became an agent of Dernburg in 1914, was editorial chief of the German Information Service and was paid $15,000 a year by the German government. He was also the Berlin correspondent for William Randolph Hearst's INS. He wrote a pro-German book in 1915 entitled *American Rights and British Pretentions on the High Seas*.

Viereck's father was a Bavarian, his mother an American. He was a talented author and wrote numerous books of homoerotic poetry. He became rabidly pro-German about 1907, and became the editor of the newspapers *The Fatherland* and *The International*. Later in 1917 he wrote that the Zimmermann telegram was "a brazen forgery planted by the British agents", at just about the time that German Secretary of State Arthur Zimmermann admitted that he wrote it. Viereck later became a Nazi sympathizer, interviewed Hitler in 1923 and 1933, and was jailed in the U. S. for failing to register as a Nazi agent during the war.

Claussen's bulletin soon caught on and about 500 newspaper editors asked for a daily copy. "Things were getting on fine", Claussen remembered in 1917. "I was the one point where the newspapers could make requests for the things they wished whether it was news, letters of introduction for the correspondents they were sending abroad, or a hundred and one other things. My phone was going day and night. I arranged interviews for the papers with Dr. Dernburg and anybody that could in any way supplement the limited wireless news."[67]

Readers of the news sheet by the German Information Service or "Pressebüro Dernburg" were kept in the dark about the man who actually directed the organization. Dernburg and Dr. Albert may have been in the spotlight as spokesmen, but the man who was actually in charge of the German Information Service was Dr. Karl Alexander Fuehr.[68] He controlled all finances and acted as linchpin with the German Foreign Office in Berlin, always remaining in the background. Described by Viereck as an "intense nervous type" and "a diplomat from the top of his hat to the tip of his toe", Fuehr had been in the German consulate service in Japan prior to the war. He claimed that he was unable to proceed to Germany from Japan. An article in Viereck's *The Fatherland* claimed: "Fuehr found himself unable to proceed further because the United States Department of State, though requested by Count Bernstorff, failed to obtain a safe conduct for him from the British authorities".[69] He remained in New York in the office of the German Consul.

In 1915, Fuehr wrote *The Neutrality of Belgium*, published by Funk and Wagnalls in New York. Later on in the 1930s, he used his best efforts to prevent publishing the memoirs of agent Franz von Rintelen, who will be mentioned later in this book, on the basis that von Rintelen's involvement in various espionage capers in the United States and the Black Tom Explosion would have a very bad effect on American attitudes toward Germany. A highly intelligent man, Fuehr married his American wife Maria N. Smart from Savannah, Georgia, about 1905, and spoke English fluently. More important, Fuehr belonged to that rare class of German official who understood American culture and psychology. When interviewed by the Justice Department on his work for the German Information Service, William Bayard Hale explicitly warned the authorities about Fuehr: "He was about as insane a propagandist as he had ever seen". On behalf of the German Information Service in New York City, Fuehr communicated directly with his former superior in Japan, Consul-General Fritz Thiel, on all daily publicity matters including the use of propaganda films. Like Fuehr, Thiel left Japan after having been attached to the Foreign Office in Berlin and was made ultimately responsible for German propaganda in the USA.

From the outset, the Dernburg propaganda committee had its mind set on highlighting specific publicity subjects. In order to gain the trust and sympathy of the American people, there should be an appeal to "fair play" and not glorification of German *Kultur*

Fig. 19. Albert Dawson on the day he left America, November 1914. Publicity picture © Brown & Dawson/American Correspondent Film Company. [Courtesy New York Public Library.]

or explicit criticism of the American neutrality policy. At a meeting on 5 November 1914, also attended by Ambassador von Bernstorff, they decided that, apart from the distribution of the daily news sheet, a fresh supply of war pictures was also necessary, as well as more encouragement and support for American correspondents to report on the German side of the war.

As a result, photographer and cinematographer Albert K. Dawson was selected to go to Germany, together with Edward Lyell Fox, a reporter for the Wildman Magazine and News Service. Born in Vincennes, Indiana, on 20 September 1885, Dawson started working as a freelance press photographer for the local newspapers. He later joined the staff of Underwood & Underwood in New York City and in 1912 set up his own stock photo agency, Brown & Dawson, in Stamford, Connecticut, which supplied pictures to newspapers, traveling agencies and advertising companies. Dawson's previous work as a ship's photographer for the Hamburg-America Line on several voyages across the Atlantic between the United States and Germany made him the obvious choice. Before the outbreak of war, Dawson had been of immense assistance to Matthew B. Claussen's publicity work for the Hamburg-America Line. According to his own statement at the time, Dawson was going to Europe, representing his photographic firm. The record however shows that he was given this assignment by the German Information Service. In a dispatch to the German Foreign Office on 16 November 1914, Dr. Albert explained: "Mr. Dawson is going over to take pictures in Germany and at the firing line. These will be sent to our press office in order to be made available to the American media. On behalf of Dr. Dernburg, I would like to express our wishes for the need of your assistance to his work. His pictures are of particular significance, because through syndication these will be published in many other illustrated newspapers. He can also judge, much better than we, which type of picture is popular with the American public."[70] This is remarkably sound advice from Dr. Albert, who was not known for having a light touch with the American public.

Thus, in the summer of 1914, America prepared to send moving picture cameramen to Europe. Donald C. Thompson, unofficially representing the *New York World* and/or the *Chicago Tribune*, or claiming to do so, had paid his own way to Belgium. Also en route were Joseph Medill Patterson and Edwin F. Weigle, who had left in August 1914. Wallace and Dawson were heading to Germany in December 1914. Others, like Durborough would leave later. But the invasion was under way.

Notes

1. Kevin Brownlow, *The War, the West and the Wilderness* (New York: Alfred A. Knopf, 1979), 90.

2. NARA RG 59, US Passport Applications 1906–1925, Wilbur H. Durborough Application 48502 dated 25 January, 1915; Record No.8383; Transcript of Church Birth Register, Methodist Episcopal Church, Camden, DE, Delaware State Archives.

3. WHD's civil service application dated 15 June 1942, Hill Field (USAAF Base), Ogden, UT, National Personnel Records Center, Civilian Personnel Records, St. Louis, MO. The vita in his file lists his other work experiences prior to 1940.

4. Christian Wiehe threatened to kill Durborough, later tried to keep the story from the press and, in the end, agreed to have Durborough take his picture. See *Cleveland Plain Dealer* (26 April 1911): 1–2.

5. The 1912 Chicago City Directory lists William (sic) Durborough's office as [Room] 507, 184 W. Washington [St.]

6. A photo Durborough personally copyrighted sourced from Underwood & Underwood that captured the essence of Teddy Roosevelt punctuating "a recent Chicago talk" with his finger appeared with an article two months later when TR was shot in Milwaukee but refused medical attention until after delivering his speech. See *Dallas Morning News* (15 October 1912): 1.

7. See article announcing the venture, *Tacoma Times* (7 October 1912): 1; another claiming the first successful aerial photo of an auto race ever taken on 5 October of the Milwaukee Grand Prix cup race, *Tacoma Times* (9 October 1912): 7.

8. Ibid, 1913, 7.

9. Scripps' [Chicago] Day Book regularly used both his photos and correspondence from the Mexican assignment starting in November and added "correspondent" to his credit byline early 1914. See *Day Book* (Chicago) 9 January 1914, 13.

10. This photo can be found online at http://www.loc.gov/pictures/item/2002707920/ accessed 28 March 2013. The Library of Congress P&P Division has many Durborough photographs taken while covering Mexico and WWI which are filed generically under NEA, the copyrighter. However, searching the Library of Congress "Chronicling America" searchable newspapers online for Durborough can readily identify many of them as Durborough's.

11. *Tacoma Times* (28 November 1913): 1; (1 December 1913): 7; (5 December 1913): 7.

12. Durborough Draft Manuscript Part 1, (hereafter cited as DDM1) Sec. 10, 1, 3, 6–7, Library of Congress, Manuscripts Division, Washington, DC.

13. DDM1, Sec. 11, 1–3, Library of Congress, Manuscripts Division, Washington, DC.

14. This photograph would result in Durborough's subpoena to testify at Salazar's trial in Santa Fe in December 1915. (See NARA RG21, U. S. District Court Records, District of New Mexico, Criminal Case Files 1912–1913, Entry 75, Case no. 2822).

15. DDM1, Sec. 11, 44, 4–7.

16. Ibid, Sec. 12, 1–3.

17. *Des Moines News* (8 January 1914): 1.

18. *Des Moines News* (3 February 1914): 1.

19. DDM1, Sec. 9, 1–3, Sec. 12, 3–7; William H. Beezey, *Insurgent Governor: Abraham Gonzalez and the Mexican Revolution in Chihuahua* (Lincoln Nebraska: University of Nebraska Press, 1973), 158, 162.

20. "William H. Raw Entertains", *St. Louis Republic*, 27 October 1904, 6. William H. Raw was a well-known photographer of stereoscopic cards for the Keystone Company.

21. *Popular Photography* (July 1948): 16, 148.

22. *New York American* (18 June 1911): 11; "London Stays up All Night for Coronation To-Day; 1,00,000 to see

Parade", *New York American* (22 June 1911): 1; Ben H. Proctor, *William Randolph Hearst: Final Edition*, 1911–1951 (Oxford [England], New York: Oxford University Press, 2007), 12; Mary Panzer, *In My Studio: Rudolf Eikemeyer, Jr. and the Art of the Camera, 1885–1930* (Yonkers, N. Y.: Hudson River Museum, 1986), 68. It also appears that Hearst first became aware of the work of George Allison from his writing on the coronation for the *New York Herald*.

23. Ansel E. Wallace, 1912. "Flash-Light Apparatus for Cameras". U. S. Patent 1,042, 856, filed 6 February 1912 and issued 29 October 1912. Wallace's device uses electricity to trigger the flash automatically when the shutter is opened, a great step forward toward the modern flash camera.

24. "Coffyn in an Epochal Flight Puts Man on Outgoing Ship: Liner is Overtaken Swiftly", *New York American* (2 May 1912): 1, 4. In spite of his risky profession and his unfortunate name, Coffyn, of the original Wright Brothers Exhibition Flying Team, died in 1960 in Palo Alto, California at the age of 82.

25. Edward Hatrick to John B. Forster, Charles D. Hilles et al, *William Howard Taft Presidential Papers*, file 494g, Library of Congress, Manuscript Division, cited by Louis Pizzitola, *Hearst over Hollywood* (New York: Columbia University Press, 2002), 457. Interestingly, Hal Reid, manager of the *Universal Animated Weekly* also asked to accompany the Presidential tour and was turned down. Whether Reid's letter, which was quite familiar, irritated Taft, or Taft simply was not ready for newsreels is unclear. The Feature Film Company was also turned down.

26. Edith O'Shaughnessy, *A Diplomat's Wife in Mexico*, (New York and London: Harper and Brothers Publishers, 1916, reprint: Forgotten Books, 2012) 131,141, 178. Edith O'Shaughnessy, *A Diplomat's Wife in Mexico: Letters from the American Embassy at Mexico City Covering the Dramatic Period between October 8, 1913 and the Breaking Off of Diplomatic Relations on April 23rd, 1914, Together with an Account of the Occupation of Vera Cruz*. (New York: Harper Brothers, 1916), 131, 141, 178; Telegram from O'Shaughnessy to Department of State, 12 January 1914, Washington, RDS, RG 59 812/10522. NARA. In Washington, the telegram was stamped by the Division of Latin American Affairs, the Assistant Secretary and The Counselor, so John Bassett Moore must have read it.

27. Ibid. 178. Edith O'Shaughnessy, Ibid., 178; Fremont Older, *William Randolph Hearst, American* (New York and London: D. Appleton-Century Co. 1936), 359–360. See also "Two Americans Arrested", *New York Times* (4 February 1914): 1. The woman, Victoria Hastings, was evidently English and earlier appeared in the newspapers as a volunteer correspondent at the American Embassy during the ten-day bombardment of Mexico City from 9–19 February 1913, which culminated in the deposition and execution of President Francisco Madero. "American Women Heroines during the Ten Days of Fighting in Mexico City", *Washington Herald* (22 February 1913): 9.

28. Terry Ramsaye, *A Million and One Nights* (New York: Simon and Schuster 1926), 658.

29. 'Joseph Medill Patterson', http://arlingtoncemetery.net (consulted 1 April 2010).

30. Joseph Medill Patterson, letter of recommendation, 23 June 1917. Joseph Medill Patterson Collection, Donnelley Library, Lake Forest College, Lake Forest, Illinois.

31. Norman Alley, *I Witness* (New York: Wilfried Funk 1941), 20–23;" Johnson Left out on 30,000 Bond", *Chicago Tribune* (16 November 1912): 2; "Find Gambling Man is Wounded", *Chicago Tribune* (14 July 1913): 3:" Clamp Lid Tight on Gambling Den: result of Expose", *Chicago Tribune* (15 July 1913): 1; "Verdict Acquits Max Annenberg", *Chicago Tribune* (8 October 1913): 3; "The Gambler's War", *Chicago Tribune* (15 July 1913): 6.

32. Edwin F. Weigle, *My Experiences on the Belgian Battlefields in the Great European War* (Chicago: The Hamming Publishing Co., 1914), 10.

33. Ramsaye, 684. For the *Herald*, another newspaper anxious to get into the newsreel business, Harold Brown produced the newsreel *Chicago Herald Movies* in 1914.

34. Not even close. Documentary footage had been shot during the Spanish American War in 1898.

35. Edwin F. Weigle, "'Laughing in the Face of Death, by Edwin F. Weigle, Eye Witness of the Battle of Vera Cruz", *Chicago Daily Tribune* (10 May 1914): G1. There is no known support for Weigle's story, but there is nothing to refute it either. The navy and marines first landed on Tuesday, not Wednesday. According to the reports of William W. Canada, U. S. Consul in Veracruz, the marines from the *Prairie* landed in Vera Cruz at about 11:20 a.m. on Tuesday 21 April 1914. It would appear that Weigle is wrong when he says that the date was Wednesday. If it were Wednesday, a day after the invasion, Weigle and Durborough would not have been on the Mexican side of the lines. In addition, the marines' first objective after they landed on Tuesday was the railroad terminal to get control of the trains before the Mexicans did (they did not succeed; the trains had been ordered out of Vera Cruz), which makes Weigle's statement that he was photographing Mexicans embarking on a train unlikely. If the date were actually Tuesday, the man Weigle saw shot could have been one of several marines or sailors. Four Americans, two marines and two sailors died on 21 April. Corporal Daniel Aloysius Haggerty died on 21 April, but Haggerty was killed at 1:30 pm on the roof of the Hotel Terminal. The other was Private Samuel Marten, born Samuel Meisenberg who was part of the landing party from the USS *Florida*. Seamen George Poinsett and John F. Schumacher, both from the landing party of the USS *Florida*, were killed the first day. Poinsett is unlikely, because he was reported hoisting the flag on the plaza when he was shot. The landing party from the USS *Florida* came ashore on 21 April about the same time as the *Prairie*. U. S. Marine Corps Muster Rolls, 1798–1940, National

Archives Microfilm T1118, Ancestry.com; Robert E. Quirk, *An Affair of Honor: Woodrow Wilson and the Occupation of Veracruz* (New York and London: W. W. Norton & Company, 1967), 93–95; Thomas Herbert Russell, *Mexico in Peace and War* (Chicago: Reilley-Britton Syndicate, 1914), 22.

36.   "The Senator Bailey is Home", *Galveston Daily News* (7 May 1914): 10; C. G. McCarthy, "Boys of the Fifth Brigade in Mexico", *Galveston Daily News* (7 May 1914): 1. Evidently the navy ship spotted the tugboat following the convoy to Vera Cruz.

37.   Victor Milner, 'Fade Out and Slowly Fade in', *American Cinematographer*, (1924): 9, 13, 14, 18, 22, cited at http://cinesilentemexicano.wordpress.com

38.   *Reading Eagle* (3 May 1914): 11.

39.   United States War Department, *Annual Report of the Secretary of War* (Washington: Government Printing Office, 1916), 312; Anne Cipriano Venzon, ed., General Smedley Darlington Butler: *The Letters of a Leatherneck, 1898–1931* (New York: Praeger, 1992); Adrian C. Duff, 'Eye Pictures of Vera Cruz City As Seen by the Man with a Camera', *Daily News* (Batavia, New York) (18 June 1914): 4; For photographs of El Tejar by James Hare, including one showing some of the correspondents mingling with the Federales, see *Colliers* (30 May 1914): 9–10. Apparently many war correspondents and other photographers either walked or took handcars to El Tejar, including Victor Milner, Richard Harding Davis, Frank Palmer Coates, Hall Simmons Starrett and Joseph Medill Patterson, editor of the *Chicago Tribune*. Patterson wrote that the Battle of El Tejar consisted of three shots. Joseph Medill Patterson, 'Terrific Battle of Three Shots', *Chicago Tribune* (4 May 1914): 3; Richard Harding Davis, 'Try to Pass my Post', *Washington Post* (4 May 1914): 1. Victor Milner may have been on the back of the photographers' handcar doing the pumping. He reported: '… a rumor reached us that the Mexicans were preparing for an attack on the water-works. We went immediately to Gen. Funston's headquarters and were given permission to accompany the troops. The soldiers were on the way and doing double time up the narrow gauge railway. There was a dozen of us with cumbersome outfits which were mostly Graflexes and other cameras. Mine with a tripod and an extra magazine, was the heaviest of all, and it was not an easy job to lug it double-time up-hill in tropical weather. It required a smart man to suggest that we find a handcar and let it work for us – and that man was Jim O'Hare of *Collier's Weekly*. How we did perspire pumping that handcar. 'Of course there wasn't any attack. Gen. Funston was a little too fast for them. The only attack that I experienced was one of "chiggers" which required a Vaseline bath in the hospital to stem their onslaught.' Victor Milner, 'Fade Out and Slowly Fade in'. *American Cinematographer* (1924): 9, 13, 14, 18, 22, cited at http://cinesilentemexicano.wordpress.com.

40.   Charles Belmond Davis (ed.) *Adventures and Letters of Richard Harding Davis* (New York: Charles Scribners Sons, 1917), 356.

41.   Mark Cronlund Anderson, *Pancho Villa's Revolution by Headlines* (Norman: University of Oklahoma Press., 1997), 241, 243, citing [Leon J.] Canova to [William Jennings] Bryan, 8 July 1914, in RDS [Records of the Department of State] 812/14805, National Archives.

42.   *Hearst Selig News Pictorial* No. 54 (3 September 1914). *Motion Picture News* (19 September 1914): 62. 'The Opening of the Panama Canal', *Bulletin of the Pan-American Union* 39 (September 1914): 363. Wallace was back in New York from Cristobal (Panama Canal Zone) on 28 August 1914.

43.   United States Senate, 66th Congress, 1st Session, Document no. 61, *Brewing and Liquor Interests and German and Bolshevik Propaganda: Report and Hearings of the Subcommittee of the Judiciary*, Vol. 2 (Washington, D.C.: Government Printing Office, 1919), 1678.

44.   E.T. Baker III, "Newsreel Man for 30 Years", *The Baltimore Sun* (6 August 1944): Sunday magazine.

45.   E.T. Baker III, "Newsreel Man for 30 Years", *The Baltimore Sun* (6 August 1944): Sunday magazine.

46.   "Finds More Thrills Turning Reel Than Plowing In Kansas", *Hutchinson Kansas News* (25 July 1935): 10; *Gould's 1908 Directory* (Kansas City, Mo.: Gould Directory Co., 1908), 481.

47.   In Edwards' scrapbooks there are several photographs from New Orleans dated 1908 and 1909. Wiegman family papers [A8a, 109a].

48.   'The Henry Ford Peace Expedition: List of members and other persons Connected with the Expedition", Copenhagen, January 1918. This seems to be an addendum to the "Henry Ford's Peace Expedition: Who's Who", December 1915. Both seem to be privately published by Ford for use within the peace conference. Swarthmore College Peace Collection, Swarthmore College, Swarthmore, Pennsylvania.

49.   Newark City Directory (Newark: Price and Lee Company, 1911) 1492. In 1912, Edwards is listed as manager, residing at 601 Broad Street while Floyd A. Walter is residing next door at 605. Newark City Directory (Newark: Price and Lee Company, 1912), 624.

50.   "Finds More Thrills Turning Reel Than Plowing In Kansas", *Hutchinson Kansas News* (25 July 1935): 10; Baker, "Newsreel Man for Thirty Years". A film frame in Edwards' personal collection shows he was interested in motion pictures as early as 1910. [A91]

51. David Nasaw, *The Chief: The Life of William Randolph Hearst* (New York and Boston: Houghton Mifflin Company/ Mariner Books, 2000), 234. According to Hatrick, he sent a cameraman named Louis de Lorme to photograph the inauguration. This is possible, but de Lorme, who worked for International Film Service, later was a writer for the animation department. Louis Pizzitola, *Hearst Over Hollywood* (New York: Columbia University Press, 2002), 101.

52. David Nasaw, *The Chief: The Life of William Randolph Hearst*, 234, citing Terry Ramsaye, *A Million and One Nights: A History of the Motion Picture Through 1925* (New York: Simon and Schuster, 1926), 654–661; Earl Theisen, "Story of the Newsreel", *International Photographer* (September 1933): 24; Raymond Fielding, *The American Newsreel 1911–1967* (Norman: University of Oklahoma Press, 1972), 70–85.

53. Kevin Brownlow, *The War, the West and the Wilderness* (New York: Alfred A. Knopf, 1979), 90.

54. "Ejercito Constitucionalista", Safe Conduct 2 August 1914 for N. E. Edwards. Wiegman family papers [A36b]

55. N. E. Edwards, "Photographer Writes of his Adventures in Filming Strike Scenes", Unknown newspaper, Wiegman family papers, [97a, 97b].

56. James Langland, ed., *Chicago Daily News Almanac and Year Book for 1918*, Vol. 34 (Chicago: Chicago Daily News Co, 1918), 571.

57. Editors Jaci Cole and John Maxwell Hamilton, *Journalism of the Highest Realm, The Memoir of Edward Price Bell* (Baton Rouge: Louisiana State Univ. Press, 2007): 226, 228, 236, 299–305; http://en.wikipedia.org/wiki/Edward_Price_Bell, accessed 22 March 2014.

58. "Fake War Pictures Stir the East Side", *New York Times* (6 September 1914): 6.

59. *Variety*, 14 August 1914, 3; *Billboard* (15 August 1914): 54.

60. "The War and the Pictures", *Moving Picture World* (15 August 1915): 964.

61. "Predicts War Picture Trouble", *Billboard* (26 September 1914): 61.

62. "Backs up National Board", *Moving Picture World* (5 December 1914): 1358.

63. "Pictures that Terrify", *New York Times* (23 October 1915): 10.

64. J.P. Morgan Jr., Wikipedia, citing Martin Horn, "A Private Bank at War: J. P. Morgan & Co. and France, 1914–1918", *Business History Review* 74, 85–112.

65. Johann Heinrich Graf von Bernstorff, *My Three Years in America* (New York: Charles Scribner's 1920), 39.

66. Barbara Tuchmann, *The Zimmermann Telegram* (New York: Viking Press, 1958, Bantam Edition, 1971), 41–42.

67. National Archives, Investigative Case Files of the Bureau of Investigation. Subject: Matthew Byrnes Claussen. Case File 65-HQ-31143. Courtesy David Wiener and Lloyd Billingsley. Hereafter given as NARA, Case File Claussen. The reason why Claussen was chosen as press agent for the German Information Service is also based on a statement by Viereck to special agent Blatchford, dated 9 January 1918. See NARA, case file George Sylvester Viereck 8000-22990.

68. National Archives, RG 65, cited in Maria Keipert, Peter Grupp, eds. *Biograpisches Handbuch des deutschen Auswärtigen Dienstes*, Vol. 1 A-F. (Paderborn: Ferdinand Schöningh, 2000), 628.

69. "The Criminal Records of Captain Guy Gaunt, C. M. G., Naval Attaché of the British Embassy", *Fatherland*, Vol. 4 no. 16 (24 May 1916): 244. Presumably, Fuehr could have gotten back to Germany if he truly needed to do so. Guy Gaunt was indeed a notable British spy, and was instrumental in breaking up a German-Hindu conspiracy during the war.

70. Letter, Heinrich Albert to Dr. Hammann, 16 November 1914. AAPA R20555/000094.

Chapter 3

Belgium

When the war was hours old, the first American journalists and cameramen were on their way to Belgium. Joseph Medill Patterson, co-editor of the *Chicago Tribune*, formed one team with Edwin F. Weigle. Others that went individually and teamed up in Belgium were E. Alexander Powell, journalist for the *New York World*, and Donald C. Thompson, cameraman.

Belgium was where the war began and the critical feature from the war correspondents' view was the chaos resulting from the Belgians being overwhelmed by an invading army they were not prepared to fight. The Belgians had no plans for handling war correspondents and would have had no time to do so even if they had. William G. Shepherd called it the "free lance days", a period of openness at the beginning of the war when anyone could catch a boat for Antwerp from elsewhere with no press credentials necessary. A lot of fakes and amateurs came to Belgium who claimed to be covering the war and there was even one individual who sent dispatches "from the front" without ever leaving his hotel suite at the Ritz-Carlton in Paris. But the situation benefited the real news gatherers who were generally free to cover whatever they wanted, unless they were unfortunate enough to meet a real martinet. For journalists, it was like Dodge City of the Old West.

Shortly after the outbreak of the war on 3 August 1914, Patterson and Weigle left Chicago for New York. In Weigle's steamer trunk were two Kodak photo cameras, three hours of unexposed film and one cinema camera, which was probably a Pathé model.[1] They sailed on the SS *Rotterdam* for Holland on 11 August. The original plan was to take moving pictures in Germany but after spending ten days in Germany trying to get permission from the authorities, Weigle found himself forbidden to shoot motion picture film of any kind. He only was allowed to shoot still pictures during a 30 August tour authorized by the Germans at Alten Grabow, the German prison camp fifty miles outside of Berlin. From the window of his Adlon hotel room in Berlin, he also got a few shots of Sedan Day on 2 September, but that was all. Because of their foreign appearance, the two Americans were eyed by the Germans with an unmistakable feeling of distrust. Weigle's cameras especially triggered the fear that he could be a spy. Because he was a photographer, Weigle was not allowed to join a group of correspondents who visited the recently captured forts of Liège.

Finally, he decided that remaining in Germany was a waste of time and left for the fighting in Belgium to see if he could cover the war from the Belgian side.

The Germans had crossed the Belgian border on 4 August, violating Belgian neutrality, and by 14 August had demolished the forts at Liège and Namur with their siege guns. By 24 August, after having taken Brussels, they headed south into France. However, while the Germans conquered the southern part of Belgium and were free to commence the massive leftward wheel of their armies into France, the Belgians still held northern Belgium and the great fortified city of Antwerp. As E. Alexander Powell, who wrote perhaps the best book on the siege of Antwerp, stated it:

> Suppose, for the sake of having things quite clear, that you unfold the map of Belgium. Now, with your pencil, draw a line across the country from east to west, starting at the Dutch city of Maastricht and passing through Hasselt, Diest, Aerschot, Malines, Alost and Courtrai to the French frontier. This line was, roughly speaking, 'the front', and for upwards of two months fighting of a more or less serious character took place along its entire length.[2]

The Germans recognized that they could not leave Antwerp, perhaps the most fortified city in the world, behind their lines on their right flank as they headed south into France. If there were any doubt of that, the Belgians quickly attacked the Germans at a number of sectors on the front, such as Aerschot, Malines and Termonde. There was also the concern the British could use Antwerp as a base for a later assault on the Germans. The Germans were therefore determined to capture Antwerp. To do so they had to seize the villages and other strong points surrounding Antwerp that would enable their massive 30.5 mortars and 42 cm. siege guns to reach Antwerp itself. It was obvious that the fight for Antwerp was going to be a big story in the fall of 1914, so Weigle and Patterson headed for Belgium.

They were not the only ones. As Germany and Britain forbade war correspondents to cover the war (Donald C. Thompson was later to say that he was arrested eight times,[3] and even the prominent pro-German newspaper publisher Joseph Patterson was arrested in Westphalia), there was a general influx of correspondents toward Belgium. After overcoming problems with the police, Weigle reached Antwerp.

Weigle was at first pleased to have finally gotten to Antwerp and was sure there were no remaining obstacles to his filming. He was wrong. When he talked to American Vice Consul Spencer, Spencer said there was no hope of getting permission to film with the Belgian forces. The previous week, Spencer had tried to obtain permission for Irwin S. Cobb and Frederick Palmer to go to the Belgian front and had been refused by the Foreign Office. Weigle did not know what to do. He tried to get help from Powell, who had excellent official connections in Belgium, but Powell turned Weigle down flat.

Weigle then had an inspiration. What if half the proceeds of the *Tribune* film were to go to the Belgian Red Cross? Weigle went back to Vice Consul Spencer, who thought it was a great idea. The Belgian military liked the scheme as well; the whole plan was finally approved by General Victor de Guise, Chief Commander of the

Fig. 20. Weigle filming from Notre Dame Cathedral, Antwerp.
[Reproduced from Moving Picture World, *12 December 1914.]*

fortified position of Antwerp. Weigle received a document with his photograph, code letters and the seal of Belgium upon it, but he was disappointed to find that the document only allowed him to take motion pictures of Antwerp and German prisoners. Still, he was pleased. He wired Patterson in Berlin, who congratulated Weigle and decided to make the deal formal. They went to the Belgian Red Cross and wrote up a binding contract. The Red Cross also agreed to furnish Weigle and Patterson an automobile and chauffeur. In addition, they received official passes to take motion pictures or still photographs anywhere in Belgium, which of course delighted Weigle.[4]

Weigle spent his first few days in Antwerp in September photographing Notre Dame Cathedral and shooting film of the pontoon bridge over the River Scheldt, over which much of the population of Antwerp as well as the Belgian and British armies escaped into Holland when the Germans finally seized Antwerp in October. After Weigle and Patterson got permission to photograph and shoot film anywhere in Belgium, they began covering the series of battles taking place in and around Antwerp as the Germans closed in on it. They would leave Antwerp in the morning by car, visit some hot spot where they would photograph and write dispatches, then return in the evening to Antwerp and the Hotel St. Antoine. In this way, they covered the battles of Termines, Alost, Aerschot, Lierre and Malines. Weigle filmed burning houses at Alost and at Lierre, a town which had been deliberately flooded by the Belgians.

According to Weigle, his first pictures of actual combat were filmed near Termonde. He had placed his motion picture camera in an abandoned house about 200 meters from the Belgian line, when suddenly the Germans opened fire. The Belgians retreated under a hail of bullets. Patterson, who usually carried the heavy film equipment, urged Weigle, who carried the camera and tripod, to dump all the camera equipment in a ditch. Said Weigle: "I kept on taking motion pictures until the Germans were too close for safety. Then I followed after the Belgians."[5]

On 15 September, Weigle and Patterson decided to go to Termonde where there was purportedly a battle in progress, but the worst of the fighting had already finished before they arrived.

> The scenes at Termonde were pathetic. Dead bodies of soldiers and of women and children were to be seen lying in the streets ... . At one point I noticed a wretched-looking woman coming along pushing a wheelbarrow. As she neared me I saw a body in the wheelbarrow. It was her child – a boy of seven. He had been struck by a fragment of shrapnel. His body was terribly torn. We spoke to the woman. She was under the impression that her son was still partially alive and she was taking him where he might be saved. We did not tell her that all life had already passed out of the limp body in the wheelbarrow even though our eyes told us that her son – her only son – was dead ... .

> While I took motion pictures at Termonde, I was unable to get 'motion' pictures in the full sense of the word; because life had passed out. Only still death was visible.[6]

Weigle and Patterson got into trouble once again. Patterson had written a story that was published in the *Tribune* and also cabled to *The Times* which the Belgians deemed pro-German. On 2 October, when the story reached General De Guise, he had Patterson and Weigle arrested and their camera equipment and film confiscated. The American Consul managed to get them out of jail and the Belgians returned their equipment and belongings, but the next day Patterson decided to leave Antwerp for Berlin, and took the film that they had shot with him to send on to Chicago. Weigle decided to stay in Antwerp a while longer.

Antwerp was surrounded by twelve forts; in addition the Belgians had made the whole area around the city a fortified zone. It was considered to be impregnable to direct assault. But the Germans had no intention of a making a direct infantry assault on Antwerp. In the series of smaller battles that Patterson and Weigle had witnessed, the Germans had gotten close enough to Antwerp to begin to shell the forts with their terrible mortars, and to use smaller guns to shell the city directly. On 6 October, the Germans began the fearful shelling of Antwerp. The Germans used their Krupp 42 siege guns and 30.5 centimeter Skoda mortars. The 42cm gun was capable of throwing a projectile sixteen and a half inches in diameter and weighing nearly a ton 27,900 feet, more than five miles. Each projectile contained 300 pounds of powder.[7] These were the weapons that had made short work of the Belgian works at Liège and Namur and would destroy the forts surrounding Antwerp. Antwerp soon became a ghost town, the inhabitants huddled in their homes or already fleeing across the Scheldt towards Holland on the pontoon bridge, the only escape route toward neutral

Fig. 21. "Fort Thompson", May 2012. Damage to Rue du Péage, as a result of the German bombardment of Antwerp, must have been substantial. Many houses in this street date from after World War I.

Holland. The Hotel St. Antoine, where Weigle and many other correspondents were staying, closed due to the barrage, and Weigle, feeling blue anyway since Patterson had left, was on his own. Donald C. Thompson had rented a pleasant house at 74 rue du Péage, and he invited E. E. Hunt, a correspondent for *Colliers Weekly* who later became active in Belgian War Relief, to stay with him, along with Weigle and D. H. de Meister, the Dutch vice consul. Unfortunately the house was located in the southeast quarter of Antwerp, closest to the German guns. Thompson had planted a large American flag in front of the building. Hunt later described the destruction of the house at 74 rue du Péage that night:

I was awakened by a tremendous roar and a shock which seemed to lift the house from its foundations. Immediately there came a distant boom! A shrill snarling whistle, then another explosion which pounded the air like storm.

Boom -wheeeeeeeeeeeeeeeeeieiei eieiekkkkkkkkBANGGGGG G! – Boom – wheeeeeeeeeeeEEEEEEEIEIEIEIEIEKKKKKKKK BANGGGGGGGGGG! Every pane of glass in the house blew out in the chaos which followed the bursting of that fourth bomb. It had hit directly across the street, less than thirty five feet from where I was hurrying into my clothes. I could hear screams and sobs; then the sound of people rushing by the house, then the rash of glass which littered the sidewalks splintering to bits as the people ran. But above every other sound clamored the continuous mad-dog snarling of the German shells ... .[8]

Weigle and the others decided to take refuge in the coal cellar in the basement, the safest place they could find in the building, and blocked the door with mattresses. Antwerp was shelled the rest of the night by German 28 cm guns working in batteries of four. Weigle related:

The next thing that happened was the falling of a mass of debris, which we knew represented the top of our building crumbling in. It followed immediately after a volley of shot. We could hear brick and other material pounding on the door of our sub-cellar. Pieces of the debris forced their way through the door and embedded themselves in the mattresses. We did not dare to get out. We could only stay there and wait until death came.

We waited and waited. The hours passed slowly. We watched the minutes pass. Suddenly at 3:30 in the afternoon, a shell struck our house with deadly crash. The entire building tumbled. Debris poured in. The dust and smoke, from the burning matter above, were suffocating. The air was clouded with smoke. We felt sure that we would smother and burn to death if we did not get out. We decided to get out rather than being burned alive.[9]

When Weigle and the others got out of the building, now unofficially known as Fort Thompson, they were amazed to see clear blue sky. Their abode, along with a whole row of houses across the street, was destroyed. They had been in the building for something like fifteen hours. Weigle grabbed his camera, by some miracle unscathed by the bombardment, and ran as fast as he could in the opposite direction of the shelling. The Hotel St. Antoine was intact, but the Hotel de L'Europe was on fire. Notre Dame Cathedral was untouched. The Queen hotel was deserted, except for a few members of the staff. Weigle went to the roof.

I rushed to the roof of the Hotel Queen with my camera. Here was a beautiful sight. The entire portion of Antwerp, from which we had come, was in flames. I also secured some splendid views of the Belgian and British armies fleeing over the pontoon bridge which extended across the River Scheldt. It was awe-inspiring to see those thousands of people rushing from Antwerp as the sun went down.

At 11 o'clock the next morning, the Germans entered the city.[10]

Weigle grabbed a tug and crossed the Scheldt into Holland, filming Belgian refugees in Kieldrecht. From there, he got to Rotterdam via the Hague. Then, from London, he arrived in New York on the SS *Philadelphia* on 25 October, and was back in Chicago by 26 October.

There is one story about Weigle's coverage in Antwerp, mentioned both by Weigle and Patterson, which could not be told until after Antwerp fell.[11] There had been gossip that the Belgians had a machine gun in the tower of Notre Dame Cathedral in Antwerp, which would give the Germans an excellent excuse for shelling the cathedral. The Belgians had no machine gun but did have a telescope. When Weigle and Patterson first arrived in Antwerp, Weigle shot a photograph in the cathedral tower showing Belgian aviation scouts observing and reporting German activities around the city. When Patterson left Antwerp, he took a copy of the photograph with him, and sent it to the *Tribune*, which caused a problem. If the *Tribune* published the photograph, the Germans would have proof that the tower was being used for military purposes. On the other hand, if Patterson telegraphed the *Tribune* and told the paper not to run it, it would be proof to the Belgians and Germans that the photograph existed. E. Alexander Powell apparently came to the rescue, explained the situation to the Belgians and showed them the photographs. They sent him to the Germans, promising that the Belgian scouts would be removed if the Germans would spare the cathedral. The Germans agreed. As a result, all scouts were removed from the tower, saving it from destruction.

On 14 November, Weigle's film *On Belgian Battlefields* opened at the elegant Romanesque Studebaker Theatre in Chicago. It was a success. According to the *Tribune*, an admittedly biased source, on the first day over 8,000 people jammed the theater, hundreds had to be turned away, and special police had to hold back the crowds on Michigan Avenue.[12] In the trade press, the exhibitor at the Studebaker said he was surprised by the success of the *Chicago Tribune* war pictures. On 5 December, it was announced that the exhibition would be prolonged for another week. Distribution of the film also apparently went well. The Central Film Company, which owned the distribution rights, announced on 19 November 1914, that Ohio had brought in $10,000. New York, New Jersey and Pennsylvania generated another $25,000.[13] Patterson later estimated that the film made $60,000 in net profits.[14]

In New York *On Belgian Battlefields* was screened for an exhibitor's preview. *Variety* reported that the film was received with lukewarm feelings. Most of the scenes looked like the familiar newsreel pictures: wrecked buildings, inspections near the front, refugees fleeing the front line and the like. Even though the reviewer found no reason to suppose that any scenes had been reconstructed for the camera, the overwhelming impression was that the movie looked "fakey".[15] The film trade people were disappointed for several reasons. One of them was the blazing publicity given to Weigle's film by the *Tribune's* copy writers. According to *Variety*, scenes of combat were extremely limited. In one particular sequence the audience saw a group of Belgian soldiers in the trenches near Malines while under fire. Some of the wounded were seen being replaced by new soldiers. "Mere scenes of unpeopled wreck [sic] are rather disappointing when one's expectations have been aroused to the point of looking for a visualisation of war's actual clash and conflict."[16] The name of the *Tribune* ("The Greatest Newspaper in the World") appeared on the credits and intertitles. Therefore, as far as *Variety* was concerned, the film was mainly a publicity drive for the *Chicago Tribune*. This seems an odd criticism, since most film intertitles of the time listed the names of the studio and producer in the largest letters possible.

Nevertheless, from a commercial point of view, the film, one of the first war documentaries shown in the United States, was a remarkable success. This was for numerous reasons. First, the film had an official stamp which was prominent in the *Tribune's* advertisements. This signified that the moviegoer would not just be seeing a lot of staged scenes or shots from a different war altogether. He would be participating, in a small way at least, in a "good cause". A lot of attention was given to Patterson's contract with the Belgian Red Cross. In one of the press releases, Van Langermeesch – the head of the Belgian Red Cross – was even described as representing the Belgian military authorities. Apparently, the *Chicago Tribune* had the

Fig. 22. Weigle's film was backed up by extensive publicity. [Full page advertisement reproduced from the Chicago Tribune, *14 November 1914.]*

exclusive right to shoot the Great War in Belgium: "The undersigned of the first party [The Red Cross] agrees to grant to no one his authorization to take cinematographic views of theatre of war".[17] Even assuming that this was part of the deal – which can reasonably be doubted – there were in fact several photographers active at the same

Fig. 23. Scene from On Belgian Battlefields.
[Reproduced from Moving Picture World, *12 December 1914.]*

time in Belgium and they all had a permit in hand. But the *Chicago Tribune* had one major advantage. By closing this contract with Belgian Red Cross, the company showed that the film was unquestionably authentic. Given that so many "actual" war pictures were faked or revamped, this was indeed a substantial asset.

Second, and even more importantly, the film supported a popular cause. In the early days of World War I, many Americans had a great deal of sympathy for "poor little Belgium", the neutral country that had been brutally overrun by the German Army, and they remembered Reich Chancellor Theobald von Bethmann-Hollweg's colossally stupid remark that the treaty guaranteeing Belgian neutrality was a mere scrap of paper. This meant that many Americans were concerned with the tragic fate of Belgium. Altogether the *Chicago Tribune* collected $20,540.00 for the Belgian Red Cross from moviegoers. The Belgian consul in Chicago declared that the exhibition of *On Belgian Battlefields* was an important factor in winning the hearts of Chicagoans for his country, and worth far more than the money.[18] It may be argued that this was hypocritical of the *Tribune*. In *Notebook of a Neutral*, Patterson had maintained that Belgium should be put under the permanent military control of France.[19]

There is one remaining issue regarding Belgium that persists after 100 years, and since the pro-German *Chicago Tribune*, for whom Weigle worked, is deeply implicated, it should be mentioned. In 1914, the *Chicago Tribune* sent a group of five correspondents to Germany to examine the charges that the German Army had committed atrocities in Belgium and northern France. This group consisted of James O'Donnell Bennett and John T. McCutcheon of the *Chicago Tribune*, Harry Hansen of the *Chicago Daily News*, Roger Lewis of the Associated Press, and Irwin S. Cobb of the *Saturday Evening Post*. In what they called a "Round Robin", they wired Chicago from Aix-La Chapelle on 2 September 1914 that they had found "absolutely no evidence of atrocities committed by the German Army against civilians in Belgium".[20]

There has been much excellent scholarship in the last ten years on the German atrocities in Belgium. Jeff Lipkes flatly states in his excellent book *Rehearsals* that the five correspondents lied.[21] In fact, the truth is more complicated.

Depending on the interpretation of their remarks, one could state that the correspondents admitted to seeing atrocities. For instance, in discussing the destruction of Louvain, Bennett says:

> A few days later Louvain lost its head. It went mad. Its civilians fired from ambuscade upon German soldiers.
>
> The deed was the supreme outrage against laws of civilized warfare.
>
> The punishment was terrible and it has put the fear of the Prussian god into every Belgian city and hamlet from Antwerp to Beaumont, from Ostend to Liege.
>
> Today the ancient and renowned university city of northern Europe lies in ashes.
>
> The halls in which so many American priests of the Roman church are proud to tell you they have studied are level with the ground. It was awful, but it was war.[22]

But was it? First of all, the charge that Germans were fired upon from ambush, like most of the *franc-tireur* allegations, has proved to be highly unreliable. But because of this incident, on 25 August 1914, the German Army ravaged the city of Louvain, burning with gasoline the city's library of 300,000 medieval books and manuscripts, murdering 248 residents and expelling the entire population of 10,000.[23] From this one can get a pretty good idea of the approach that Bennett took. He said that he saw no evidence of atrocities, but he said that if they occurred, (1) they were not atrocities, or (2) they were justified. He also takes a very strict definition to what constitutes an atrocity. A few sentences further on, he comments: "Always on our march the facts relative to the German atrocities evaded us. Always it was the next village that a woman had been outraged, a child butchered, or an innocent man tortured. Arriving at that next village, we could get no confirmation from the inhabitants." This tends to substantiate the allegations that the really lurid stories of atrocities – nuns raped, children bayoneted, hands cut off and so on – were false. It does not address the issue of shooting and hanging alleged *francs-tireurs* out of hand. Bennett was not the only one who hedged on what constituted an atrocity. Irwin S. Cobb, another of the five correspondents, who was accompanying von Kluck's army, watched from a window as six hostages were shot.[24] Later, after America entered the war, he reported the issue a little differently:

> But I was an eyewitness to crimes which, measured by the standards of humanity and civilization, impressed me as worse than any individual excess, any individual outrage, could ever have been or can ever be; because these crimes indubitably were instigated on a wholesale basis by orders of officers of rank, and must have been carried out under their personal supervision, direction and approval. Briefly, what I saw was this: I saw wide areas of Belgium and France in which not a penny's worth of wanton destruction had been permitted to occur, in which the ripe pears hung untouched upon the garden walls; and I saw other side areas where scarcely one stone had been left to stand upon another; where fields were ravaged; where the male villagers had been shot in squads; where the miserable survivors had been left to den in holes, like wild beasts.[25]

And of course, the correspondents made naive comments on their fact finding trip in September 1914. First they complained that when interrogated, the Belgians did not come forth with any charges against the Germans. This leaves aside the Belgians' natural reluctance to comment openly to correspondents on what happened, since the journalists would not be there when the Germans might take possible reprisals against tale tellers.

Additionally, the correspondents were not taken to towns that suffered especially from atrocities, but instead went to points south of the German line of march. In their cablegram, their destinations included Landen, Louvain, Brussels, Nivelles, Binche, La Buissière, Hantes Wiheries, Merbes-le-Château, Soire-sur-Sambre and Beaumont.[26] None of these towns reported major atrocities, although the home page of Merbes le Château does mention that damage from heavy fighting destroyed some of the Roman ruins. Soire-sur Sambre is listed as a castle. The correspondents do list going to Louvain, but they did not go to Aarshot (156 dead), Andenne (211 dead), Tamines (383 dead), or Dinant (674 dead). It also is rather remarkable that five correspondents on a fact-finding trip like this did not include a photographer or a cinematographer. Patterson's own stance can be suggested by what Bennett says about him in his report of 12 September 1914 to the *Chicago Tribune*:

> Last Sunday night I had the pleasure of seeing Joseph Medill Patterson in Aix. He came up from Berlin under military escort with five other American correspondents and was permitted to view the forts at Liège [the ones which Weigle was not allowed to film].

> He was much discouraged about the war correspondents' game and says the jig is up, and that no armies will longer tolerate them.

> He was so kind as to say, however, that if my anti-atrocities story, which should, as I said, reach you tomorrow evening, did get through to Chicago it would be worth the trip I made from London.[27]

And even more remarkably, Bennett quotes Patterson as follows:

> All the men in the groups of Americans here have been convinced by a fortnight's observation with the troops on the countryside and with the citizens in this town that the situation involves nothing less than the reshaping of Europe by Teutonic hands. It is a new European empire swinging into being, and if Europe doesn't like it, Europe will have to fight over the matter for the next five and twenty years.

> To us the German ascendancy seems as inevitable as sunrise tomorrow. God save us, but the system and the power behind the system are just as incredible, and the spirit of the people is overpowering.

> What Joe Patterson had seen had him talking last Sunday night in precisely the same strain I am writing to you tonight – a strain that may seem to you hysterical, but that is in truth very, very grave.[28]

This may be the letter that when it was printed in Chicago, impelled the Belgians to arrest Weigle and Patterson and encourage Patterson to leave Belgium.

It might in addition be fairly charged that Weigle's book, *My Experiences on the Belgian Battlefields*, is not as even-handed in its description of the war as it seems, more because of what it does not say than by what it says. Weigle shows compassion for the refugees, but always avoids mention of the cause of their misery. In his book

Fig. 24. "That orgy of lust and blood". Powell in his car, amidst the ruins of Aerschot.
[Reproduced from Fighting in Flanders *(New York City/Charles Scribner's 1914).]*

on page 31, there is a photograph of a group of Belgian refugees with the caption 'Belgians Forced out of Homes by War', which seems an evasive way of stating things. Jeff Lipkes' book on the atrocities committed by the German army in Belgium only covers August 1914, and not September when Weigle started filming. Nevertheless, Weigle photographed at Aerschot (Aarschot) when the atrocities were still going on or had just ended. Lipkes spends an entire chapter on Aerschot. The Germans murdered between 150 and 180 civilians including men, women and children in three mass executions, raped countless women, and deported 300 civilians, including Aerschot's priests, to concentration camps in Germany. On 10 September, E. Alexander Powell and the American photographer Donald C. Thompson were permitted to enter Aerschot, and found a ghost city. Powell said:

> In many parts of the world I have seen terrible and revolting things, but nothing so ghastly, as terrifying as Aerschot. Over two thirds of the houses had been burned down and showed unmistakable signs of having been sacked by a maddened soldiery before they were burned. Everywhere were the ghastly evidence. Doors had been smashed in with rifle butts and boot-heels; windows had been broken; furniture had been wantonly destroyed; pictures had been torn from the walls; mattresses had been ripped open with bayonets in search of valuables; drawers had been emptied upon the floors; the outer walls of the houses were splattered with blood and pock-marked with bullets; the sidewalks were slippery with broken wine bottles; the streets were strewn with women's clothing. It needed no one to tell us the details of that orgy of blood and lust. The story was so plain that anyone could have read it.[29]

All Weigle wrote about Aerschot is that 'We spent a few days in trips to Aerschot and Malines, where we found that the destruction wrought by the big guns had brought down beautiful buildings'.[30]

Donald Thompson arrived in Belgium supposedly armed with credentials from the *Chicago Tribune* and *Leslie's Magazine*, although Patterson never mentions him as accredited to the *Tribune* in Belgium. According to Powell, Thompson's credentials consisted of his passport, an Elk's Club card, and a letter from Colonel Sam Hughes of the Canadian Royal Militia, authorizing him to take pictures of Canadian troops wherever found.[31]

Donald C. Thompson is one of the most celebrated film cameramen in World War I, and there are a stack of newspaper articles about him written both at the time of the war by the Kansas press and later. He is often mentioned in E. Alexander Powell's *Fighting in Flanders*. He has been the subject of two excellent articles, the first being by David Mould, and then the second article written jointly by David Mould and Gerry Veeder.[32] He was once described by journalist Charles Wheeler as "the last word in impertinence and gall when he landed on the shore of Europe and asked where the war was at".[33] A more characteristic description couldn't be given of the young man who soon made a name for himself as one of the most remarkable American film correspondents of the First World War.

Fig. 25. Donald C. Thompson with Graflex camera. [Reproduced from Leslie's Weekly, *11 November 1915.]*

However, while Thompson should have been easy to research, with a thick file at the Kansas Historical Society and another at the Topeka and Shawnee County Public Library, his story presents many problems. For instance, it is very difficult to say who his father is.

Donald C. Thompson was born in Topeka, Kansas, on 19 January 1884 according to all reports, although the birth certificates do not go that far back in Shawnee County, Kansas. At times he said that he was the son of C. L. Thompson, one of the pioneer settlers on the Kansas prairie near the Delaware River. In 1865, C. L. Thompson had erected a corn mill on the site of an old Mormon settlement which was thereafter called Thompsonville. Donald Thompson, who was proud to be from Kansas, probably told this story many times, at the time when his reputation as a war photographer was growing. Unfortunately, the story is too good to be true since C.

L. was married to someone else besides Donald's mother, and had children of his own. Other records including some of Donald's passport applications claim that his real father was Harry E. Thompson, born in Oxford, Ohio, occupation unknown. However, this is evidently not true either.

Donald's mother was named Sarah Alice, commonly known as "Essie". Thompson claimed that Sarah and Harry married around 1880. However no record exists of a marriage license for Sarah and Harry in Topeka. Sarah came from a large family called Conkling and occasionally Conklin that had come to Kansas from Butler, Ohio. There is a marriage license in the official records of Topeka for a union between Thomas A. Thompson and Sarah M. Conklin on 14 November 1880.[34] There is something fishy about the license. The wedding was performed in Grantsville, Jefferson County, Kansas, but the license was recorded in Shawnee County. This is irregular. If the wedding was performed in Jefferson County between two citizens of Jefferson County, then the license should have been recorded in Jefferson County. In addition, there is no Sarah M. Conklin listed in Grantsville, Thompsonville or anywhere else in Kansas at the time, although there are plenty of listings for Sarah A. Conklin.

Thomas is fairly elusive himself. There are records showing that he was born in Grayson, Carter County, Kentucky in 1851, was a doctor, that he lived in Grantsville in Jefferson County which is outside of Topeka, located in Shawnee County. Thomas attended and graduated from the Medical College at Cincinnati in 1875.[35] He also had another wife, Susan, in Kentucky who died in 1916. He evidently never lived in Topeka with Sarah. Later, he went back to Kentucky, but in the end returned to Topeka where he died in 1922. For many years, Sarah was listed in the Topeka City Directory as "Sarah Thompson, widow of Thomas A. Thompson", even before Thomas died.[36]

The authors do not add this information because of their great passion either for genealogy or scandal, but because the record shows that from the beginning, Donald Thompson (and perhaps his family before him) constructed his life and his history as he went along. In a letter to Ron van Dopperen dated 9 September 1991, Serbian film historian Dejan Kosanovic of Belgrade was the first to describe him as "… a little mythomaniac".[37]

In fact he was a lot mythomaniac, and his mythomania was essentially the cause of his success. He could – and did – say almost anything to the press, or for that matter, to anyone. As a shining example, Thompson claimed he made the first war films in motion picture history while on a roving assignment to Europe during the first Balkan War in Turkey. In reality he had probably never left the country then and remained in Topeka, Kansas.[38] His remarkable appearance was also part of the same flamboyant persona. He was more than an ordinary photographer: not only was he adept at selling his films but also – if one may put it this way – himself. The presentation of a news item is in itself a part of selling the film. In Thompson's case, it went much further.

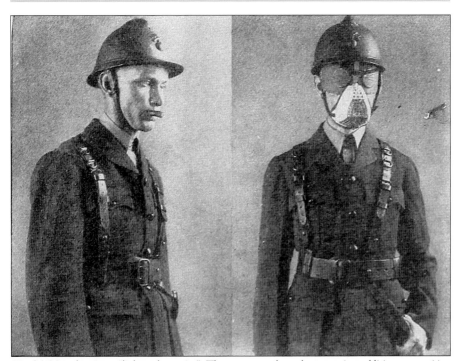

Fig. 26. More than just a "little mythomaniac", Thompson was always keen on using publicity opportunities. Here he poses for a photo shoot for Film Fan Magazine, *December 1916.*

He used his natural tendency to heighten his self-esteem to help him appear as a star photographer. And the public, watching the rise of cinema celebrities such as Chaplin, seemed to have relished the exhibition. As the war started America needed heroes. Thompson became one, and not one newspaper ever appears to have questioned the veracity of his tales.

Donald Thompson grew up in Topeka at 411 West Seventh Street and attended Harrison School. Judging by the local papers, Donald possessed a rudimentary education. His nickname at school was 'Shrimp', because he was only five feet four inches tall. This he compensated for with what the *Kansas City Star* called: "the prescience of a sixth sense, [he is as] tricky as a fox, blessed to a marvelous degree with shrewdness and native adroitness".[39]

In 1903 Thompson claimed to have had his first experience with the camera when the Kaw River flooded the Topeka area. He started making some notes about the disaster, which he brought in to the city editor of the *Topeka Daily Capital*. After the reports came his pictures. However, a search of the *Topeka Daily Capital* shows no evidence of any byline to Thompson or of any photographs by him of the flood. Most of the photographs of the flood, which were very good, were taken by John M. Strickrott, who also published a book of his photographs. Nevertheless, Thompson evidently sent some pictures to the paper which used his shot of the newly constructed state capitol. It was the first of many as he continued freelancing as a photographer for this local newspaper.

On 12 June 1906, Thompson married Elizabeth Elsie Bauers with the document giving his address as New York City and, since Thompson was still a minor, his mother's consent.[40] The following year he started freelancing for the *New York World*. A breakthrough came in 1912 when he was reportedly engaged with the assignment to cover the presidential elections. A contemporary news report indicates he was a staff correspondent for the *Washington Herald* working on publicity stories for the local business communities.[41] At the Baltimore Democratic Convention that year, Thompson said he took his first flyer into film. He evidently freelanced so well that he became a charter member of the Unusual Angle Club. And, according to *Motion Picture News*, he soon was welcome in the offices of many editors.[42]

In September 1909, Thompson was arrested by the police in Norfolk, Virginia, on the charge of having impersonated artillery officer Lt. Earl McFarland. Using this name and several other aliases, Thompson had cashed false checks throughout the country. Arraigned before a U.S. commissioner, Thompson waived examination and asked to be sent to Los Angeles on bail. The *Washington Post* reported: "Thompson, in his neat suit of gray and cleanly shaven and in no way looking like a prisoner asked the deputy marshall if he was not entitled to a blanket at night. 'I cannot sleep in my clothes and when I take them off, there is nothing to do but to shiver. I don't want any favors, but I do want what is coming to me.'"[43]

Thompson was sent to Leavenworth Prison where he was evidently a model prisoner.[44] However, while he was incarcerated, the warden received a pathetic letter (spelling mistakes are left unchanged) from Thompson's wife Elizabeth Elsie, which would suggest that Thompson could be pretty brutal:

> To the Warden
>
> Dear Sir: –
>
> I received a letter from my husband, Mr. Thompson. The letter is an insult to me. Sir if you only knew all I have suffered by that man's hands you would not blame me for wanting a divorce. I have proof that he deserted me twice, and the last time he left me with a deasease.
>
> Please pardon me for writing so plain but I only want you to know the side of my story.
>
> I have one child and I have taken care of her since she was 9 months old. I still have the ring and did not sell it I can keep that ring toward the support of my husband. If I return this ring his mother has lots of jewelry that came from the same place. If he stold the ring I don't want it. But he says he has charges against me I would realey like to know what they are.
>
> My father and Mother have done more for that man and than any other person in this world. My father has a charge against him [presumably Thompson] at the presant for forgery. And then he writes me such a letter.
>
> Please write me and let me know just what to do. I will be so thankful to you.
>
> Of course if this ring will cause me any trouble I will return it. But I think I am as much entitled to it as aney if his people or friends.

> Hoping I am not asking to much of you and have not burdened you with my troubles, but am a poor woman and have no one to turn to.
>
> I beg to remain/ A friend
> Elizabeth Thompson Delia, Kansas[45]

The warden wrote back and advised her that she was certainly justified in divorcing Thompson, which she did. Donald and Elizabeth Thompson were divorced on 19 May 1910, the decree to become final six months later.[46]

Thompson was released from Leavenworth on 27 June 1911. However upon his release he was arrested at the gate.[47] He had been arrested and convicted by the Federal authorities for impersonating an officer, but he was also wanted in Ohio on the charge of obtaining money under false pretenses, as well as in Saint Louis on a charge of defrauding mercantile houses while impersonating an officer of the Coast Artillery and claiming to be stationed at Fort Riley, Kansas. It is unclear if he had to serve further time.

It might be worthwhile to discuss briefly Thompson's felonies. His general pattern was to assume a false identity and then run some variation of a check forging scheme. One sheriff called him a "small-check man". Interestingly, the identities he assumed follow a pattern. They were usually officers, such as captains, lieutenants or federal agents. Thompson tended to impersonate men in positions of authority, fairly smart and "macho" types who would command attention and respect in the community. Later during the war, Thompson called himself "Captain Thompson", with a commission from the Nebraska National Guard, but he had never been in the armed forces. It appears as if the assumption of this particular sort of identity might have been as important to Thompson as the actual theft of jewels or money.

In any case, by 1913 he had gone west as a photographer for the *Pueblo Chieftain* to take pictures of the Colorado Coal Field strike. He also appears to have worked for the Associated Press. The highlight of his career came a year later with the beginning of the First World War.

Donald Thompson belonged to a handful of American photographers who longed to get into the war. On 24 July 1914, he left on the SS *Teutonic* for London. From a newspaper in Montreal, he had been given an assignment to take some important business papers to England as a courier. When Germany declared war on Russia on 1 August, he decided to cover the war himself. He wired *Leslie's Weekly* in New York and asked for financial support. The wire was delayed and Thompson decided to sell everything he had. He pawned his watch and bought a complete photographic outfit. All of his three Kodak Eastman cameras were large ones, "to prevent the possibility of any one accusing me of being a spy", as he later explained.[48]

Thompson had a point there. War correspondents were not welcome anywhere near the front. But the journalist carrying a camera had to confront another disadvantage because the camera was frequently looked on as the badge of a spy. As we shall see later, Thompson often was in fact treated as a spy. All in all the most important obstacle he had to cope with was not so much the physical danger of war but simple human distrust.

After arriving in London, the photographer made his application to the British Foreign Office. There he presented the credentials he had obtained from General Sam Hughes, who had given him permission to film the Canadian troops. In London, the young American was told that he would be allowed to go to the front as soon as the French authorities gave permission. Upon reaching Paris, Thompson soon found just how much the military officials liked the idea of a civilian filming their war:

> "They told me that they would be only too glad to have me go to the front as soon as the English war office gave permission. I realized at once that no photographer was going to be permitted at the front, so I pawned the last piece of jewelry I had and left Paris for the front on my own responsibility."[49]

As a typical freelance cameraman, he depended on his own efforts. And he would hardly let himself be fooled by the British War Office with such a hackneyed lie. So he tried to reach the front on his own. As mentioned earlier, he was arrested approximately eight times and spent eight nights in guard houses. A correspondent who was with Thompson until the fall of Antwerp described a typical example of this photographer trying to leave Paris:

> "On another occasion he explained to the French officer who arrested him that he was endeavoring to rescue his wife and children, who were in the hands of the Germans somewhere on the Belgian frontier. The officer was so affected by the pathos of the story that he gave Thompson a lift in his car. As a matter of fact, Thompson's wife and family were quite safe in Topeka, Kan."[50]

After the eight arrests, the French authorities got tired of this troublesome American. Escorted by two gendarmes, he was sent to Amiens. The gendarmes saw him buy a ticket to London and felt that their mission was accomplished. But it wasn't the end for the man arrested. Shortly after midnight, a British military train pulled into the station of Amiens. Thompson started a friendly talk with the Tommies who proudly posed for his camera. Soon after, another train loaded with artillery came in. Aided by the British soldiers, the photographer slipped under the tarpaulin covering a field gun and fell asleep. When Thompson awoke next morning, he found himself near Mons in Belgium.

Being not only resourceful but also lucky, Thompson had managed to reach the front. As it turned out, Mons was one of the most interesting places to visit for a war correspondent in 1914. The Entente forces, extremely surprised by the rapid encircling movement of the German armies through Belgium, had to make a stand near Mons in order to cover their retreat to the river Marne. The result was a fierce engagement and it was only with great risks that the armies saved themselves from being completely overwhelmed. The small professional British army took heavy casualties, so it is not surprising that it did not want photographs or film of the occasion. The British pointedly remarked that an angel had saved the army at Mons. Donald Thompson was one of the very few photographers to photograph the battle.[51]

He states that his first pictures were made with the British Fifth Royal Scots, whom the Germans called "The Ladies from Hell".[52] After marching for two hours, he had followed the regiment into the first line. How he managed to accomplish this is unknown. It took him about five minutes to explain his presence at the front, but the officers let him go along in the end. Perhaps he was looked on as a strange sort of mascot: Thompson had just put on his newly acquired Scots fatigue cap.

Upon arriving in foremost position, the American almost immediately came under heavy artillery fire. Judging from the trade papers, he must have had as much courage as the soldiers. When asked in an interview if the work wasn't dangerous, he calmly declared: "Yes, I suppose it is, but if you're going to be killed you will be, so why worry?"[53] In another article there is even mention of him staying behind after the last British soldier had fled, with Thompson grinding behind his film camera, opposite the attacking Germans.[54]

These stories are very unlikely to have happened that way. The articles mentioned here were probably written by publicity agents of the company that marketed Thompson's first war film. Thompson himself wasn't very modest either, certainly not when promoting his own films. As he knew, by stretching the truth – or breaking it altogether – about his exploits he could present himself as a first class "star" photographer. This presentation – the casual 'devil may care' attitude – would increase public interest in his films.

A more plausible interpretation of Thompson's experiences at Mons is to be found in an interview with the *New York Times*. It shows that he probably wasn't as reckless as he later suggested. In reality, Thompson must have been wise enough to leave the firing line when things could get out of control. Said Thompson:

> ... For eighteen hours the Germans pounded us with the biggest part of their artillery, and I don't want to see anything hotter. You see, without knowing it I'd walked right into the battle of Mons. Well, after a couple of days I saw that the Germans were concentrating most of their fire on the British army, so I moved over to visit the French for a while. I hadn't been with the French very long though, before I ran into a lieutenant who had arrested me in Paris. That was nothing out of the way for me, for I was arrested eight times while I was there and spent nearly every night in jail; but this fellow remembered me and said I'd have to be shipped back to Amiens.[55]

At Amiens, Thompson was transferred to a train bound for England, with the polite remark that he might find that country healthier than France. The train was crowded with refugees and the American found it more comfortable to get a seat in the compartment which had been reserved for a Russian lady. His impertinent behavior once again saved the day. Tumbled out on the station platform at Boulogne and stripped in full view, he was clearly treated as a German spy. But his films were not found. After paying the Russian lady 250 French francs and a roll of cigar coupons (which he claimed to be U.S. war currency), she hid the celluloid for Thompson in her personal luggage. "Believe me", Thompson said, "I wanted to get them back before she tried to cash those coupons".[56] This is another of those stories that

Fig. 27. Donald Thompson (left) and New York World *correspondent E. Alexander Powell.*
[Reproduced from Fighting in Flanders.*]*

Thompson told again and again. Although it is a marvelous story, it should be noted that there is absolutely no independent support.

For Thompson, getting to the front was a personal victory. Undaunted by military regulations, he had been one of the few cameramen to reach the front with a film camera. With his personal reputation growing, he now began freelancing for several newspapers and once again visited Belgium. Claiming that he represented a German press syndicate, he successfully used another *ruse de guerre* to cross the front lines. He had his best chance when he met E. Alexander Powell, a journalist for the *New York World* who was with Thompson until October 1914 and gave him extensive publicity. The photographer's first reaction was a typical example of his cunningness: "I noticed that Mr. Powell had a Belgian military car and that the soldiers jumped at his bidding. I thought that was the way I ought to travel."[57]

Powell also had what appeared to be love at first sight for Thompson:

> I met [Thompson] while paying a flying visit to Ostend. He blew into the consulate there wearing an American army shirt, a pair of British officer's riding-breeches, French puttees and a Highlander's forage-cap and carrying a camera the size of a parlor phonograph. No one but an American could have accomplished what he had and no American but one from Kansas. He had not only seen war, all military prohibitions to the contrary, but he had actually photographed it.

> Thompson is a little man, built like Harry Lauder; hard as nails, tough as raw-hide, his skin tanned to the color of a well-smoked meerschaum, and his face perpetually wreathed in what he called his "sunflower smile". He affects riding-breeches and leather leggings and looks, physically as well as sartorially, as though he had been born on horseback. He has more

chilled-steel nerve than any man I know and before he had been in Belgium a month his name became a synonym for coolness and daring.[58]

The privileges that Powell enjoyed from the Belgian authorities were remarkable. After reading his book *Fighting in Flanders*, there is not much doubt left as to the reason why. Although many of his American colleagues disagreed, Powell believed the atrocity stories, some of which are described above. Thompson was aware that the atrocity issue had a propagandistic value and he may have used it for his personal benefit. According to Powell, the photographer had only been in Antwerp for 24 hours when he received a pass to film the war without any restrictions. In the introduction of his book *Donald Thompson in Russia*, Thompson described how he managed to get these permissions for the front. It all pointed towards the familiar but utterly false notion that the camera doesn't lie. As he wrote, describing the strange meeting he had after a ten hour wait at the Royal Palace:

> I noticed a tall gentleman sitting at a writing desk, a green lamp casting its reflection over him. Stepping up to the desk, I met his gaze. He asked me what I wanted. I replied that I wished to see King Albert of Belgium. 'I am Albert, King of the Belgians', he said. A few years before I had been husking corn in Kansas. For a few seconds I could not speak a word. The first thing that came into my mind was this: 'King Albert', I said, 'I have never met a king before in my life'. (It was hard enough for me to hold a pair of jacks in a poker game). 'I do not know what to say except to tell you that I am here and what I want to do.'

> I then explained that the world at large would believe the stories of Belgium's heroic fight against the Germans, but the stories of German atrocities were so awful that the people would doubt them. If he had photographs however, the world could see what the German armies were doing in Belgium.[59]

The story is beautiful, but again, it seems highly unlikely that it is true. It was written in 1918, almost one year after the American intervention into the war, and pro-Belgian and anti-German feelings were running high then. Knowing Thompson's sense of drama, he probably gave a twist to his talk with the Belgian king. It is certain anyway that Thompson – even if his intentions were sincere – wasn't able to deliver any evidence of the German atrocities, and this he openly declared to the American press in 1914–1915.[60]

After receiving his pass, Thompson followed the Belgian army right down to the siege of Antwerp. There the Belgians had withdrawn their troops and were trying to harass the German lines. All attempts at defense came to an end when the same big howitzers that had smashed the forts of Liège came into action. Thompson was in Waelhem, one of the outposts of Antwerp, when the bombardment began. The shelling started as he was dining with some Belgian officers. Their appetite quickly vanished when the ceiling went to pieces and the bodies of dead soldiers fell on the dinner table. Thompson had a close call. But even more extraordinary were his experiences in the city of Antwerp. Together with Edwin Weigle he underwent the night-long imprisonment in the small cellar of the house at 74 rue du Péage described above.

In the end, both American film correspondents survived the German bombardment. Thompson, being a freelancer, now changed sides when the German troops took

Fig. 28. German infantry on the border between Belgium and France, probably photographed by Donald Thompson. [Reproduction from Fighting in Flanders.*]*

Antwerp. He followed them on their march to the coast and sat in a hotel on the Ostend waterfront when the British in their turn started to fire their rounds. While dining with some officers, he reported that a shell fell into the party and wounded him in the face. Thompson stayed with the Germans, but not for long.

And so Belgium was conquered, but it did not surrender. The Belgian army held out in a narrow strip on the coast until the end of the war. Regardless, there were no stories for the American correspondents; they headed for other battlefields.

As far as anyone can tell, no motion pictures shot by Thompson in Belgium have survived or were reported in the American film trade press, so perhaps he stayed with his oversize still cameras. But there is an illustration (not a photograph) of him with a Moy camera at Mons when he was with the Highlanders.

When Weigle and Thompson moved on from Belgium, they left a land where 6,000 Belgians would be killed as well as 25,000 homes and other buildings in 837 communities destroyed by the end of the war. Eventually 1,500,000 Belgians, 20% of the entire population, fled from the German Army.[61]

Notes

1. Parke Farley, 'The War Photographer's Job', *Photoplay Magazine* (February 1915): 163.

2. E. Alexander Powell , *Fighting in Flanders* (New York: Charles Scribner's Sons, 1914), 27.

3. Powell, *Fighting in Flanders*, 15.

4. Weigle, *My Experiences on the Belgian Battlefields* (Chicago: Hamming Publishing Company, 1914), 32–35.

5. Weigle, *My Experiences on the Belgian Battlefields*, ibid., 43. Patterson, in the introduction to Weigle's book, substantiates Weigle's story.

6. Weigle, *My Experiences on the Belgian Battlefields*, ibid., 37–38. *In Fighting in Flanders*, Powell tells the same story,

and there is a photograph of the dead boy and his sister in the wheelbarrow. All the photographs in *Fighting in Flanders* are credited to Donald C. Thompson. Powell, *Fighting in Flanders*, 173.

7. Herbert Jäger, *German Artillery in World War I* (Ramsbury, Marlborough (Wiltshire): Crowood Press Ltd., 2009), 57, 68.

8. Edward Eyre Hunt, *War Bread* (New York: Henry Holt & Co., 1916), 87. The shelling of 74 rue du Péage was probably one of the most well documented events in the Great War. While insignificant in itself, it is representative of the intense German shelling of Antwerp between 6 and 10 October 1914 when the city finally surrendered. Weigle wrote about it (infra), E. E. Hunt wrote about it, Horace Green wrote about it, and James H. Hare, another famous war photographer, photographed the battered facade of 74 rue de Péage, American flag still flying, for *Leslie's Weekly*. His photograph is reproduced in Hunt's book. See also Horace Green, *The Log of a Noncombatant* (Teddington, Middlesex: Echo Library, 2008; first published 1915), 46–52. Arthur Ruhl of *Colliers* wrote about it, *The New York Times Current History of the War*, Vol. 2, 1915, (New York: Chadwyck-Healey New York Times Company, 1915), 686.

9. Edwin F. Weigle, *My Experiences on the Belgian Battlefields*, 54–55.

10. Ibid.

11. Joseph Medill Patterson, '"Tribune" Photograph Saves Antwerp's Fine Cathedral', *Chicago Daily Tribune* (21 October 1914): 1; Weigle, *My Experiences on the Belgian Battlefields*, 28.

12. '8,000 Persons Jam Theater to see War Films', *Chicago Sunday Tribune* (15 November 1914): 9.

13. 'Chicago Letter', *Moving Picture World* (5 December 1914): 1362; 'War Pictures Sweep United States', *Billboard* (28 November 1914): 58.

14. Joseph Medill Patterson, letter of recommendation for military service, 23 June 1917.

15. "War Pictures 'Fakey'," *Variety* (21 November 1914): 7. See also a similar article in *Variety*, (28 November 1914): 22. *Variety* watched the newspapers enter the documentary and newsreel business with an unmistakable sense of distrust. Whether the films were as bad as it says, or the trade paper was trying to protect the studios, still their major source of advertising, is unclear.

16. "Belgian War Pictures", *Variety* (4 December 1914). See also *Moving Picture World* (12 December 1914): 1507.

17. *Moving Picture World* (21 November 1914): 1113.

18. *Moving Picture World* (21 November 1914): 1113.

19. Joseph M. Patterson, *Notebook of a Neutral* (New York: Duffield & Co. 1916), 77, 45. Weigle, *My Experiences on the Belgian Battlefields*, 46.

20. C. Hartley Grattan, *Why We Fought*. (New York: The Vanguard Press, ca 1929, Reprint Bobbs-Merrill, 1969), 71–72. Grattan's book reprints the cablegram in its entirety, citing *Foreign Relations Supplement* (1914): 801–802; Arthur Ponsonby's *Falsehood in War-Time*. The United States suppressed the report when it entered the war. Grattan's book, written at the height of the antiwar feeling in the late 1920s and 1930s, was reprinted in 1969 when revisionists in America were taking another long hard look at Vietnam. Thus time's wheel continues to turn.

21. Jeff Lipkes, *Rehearsals: The German Army in Belgium, 1914* (Leuven: Leuven University Press, 2007). For additional excellent recent scholarship on the atrocities in Belgium, see also John N. Horne and Alan Kramer, *German Atrocities 1914: A History of Denial* (New Haven, Yale University Press, 2001); Larry Zuckerman, *The Rape of Belgium: The Untold Story of World War I* (New York: New York University Press, 2004).

22. James O'Donnell Bennett, "German Atrocities are Fiction", *Chicago Tribune* (2 September 1914), reprinted in George William Hau, *War Echoes or Germany and Austria in the Crisis* (Chicago: Morton M. Malone, 1915), 252.

23. Wikipedia, citing Spencer Tucker, P.M.R. (2005) World War I: Encyclopedia, Volume 1, ABC-CLIO/Greenwood, 714. The reprisals arose because of a German claim that Belgian irregular troops fired upon German troops from an ambuscade but this was never proved. The Belgians claimed that two units of German troops fired upon each other. See also Barbara Tuchman, *The Guns of August* (New York: Macmillan, 1962), 313–322.

24. Tuchman, 315.

25. Irwin S. Cobb, "*Speaking of Prussians –*" (New York: George H. Doran, 1917), 33.

26. C. Hartley Grattan, *Why We Fought*, 1–72.

27. James O'Donnell Bennett, "Tribune give New Light on German Spirit", *Chicago Tribune* (12 September 1914), reprinted in George William Hau): 247.

28. Ibid., 246.

29. Jeff Lipkes, *Rehearsals: The German Army in Belgium, 1914*, 170, citing Powell, *Fighting in Flanders*, 85–88.

30. Weigle, *My Experiences on the Belgian Battlefields*, 46.

31. Powell, 15.

32. David H. Mould, "Donald Thompson: Photographer at War", *Kansas History, a Journal of the Central Plains*, Volume 5, No. 3. (Autumn 1982): 154–167; David H. Mould and Gerry Veeder, "The Photographer-Adventurers: Forgotten Heroes of the Silent Screen", *Journal of Popular Film and Television*, 16: 3 (Fall 1988): 118–129.

33. "Kansas Boy Likes the War", *Kansas City Star* (29 January 1915).

34. Marriage License, T. A. Thompson, Grantsville and Sarah M. Conklin, Thompsonville, at Thompsonville, Jefferson County, Kansas, 14 November 1880, No. 1105, Kansas Historical Society, Topeka, Kansas. See also Sharon Schertz Iamele, *Conklin Cousins: The Many Children of Joseph and Mary Conkling* (Worthington, Ohio [563 Meadoway Park, Worthington 43095]: S. S. Iamele, 1999), 126.

35. *60ᵗʰ Annual Catalogue, Medical College of Ohio*, Cincinnati Ohio, 1880–81. AR. GOV. 01, AAMC Series 3: Historical Documents Box 2 Folder 32, Kansas Historical Society, Topeka, Kansas.

36. "Thompson Sarah A. (Wid. Thomas A.) res 411 W. 7ᵗʰ", *Radges' Topeka City Directory for 1912*, p. 510. Thomas A. Thompson died in Topeka in 1922. Ancestry.com.

37. Dejan Kosanovic, letter to Ron van Dopperen, 9 September 1991.

38. "Around the Plaza", *San Antonio Light* (23 April 1933): 1

39. "Kansas Boy Likes the War", *Kansas City Star* (29 January 1915).

40. Marriage License, T. A. Thompson, Grantsville and Sarah M. Conklin, Shawnee County, Kansas, 12 June 1906, no. 1191. Kansas Historical Society, Topeka, Kansas.

41. "Washington Paper Plans Write-Up of Frederick", *Frederick Post* (23 February 1912): 3.

42. "Cameraman Thompson off to War for Paramount", *Motion Picture News* (6 November 1915): 46.

43. "California Gets Him", *Washington Post* (21 September 1909): 19.

44. Donald C. Thompson, number 6754. Records of Leavenworth Penitentiary, National Archives, Kansas City, Central Plains Division, Kansas City, Missouri.

45. Elizabeth E Thompson, letter to R. W. McClaughtry, Warden of Leavenworth Penitentiary, 7 February 1910.

46. Elizabeth E. Thompson vs. Don C. Thompson, Petition for Divorce, Jackson County Kansas Number 5025, 19 May 1910.

47. "Arrested at Prison", *Washington Post* (18 July 1911): 1.

48. "Donald C. Thompson Home from War", *Moving Picture World* (26 December 1915): 2375.

49. Donald C. Thompson, *Donald Thompson in Russia* (New York: The Century Company, 1918), viii.

50. "Calls Don Thompson the Greatest of all War Photographers", *Topeka Capital* (26 December 1915).

51. The only other cameraman working near Mons at that time was George Ercole, film correspondent for Pathé. According to *Moving Picture World*, Ercole was told by a British major that "if he didn't make himself scarce he would be shot. They didn't want films then, and none of the Belgian pictures saw the light" (14 September 1918, 1550).

52. Once again, Thompson manages to confuse matters. There was no unit called the Fifth Royal Scots at Mons, although there were plenty of Scots. One source says that the only Highlanders at Mons were the Gordon Highlanders, although there was the Fifth Brigade which was part of the Highland Light Infantry. The First Brigade, part of I Corps under the command of General Douglas Haig included the 1st Scots Guards and the 1st Black Watch. Also listed in the order of battle was the 2nd Argyll and Sutherland Highlanders. II Corps, under General Horace Smith-Dorrien, included several units of the Royal Scots, the 2ⁿᵈ Royal Scots and the 1ˢᵗ Royal Scots Fusiliers. The Germans called all kilted units "Ladies from Hell".

53. "Paramount Photo News-Man", *Moving Picture World* (6 November 1915): 1114.

54. "Donald C. Thompson Home from War", *Moving Picture World* (26 December 1915): 2375

55. "Paid a War Bribe in Cigar Coupons", *New York Times* (16 November 1914): 4.

56. Ibid.

57. Donald C. Thompson, *Donald Thompson in Russia*, viii.

58. Powell, 13–14.

59. Donald C. Thompson, *Donald Thompson in Russia*, x.

60. See for instance Thompson's comments, as quoted by the *Topeka State Journal*, 30 January 1915: "Thompson denied having seen any atrocious crimes committed on the part of the Germans. 'The German soldier is too well disciplined to break loose like that'." Actually this is rather odd if Thompson accompanied Powell to Aerschot and Louvain. Perhaps he did not, although there are photographs from both places in Powell's book.

61. Jeff Lipkes, *Rehearsals*, 13.

Chapter 4

William Randolph Hearst and the War

As previously noted, William Randolph Hearst was pro-German, anti-English, and not a supporter of World War I. Hearst may have been ideologically driven to support Germany. However he would never pass up a good story, even if it came from the side of the Entente. For example, a *Hearst-Selig News Pictorial* newsreel of the German naval raid on Scarborough, England, in December of 1914, widely felt to be an example of German barbarism at the time, still survives in the John E. Allen Collection. Hearst was primarily a businessman interested in selling newspapers, so the fact that one of his cinematographers, Ariel Varges, ended up covering the war with the British did not bother him excessively. But in this chapter we will discuss two cinematographers who went to cover the German side of the war for Hearst (Colour Plate 5).

Ansel Earle Wallace

One of the most fascinating stories about the Americans in Germany involves Wallace, Dr. Lewis Hart Marks, American Ambassador James W. Gerard and Count J. M. de Beaufort. Offstage pulling largely invisible strings, we have William Randolph Hearst and Mumm von Schwarzenstein, press chief of the *Auswärtige Amt* or German Foreign Office. To a lesser degree Woodrow Wilson and Kaiser Wilhelm II were involved. For a while, these wildly dissimilar figures used each other to achieve their goals in wartime Germany.

World War I started in August 1914. Wallace's employer, William Randolph Hearst, in spite of any short-lived anglophilia he had experienced during the coronation of George V, was very interested in sending cinematographer Wallace to Germany. On 10 November 1914, Ambassador von Bernstorff wrote a warm letter of introduction for Wallace to Press Secretary Dr. Otto Hammann in Berlin, and on 11 November 1914, Bernstorff's signature appeared on the lower left hand corner of the passport for Wallace, authorizing him to travel in Germany.[1]

Wallace, armed with impeccable credentials, nevertheless encountered the problem confronting every foreign reporter and cameraman who came to Germany in 1915.

Fig. 29. Shot of A. E. Wallace from the Boston American, *29 August 1915.*

The German Foreign Office welcomed him but the German General Staff did not. As the war continued and the military slowly expanded its power over all parts of German civilian life, the repercussions were quickly felt by the press, both German and foreign.

Wallace, like practically every other correspondent in Berlin, stayed at the Adlon Hotel. He wasted no time in trying to pull a few strings. On Adlon stationery, Wallace wrote a remarkable letter to Freiherr von Mumm, which demonstrates how deeply involved Hearst was with the Germans:

> December 7, 1914.
>
> To his Excellency Freiherr von Mumm, Auswärtiges Amt, Berlin
>
> Your Excellency,
>
> Referring to your request that I send you a statement as to the purpose of my mission to Germany I beg to state that Count von Bernstorff has arranged with Mr. William Randolph Hearst for the publication of my reports and photographs in the papers and magazines owned or controlled by Mr. Hearst, which include the following:
> The New York American,
> New York Evening Journal,

Morgen Journal,
Boston American,
Chicago American,
Chicago Examiner,
Los Angeles Examiner,
Los Angeles Times,
San Francisco Examiner,
San Francisco Call,
Atlanta Georgian,
Cosmopolitan Magazine,
Hearst Magazine,
Good House-keeping Magazine,
and the International News Service which supplies over 600 daily papers with news and illustrations throughout the United States.

Furthermore, I was to take cinematographic pictures for the Hearst-Selig News Pictorial, which is controlled by Hearst, and which is a moving picture film shown twice a week in the moving picture theatres in all larger cities of the United States and Canada, depicting the news events of the world.

Up to the present time we have had practically no illustrations or pictures from Germany of any kind, while the country has been flooded with news and pictures from England, France and Belgium.

Mr. Hearst offered to Ambassador von Bernstorff the entire Hearst service as a channel for such news and pictures as the German authorities would care to have published in the United States.

This offer was accepted by the Ambassador and my visit to your country arranged. Count von Bernstorff assured us that we will have all the help necessary and that I will have no trouble in making such photographs, moving picture films and collecting such other material as you would care to have sent to the United States.

To counteract the impressions which are held in America based on reports so far received from other than German sources I have been instructed to do the following things:

To make films and still pictures here in Berlin and other German cities, showing the crowded busy streets, motor cars which we were given to understand have been entirely suspended.

I am also expected to visit some of the large prison camps where the English, French and Russian troops are interned, particularly those showing the black and white men who are fighting against Germany.

I then expect to go to the Eastern Scene of war and anywhere else that you may care to have me go and make pictures of the troops in action. Particularly I would like to show the damage done to the villages in East Prussia by the Cossaks [sic]. It is understood by Mr. Hearst and, I agree that all pictures, films or news, prepared by me shall be developed by you and receive your approval before they are sent to America.

I should like to begin this week at the earliest possible date. The steamer Rijndam sails on December 19 from Rotterdam and if it were possible to prepare a few films showing Berlin at present, my friend Congressman Metz, who sails then, has promised to take them so that they can be shown in the United States during Christmas Week in the American cities.

My work in and around Berlin could be done in two or three days, so I could leave for the eastern front in a very short time.

Awaiting your instructions in the matter, I am,

Very respectfully,

Your obedient servant,

[sig.] Ansel E. Wallace[2]

Thus in December 1914 Wallace was sitting at the Adlon, chafing to get a chance to do his job in Germany, surrounded by fellow journalists also stuck while waiting for permissions from the German government. Later, Director Josef Schumacher, head of the Picture Section of the ZfA, wrote an eloquent letter to Freiherr von Mumm on the plight of foreign film men in Germany. He might not have had Wallace expressly in mind, but his words could apply to any of the American cinematographers trapped in Berlin:

> If our film propaganda still has not met all requirements up to now, there are generally two reasons: (1) the lack of motives. This is based primarily on the very limited understanding that up to now our desire for the granting of permission for cinematographers to go to the front has been met with by the military. So, individual Americans, in part at the cost of the ZfA have been here for weeks and months without being able to travel to the front. On top of this many times the most interesting shots were deleted by the military censors. Only recently has there appeared, perhaps prompted by the great success of the Austrians, a greater understanding of the situation by our military authorities; grasping for instance the importance of working up a stronger film propaganda by the Ministry of War for the Balkans. (2) Another obstacle is the question of costs. Film propaganda is an extraordinarily expensive sport.[3]

Lewis Hart Marks

Sometime around early December 1914 a frustrated Wallace began to try to figure out alternate methods to do his job in Germany. There were other and perhaps more useful agents than the barmen and servants at the Adlon, and this is where Dr. Lewis Hart Marks, who was introduced in Chapter 1, enters the scene. In an article published on 4 July 1915 the *New York Times* reported on the rich mixture of characters at the Adlon, and commented:

> A conspicuous figure about the lobby of the Adlon is Dr. Louis [sic] H. Marks, an American physician and former assistant of Dr. Ehrlich. Dr. Marks, who is the director of a scientific research institute in Frankfort [sic], has already lost in battle several of his ablest German assistants, who abandoned science at the call of the Kaiser. Mrs. Marks, who was a Miss Strauss of New York, will leave Berlin this week for a visit in Frankfort.

> The Adlon now has become the undoubted news centre of the German Empire, for the dwindling band of American journalists has almost without exception sought refuge under its roof. The old guard, in addition to THE NEW YORK TIMES correspondent, consists of two representatives of the Associated Press, a special correspondent of the New York World, and the correspondent of the Chicago Daily News. There are also three photographers from Chicago.[4]

The meeting of Wallace and Marks seems to have been a marriage made in heaven. Wallace came to Germany with nearly the finest credentials as one could get from William Randolph Hearst and Ambassador Bernstorff, while Marks after more than six years in Frankfurt am Main, had excellent contacts, both in the civil and military

Fig. 30. New army being drilled at Frankfurt, Germany. Scene from a newsreel filmed by Wallace.
[Reproduced from Motography, *13 February 1915.]*

world. Marks decided to make them available to Wallace for an assault on the German Foreign Office and the Army General Staff.

According to a telegram by the local military, on 10 December Wallace arrived in Frankfurt. Marks must have paved the way for his arrival. The authorities there had no problems with him taking still pictures of the troops in training, but they did apparently object to films.[5] However, Wallace must have succeeded in changing the minds of the local authorities, because in an interview given later, he related:

> At Berlin, I had to put up with the usual wait until they investigated me. I got sick and tired of it and broke away, beating it to Frankfort-on-the Main [sic]. There I was lucky enough to get to the Prince and Princess Friedrich Carl von Hessen. Through them I was able to film the German barracks where I got a fine group of pictures of the German troops in training.[6]

Against all odds some of the newsreels that he took of the German troops in training at Frankfurt am Main survive in the John E. Allen collection, complete with an intertitle that includes Wallace's name, although his initials were transposed to "E. A." Wallace.[7]

But Wallace's explanation raises more questions than it answers. By and large, newspaper men do not 'get to' German nobility without a lot of help. Again, the likely explanation is that Marks paved the way.

By that time Wallace had become pretty much disgusted by the lack of cooperation from the German officials in Berlin. He said so in his interview in the *Boston American*, and it is also mentioned in a letter by Wilhelm Merton dated 11 December 1914 to Mumm. Wilhelm Ralph Merton was a power to be reckoned with; he served on several committees regarding German propaganda. His family had emigrated to Frankfurt am Main from England in 1837 and his father changed his name from Moses to Merton when he received German citizenship. In 1881 Wilhelm founded

Metallgesellschaft, a corporation which quickly became a world empire with subsidiaries around the world. He became one of the best known financiers in Germany, but remained a Social Democrat and helped to found the University of Frankfurt. He must have been a friend of Marks. Merton's letter was most convincing:

> Most honored Excellency,
>
> I take the liberty of turning to you in the following matter:
>
> Today, through the acting Generalkommando here [Frankfurt am Main], Mr. Wallace of the Hearst press was introduced to me. He told me that in Berlin – in contrast to Frankfurt, where he was shown the greatest cooperation by both the Generalkommando and the initiatives of Prince Karl von Hessen – here, he has run up against all possible difficulties with reference to the permission to view prison camps, to photograph streets and above all, to go to the front. In the greatest disappointment he then traveled here with the purpose of returning to New York, since he certainly can accomplish nothing here, although the Ambassador Bernstorff informed him that everything would be in order and there he would find every accommodation.
>
> Whatever one may think about the Hearst Press and Herr Hearst personally, in any case from what I have heard he represents a huge power in the United States, and for us to win that is all the more essential, since he is the only one that still does not fall into dependence on England, and as Hearst's political interests, as I reliably hear, temporarily center on winning political influence through German-American and Irish opinion.
>
> How much the matter interests him is shown in that he has allocated huge resources into this trip and every week a courier is supposed to go with films from Rotterdam to New York, a sign of how important speed is to him. In this we have certainly a still greatest interest and since once again the Americans are, sadly, especially effective in working with pictures, we must not let this truly good opportunity go by.
>
> We can here as before, as matters stand, complete our information service in the most effective way, yet on top of everything, without it costing us anything.
>
> If I plead for this, this does not come from love for the Americans or certainly for their methods. But what are we supposed to do?
>
> From Herr Ballin, I heard that the representatives of the Hamburg-America line, who came here from New York, have already gotten permission to go to the front with a photographer [Edward Lyell Fox and Albert K. Dawson]. As extraordinarily useful as this is, it has understandably nothing approaching the importance as when the representative of the Hearst press receives the opportunity to make photographs and reports.
>
> From the conversations with Wallace it came out that he is also insulted that the General Staff offered him only a trip to the front with a large number of correspondents, and in the bargain, possibly at some remote point in time.
>
> I believe you should dedicate yourself urgently in granting Wallace all support, so that his wishes will be complied with. Indeed, he would like to spend Christmas near the front, and before that, get shots of the prison camps, street life and so on. In addition he wants to make shots in East Prussia and Poland, in order to show these things in the United States.
>
> I remark also, that Herr Wallace was on the point of traveling further, that he allowed himself by the gentlemen here to be persuaded to wait a few days to stay and wait to see what answer he gets from Berlin.
>
> It will also interest you to hear that Herr Wallace was surprised to the highest degree by the

situation that he sees here in public. In the United States people think generally that Germany has gone to the dogs.

I would be very thankful for a telegram, to be able to give Herr Wallace an answer and remain, most honored Excellence, with warmest regards,

Your Completely Devoted

W. Merton

[Partially illegible, but evidently Merton sent a copy with handwritten note to Matthias Erzberger.][8]

Merton's letter clearly set off a spark. According to a letter by Freiherr von Mumm to the German police dated 13 December 1914:

The American citizens Herr E. A. Wallace [sic] and Herr Dr. L. H. Marks want to make photographs and film in Germany. Both gentlemen are extremely heartily recommended, Herr Wallace as representative of the Hearst newspaper enterprises in the United States, by the German Ambassador in Washington; Herr Marks, the general practitioner in Frankfurt am Main, through a German Propaganda Committee in Frankfurt am Main, and through the royal president of the government in Wiesbaden.

In addition, according to reports, Princess Friedrich Karl von Hessen has expressed an interest in the quest of the above mentioned gentlemen and has written a personal letter to His Majesty the Kaiser. Also on the part of the Auswärtige Amt, the endeavors of both men, whose attempts to produce a German propaganda in conformity with the truth, appearing useful in neutral countries abroad, has caused lively interest.

The Auswärtige Amt therefore respectfully asks the Royal Polizeipräsident to furnish with all possible speed all necessary permissions for both gentlemen, and especially, permissions with reference that the gentlemen want to make shots of streets, public places and so forth, insofar as these shots do not interfere with military matters.

The Secretary of the Auswärtige Amt,

Freiherr von Mumm[9]

This is the kind of ammunition that not even the most hardened Army General Staff member could ignore.

Count van Maurik de Beaufort

De Beaufort is another major player in this drama. If Marks was a bit shady, as alluded to in Chapter 1, de Beaufort was totally bogus. Known as Count van Maurik de Beaufort, he spoke with a plummy British accent, sported a monocle, a top hat and white-topped shoes. Evidently he was not without charm. In 1909 he married Irma Kilgallen, the daughter of M. H. Kilgallen, a Chicago steel magnate, real estate developer and millionaire. Going about Chicago in an open car with his bull terrier pup Bob, he was what Americans call a character, and was always good for a story in the Chicago papers. Unfortunately his domestic life with Irma was marked by strife – Irma suffered a broken arm and leg during their marriage – and he was sometimes hauled into court. Eventually someone checked out an Almanach de Gotha, and there was no such Count de Beaufort listed. In reality the Count's name was Jacques Albert Uilenbroek, an ordinary Dutch citizen who had emigrated to the United States after deserting the army. In Chicago his marriage to Irma Kilgallen ended in an extremely messy divorce, and evidently Kilgallen Père had de Beaufort beaten up several times when de Beaufort refused to divorce his daughter.

Count de Beaufort then turned to creative ways to plead his case and make a living. With Bob at his side, he appeared in vaudeville at the American Music Hall in Chicago in November of 1910. The *New York Times* previewed his act:

> De Beaufort will sing a song, recite a piece entitled 'the Battle', and deliver a monologue, in which he will describe as far as he may what he terms the 'trials and tribulations' of his courtship of and marriage to Miss Irma Tracy Kilgallen and his final expulsion from the Kilgallen

COUNT DE BEAUFORT, SLAIN IN BATTLE, ONCE A CHICAGOAN

Count Jacques Alexander Dudley von Mourik de Beaufort, who met death while fighting near Nieuport, Belgium; Irma Kilgallen, the former countess and Chicago heiress, and "Bob," the dog which was the constant companion of the count and was as well known as the count himself

Fig. 31. Count de Beaufort and his bull pup Bob, not to mention his former wife Irma Kilgallen, after his reported death in Belgium. He turned up alive after all.

home, 3,230 Michigan Avenue, after the Countess had suffered her broken arm and leg. He will also dwell on his arrest at St. Luke's hospital, where the Countess is recovering, and how he expects to become reconciled to her. The dog will perform tricks his master has taught him.

Evidently he was a hit. The *San Francisco Call* wrote a review entitled, 'Count is Hit on Vaudeville Stage; Creditors Cheer'.[10]

In December 1910 de Beaufort managed to obtain an exclusive contract to appear in motion pictures. His first and only film was called *The Romance of Count de Beaufort*, and of course Bob was a co-star. Carl Laemmle of IMP signed his contract, and according to *Moving Picture News* the Count earned so much money that as a producer Laemmle did not make any profits, but this claim is from an advertisement by IMP and may have been motivated by publicity. The movie was released on 21 December 1910.[11]

After an eventual divorce in 1912 de Beaufort then turned up in New York and Philadelphia where he took up newspaper work. Since he habitually wore a top hat, monocle and spats, he became known as "The Dude Reporter". He also appeared in newspaper stories himself, the stories often involving altercations of one sort or another.[12] He went to Europe to cover the war, saying he was working for the British newspaper *Daily Telegraph*, but he was also working for Hearst and INS. His stories came from within Germany, which certainly would have forbidden a correspondent from a British newspaper to enter, and their tone in the Hearst papers in 1915 is remarkably

Fig. 32. Count de Beaufort as a movie star. "His object is to prove to his daddy-in-law that he can make money as any American", commented Moving Picture World.
[Reproduced from an advertisement, published on 10 December 1910.]

more neutral than the writing in his book *Behind the German Veil*, published in Britain in 1916 and in the United States after America entered the war. Even if de Beaufort was a con man and swindler, his book is well-written, very entertaining and sometimes informative. Even the Secret Service man who wrote a report on him liked his book. He was also to be very much involved in the Wallace saga.

On 25 December 1914 Wallace sent his first big story from Berlin, stating that he had been granted a personal interview with Helmuth von Moltke, Chief of the German General Staff. The story started with von Moltke's assertion that Germany was fighting England for its existence, as well as that of European civilization, that Russia had already been beaten on the eastern battlefields, and so forth:

> These striking statements were made to me today by General Moltke in the first interview he has granted to any representative of the press since the war began. Gen. von Moltke is on temporary leave here. Shortly after my arrival in Berlin, the head of the greatest military organization in the world kindly consented through his adjutant to give me an exclusive

interview for the International News Service. This had to be postponed until today because of the General's illness. He received me this morning in his private apartments in the general staff building itself … .

And after other statements explaining and defending Germany's position in the war, maintaining among other things that Germany was the Liberator of Europe, and that it had been 'German militarism' that had kept the peace in Europe for the last forty-three years, von Moltke terminated the interview.

At the conclusion of the interview General von Moltke affixed his signature and shaking my hand warmly said he wished me a safe journey.[13]

Which would have been fine, except it appears that the "interview" appears to have been staged. This brings us back to Mr. de Beaufort. In his book he describes a discussion he had with Professor Ludwig Stein, one of the founders and an assistant editor of the *Vossische Zeitung*, one of the government's favorite newspapers. The conversation concerned some of the interviews that had appeared in the American press.

Referring to Wallace's spurious interview with von Moltke, Professor Stein told de Beaufort:

'The interviews with the Crown Prince, the Crown Princess, Admiral von Tirpitz, von Moltke, the German Chancellor, General von Bernhardi, and many others, were merely political moves on the great chess-board of war. They were, every one of them, carefully thought and mapped out beforehand, and then in most cases the finished article, translated and typewritten, was handed over to the 'interviewer' – i.e., to the man who represented these papers which would give the 'interview' the greatest publicity. Needless to say, that he must practically guarantee beforehand that it would be printed without alterations or corrections of any kind whatever. I myself arranged the interview with General von Moltke. The American journalist received his interview, written out, ready for mail or cable….'

In a footnote on the same page relating to the "American journalist", de Beaufort added: "The man who got this interview was not a journalist at all, but a photographer and moving-picture operator, representing the Hearst interests. He did not speak a word of German."[14]

De Beaufort attributed the interview to a certain Graf von Hessenstein, a nephew of von Moltke, also known as 'Whispering Charlie', who had written the story in a first-person style so that it appeared that the general had given Wallace a personal interview. In a way the description of von Moltke's 'affixing his signature' gives the game away, as von Moltke would only have signed a statement. It should be added that this type of press manipulation was not unusual. Stein, above, alludes to a similar interview with General von Bernhardi. In all likelihood that interview was granted to Wilbur H. Durborough, who did not speak a word of German. Edwin F. Weigle obtained film in Germany, including the erection of the statue of von Hindenburg, that was shot before he even got there.

On the other hand, as de Beaufort reports that Ludwig Stein admitted that the press office was the author of the fake interview, it seems odd that he would then attribute it to Graf von Hessenstein. According to de Beaufort:

Fig. 33. "Kaiser Wilhelm visits the Belgian front and poses for the Hearst-Selig cameraman." The scene was probably bought by Wallace. [Reproduced from Motography, *16 January 1915.]*

[Hessenstein's] transactions stirred up a very nice little hornets-nest between the General Staff and the Berlin Foreign Office. It appeared, and was conclusively proved, that 'Whispering Charlie' [Hessenstein] was a dealer in special privileges. If a journalist felt neglected Charlie was the doctor – for a consideration, of course. An American cinema operator, who suddenly grew ambitious to blossom into a journalist, approached Charlie in the proper manner, and lo! Five days later American papers published an 'interview' by him with General Moltke. It is of course a mere matter of detail that the 'interview' was a typewritten affair, presented to him by von Moltke – who knew as much English as Mr. Cinema Man knew German, i.e., nil – with a 'How do you do' and 'Good Bye' thrown in. It proved what Charlie could do. For an additional £50, plus a commission on a sale of a motor-car, bought by the Cinema man from Captain von Brauwitz, of the Railroad Department of the Berlin General Staff, Charlie furnished the American with a pass for a two weeks' visit to the eastern front including a hundred feet of film, which he was able to take of General Hindenburg and his staff. He also filmed the Kaiser's sister, Prince von Bulow, and various other notabilities – cheap at the price![15]

Although a frame enlargement of the Kaiser footage credited to Wallace does survive, the newsreel from which it is taken does not:

HEARST-SELIG NEWS PICTORIAL. NO. 2 (Jan. 7, 1915) ... More of A. E. Wallace's pictures from interior Germany, show the arrival of Christmas gifts for the German soldiers. German soldiers are seen loading captured Belgian cannon on cars to be shipped to Berlin. Kaiser Wilhelm himself visits the Belgian front and poses for the Hearst-Selig cameraman as he reviews the crack Prussian troops and just as he enters his automobile to be whirled away by his military chauffeur. With him are seen the officers of the famous German general staff.[16]

Since, according to de Beaufort, 'Whispering Charlie' also offered to persuade the Kaiser to pose for his camera for 2,000 marks, this story may have something to do with the Hearst-Selig newsreel mentioned above. Since there is no evidence that Wallace reached Belgium to shoot film with the German army, or that he actually took pictures of Kaiser Wilhelm, this may be some of the film that was sold to him.

Finally Wallace and Marks got a chance to travel to the eastern front from 15 to 21 January 1915. Wallace did not write many articles after his "interview" with von Moltke but we are fortunate that he gave an interview to Hearst's *Boston American* in August 1915 regarding his trip to Poland. His final destination was Lowicz, but according to the article, he ended up in Lodz. The German army had already started its drive across Eastern Poland subsequent to its victories at Tannenberg and the First Battle of the Masurian Lakes. The Germans probably decided to send Wallace to Lodz right in the aftermath of what later was called the Battle of Lodz, in which the Germans narrowly escaped being encircled in the city by the Russians. The Russian drive on Silesia stopped when the Germans decided to break off their attack on Warsaw. The Russians abandoned Lodz on 6 December 1914. The battle was a stalemate at best but Ludendorff was able to sell it as a German victory, and this is probably why the German General Staff was willing to send Wallace as well as several military attachés (*infra.*) to the theater.[17]

Wallace claimed that von Moltke telephoned Paul von Hindenburg to tell him that Wallace was coming, rather a remarkable thing for a German general of von Moltke's rank to do, and one wonders if this is again the fine hand of Marks. In any case Wallace first traveled to Posen to von Hindenburg's headquarters, but von Hindenburg was too busy to see him, so Wallace went to Allenstein in East Prussia, 'the city that the Russians took and held for a day before they were booted out of it', then on to Soldau, Niedenburg and Mlawa.

Wallace's comments on the campaign were pro-German. He claimed that the Germans set up soup kitchens to feed the Poles, and established a system whereby they received immediate payment for any items requisitioned by the Germans. In fact the Poles were living by barter and were starving. Colonel Ernest P. Bicknell, Wickliffe Rose and Colin Herrle of the American Red Cross and representing the Rockefeller Foundation Commission were in the vicinity at the same time. Bicknell later wrote, "And I am not exaggerating when I say that we have seen in the past three days a degree of destitution, misery and squalor which surpasses anything we have observed in Belgium or any other country".[18] In addition Wallace reported Russian atrocities, claiming that both at Soldau and Niedenburg, the Russians had cut the tendons in the right arms of German boys so that they could never bear arms. He claimed to have seen three victims, but said that they were in such bad shape that he could not photograph them. However, Bicknell, Rose and Herrle were in the vicinity at the same time, and Bicknell stated definitely that the Red Cross had heard of no atrocities committed by either the Germans or the Russians.[19] Wallace continued:

> 'Up to this time I was rather disappointed, as I wanted to get some actual fighting. I motored to Lodz and saw wonderful sights along the roads – miles of transportation trains, motor trucks and carts by thousands, thousands of men, thousands of Russian prisoners, wounded soldiers in carts and autos amid the snow and ice.'[20]

When he finally got to Lodz Wallace filmed General von Mackensen, who had just received the *Pour le Mérite* for his heroic actions in saving the day at Lodz. "He is modest, even more so than General von Hindenburg. It happened, luckily for me, that 20,000 Austrian cavalry came through the city the next day and I got the general reviewing them."[21]

On 22 March 1915 Hearst-Selig released a story on the Austrian cavalry boarding trains from Lodz to move against the Russians near Warsaw. The same newsreel includes a story on Austrian 32 cm. guns, filmed at Bolimow. Both of these were probably shot by Wallace earlier in January, possibly from the time that he encountered von Mackensen and his Austrian soldiers.

Wallace photographed Russian prisoners in Soldau as well as the destroyed city. When he was staying at the house of the Chief of the Fire Department in Skierniewice, the Chief's wife told stories about the general slackness of Russian officers who had lounged about the house with their mistresses, played cards all night and slept all day. At one point, his hostess said that Grand Duke Nicholas himself entered the house, slapped two Russian officers there and ordered them into the trenches with their men. At Lowicz Wallace shot various newsreels, including one that still exists and was released in February 1915.[22]

Wallace also finally caught up with General von Hindenburg, apparently in Posen. When Wallace asked him why he had not captured Warsaw, von Hindenburg smiled and said: "Because we don't want it. What we want is the Russian army and we are going to keep after them until we get it." As it turned out, the Germans got Warsaw anyway in August, but they did not get the Russian army, at least not enough of it to keep it out of the war for too long.

Wallace filmed von Hindenburg, but in an advertisement for the newsreel (which unfortunately is all that remains of the film) von Hindenburg does not look entirely pleased about being on film. Edward Lyell Fox mentions that "… An American 'movie man' finally induced Von Hindenburg to stand before a camera. He did it in a way that made you think of the old J.P. Morgan who wanted to smash every camera he saw." The "movie man" was probably Wallace.[23] Wallace continued his filming:

> I could hear the booming of the guns night and day, and I was anxious to get to the firing line. I ran across a German artillery position. The officers, when I asked them to fire the guns, so I could get pictures, said the Russians had nearly located their stand and said they must keep quiet for a time. But finally they consented and I got my pictures.

> Hardly had the boom-booms died away when the Russian retort came, and two shells struck a house about 300 yards away from us, blowing the building into oblivion. They refused to let me photograph the wreckage.

> I was in on the wiping out of a Russian artillery position. I mean, I was there when it was done, a witness. It was a most thrilling spectacle – aeroplanes overhead, signaling the position of the Russian with colored lights, shrapnel bursting around the aircraft, then a boom, another boom and then [so] on – until the Germans had the range, and then a crash – and the position was wiped out.[24]

Wallace reported in the same article that somewhat later, "outside Rawa" (probably the Rawka River where Wallace was trying to film another artillery engagement) he

YOU CAN BE NEUTRAL

AND STILL SHOW
YOUR PATRONS THE

IDOL
OF THE
GERMAN ARMY

The master mind on which the
hopes of the German Empire rest—
the man, who every day, bears the
greatest weight of responsibility ever
placed upon the shoulders of a
human being—

Field Marshal
VON
HINDENBERG

The first motion pictures of this Colossus of the
Military World, taken at Army Headquarters in
East Prussia by Staff Photographer A. E.
WALLACE, will appear in the

HEARST-SELIG
NEWS PICTORIAL
Number 19
Released Monday, March 8th

Another Scoop for the World's
Greatest News Reel!

*Fig. 34. Von Hindenburg, not looking overjoyed to have his picture
taken. Whether this was a photograph of the Field Marshal by
Wallace is not known, although Wallace gets a by-line in the
advertisement.*
[Reproduced from Moving Picture World, *13 March 1915.]*

ran into General Curt von Morgen, who had distinguished himself at the Battle of Lodz. Von Morgen asked him, "'Hey – Do you want to get shot?' His perfect English surprised me as much as did his interest in my fate. 'We're having a little battle and you should be able to get some pictures', he said." Curt von Morgen in his book *Meiner Truppen Heldenkämpfe* reported that early in 1915 he had some interesting visitors, including three Americans who were supposedly investigating conditions in Poland for the possible purpose of opening an aid facility for the Poles. They were the previously mentioned Dr. Rose, Ernest Bicknell and Colin Herrle, who were warmly welcomed by von Morgen and his staff.[25] Wallace and Marks also appear to have been with General von Morgen for a while, judging from several pictures taken by the INS at his headquarters.

Von Morgen reported that soon after came a group of military attachés, including Colonel Moritz von Wattenwyl from Switzerland, Colonel Ludovic Mircescu from Rumania, a Lieutenant Colonel from Argentina and Colonel Luigi Bongiovanni from Italy (shortly before Italy entered the war on the Entente side on 23 May 1915). It is worth noting that all these attachés were pro-German, and Wattenwyl was later cashiered from the Swiss Army for spying for Germany. Also there, although not mentioned by General von Morgen, was Major George T. Langhorne, the military attaché from the United States. Wallace filmed these attachés and they appeared in *Hearst-Selig News Pictorial* No. 28, released on 8 April 1915. In addition, a photograph of the military attachés in Poland, including the American attaché Major George T. Langhorne, appeared in the *New York Times Mid-Week Pictorial* on 15 April. The photograph was copyrighted by INS and was almost certainly taken by

Fig. 35. General Kurt von Morgen and his troops. Picture by A.E. Wallace, reproduced from George William Hau's pro-German book Echoes of War *(Chicago/ M. M. Malone c. 1915).*

Wallace. Major Langhorne was pro-German. During his stay in Berlin he allowed the spy and saboteur Franz von Rintelen to send Langhorne's messages to the United States encrypted in secret code via the German transmitters at Nauen. Langhorne wanted to avoid British censorship. Von Rintelen promptly cracked all the American codes. When this was discovered Major Langhorne was recalled to the United States.[26]

On 31 January, just after Wallace's departure from the front, the Germans fought the Battle of Bolimow, generally considered to be the beginning of the second Battle of the Masurian Lakes. If Wallace had been there a week later, he would have witnessed Germany's first unsuccessful attempt to use poison gas.

Wallace's time at the eastern front resulted in some spectacular photographs and newsreel footage for Hearst. But upon Wallace's and Marks' return from the front, things rapidly began to go sour for Wallace.

In several of the aforementioned quotes involving the payment for the interview with von Moltke, Count de Beaufort explicitly stated that Wallace accused Marks of taking money from him in exchange for being sent to the front. Independent sources verify that de Beaufort made the accusation although they could not verify if it were true. It appears that de Beaufort himself got into this scheme, paying 2,000 marks for a two week trip along the battlefields on the western front, although later he tried to justify himself by claiming in his book that he only did it to prove to Berlin that such deals were going on. According to de Beaufort, Wallace drank too much German champagne one evening and described the transaction to Herr Stein, who became

Fig. 36. Wallace with his movie equipment, sitting in a droshky. Eastern front, January 1915. [Reproduced from Boston American, *29 August 1915.]*

upset. De Beaufort then reported the whole transaction to the Foreign Office and the Press Department of the General Staff, to their consternation. It was apparently on or about 10 February 1915 that de Beaufort went to Conrad Frederick Roediger, a civil servant of the AA, with his story. Roediger wrote a report on 12 February, which was then sent as a private letter to Count von Bernstorff on 16 February. Roediger had interviewed Americans who were known to be friendly to the Germans and asked them about de Beaufort. They reported the general information about de Beaufort's unusual marriage, general unreliability, shady doings and so forth, but then went further. Roediger reported:

> … From all Americans with whom I just spoke about Beaufort, he is described as an extremely dangerous man who attempts everywhere to cause discontent, and whose expulsion as an annoying foreigner would be warranted. As for his relevance as a journalist, it is said that when one learns his history one generally laughs at him.

> The following story seems characteristic of de Beaufort. He came to me on 11 February in the evening, apparently very upset, and explained he had received an offer from a German gentleman by which Beaufort and Wallace, in exchange for some 1800 marks, would get to the front within four days by means of the mediation of this man. He did not want to name the man, but he then identified him as Count Hessenstein. De Beaufort felt that this was unbelievable and felt it was his duty to let the Auswärtige Amt know of this misconduct. He even saw a receipt in the hands of Herr Wallace. And this gold was the payment for a trip to the eastern front. After the return of Herr Wallace and after a few of his film shots were not passed by the military censors, Count von Hessenstein promised that for 500 marks he would arrange for the films to be passed by the censor.

Roediger, who seems to have been a fairly clever individual, was smart enough not to rely on de Beaufort and went to two Americans he trusted, Marks and Edward Lyell Fox, to get the story from them. Roediger continued:

> A certain Count Alfred Hessenstein, who makes the rounds through the Hotel Adlon, sold Wallace two stories for 400 marks and made out a receipt. This is the receipt of which de Beaufort spoke and handed to me, and which I nevertheless had to hand back. De Beaufort learned somehow about the matter and, as Count Hessenstein explained it to the two Americans, de Beaufort in his turn went to Hessenstein with the request to do something for him and his trip to the front. According to his version money was not promised. There is supposed to have been no money paid. Today, de Beaufort explained that he talked it over with Herr Professor Ludwig Stein. And so the matter draws in other parties.

> The two Americans describe Count Hessenstein as a somewhat senile man who plays a somewhat remarkable role. They consider the version of Herr de Beaufort as completely untrue. At my suggestion, they confidentially warned Count Hessenstein for the time being to get somewhat less involved with Beaufort.

> The way it was told to me, Wallace and de Beaufort plan soon to travel to some city in West Germany where they are supposed to shoot the following:

> The "Count" de Beaufort, American War Correspondent, arrives in the village, in which the family castle is located. The population of the village, previously rehearsed, will greet the "Count" with stormy applause and cover him with flowers.

/s/ Roediger[27]

A week later on 19 February 1915, Roediger, after further investigating, wrote an additional report on the doings of de Beaufort, who was supposed to be deeply involved with two unsavory alleged Americans, Paswell and "Spitz" or "Spiess". Spitz was said to have wormed his way into the good graces of Prince Reuss. But the statement in Roediger's report which must have made the AA and the General Staff shudder most was his comment:

> Beaufort and Wallace continually expressed the view that every journalist who gets to the front has succeeded by bribery. The two may spread this opinion in order to fish in troubled waters.

> As has been imparted in an earlier note, de Beaufort is not taken seriously. At the same time several journalists here, especially Corey and Fox, are ready, if necessary, to call attention to Beaufort's behavior in Germany by telegraphing American newspapers in order to paralyze an eventual scandal report of de Beaufort in the Hearst press. Such material would especially be for the [New York] World a windfall [gefundenes Fressen].

> Roediger[28]

Graf Alfred Hessenstein, the supposed villain of the piece, was having none of it. On 3 March 1915, the AA obtained his statement:

> I met Dr. Marks through the Baronin von Arnswald. I discovered from him that he was active for the American press on the pro-German side. Since I am a writer, I wrote a few articles for Dr. Marks and received 800 marks (not 300 dollars). I submitted a receipt. This receipt probably came up with the delivery of the denunciation in question when presented for discussion. Of an interview that I am supposed to have composed for Herr Wallace with Generaloberst von Moltke, I know nothing. Wallace cannot speak a word of German. On the other hand, Dr. Marks speaks German and has also consulted with Generaloberst von Moltke.

I had nothing to do with Wallace, and have also received no money from him. As for the procurement of passes for Herr de Beaufort – whose name by the way is counterfeit and who is a person with a terrible reputation – is concerned, the matter has also been falsely presented. De Beaufort asked admittedly whether he could get passes for a trip to the front. I refused to get involved in that in any way.

The third point, that I promised Herr Wallace to get his film through the censors is completely preposterous, since I have no means through which I could accomplish such a thing. It has already been said by Dr. Marks that de Beaufort would undertake something against me. Baron Bernard Uexküll who lives at Friedrich-Wilhelmstrasse 13 can give more exact information.

Graf Alfred Hessenstein

a.u.d.

Koch[29]

Needless to say, de Beaufort's version was somewhat different:

The outcome of the affair was that the cinema man was first urged to withdraw, or rather repudiate all his statements about the help received from Count Hessenstein. If he would do that, he would be given a universal pass to travel anywhere in Germany and take all the photographs and cinema pictures he liked. I happen to know that he felt much inclined to accept such a generous offer, but the difficulty was that I was in possession of all his receipts for money paid to Hessenstein. The upshot was that his filming career was cut short, and that he withdrew to the neutral territory of Holland. It had been a lucky day for me when I got hold of these receipts, because but for these I would have had no evidence at all after the American left the country. I made several affidavits, and Whispering Charlie and his partner, Dr. Marx, or Marks, disappeared for the time being from the Adlon field of operations.[30]

It is worth pointing out that while the receipt seems to have existed, not even de Beaufort claims to have seen Hessenstein in possession of it. This and other material strongly suggests that if anyone financed a trip to the front, it was Marks. A previous letter to Roediger dated 26 January 1915 comments that Wallace and Marks, back from the front and still at the Adlon, were no longer friends.[31] This could be a reference to resentment Wallace may still have felt for paying Marks to get to the front.

The authors were fortunate enough to have found and purchased a scrapbook entitled "German-Russian World War I Photographs", owned by A. E. Wallace. The material in Wallace's scrap book indicates he paid Marks, even though Hessenstein may not have received anything. Many of the photographs in the album were not actually taken by Wallace, although most have an INS stamp on them. What is most interesting in the scrapbook is a number of official documents, bills and vouchers. These include an official *Ausweis Nr. 112* giving permission for A. E. Wallace and "H. Lewis Marks" [sic] to travel to the eastern front from 15 to 21 January 1915 to Lowicz for the purposes of film and cinematography. Lowicz was German Army headquarters in the east at the time. It was signed by the Head of Department IIIb of the Acting German General Staff Karl Brose, the man so disliked by Freiherr von Mumm.

Fig. 37. Russian prisoners at Skierniewice.
[Photograph by A.E. Wallace, reproduced from the Bain Collection at the Library of Congress.]

There may have been reasons for Brose to sign the *Ausweis* other than official pressure. And when one thinks about it, although it may not have been impossible for an underling in the General Staff to be involved in a bribery scheme, the idea of Brose, who ended the war as a major general, accepting a bribe of this nature seems unlikely. As we discussed in Chapter 1, Karl Brose's Department IIIb was in charge of intelligence, especially against the Russians. Brose had been in charge of Department IIIb for over ten years and had been trained in intelligence, not public relations. This raises the question whether at least part of this trip was for Department IIIb intelligence purposes, as well as propaganda ones, especially in light of the report probably written by Marks that was later to turn up in New York (infra). It also suggests that nobody had to pay the Army Chief of Staff anything. This trip to the eastern front may have been a Department IIIb project to obtain information from the beginning.

Nevertheless there is also a bill from A.C. Steinhardt, one of the finest haberdashers in Berlin, to "*Herrn Dr. Marx wohlgeboren*", on 28 December 1914 for 530.75 marks for a complete set of clothing appropriate for roughing it at the front. The fact that Wallace had the bill at least implies that Wallace paid it.

James W. Gerard

Somewhat later, the American Ambassador to Germany, James W. Gerard, developed what could be called a near phobia about Marks. On 8 September 1915 he sent a telegram to President Wilson:

> Hear again definitely that Emperor refused to see me as long as America delivers arms. To emphasize matter Emperor has lately received an American propagandist named Nilbuhr [Niebuhr] and an American spy named Doctor Marx [sic] who hangs about Hotel Adlon and is a medium of communication between American correspondents here and General Staff, lending correspondents money and otherwise corrupting them. (I beg you) to back me up and

notify Bernstorff that President will not see him or allow him to enter White House until Emperor receives me. It is customary here that foreigners must be presented by their Ambassadors. I also want authority in my discretion to take up the passport of Doctor Marx giving him emergency passport to United States. Above is not fault of Foreign Office or Chancellor but of military who surround Emperor and keep him out of Berlin.

Gerard, Berlin

To which President Wilson enclosed with a note to Edith Bolling Galt: "Ordinarily our Ambassador ought to be backed up of course, but – this ass? It is hard to take seriously."[32]

But later Ambassador Gerard at least roughly confirmed de Beaufort's prior accusations, although he could not of course verify them. On 7 December 1915, evidently ignored by President Wilson, Gerard wrote a dispatch to Robert Lansing, Secretary of State, on the subject of Dr. Marks, asking for authority to take up his passport:

> … I cabled you once asking authority to take up the passport of one Dr. Lewis Hart Marx, and you asked for more details; these now follow. Ex-Congressman [Herman] Metz represents in America the great chemical and dyestuff works of the 'Hoechst' Company at Frankfort [sic]. This company, or the people interested in it, also manufacture various medicines particularly those made from coal tar. Wishing to take advantage of the reputation of Dr. Ehrlich, of 606 fame, they established 'an Institute for Medical Research' with Dr. Marx, a young Jew about 30, who had, I believe once studied under Ehrlich, at the head. The game was to announce that 'Dr. Marx, pupil of Ehrlich, has discovered a cure for malaria', and then sell the 'cure' all over the U.S.A. For some reason, the public would not bite. Metz, when here, tried to get me to ask the Emperor to give the coveted title of 'professor' to Marx, and Marx persecuted me with tales of his own celebrity, but I 'side-stepped', sheltering myself behind the State Department regulations. This has probably rather incensed the 'doctor'. After the outbreak of the war the Doctor took up his quarters in the Adlon Hotel. He was accused by a Hearst newspaper man named Wallace of taking money from him to get him sent to the front, and of introducing, as part of the scheme, a sort of aristocratic loafer named Count Hessenstein, as the nephew of Moltke, head of the General Staff. Later another Hearst man, 'Count' de Beaufort threatened to expose all this, and I helped Baron Mumm of the Foreign Office, to hush up the scandal by taking up 'Count' Beaufort's passport and sending him home. A good secret service man can get the story from 'Count' de Beaufort in New York.
>
> Dr. Marx then more and more devoted himself to American correspondents here. He arranged with the General Staff to have Herbert Corey sent to the front; you may remember Corey's subsequent violently pro-German articles. Dr. Marx has also been busy (although not a Red Cross doctor) in getting medical supplies for the Germans. The doctor now seems to be employed by the General Staff to 'attend' to American correspondents. He lends them money, etc. I know of some instance he lent one correspondent 700 dollars in gold. Finally he invited all the correspondents here to a supper, and proposed, entirely from altruistic grounds, a correspondents' union. [Seymour] Conger of the Associated Press, was elected President in his absence, but of course refused and they broke up the union. Marx has admitted to me that he is working for the German government, and is bitterly opposed to the President. He lately obtained an audience with the Emperor, through the latter's sister, Princess Charlotte of Saxe-Meiningen, with whom Metz has a 'pull'.…[33]

As will be related in more detail later, Heinrich Albert, newly appointed propaganda chief, left his briefcase full of documents relating to top secret German interests in

America, including propaganda efforts, on the New York subway, and when he got off they were snatched by an American secret service agent.[34] From then on, he was nicknamed "the German minister without portfolio". It was decided to leak the documents to the *New York World*, which started to publish the contents on 15 August 1915, and continued doing so for almost a week.

Among other documents in the briefcase was a memorandum proposing the formation of a syndicate, to control German war photographs and film for the American market. It proposed also that snapshots be distributed to German soldiers: "During my trip to the East in company of the American photographer Wallace, I have become convinced that a real necessity for these photographs on the part of the soldiers exists." Unfortunately the author of this memorandum is not mentioned, nor does the name appear in the original Albert documents at the National Archives.[35] In light of the *Ausweis* mentioned above, Marks' reported membership on a German committee to develop propaganda for use abroad, and all of the other matter in the German files, it seems extremely likely that it was Dr. Marks.

Marks' work behind the scenes seems to have contributed to an important alteration in the German approach to World War I journalism. United Press correspondent William Shepherd reported in 1917:

> It was a light that dawned in Germany, spreading through the war offices of Europe, which finally dispelled the gloom of the 'dark ages'. The British kept their first battle of Ypres a secret from the world for four months. But the Germans were guilty of a stupidity almost as great, for von Hindenburg's first defeat of the Russian army in the Mazurian Lake region did not reach the world until Karl von Wiegand, then of the United Press, discovered the battle as a news story, and persuaded the German War Office to let him go to Eastern Prussia and make a news story out of the victory. That one story served to prove to the Germans the value of proper publicity. Within a short time they had appointed a man in the War Office whose sole duty was to arrange for trips for war correspondents to the various fronts. The Allies soon felt the force of this German move. While desperate correspondents on the Ally side were either sending out fake and imaginative stories, or were passing their days in idleness in the Ally capitals, the correspondents in Germany were glorifying German arms by their stories of German doings. To offset the German propaganda, the Allies began to grant certain privileges to correspondents, and these privileges exist today.[36]

But whatever Marks accomplished on behalf of the Germans in 1915, his friend Congressman Herman A. Metz was no longer trying to help him after America entered the war. Following an interview with Metz, in the extremely useful Bureau of Investigation report dated 5 October 1917, agent Ed. L. Newman revealed:

> … Mr. Metz also said that Marks had known quite a number of American war correspondents there – amongst others he mentioned A. E. Wallace, Edward Lyal [sic] Fox. The former he succeeded in introducing to Emperor Wilhelm's second sister, not Charlotte of Saxe-Meiningen.

> Marks, according to Mr. Metz, being a Jew, would be barred from German court circles, so far as Metz knew, and any connection which Marks might have claimed to have had with royalty would be effected through the disreputable and bankrupt Count Boudessen [von Hessenstein?]. Mr. Metz also stated that Marks, as he later learned, was in league with a lot

of men who are considered nothing but a common, low set of grafters, who posing to know royalty and nobility through this count have often promised to perform different tasks which he knew could seldom, if at all, have been accomplished.[37]

Newman commented that Metz had described Marks as having no particular research ability, and as having done little to help Dr. Ehrlich, but said, "In this report, Mr. Metz further admitted that Marks had sufficient influence with the police of Berlin and Frankfort [sic], and in that way he (Mr. Metz) was able to get the German government's permission to take out the first war film pictures that were brought over to this country".[38] Metz probably brought these films to the United States on the SS *Rijndam* when he sailed from Europe in December 1914.

On 28 December 1915, Gerard sent an additional dispatch to Robert Lansing referring to the Hotel Adlon "'spy nest headed by Dr. Marx":

> Anthony Czarnecki, a very intelligent Chicagoan, an American of Polish descent, is here representing Victor Lawson and the Chicago 'Daily News'. He informs me that the Spy Nest is contemplating an attack on the Administration because of the taking away of Archibald's and other passports, and he wants word sent immediately to Mr. Denis [Charles Dennis], manager of the Chicago 'Daily News', to the effect that, after investigating the situation, he is strongly in favor of the taking away of passports of Americans who abuse the Administration and America or act in an unneutral matter. Please get this to Mr. Denis. He is afraid [Oswald F.] Schütte, correspondent here of the Chicago 'Daily News', who is in the toils of Dr. Marx, may send an attack … . I have your cable of authorization re Marx but will go very slow in the matter.
>
> It might make a good story for the New York 'World' if they would send a man to stop at the Hotel Adlon, fall in apparently with the designs of the Spy Nest, and see how much money Marx would give him and with what members of the German Government Marx could put him in touch. The 'World' envoy might say that he had come to Germany to get a quick view [of] the German side … .[39]

If the Americans were not thrilled by Marks, the Germans also had their doubts, and these eventually reached a critical level. Dr. Wilhelm von Radowitz was the highest-ranked advisor to Wilhelm von Stumm, chief of the political department of the AA. He was also their chief councilor from 1914 and in 1915 was assigned to secret subjects such as espionage and given the title *Geheime Legionsrat*. Radowitz made inquiries about Marks. Roediger replied:

> To Herr G.L.R. von Radowitz
>
> Berlin, 7 January 1916
>
> G. A.
>
> Dr. Lewis Hart Marks, an American citizen, is a familiar person here at the information department of the Ministry of Foreign Affairs; we have known him since the outbreak of the war. Marks used to be a physician, and has lived in Germany now for about eight years. He worked for Ehrlich's Institute in Frankfurt am Main. Dr. Marks is now working for the War Office (Rittmeister von Lustig) on the procurement of serum for the German and Austrian Army.
>
> Dr. Marks has come to this office several times, giving recommendations on matters concerning American correspondents. He has given us some useful pieces of information and advice

on some of these journalists. Generally speaking however he is considered a pompous ass who likes to pretend that he's very important. His position here isn't quite clear. According to Dr. Marks himself, he has advanced several of these correspondents sums of money as a favor. It also appears that he has been a middle man on the buying of news stories and that he has tried by different ways to arrange permits for the American correspondents to get to the front. On several occasions we suspected that he used his position for his own financial benefit. We have not found any conclusive evidence however to substantiate this. In the summer of last year [1915], we received a confidential report by agent Krebs, in which he warned us about Dr. Marks and stated that Marks was in contact with the New York World. Recently Rittmeister Warnecke – acting Commanding General of the 18th Army Corps – also mentioned he has some doubts about Dr. Marks, because he does not appear to be rich and it seems very dubious where he finds all the money for his expensive stay in Berlin [at the Adlon Hotel] and the loans to the correspondents. There is however no definite evidence to the disadvantage of Dr. Marks. He is being recommended by a Member of Parliament, Haeckscher.

A few months ago, we were told that Marks tried to organize the correspondents but this attempt was not successful.

On the whole, it is advised to be somewhat careful while dealing with Dr. Marks although we consider him useful because of his confidential statements on the American correspondents.

Roediger[40]

Thereafter come several mystifying articles in *Moving Picture World*, the first on 30 January 1915 and the second on 20 February 1915. Both described Wallace's harrowing experiences on the western front, and preview the exciting stories from there that would soon be shown in the *Hearst Selig News Pictorial*.[41] Both these reports would seem to be almost totally false. Wallace was at the eastern front until 21 January 1915. While the beginning of the first letter, concerning Wallace's problems with red tape and in getting to the eastern front is true enough, there is absolutely no evidence that he ever filed any footage from France or Belgium between January and February 1915. Wallace was in Rotterdam on 15 February 1915, according to his visa stamped at the Consulate-General. On the other hand, on 14 March one of the AAPA records contains a statement on the American journalists Wallace and Fox living in the Adlon, who purportedly paid some 1500 marks for the furnishing of a pass to the front. One of the receipts was apparently sent by de Beaufort to the United States. This probably implies that Wallace returned to Berlin and stayed there until March and only left the country with August F. Beach in March 1915. But there is no evidence of Wallace's having made a trip to France or Belgium.

De Beaufort is unfortunately unclear on the specifics of Wallace's departure, simply stating that "the upshot was that his filming career was cut short, and he withdrew to the neutral territory of Holland".[42] In the records at the German archives there is no overt complaint by the Germans about Wallace's behavior. But it may be that the German government made it clear to Wallace that his previous contacts would no longer be available, and thus he may have decided to withdraw from Germany, at least for a while.

Alternatively, there were numerous complaints about de Beaufort. De Beaufort's accusations had caused a small firestorm in Berlin. After all, one is not meant to be able to bribe the German General Staff or the Foreign Office. In addition, the matter laid bare the conflict between the Foreign Office and the German Army on the subject of ultimate responsibility for German propaganda for neutrals. In fact de Beaufort caused a flurry of notes, queries, and questions, Mumm saying that de Beaufort gave him "many headaches". The German government, both the General Staff and the AA, knew that de Beaufort was a questionable character early on and yet they had handled him with kid gloves for the same reason that they were kind to Wallace. He was a Hearst correspondent, they did not know how much clout he had, and they did not want to anger Hearst. It was only after von Bernstorff asked Hearst directly about de Beaufort and Hearst responded that he had no interest in him that the German government took strong measures.

The AA inquiries did solve some things. De Beaufort got into Germany in the first place by first approaching von Bernstorff at the American Embassy. Von Bernstorff, apparently on the basis of his being a Hearst journalist, gave him a letter of introduction. Somehow de Beaufort found his way to Italy, where he approached the German Embassy in Rome and received a letter of introduction dated 15 January 1915 from Herbert von Hindenburg, the Field Marshal's nephew, who acted on von Bernstorff's recommendation. With this he had no trouble getting into Germany. There is even a photograph of the letter from Herbert von Hindenburg in de Beaufort's book, and elsewhere de Beaufort describes the letter as his "magic key".

After the Wallace imbroglio, de Beaufort, in an amazing display of chutzpah, went first to Poland in March of 1915 and then to Kiel and the other German North Sea ports without ever getting any permissions either from the AA or the General Staff. He used the letter of introduction from Hindenburg's nephew and the name von Hindenburg apparently scared the German army so much that it let de Beaufort bluff his way through both trips. According to de Beaufort, he got an exclusive interview with Field Marshal von Hindenburg, although his fellow journalists doubted that he ever interviewed von Hindenburg, and the Germans later flatly denied any such interview took place. Both the *Norddeutsche Allgemeine Zeitung* and *Der Tag* said that de Beaufort's supposed interview with von Hindenburg was an invention. He only got as far as Lötzen on 15 March 1915, where he was sent back to Berlin by the German authorities, and then expelled from the country.[43] *Der Tag* was especially incensed by de Beaufort's alleged interview because he reported that von Hindenburg's face was "cruel"; "Anyone who dares to describe in such a way the face of such a great man – a giant among leaders in this titanic world struggle clearly shows that his own personal appearance isn't worthy of the dignity that goes with the aristocratic title of the family of de Beaufort."[44] The reporting by de Beaufort on the North Sea ports is amazingly detailed, even if very few details are given about how he got there or what his sources were, and it was good enough to later become the subject of an article in the London *Quarterly Review* in October 1916. On his return to Berlin de

Beaufort was firmly invited to leave, both by the German and American governments (statement by Ambassador Gerard, *supra*). Typically, de Beaufort makes high drama out of his departure:

> As to my arrest, the various interrogations, my explanation as to how the incriminating article appeared, my arrest, my release, re-arrest, release again, but under orders not to leave Berlin: their demand for my parole – which, need I say, I refused – and my ultimate escape across the Baltic; the harassing days of my trip across the North Sea in the tramp steamer Flora in fear of a German submarine that would press me to return; and finally my safe landing in Hull – well, over these incidents and sensations I must, at least for the present draw a veil.[45]

After Wallace left, the open feud described in Chapter 1 developed between the reporters and Ambassador Gerard, who was angry and convinced of the pro-Germanism of some of the correspondents, especially Raymond Swing (later known as Raymond Gram Swing), Oswald Schuette and Walter Niebuhr. Carl W. Ackerman and Herbert Bayard Swope remained on Gerard's side in the feud. Ackerman later reported that after America entered the war on 26 April 1917, in an address to the American Newspapers Association in New York, Gerard summed up his feelings: "Most of the American correspondents became super-Ambassadors and proceeded to inform the German Government that they must not believe me – that they must not believe the President – that they must not believe the American people – but believe these people, and to a great extent this war is due to the fact that these pro-German Americans, a certain number of them, misinformed the German government as to the sentiments of this country".[46]

On the English Channel

It was Wallace who showed the English Admiralty and the world that not only had Germany built super-submarines but they were also in action.

On 4 February 1915 the Germans decided to make the English Channel, including the area off the coast of Holland and Belgium, a war zone in which enemy ships would be destroyed and neutral ships could be searched, seized and held as prizes by the German government. It was the first tentative German effort to use U-boats on neutral merchant shipping. In accordance with this "new commercial warfare", the *U-28*, commanded by Commandant Georg-Günther Freiherr von Forstner, took up patrol duties off of the coast of Holland, first sinking SS *Leeuwarden* on 15 March by gunfire and with no casualties.[47]

In the meantime Hearst sent his London representative August F. Beach to Germany to collect the remains of James Creelman, a famed Hearst representative in Berlin, and to bring them to Holland, as well as to "settle the matter of De Beaufort".[48] Wallace travelled along with Beach to London from Rotterdam on board the SS *Batavier V*. On 18 March, three days after the *Leeuwarden* sinking, on a pleasant spring day, Wallace had just come to the deck after a hefty breakfast. He was looking around the vast sea when suddenly a submarine emerged from the water right next to the steamboat. When it approached, several persons appeared in the turret and

THE START: TAKING IN OIL FROM HER TENDER

PREY NUMBER TWO: APPROACHING THE ZAANSTROOM

THE CHASE: FOLLOWING IN THE WAKE OF A DUTCH STEAMER

OVERHAULING HER PREY: ROUNDING THE BOW OF THE BATAVIER IV

ABOUT TO BOARD THE PRIZE: THE PILOT LEAVING THE TENDER FOR THE STEAMER

THE SUMMONS TO SURRENDER: CALLING UPON THE STEAMER TO HEAVE TO

THE TRIUMPH: THE SUBMARINE LEADING THE WAY THROUGH MINE-FIELDS INTO ZEEBRÜGGE

VON FORSTNER'S SUBMARINE (U 28)
A Series of Photographs taken from

IN ACTION IN THE NORTH SEA
the Deck of One of her Victims

Fig. 38. German submarine U-28 in action. Sequence of photographs by Wallace from the London Graphic, *27 March 1915.*

ordered the *Batavier V* along with the SS *Zaanstroom* to stop. Beach reported the incident for Hearst's *Chicago Examiner*:

> Wallace and I, bound from Berlin to London via Rotterdam had just come on deck after breakfast Thursday when we saw a German submarine of the largest type, the U-36 cutting across our stern at a twenty knot gait. Wallace dived below to get a kodak and cinema camera, and the fun was on. The captain of the *Batavier* had ordered the engines stopped and was standing aft to receive the Germans … . A smiling German lieutenant and party came aboard to inform the crew and passengers that their ship was war booty, hoisted several flags and started semaphoring to the U-boat.
>
> All this time Wallace was grinding away at the moving picture camera. Next to the German visitor he was the busiest man on the North Sea. The *Batavier* stopped and heaved her anchor and the submarine, shaping a swift course for the south, a few minutes later struck a course due east in the direction of a blotch of black smoke directly off our stern, which was the *Zaanstroom*.[49]

Actually the U-boat was not the *U-36* but the *U-28*, commanded by von Forstner. Von Forstner also described the incident and the encounter with the 'Hearst reporter' in a diary he kept which was published in German and in an abridged form in the United States. Subsequently the *U-28* and several submarine tenders escorted both the *Batavier V* and the *Zaanstroom* to Zeebrugge through what Beach described as a "dense minefield". Edward Hatrick, head of the Hearst newsreel section, described the scene somewhat later:

> Wallace did not waste any time inspecting the new arrival. His first thought was – a picture. Therefore he dived below and soon reappeared with his camera. While no shots had been fired, Wallace did not want the unwelcome visitors to mistake his camera for a new type of a machine gun. So he 'set up' in the shelter of the aft deck house, and as soon as the submarine approached he began cranking and kept it up until a German officer climbed over the side of the ship and informed the captain that his ship was a prize of war and that the Germans would take it to Zeebrugge. With the appearance of the German officer Wallace ducked below and began taking pot shots with his camera at the submarine out of the porthole of his stateroom.
>
> A few miles out from Zeebrugge, a submarine tender drew alongside.
>
> 'What have you here?' the tender commander enquired of the German officer aboard the Batavier V. 'A fine haul, captain', came the answer. 'Pork, cheese, butter, beer, sauerkraut, eggs, Belgians and French.'
>
> Wallace and his companion were standing on the deck directly below the officer and at this point Wallace's companion chimed in and said: 'And two Americans'. Then came the bombshell from the German lieutenant. Looking down at Wallace, he said, 'Yes, and you have taken pictures of the whole performance'.
>
> Wallace looked at the officer and grinned. There was nothing else to do. He immediately had visions of spending some time in jail, but worst of all, he would lose his film.
>
> On the way into the harbor he brought his cameras and other luggage on deck. He had made up his mind to lose everything without any protest if they did not insist on searching him personally. The only thing on his mind was that precious two-hundred-foot roll of film.
>
> When they arrived at the dock they were lined up with other passengers for examination, and were then told to stay aboard the steamboat. Here they remained for two days, and then came another surprise. Wallace and his companion were given a pass with a German officer for an escort and ordered to leave that afternoon for the Dutch frontier.
>
> There was no further examination of their baggage and they started on their way with film and cameras intact. Whether the German officer failed to report the incident of taking pictures or whether they let the pictures slip through Wallace never knew, nor did he stop to enquire. They made their way to Holland and several days [later] arrived in England.
>
> Here they did not receive the same treatment. Their luggage was seized and as soon as Wallace explained what he had the films were taken to the Admiralty office where they were developed and later projected for the benefit of the officials. A few weeks later the films were released by the British authorities, and Wallace started home with the biggest 'scoop' of the war in his suitcase.[50]

Von Forstner was amused by "the reporter's" (probably Beach's) reaction to the *U-28*'s trip through the "alleged minefield" off Zeebrugge. Every time the U-boat slowed down to sound its depth, the reporter thought the boat had just slipped by a deadly mine. Later when the reports came out, Beach had reported on "our trip through the minefield! An audacious feat!"[51]

From mid-March through April, Wallace was in England. When he arrived, he must have come in contact with George Allison. Allison was chief of INS operations in London, and bought thousands of newsreels and photographs, virtually everything he could get his hands on, for William Randolph Hearst.[52] Allison also reported the

Batavier V incident and said he made the newsreel films available to the British Admiralty. He felt that he had the pro-German Hearst organization working for the British and its allies, a good example out of many of a newspaper editor's politics being sabotaged by his reporters and staff. Von Forstner reported that Wallace's photographs first appeared in the London *Daily Graphic* on 27 March 1915, so Allison must not have wasted much time in circulating the pictures. The *Daily Graphic* photographs were included in the English translation of Forstner's book. Forstner also mentioned that the pictures were widely distributed in many newspapers in the United States, as indeed they were. The *New York Times Mid-Week Pictorial* ran a full page of photos of the U-boat on 15 April 1915. The study of the films by the British Admiralty might suggest why Wallace's films did not run until May in no. 34:

> Off Zeebrugge. A German submarine captures the Batavier V and the Zaanstroom, Dutch vessels, and sends them into port under pilots sent out by the submarine. Pictures made by staff photographer, A. E. Wallace.[53]

Italy

In April Wallace arrived in Italy, an excellent spot for a correspondent since it was clear that Italy was going to enter the war very soon, although no one was quite sure on which side. Wallace lived lavishly, staying in Rome at the Hotel du Quirinal from 24 April to 7 May, and the Hotel Windsor on the Via Veneto from 22 May to 26 May 1915. Italy declared war on Austria-Hungary on 23 May 1915. In Wallace's scrapbook there are a group of photographs from Rome, probably taken when the official announcement was made of Italy's taking up arms. In June of 1915 Hearst-Selig ran Wallace's filming of Rome when war was declared as well as the Italian government's calling out troops to protect the Austrian Embassy from the crowds. On 1 July the *New York Times Midweek Pictorial Review* released some of the same photographs, including the one that *Hearst-Selig* had used to publicize Wallace's newsreels.[54]

Wallace left Rome bound for Venice on 26 May 1915. This was the logical course for him to head for the battlefront since most of the early fighting between Italy and Austria took place in the Carnic Alps or toward Trieste and the *Terra Irredenta* along the Adriatic coast. Wallace was present in Italy during the first abortive Italian attempt against the Austrians on the Carso Plateau and during the First Battle of the Isonzo. But Wallace filed no stories nor made motion pictures from any Italian battlefront. The possible reasons include Italy having entered the war totally unprepared and probably without any provision for foreign cinematographers. Also General Luigi Cadorna, Supreme Commander in Italy and possessing near dictatorial powers, wanted to ban all journalists from the front. Then on 23 May 1915 the leading Italian newspapers petitioned the government and general staff for permission to file stories after the Supreme Command had approved them, but only they would be allowed to do so. And, similar to Germany's system, the correspondents were only allowed

Fig. 39. Declaration of war in Rome, May 1915. This shot appeared credited to Wallace in Motography, *17 July 1915, and also appeared in the* New York Times Mid-Week Pictorial, *1 July 1915, which is reproduced here.*

to visit the front in large groups and under close military escort. The favorite government paper was the *Corriere della Sera* which got many special favors and preferential treatment. It is doubtful that Hearst was able to call in many favors from the Italian government. If this was not already a sufficient deterrent to Wallace, the War Powers Act of 22 May 1915 allowed the government to examine and seize any publication as well as postal, telegram or telephone communication that might be "prejudicial to the supreme national interests". And worst of all, the publication of any information not from official sources was forbidden.[55] There are a number of photographs of the Italian campaign copyrighted by INS that made their way into the *New York Times Mid-Week Pictorial* in June 1915, but it is not known whether Wallace took these photographs himself or purchased them from the Italians. In his scrapbook there is one photograph of Italian *Bersaglieri* with a machine gun, but there is no evidence that Wallace took it. Under these circumstances Wallace can be excused for not shooting any moving pictures. He was in Venice during one of a series of air raids it experienced in the summer of 1915. Venice was not totally unprepared with guns and other weapons on the Doge's Palace and search lights on the Saint Mark's Cathedral, now encased in steel girders and covered in sandbags. Venice was "spy-mad" according to Wallace, and he was refused permission to make still photos or shoot film. He was staying at the Grand Hotel with a fellow American and his wife when the Austrians started dropping bombs and steel arrows on the city, which he reported on 10 July after he arrived in New York on the SS *St. Louis* on 5 July 1915. It is perhaps significant that he was safely out of Italy when he filed his story in New York and his many photographs appeared in the *New York Times*.[56]

After returning to the United States Wallace covered similar stories for Hearst that he had filmed before the war, with little fanfare. He photographed the militia in

Boston, and on 15 August 1915 he flew with Lawrence Sperry, the son of Elmer A. Sperry who developed the Sperry gyrocompass, in his Curtiss Flying Boat at Amityville, Long Island.[57] According to Justice Department files, Wallace left Hearst's employment in late 1917 and had returned to Evansville, Indiana, by September 1918. No record of military service has been found.

And thus Wallace's war ended. He had spent about three months in Germany and managed to get to the eastern front in Poland for one week, with his most famous photographs coming from an unsought opportunity as he was leaving Germany.

Hearst must have been disappointed with the Germans' response to what was a huge gift on a platter to Germany. Instead of sending another journalist into the abyss as it were, he wanted a prior arrangement with the Germans so future cameramen would have a fixed assignment before arriving in Germany.

Nelson Edwards

With A. E. Wallace back in America, Hearst and Hatrick arranged for another Hearst representative to film in Germany. According to most sources, in December 1915 Hearst wrote a personal note to Ambassador Count von Bernstorff asking for his help since the two men had met socially and got on.[58] However, the December date may be incorrect or von Bernstorff may have independently realized that an American cameraman representing Hearst interests in Germany would be a very good idea because long before then the machinery to send Edwards to Europe was in motion.[59] On 21 October 1915 Edwards received the following terse, yet enticing telegram while covering the Exposition at San Francisco:

> cb New York Oct 21 15
>
> Nelson Edwards
>
> Call San Francisco
>
> How would you like to take a trip to Germany and Austria please wire
>
> E. B. Hatrick[60]

It may be assumed that Edwards liked it very much. He immediately started making preparations to leave and applied for a passport. On 4 November 1915 von Bernstorff had already granted Edwards permission to represent the *New York American* and the International Film Service, making any personal note in December from Hearst to von Bernstorff unnecessary. According to the *Editor & Publisher:*

> The intimate friends and co-workers of Nelson E. Edwards, of the Call art staff, and moving picture operator of the International Film Service, gave him a farewell dinner Saturday evening in a downtown café to speed him off for the Balkans where he will take war pictures. Edwards left , October 23, for New York, where he will sail for Rotterdam. While here he represented the Call and Post and the Hearst-Selig Pictorial Weekly making films of the Exposition Events for that service. In taking war pictures Edwards will be attached to the Austro-German armies … .[61]

Proof again, if more is needed, that Hearst and Edwards knew his specific assignment in the Balkans before he left. Edwards was to sail for Europe on the SS *Rijndam*, but the plan changed. That fall Henry Ford arranged to send a Peace Ship with a large number of prominent pacifists aboard to Europe to establish a permanent commis-

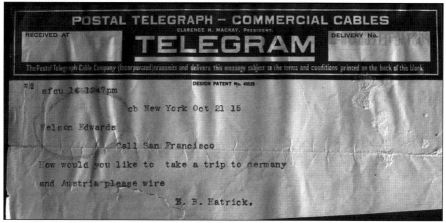

Fig. 40. Telegram from Hearst's newsreel chief Hatrick, inviting Edwards to war-torn Europe.
[Courtesy Wiegman family.]

sion in The Hague and create a permanent committee to persuade the combatants to stop the Great War. While the concept was good, the whole enterprise received tremendous ridicule from its inception. Ford's general ineptness and the bickering among the peace delegates did not help matters. Ford could not persuade most of the really important people he wanted for the trip to accompany him; they probably sensed failure. Ford also invited a large number of reporters, correspondents and photographers to accompany the mission. On 1 December 1915 Hatrick telegraphed Louis P. Lochner, then secretary for Henry Ford, asking that Edwards be the INS representative on the Ford Peace Ship leaving for Europe.[62] This was evidently agreeable, and the INS sent Edwards to Europe on the Henry Ford Peace ship, the *Prinz Oscar II.* It sailed from Hoboken on 4 December 1915. Louis Lochner, Ford's secretary, said three cinematographers were aboard but only Joseph T. Rucker, indeed a fine cameraman, was listed.[63] A newsreel cameraman for Universal, he had covered the opening of the Panama Canal in 1915 and later won an Academy Award for cinematography in 1930. Berndt G. Phillips was also aboard but little is known except that he was a still photographer working for Underwood & Underwood in New York. The three were the subject of a poem in a photography magazine:

Rucker, Edwards and Phillips

Sailed to end the War,

On Oscar the Second,

With a few dozen more.[64]

The fourth cinematographer was Lawrence J. Darmour, a cameraman for Mutual. Pell Mitchell, head of newsreels for Mutual had gotten him aboard as what must have been a last minute addition. His passport was only issued on 3 December 1915, the day before sailing. He had photographed the Standard Oil strike with Edwards.[65] On

8 December 1915 the expedition set up what now would be called a "photo op". The *Argosy*, the Expedition's ship's newspaper, reported on 8 December:

OUR PLACE IN THE SUN

The activities on deck this morning included taking moving pictures. The presentation of the flag from Philadelphia was duplicated, Mrs. [Joseph] Fels presenting it to Mr. Ford. After that Mr. Ford and office force of about 25 were photographed. Later Mr. Ford was taken standing at the wheel.[66]

The Ford Peace Ship had landed in Christiana, Norway on 19 December 1915, where the members of the expedition stayed until they took a train for Stockholm on 23 December and from there went on to Copenhagen and through Germany to The Hague. Edwards stayed with the group in Sweden and was photographed at a banquet at the Grand Hotel in Stockholm. But

Fig. 41. Edwards and Mutual cameraman Larry Darmour (left) aboard the Ford Peace ship, December 1915. [Courtesy Wiegman family.]

he had to leave the group since he could not take his camera into Germany.[67] So in Sweden he managed to get a small 100-foot boat, which possessed neither lifeboats nor life belts, to take him to Rotterdam through some of the coldest and choppiest water anywhere, a trip which took three days. From Rotterdam, he made it to The Hague, but did not stay long. He had received permission to enter Germany with his camera. The trip on the Peace Ship was not a waste. *Hearst-Vitagraph News Pictorial* No. 1 featured Ford's ship in its very first issue, and Edwards' coverage included the extremely dignified and prominent ministers Charles F. Aked and Dr. Lloyd Jenkin Jones playing leapfrog on deck. The footage received hearty laughter when projected.[68]

As with several other American news photographers before him, once Edwards was in Germany, the Germans did not seem to know what to do with him. As his fellow cameraman Albert K. Dawson remarked, the Germans displayed a reluctance to send American cinematographers to the real hot spots. While Edwards was in Germany, the bloodbath at Verdun was at its height, and the battle of the Somme started on 1

July, but Edwards was never sent to either place. According to his later recollections, he did however see some combat in spite of German restrictions. On one occasion the special car in which he was being conducted along the western front ran into heavy French artillery fire along a half-mile stretch of exposed highway. Edwards and a German officer lay on the back seat, across each other. When they sat back up, they found that the shellfire had torn to shreds the back of the seat where their heads would have had been. Another time Edwards visited the front and attracted a crowd of German soldiers, who in turn attracted French artillery. An officer told the men to take cover. "He hadn't more than got that out of his mouth when I heard those things whistling", Edwards says. "I left my camera there and ran for a dugout because when I see those things clipping the limbs off of trees I'm out in front." The shells felled some trees and killed some Germans.[69] In March, after a very brief stint in Berlin and environs photographing the obligatory prison camps, he was sent to cover Turkey, Germany's friend and ally.

At the time Germany was anxious to direct a thorough film propaganda effort toward its allies in the Balkans and the Near East, whom they had essentially ignored. The Germans were especially worried about Turkey, where it appeared that Russia might accomplish its drive through the Caucasus and attack from the east, along the Black Sea. Germany was very worried about the influence of Austria-Hungary's propaganda in Turkey, and wanted to counter it. The ZfA started what Conrad Barkhausen called "*Der – Orient – Kino – Verband*". Joseph Schumacher enlisted *Messter-Film* to distribute the films to the Near East.

In addition, the German navy, always interested in the Dardanelles, was enthusiastic about film exhibitions, especially in Turkey. Schumacher's *Auslandszentrale* was already distributing films there through *Messter-Film*. A deal was made with Schumacher to use film which would be taken by Edwards in Turkey. These films, primarily taken for Hearst in America, would now also be offered to the news service of *Reichsmarineamt*, under the leadership of *Korvettenkapitän* Hans Wittman, to be released in Turkey, Bulgaria and Germany as well.[70] It speaks to Hearst's pro-German sentiment that he willingly allowed German use of these films.

"The Turk and the Teuton"

In the latter part of 1915 Field Marshal August von Mackensen, commanding a force comprised of Germans, Austrians and the Bulgarian First Army and named Army Group Mackensen, had attacked Serbia in a campaign called the Second invasion of Serbia. It was a great success for the Central Powers, and Belgrade fell on 9 October 1915. The Serbs' only rail connection to the Entente forces at Salonika was also cut off, leaving the Serbs no choice but to admit defeat and retreat to the Adriatic coast. The Bulgarians captured the section of the famed Berlin-Baghdad Railway, one of the Kaiser's pet projects before the war, that had previously been in the hands of the Serbians, thus re-opening the railroad from Berlin to Constantinople. On 1 July 1916 *Billboard* reported:

Nelson G. [sic] Edwards, staff camera man of the Hearst International News Pictorial with the Turkish Army at Constantinople is responsible for a number of remarkable photographs showing Turkish infantry in the field.

When Turkey entered the Great War the 'Sick Man of Europe' was not taken seriously by any of the students of the conflict. Turkey was supposed to be hopelessly corrupt and ravaged by traitorous and grafting political profiteers, for which the Far East is notorious. Its army, brave enough as a whole, was sadly disorganized and poorly equipped. Then came Liman von Sanders, Teuton, and reorganized the half-hearted and dissatisfied fighting force. With the assistance of German officers, German equipment and German efficiency methods he accomplished the impossible, and from a horde of disgruntled renegades made the Ottoman forces a powerful and efficient unit, as witness the defense of the Dardanelles. The failure of the allies at Gallipoli [was what] led Nelson G. [sic] Edwards, staff camera man for the Hearst International News Pictorial, with the armies of the Kaiser, to Constantinople and the Turkish Battle Fronts in Persia.[71]

The *Billboard* article, obviously written by a Hearst PR man, is remarkable for its errors as well as its patronizing attitude toward the Turks. The Young Turks had started a revolution in 1908 against Ottoman corruption in Turkey with no German help. They and especially Kemal Atatürk would have been interested to learn that Liman von Sanders and the Germans were solely responsible for the victory at Gallipoli, or for that matter that Turkey was in the "Far East". But it did appear in the early spring of 1916 that the Turkish and German forces were on the verge of a breakthrough, both against the British-held Suez Canal and in Persia. Gallipoli had fallen; the Turks had besieged General Charles Townshend's British forces in Mesopotamia at Kut-El-Amara. The Germans evidently planned to use Edwards to publicize the defeat of Serbia, the re-opening of the railroad, the resulting celebration of German-Turk amity and the possibility of victory in Persia and the Suez. As part of this scheme, the Germans sent Edwards to Constantinople by the reopened Berlin-Baghdad Railway, or *Balkanzug*, where he stayed for several months. His pass for the train stated that he did not need to be deloused, which must have pleased Edwards no end.

In an extensive and excellent article that appeared in the *Philadelphia Record* on 3 December 1916, Edwards reported that he arrived in Ottoman Turkey just about the time that Field Marshal von Mackensen also arrived there as the Kaiser's emissary.[72] In February 1916 the Kaiser had appointed Sultan Mohammed V of Turkey a Field Marshal and delegated von Mackensen to deliver to the Sultan the Field Marshal's baton and his personal letter. The Sultan received von Mackensen when he arrived in Constantinople on 20 March, whereupon von Mackensen delivered the baton and the letter from the Kaiser. The Sultan gave him a reception at which Enver Pasha, the Minister of War, was also present, and the Sultan conferred the Osmanieh Order in Brilliants on von Mackensen. Later, von Mackensen attended a tea given him by the German colony in Constantinople at the *Deutsches Haus Teutonia*. In answer to a formal statement of thanks for opening up the Berlin-Baghdad Railway, he stated that most of the credit belonged to his men, and that

God had been with them. A scene showing von Mackensen's visit to Constantinople, together with a view of Turkish troops, appeared in *Hearst International News Pictorial* No. 48 which was released on 16 June 1916.[73] Edwards was also very active as a still photographer. Edwards photographed von Mackensen's arrival in the Constantinople train station. He was quite taken with von Mackensen. The *Philadelphia Record* quoted Edwards:

> Edwards has a very great respect for this man von Mackensen, who is much talked about right now on account of his marvelous campaign in Rumania. The photograph which the American movie man made of the great German strategist is perhaps the most striking likeness of Mackensen that has come to this country. The picture looks like what Mackensen is – a man of indomitable pluck and courage, a fierce, swift fighter; a brilliant strategist; a doer always of the unexpected. 'If von Mackensen wants to take Rumania' is Edwards' way of putting it, 'Rumania is as good as taken'.[74]

But aside from the parades, ceremony and human interest photographs in Constantinople, the Turks did not know what to do with Edwards, either. As previously mentioned, the Turks were engaged in a very successful campaign against the British in Mesopotamia, which climaxed when the Turks besieged and captured Townshend's British Army at Kut, which surrendered to the Turks on 29 April 1916. The historian Martin Gilbert calls this as great a victory by the Turks as Gallipoli had been, but still the Turks seemed reluctant to send Edwards to that theater.[75]

Articles that run in Sunday magazines generally are written on the light side, and this was as true in 1916 as it is now. But there is a dark side to Edwards' stay in Turkey that can clearly be read between the lines of the *Philadelphia Record* story. Edwards tells a funny story about a fake crank he developed for his newsreel camera, but it is not without significance:

> It was made very clear to [Edwards] what he might and what he might not photograph. He would have wasted a good many thousand feet of film, had not his American ingenuity come to the rescue. For a Turkish officer would say 'Now turn the crank' and turning the crank of course, meant exposing the ribbon of film in his moving picture camera. So he fixed up a little device on the crank of his camera by means of which he could throw out the mechanism at will. So when the Turkish officer would order 'Turn' with a menacing edge on his voice, while the object to be photographed was still four or five hundred feet beyond range, Edwards would diligently turn the handle – and that would be all.[76]

The article makes clear how difficult it must have been to photograph in Turkey. Edwards reported that most of the windows on the train were sealed upon his trip from Berlin, and a seal was placed on his camera so he could not photograph.[77] Edwards was greeted upon arrival in Constantinople by the criminal police in Constantinople and told to report to police headquarters. When he arrived, they informed him that there were strict orders that no photographers were to be admitted to Turkey. The border guard who had let him into Turkey did not know what the word "kinematographer" on his pass implied. In any case, the police ordered him to leave Turkey immediately. The only thing that saved Edwards was a letter from the

Turkish Ambassador. He was allowed to stay and, according to him, given every privilege.

But the fact was that the Turks had very little militarily that they wanted photographed. Unfortunately for the Turks and Germans, in spite of Kut-El-Amara, the autumn of 1915 was the high water mark of German aspirations in the Middle East and Mesopotamia. The English, Russian and French forces soon woke up to the Germans' buildup of forces in Persia, and sent in extra forces to secure these areas. The German-Turkish attack on Suez was also a failure. The Germans simply could not send enough men or materiel on the still unfinished Berlin-Baghdad Railway to launch a major campaign on the Sinai Peninsula. In part because far too many Germans displayed the same kind of short-sighted arrogance evidenced in the *Billboard* article, Ottoman resentment of the Germans had increased to the point where Germans were often attacked, and Germans were officially advised not to travel alone in Turkey. The Shah of Persia, who had seemed on the verge of entering the war on the side of the Central Powers, lost interest. In the Caucasus, the Russians had taken Erzerum and took Trebizond on 18 April 1916, about the time Edwards left Turkey. Even the British in Mesopotamia, after a short lull to rebuild their forces, resumed their push on Baghdad. And perhaps most damning of all, Sheriff Hussein in Arabia, occupying the most holy cities of Mecca and Medina, revolted against Ottoman rule and came out for the British. This meant that the Ottoman Sultan, the nominal Caliph of all the Muslims, had been rejected in his own holy land.[78] There were very few triumphs in Turkey for Edwards to report. Adding to the situation was the Turkish massacre of the Armenians. While most of the killing took place in Armenia, many Armenians had been working on the railroad upon which Edwards travelled, and the Turks must have been very worried about what Edwards saw, let alone photographed. It is no wonder that the windows of Edward's train and his camera were sealed.

What he did report is short on facts; instead, he tells human interest stories. But his photography was very beautiful. He photographed the Sultan, the Sultan's harem, Turkish cavalry and artillery either on maneuvers or in battle, Turkish medical personnel performing an operation, an amputation, possibly the one he mentioned in the *Philadelphia Record* article, as well as prominent Turkish members of the government, including the Mayor of Constantinople, the Sultan, the Turkish foreign minister, Mackensen and Talaat Bey, the Minister of the Interior.[79] Talaat Bey, whose photograph is prominent in the *Philadelphia Record* piece, was a controversial figure. Edwards reported that Talaat Bey helped him get a couple of newsreel stories to Germany past Turkish censors. Edwards had made friends with Talaat while photographing him on some of his favorite horses at his country estate, and "… when the authorities held up the films, the movie man called Taloat [sic] on the phone. The films went out on the same train with their owner." Talaat Bey was a member of the Young Turk movement, and was on the one hand reported to have helped British

Fig. 42. Edwards's photograph of Turkish artillery, 1916.
[Courtesy Wiegman family.]

and French citizens who were trapped in Turkey after the beginning of the war and the subsequent declaration of Turkish jihad against the citizens of the Entente. Although Americans were neutral, they sometimes had difficulties with the regime, and he was often helpful to them as well. Nevertheless, he was later accused of having engineered the Armenian genocide by decreeing the relocation of Armenians on 30 May 1915. After the fall of the Ottoman Empire, he fled Turkey and took refuge in Germany, where he was gunned down by an Armenian in 1921.

On Edwards' return to Berlin, evidently with the newsreels that Talaat Bey had approved for release, Edwards agreed to let *Messter Woche* newsreel use them by a letter of agreement dated 20 April 1916.[80] A selection of these war scenes probably reached the American theatres two months later. On 20 June 1916, *Hearst International News Pictorial* No. 49 showed Turkish infantry going into action in the mountains, many of the soldiers returning wounded and being cared for by Red Crescent nurses. Although his name is not mentioned in the synopsis of the newsreel, the footage was probably shot by Edwards.

Edwards returned to Germany at the end of April 1916 and visited the huge prison camp in Darmstadt on 15 May. In his album, there is a photograph of General von Moltke's funeral in Berlin on 18 June 1916, but it is not certain that Edwards took it. The first time Edwards received a byline in the synopses of Hearst-International News Pictorials that appeared in the trade journals was in *Hearst International News Pictorial* No. 61 (1 August 1916), which cited Nelson Edwards' film showing the training of troops at Barnstädt, a Zeppelin flying over the German capital, and the "monster" statue of von Hindenburg erected in Berlin.[81]

Filming the German Navy

After Edwards returned to Berlin from Constantinople, he worked unceasingly to secure permission to photograph the German fleet at its bases on the North Sea. He finally got permission to do so from Chancellor Bethmann-Hollweg, probably not

Fig. 43. Edwards, filming Admiral von Hipper, one of the German top naval commanders.
[Courtesy Wiegman family.]

only due to Edwards' powers of persuasion but also because the Germans were elated by what they felt had been a major naval victory. The Battle of Jutland or the *Skagerrakschlacht* was fought between the British and German navies between 31 May and 1 June 1916. Both sides claimed victory, although the outcome was inconclusive. The Germans still celebrate the battle as a victory, since the British lost more ships and twice as many sailors as the Germans. The British, while unhappy generally with the battle with the German fleet, took the position that Jutland changed nothing. They had hurt the Germans. The German navy had fought a battle which still left the British navy predominant, then retreated to its North Sea ports where it remained bottled up until the end of the war. Nevertheless the German navy was in a celebratory mood, and when Edwards arrived at Wilhelmshaven, he became the personal guest of Admiral Scheer himself for three days aboard the battleship *Friedrich der Grosse*.[82]

The Germans' good mood may explain why Admiral Franz Ritter von Hipper looked so happy when Edwards photographed him on board the battleship *Westfalen*. Admiral von Hipper had been in charge of Scouting Group I and although his flagship had been shot to bits, his ships had sunk three British battle cruisers. The Kaiser had awarded him Germany's highest military award, the Pour le Mérite, which appears around von Hipper's throat in Edwards' film. *Hearst International News Pictorial* No.

63 (8 August 1916) some of which featured the battleship *Prinzregent Luitpold*, included "… first of a series of exclusive pictures by staff photographer Nelson E. Edwards, of the Kaiser's fleet, showing the best of the German empire's fighting ships in trim for battle, Wilhelmshaven, Germany".[83] No. 64 (11 August 1916) included "exclusive picture by staff photographer Nelson E. Edwards, showing a day in the life a German sailor Wilhelmshaven, Germany".[84] Number 65 (15 August 1916), the third of the naval series, featured film by Edwards showing activities on board the flagship of Admirals Scheer and von Hipper at Wilhelmshaven. Edwards got shots of Scheer and his staff.[85] On 15 July the press section of the Admiral's staff of the German Navy even provided a pass allowing Edwards to travel from Berlin via Kiel to photograph the U-boat school in Eckernförde.[86] Any photography of German U-boats until then had been strictly prohibited.

Shortly after Edwards' return, the *New York American*, Hearst's flagship newspaper, reported Edwards' comments on the experience. The statement lacks Edwards' normal exuberance and has the rather stilted sound of a thank-you note, but it seems accurate enough:

> Of all my unusual experiences and adventures I am proudest of the fact that I am the only foreigner to have visited Kiel Canal and Wilhelmshaven, the great naval strongholds of the German fleets. I was at both places soon after the sea fight between the British and German fleets off the Skaggerak. There I made films of the battleships, torpedo boats and submarines. This rare privilege was granted to me for the International Film Service through the courtesy of Captain Boy-Ed, former naval attaché of the German Embassy at Washington. The German officers, from Admiral Scheer to the enlisted men, were extremely courteous and aided me to make the films for exhibition in America.[87]

Edwards somewhat later was sent to the Vosges. He photographed battles for mountain trenches which were featured in *Hearst International News Pictorial* No. 77 and 78 (26/29 September 1916). A detailed army report on his trip to the Vosges still exists:

> Berlin, 10 August 1916

> Report on the Journey by a Neutral Cinematographer to Strassburg and the Vosges Front, 5–8 August 1916.

> Guide: 1st Lieutenant von Donat

> Participant: Nelson Edwards, Cinematographer for the Hearst Press

> 4.8.1916 9.44 A.M. Departure from Berlin, Anhalter Station.

> 5.8.1916 12.00 A.M. Arrival in Strassburg, where we immediately reported for duty at the Intelligence Officer of A.O.K. From him, we received a railroad ticket to Heilig Blasien (1, 07) and a sealed letter for the General Staff of 4th Reserve Army Corps.

> At Heilig Blasien, we reported at the Railroad Officer, from there we took a truck to General Command HQ, and received further instructions to go to the 30th Division on 6 and 7 August and to the 39th Division on 8 and 9 August. Travel by truck, accompanied by a staff officer, to the 30th Division in Belval.

> Arrival around 5 PM, then we had tea with His Excellency von Krause [probably Ernst von

*Fig. 44. Picture from Edwards' personal scrapbook, dated 8 August
1916. A German military report describes how on that same day he
filmed an infantry charge in the Vosges. [Courtesy Wiegman family.]*

Krause]. Next, we went to Senones, where we were quartered for the night. Sightseeing around
this place and dinner at the officers' mess.

6.8.1916 A.M. Trip by truck to the new cemetery for civilians and soldiers, accompanied by
a staff officer. Film report of His Excellency von Krause visiting a memorial monument and
attending a military funeral, together with other officers.

Trip and film report of the forward trench lines, as well as the area behind the front, on the
mountain heights. In the afternoon, we were guests at the officers' barracks in Senones. Film
report of officers drinking coffee around the mess table. In the afternoon, we went to Divisional
Staff and took motion pictures of the staff officers watching a plane. Film report of soldiers
playing games, such as horse riding, cock fights; also competition in throwing dud hand
grenades.

These scenes were all taken on a location where trees had been cut down in the forest. Back to Senones where more films were made, while His Excellency von Krause was attending; canteen scene in the open field. Dinner as guests in the officers' quarters.

7.8.1916 A.M. Film report on the departure of the regimental staff. By truck, we toured the immediate area and took motion pictures of fatigue work, such as men felling trees and soldiers working in the quarry, also the transport of wounded to Field Hospital. Arrival of munitions by rail road and transfer to a motor vehicle. Around midday, we were in the officers' quarters.

P.M. By car, we toured to Headquarters of the 39th Reserve Division. From there, we immediately went to HQ of the 9th Reserve Brigade, commanded by his Excellency Mark, in Lubine. Arrival around 5 P.M. Sightseeing of the "Pioneers Park" [probably barracks of engineer troops]. Quartered for the night in Lubine.

At 7.30 P.M. we were welcomed by His Excellency Mark, and had dinner with him. Motion picture report of musical band, playing in front of Regimental HQ, and daily life in the streets of Lubine.

A.M. Journey with a horse-drawn wagon to the trenches on the heights, east of St. Dié. While taking that trip, films were made of the attack by an infantry company on these mountain heights. Scenes showing soldiers attending the horses, building new barracks, departure of a mixed group of horses, mules and donkeys, observation post in the woods, French shrapnel attack on a German airplane, the arrival of wounded soldiers and their transfer by cable car. Because this scene was taken while we under artillery attack film work had to be stopped immediately. We arrived in Lubine safely. At 2 P.M. we were with His Excellency Mark.

P.M. Films were made of haying activities in the fields, soldiers washing up, men and women working on the harvest, funeral scene also showing children. Dinner with His Excellency Mark accompanied by music.

8.8.1916 A.M. At 8 o clock, we left Lubine and went to Weiler to visit the Field Recruiting Depot of the 39th Bavarian Division. There films were made of an infantry charge on fortified trenches, sanitary works, an attack with hand grenades, explosion of mines, a group of soldiers resting, wearing their new steel helmets. Close up shot of one of these men while on an observation post.

Return trip to Weiler. There we had breakfast in the officers' barracks, accompanied by music.

P.M. Trip to the train station. Departure by train at 12.44 to Strassburg. Arrival there at 3 P.M. and reporting at A.O.K. Departure from Strassburg at 6.38 P.M. to Berlin, via Frankfurt. Arrival at Friedrichstrasse Station at 9. A.M.

NOTE:

The cinematographer was very satisfied, especially because all formalities had been taken care of quickly. In short, everything pleased him very much. His only concern was that he couldn't make any films of the artillery, which is something, he complained, his competitors were allowed to. The weather was magnificent. Everyone at the front followed the film work with great interest and was actively helping the cameraman with his work, so that he could make a success out of it.

(SIGNED)

Donat

1st Lieutenant

Copies to:

Head IIIb [Military Intelligence]): 1

Head Military Press Office: 1

Information Desk Foreign Office: 1

Id: 1

SPECIAL NOTE

On the cinematographer Mr. Nelson Edwards I have the following observations: he is an easy-going, unpretending man, with few needs and a great stamina. He seems to be used from an early age to doing hard, physical labor and is always ready to pitch in. To me, he seems to be an honest man with an open minded character.

I have no further remarks or recommendations for any upcoming trips to the front, because this journey was wonderful.[88]

The description in *Moving Picture World* makes the coverage in Edwards' newsreel number 78, shot in the Vosges, sound both unrehearsed and graphic:

On the West Front. – Exclusive pictures by Nelson E. Edwards, showing the actual progress of a desperate battle for possession of mountain trenches. The camera catches the bursting shells immediately over the first line trenches and shows the men, bewildered by the incessant shell fire and crazed by the prospect of sudden and certain death, running wildly about the explosion-torn battlefield.[89]

Three weeks after his arrival back in America, Edwards' last films from Europe were shown in No. 86 (27 October 1916). This newsreel pictured women doing men's work in the German capital, French women harvesting crops in occupied territory and General Krause meeting a fellow officer in the crowded streets of Berlin.[90] At least some of the footage which appeared in No. 79 and No. 81 (3 and 10 October 1916), and No. 86, (27 October 1916), especially that dealing with the hand grenade training, shots of General von Krause and the women working in the field, was probably shot by Edwards on his tour with Lieutenant von Donat.

One of the most successful films that Edwards made while he was in Europe was his coverage of the return of the submarine *Deutschland* to Germany. Earlier in the year, the Germans had sent the super-sized merchant German submarine to Baltimore with an extremely valuable cargo of dyes. It had arrived on 9 or 10 July 1916, and stayed until 2 August. The trip had been a good-will mission as well as propaganda, because the *Deutschland's* successful voyage showed that Britannia did not totally rule the waves by any means. While Edwards was in Germany, on 24 August, the *Deutschland* returned from America, arriving at Bremerhaven to much fanfare there. Baltimore took a proprietary interest in the *Deutschland,* so the *Baltimore Sun* gave Edwards' coverage some fanfare as well:

Exclusive motion pictures of the arrival at Bremen of the German super-submarine line *Deutschland* are contained in the Hearst International News Pictorial No. 75, just released.

The latest pictures of the Deutschland were made by Nelson E. Edwards, staff photographer of the Hearst International News Pictorial in Germany. Edwards had the special permission of the German Government. His pictures show the Deutschland, decorated with German flags, ascending the river to Bremen, the crowds along the banks cheering madly. The lens of his camera also caught the welcome extended to Captain Koenig, the intrepid commander of the Deutschland, and his heroic crew as they landed.

Officers in high military circles, Government officials and enthusiastic thousands hailed the submarine commander. Flowers and gifts were showered upon the sailors and they became the men of the hour in Germany.[91]

Edwards and the German company as well as the Navy tried to work out an arrangement so Edwards could return to the United States on the *Deutschland*. Sadly, the German authorities rejected this idea, as the Germans were having enough trouble with the Wilson administration without the possibility of an American citizen getting killed traveling on a German submarine in wartime. Instead, Edwards sailed on the *Nieuw Amsterdam* from Rotterdam and arrived in New York on 3 October 1916.

William Randolph Hearst had sent two of his best cinematographers to Germany. Although both cameramen did yeoman service, he must have been disappointed by the results. After the *Lusitania*, Germany grew increasingly unpopular in the U.S. By the autumn of 1916, Hearst was interested in running for a political office in America, and his anti-British and pro-German stance was beginning to hurt him with the voters. He was falsely accused of wining and dining Captain Boy-Ed and Franz von Papen, future member of Hitler's cabinet, before they were deported for espionage and sabotage activities in New York. It is the kind of accusation that sticks. It is also reported that in many cases, gangs set Hearst newspapers on fire before they could even be sold. He may have decided to soft-pedal his politics. In any case, he did not send any more film correspondents. Since the German military remained for the most part hostile to film correspondents, and as relations worsened between the United States and Germany, both the newspapers in the United States and the German Foreign Office lost interest. The scene would again shift elsewhere.

Notes

Ansel Wallace

1.   Bernstorff to Hammann, 10 November 1914, AAPA, WK Nr. 3, Bd. 5, 000030; A. E. Wallace, Visa dated 11 November 1914, no. 4 3936, photocopies in possession of authors. AAPA, WK Nr. 3, Bd. 5, 000031-000034.

2.   Wallace to von Mumm, 7 December 1914, AAPA, WK Nr. 3, Bd. 5.000031-000034.

3.   Josef Schumacher to Freiherr von Mumm, "Vorschlag zur Umgestaltung der Aufklärung durch das Bild", 7 July 1916, BA R901, 1302 Bl. 174–176, cited in Ulrike Oppelt, 108.

4.   "Many Americans Remain in Berlin: Adlon Colony Includes the Rockefeller Commission and Two Diplomats", *New York Times* (4 July 1915): I, 4. The *New York Times* correspondent who filed this story was probably Cyril Brown; one of the Associated Press representatives was Seymour Conger; the *Chicago Daily News* correspondent was probably Oswald F. Schuette; at least two of the Chicago photographers were probably Wilbur H. Durborough and Irving Guy Ries, shortly to leave for the eastern front. The photographer Edwin F. Weigle was from Chicago and stayed at the Adlon, but had left Berlin in May for Austria.

5.   Telegram from General Staff to AA, 10 December 1914, AAPA, WK Nr. 3, Bd. 5 20555.

6.   Boston American Man Tells How He Trailed Germans on Great Drive through Poland, *Boston American* (29 August 1915): I, 9.

7.   *Hearst-Selig News Pictorial*, No. 9, 1 February 1915. *Moving Picture World* (13 February 1915): 1038; John E. Allen Archives, ID 11564, Ubit ID 19200136, Tape ID 1W06, TC 12:58:01; and ID 11565, Ubit ID 19200137, Tape ID 1W07 13:00: 14.

8.   William Merton to Freiherr von Mumm, 11 December 1914, AAPA, R, WK No. 3, Bd. 5, 000072-000074. For more on Wilhelm von Merton, see Hans Achinger, *Wilhelm Merton in Seiner Zeit* (Frankfurt am Main: Waldemar Kramer, 1965).

9.   Freiherr von Mumm to Polizeipräsident, Berlin, 13 December 1914, AAPA, R, WK Nr. 3, Bd. 5, 000088-89.

10. "De Beaufort in Vaudeville", *New York Times* 19 November 1910, 1; *San Francisco Call*, Volume 108, no. 175 (22 November 1910): 1.

11. Count Alex Albert von Mourik de Beaufort, "Why I Am Making a Fool of Myself", *Tacoma Times* (12 December 1910): 4; "Identified by His Dog", *Tribune New York* (26 April 1910): 9. For information on the film, see *Moving Picture News* (3 December 1910): 4, 14–15. For a good synopsis of the film, see *Sag Harbor* (New York) *Corrector* (December 1910).

12. "De Beaufort Saved by Franko's Fists", *New York Times* (23 July 1913): 7.

13. Ansel E. Wallace, "Germany Wars For Liberty", *Rockford Republic* (11 January 1915): 1.

14. J. M. de Beaufort, *Behind the German Veil* (London: Hutchinson & Co., 1917), 32–33. The American edition of this book removes the reference to the Hearst interests. The comments by Professor Stein suggest that the interview that Wilbur H. Durborough obtained from General von Bernhardi was equally bogus. "Gen. von Berhardi [sic] Germany's famous Military Genius and Author, Discusses the War with Durborough", *Reno Evening Gazette* (16 August 1916): 3, cited in Graham, "The Kaiser and the Cameraman", *Film History*, Vol. 22, no. 1 (2010): 28–29.

15. J. M. de Beaufort, *Behind the German Veil*, 50. De Beaufort mentions later that Hauptmann von Brauwitz was head of the railroad division at the German General Staff. De Beaufort, 205. No other mention of von Brauwitz has been found.

16. *Moving Picture World* (23 January 1915): 555. In the Wallace scrapbook, there is a photograph of the Kaiser visiting the Crown Prince at his headquarters along with Prince Oskar. The photograph has an INS number C9917-X-©, so Hearst apparently bought the rights for the U.S., but the original photograph was taken by court photographer G. Berger of Potsdam, and was distributed by the Neue Photographische Gesellschaft, control no. 5116. http://bildpostkarten.uni-osnabrueck.de.php?pos=-14594. Many shots of the Kaiser's visit on this occasion exist, all apparently shot by Berger.

17. Norman Stone, *The Eastern Front 1914–1917* (London: Penguin Books, 1998), 107.

18. Ernest P. Bicknell, *In War's Wake* (Washington: American Red Cross, 1936), 84–85; "Poland Another Belgium", *New York Times* (24 January 1915): 3. Rose and Bicknell substantiated Wallace's claim that there were soup kitchens for the Poles, but maintained that the rations were severely limited, the bread ration for instance being one-fifth of a pound.

19. Ernest P. Bicknell, *In War's Wake*, 84–85.

20. *Boston American* (29 August 1915): I, 9; *Hearst Selig News Pictorial* No.28 (8 April 1915) … "Soldau. East Prussia – German soldiers raze walls of buildings wrecked by Russian shells. Skierniewice, Russian Poland. – Military attaches of various nations are guests of Germans on east front. Lodz, Russia – Gen. von Mackenson [sic] of the Ninth Army reviews division of Austrian cavalry on their way to fight the Russians …", *Moving Picture World* (1 May 1915): 778; Edward Lyell Fox, *Behind the Scenes in Warring Germany*, 279.

21. *Hearst Selig News Pictorial* No. 23 (22 March 1915); *World Moving Picture* (17 April 1915): 446

22. Another story that Wallace shot was another newsreel that survives in the John E. Allen collection at the Library of Congress: "Hearst-Selig News Pictorial. GERMAN WAR MACHINE SENDS HORDES OF MEN TO EASTERN FRONT. LOWICZ, RUSSIAN POLAND. – Fresh troops brought up to push the attack of Gen. Von Hindenburg are detrained and started to the trenches." *Hearst Selig News Pictorial* No. 21 (15 March 1915). Nitrate film at Library of Congress, M/B/RS Division, MAVIS 186455; Tape at John E. Allen Archives, ID 12125, Ubit 19200530, Tape ID 1W19, TC4:56:16.

23. Advertisement for *Hearst Selig News Pictorial* No. 19, released 8 March 1915, *Moving Picture World* (13 March 1915): 1698; Edward Lyell Fox, *Behind the Scenes in Warring Germany*, 279.

24. *Boston American* (29 August 1915): I, 9.

25. Curt von Morgen, *Meiner Truppen Heldenkämpfe* (Berlin: Mittler und Sohn, 1920), 48–49, Ernest P. Bicknell, *In War's Wake*, 100–101.

26. Captain von Rintelen (Franz Rintelen von Kleist) *The Dark Invader* (London: Lovat Dickson Limited, 1933), 58–60.

27. Roediger, note dated 12 February 1915, sent as private letter to Count von Bernstorff 16 Feb 1915, AAPA, Vereinigte Staaten von Amerika No. 6 No. 2, R17239.

28. Roediger, note dated 19 February 1915, AAPA, Vereinigte Staaten von Amerika No. 6 No. 2, R17239. Joseph Pulitzer's *New York World* was famously anti-German. Frank Paswell was described by de Beaufort as a German propagandist spy in Russia in the service of Matthias Erzberger. *Behind the German Veil*, 76.

29. Hessenstein, statement to AA, 3 March 1915, AAPA, Vereinigte Staaten von Amerika No. 6 No. 2, R17239. Baronin von Arnswald is probably Bertha Baronin von Arnswaldt, who ran the most famous literary salon in Wilhelmine Germany.

30. J. M. de Beaufort, *Behind the German Veil*, 50–51; *Syracuse Herald* (18 October 1917): 4.

31. Baerecke to Roederer, 26 January 1915, AAPA, Vereinigte Staaten von Amerika No. 6 No. 2, R17239.

32. Arthur S. Link, Ed., *The Papers of Woodrow Wilson, Vol. 34, July 21 – September 30, 1915* (Princeton, New Jersey: Princeton University Press, 1980), 441–442.

33. Gerard to Lansing 7 December 1915. National Archives, College Park, MD. State Department Records, RG59, 763.72/2342 ½, DNA. There was another factor making it unlikely that von Moltke gave an interview. In September, 1914, von Moltke had been sacked as Chief of Staff, following the German failure in the Battle of the Marne, and was replaced by Erich von Falkenhayn. He was formally relieved on 3 November 1914, but the news was kept from the German public for several months. Following his dismissal, von Moltke, who was in very poor health and suffering from a gall bladder infection, had a complete mental and physical breakdown. He had insisted on staying in headquarters in Mezières, but on 1 November 1914, he accepted the Kaiser's offer to stay in one of the Kaiser's palaces in Bad Homburg, in the Taunus near Frankfurt am Main, far from Berlin. In any event, even if von Moltke was in Berlin by December 1, his consent to granting a personal interview to an American photographer, as well as his still clinging to the title of Chief of Staff, considering his formal dismissal almost two months before, seems remote. For more on Herman Metz, see Mira Wilkins, *The History of Foreign Investments in the United States, 1914–1945.* (Cambridge, Mass.: Harvard University Press, 2004), 239; for more on Herbert Corey's and Edward Lyell Fox's articles in American newspapers, see "Telegramme an Amerikanische Zeitungen über die Zustande in Deutschland und an der Ostfront im Februar 1915", Berlin State Library, [no publisher given, 1915]. A lot of Herbert Corey's newspapers are at the Library of Congress, in deplorable shape.

34. Barbara Tuchman, *The Zimmermann Telegram* (Bantam Books Edition: The Macmillan Company, 1958), 82–83; "How Germany Has Worked on U. S. To Shape Opinion, Block the Allies and Get Munitions for Herself, Told in Secret Agent's letters", *The World* (New York) (15 August 1915): 1–3.

35. *The World* (New York) (15 August 1915): 1. Complicating this anonymous memo, Herbert Corey in an unpublished manuscript of his experiences in World War I says that when he read the *World*, he clearly recognized some of his own words and ideas in the memo, which he had imparted to an unidentified woman in Berlin. She was possibly Mary Ellen Donahue, who had married Heinrich von Schroeder, a former Prussian army officer, and was well-known in Berlin society as a lady with a flair for politics. According to Ambassador Gerard, the "American Baroness", as she was called, was an amateur spy for the Germans and closely linked to Lewis Marks. Herbert Corey, "Perfectly Irresponsible" 48–49. Herbert Corey papers, Library of Congress, Washington, D.C; Gerard to Lansing 7 December 1915. NARS, SDR, RG59, 763.72/2342 ½, DNA; Susan Saperstein, "Baroness von Schroeder, Rambling Bits of History", http:www.sfcityguides.org.public_guidelines.hmtl; Carl W. Ackerman, "Gerard Weeds Spies out of American Embassy", *Binghamton News* (21 April 1917): 9.

36. William Shepherd, *Confessions of a War Correspondent* (New York/London: Harper & Brother Publishers 1917), 118–119.

37. In Re Lewis Hart Marks: German Activities. Agent Ed. L. Newman, 6 October 1917, Bureau of Investigation File 27865, MID file 9140-734. No Count Boudessen has been found.

38. Ibid.

39. Gerard to Lansing 28 December 1915. Records of the Department of State Relating to World War I and its Termination, 1914–1929, NARA, Group 59, NARA 367, Roll 0025, International Relations, Serbia and Austria 763.72/2346, 1. James W. Gerard also cites de Beaufort's account: "The spies and influencers of American correspondents made their headquarters at a large Berlin hotel. A sketch of their activities is given by de Beaufort in his book 'Behind the German Veil'". James W. Gerard, *My Four Years in Germany*, 306.

40. Roediger to von Radowitz, Auswärtiges Amt, Politisches Archiv, Berlin, 7 January 1916. 'Agent Krebs' is Franz Hugo Krebs, a pro-German newspaperman who worked for McClure's. Haecksher is Siegfried Heckscher, liberal member of the Reichstag, member of the foreign relations committee and an authority on Germany's foreign relations. He also became publicity director for the Hamburg-American Line. Oswald F. Schuette wrote Heckscher after he recommended Schuette for a trip to Trier to counter foreign propaganda aimed at 'peaceful German cities'. For six weeks Oswald tried to arrange a trip to occupied Flanders, but the trip was, typically, turned down by the General Staff. Schuette also asked to be remembered to Doctor Marks. AAPA, WK Nr. 3, Band 10, 000179-000182. Elsewhere, Oswald comments on some of Heckscher's activities which included press relations between America and Germany. *Chicago Daily News* (22 February 1917). Schuette also reported that Heckscher urged closer ties with Tsarist Russia, citing himself as a spokesperson for the liberals and radicals in the Reichstag. Oswald F. Schuette, 'Germany Confident of Resisting Drives: Oswald F. Schuette Sees "Peace Crisis" as Logical Outcome of Deadlock; Crops Avert Starvation', *Chicago Daily News* (28 August 1916). Courtesy James Castellan.

41. *Moving Picture World* (30 January 1915): 689; *Moving Picture World* (20 February 1915): 1147.

42. J. M. de Beaufort, *Behind the German Veil*, 52.

43. Von Mumm to Hammann, 23 January 1915, AAPA, Akten R17238, Vereinigte Staaten v. Amerika no. 6 no. 2, Bd. 5.

44. De Beaufort's fellow writers doubted that de Beaufort actually got an interview with von Hindenburg. In addition,

in comparing Oswald F. Schuette's story on von Bissing and Edward Lyell Fox's Hindenburg interview with de Beaufort's Hindenburg interview, there is some suspiciously similar dialogue and choice of subject matter. FBI de Beaufort File, 8000-40868; Edward Lyell Fox, *Behind the Scenes in Warring Germany*, 277–278, de Beaufort, *Behind the German Veil*, 159–160. Schuette, *Chicago Daily News* (7 April 1915). Schuette, Fox and de Beaufort use the story about the orderly to the cranky general who could get along with him because he used to be a wild animal trainer. Schuette and Fox use it in relation to Governor General von Bissing, in charge of occupied Brussels (168–169), and de Beaufort, two years later, uses the same story in relation to von Hindenburg (158). Dutch newspapers reported on the German report that de Beaufort's interview was completely false. *Algemeen Dagblad* (Netherlands) (21 September 1916): 5; *De Tijd* (Netherlands) (2 September 1916): 5. The *Norddeutsche Allgemeine Zeitung* also reported that de Beaufort's report featured in the British *Sunday Pictorial* on 13 August on attending a church service with the Kaiser in March 1916 was absolutely false. De Beaufort was not even in Germany in 1916. 'Der Wert englischer Reporterberichte', *Norddeutsche Allgemeine Zeitung* (31 August 1916): 1. De Beaufort's report does sound similar to Ludwig Ganghofer's report on attending a church service with the Kaiser. Ludwig Ganghofer, *Reise zur deutschen Front*, no. 4, 19 January 1915 (Berlin: Ullstein & Co, 1915)

45. *De Tijd* (2 September 1916): 5. De Beaufort published essentially the same interview in *Behind the German Veil*, 159–160. J. M. de Beaufort, *Behind the German Veil*, 362–363.

46. Carl W. Ackerman, *Germany, the Next Republic?* (New York: Grosset & Dunlap, 1917, 1918), 281. Citations are to the 1918 edition.

47. Robert K. Massie, *Castles of Steel: Britain, Germany and the Winning of the Great War at Sea* (New York: Ballantine Books, 2004), 518–519; Günther-Georg Freiherr von Forstner, *Als U-Boots-Kommandant gegen England von Günther-Georg, Freiherrn von Forstner* (Berlin and Vienna: Ullstein Verlag 1916), 76–77, 107.

48. Freiherr v.Mumm to Stellvertretenden Generalstab der Armee, Presseabteilung, 14 March 1915, AAPA, R17239.

49. 'Examiner Correspondent Captured by Submarine', *Chicago Examiner* (24 March 1915): 3; 'Submarine seizes 2 N.Y. American Reporters', *New York American* (24 March 1915): 1. George F. Allison, *Allison Calling*, 28 (London: Staples Press Ltd., 1948), cited in Pizzitola, *Hearst over Hollywood*, unpaginated).

50. Edgar B. Hatrick, "The Real Heroes of the Movies", *New York American* (15 February 1920); *American Weekly* Section (unpaginated). Forstner, 138.

51. Forstner, 138.

52. George F. Allison, *Allison Calling*, 139.

53. Forstner, 138. George F. Allison, *Allison Calling*, 27–28. Allison evidently gave Wallace a number of INS-stamped photos of events taking place between March and June 1915. It is assumed that many of the pictures in Wallace's scrapbook came from Allison, since many of the photographs, such as the sinking of the HMS *Majestic* at Gallipoli, the Gretna Railroad disaster and the sinking of the SMS *Dresden* off the coast of Chile would seem to be of particular interest to the British. There would have been no way that Wallace could have shot films or pictures in Gallipoli and Chile, or even the Gretna Rail Disaster, since it happened after Wallace left for Italy.

54. *Hearst – Selig News Pictorial* no. 49 and 50, 1915 (June 2-); *World Moving Picture World* (10 July 1915): 372, 374; *Hearst – Selig News Pictorial* no. 51, 1915 (28 June 1915) *Moving Picture World* (24 July 1915): 708.

55. Mark Thompson, *The White War* (London: Faber and Sons Ltd: New York: Perseus Books, 2008), 211–212.

56. A. E. Wallace, 'Venice, Spy Mad, Like City of Dead, Says Photographer', *Syracuse Herald* (11 July 1915): 3; New York Passenger Lists 1820–1957: Record for Ansel Earle Wallace, Ancestry.com; *New York Times Pictorial Review* (1 July 1915).

57. 'Sperry Flies from New York to Amityville – Will Try for Curtiss Marine Trophy', *Aerial Age Weekly* (23 August 1915): 543–544.

Nelson Edwards

Items from the Wiegman family papers are marked with an internal number, such as A59a. This refers to page numbers devised by Nelson Wiegman to guide researchers to items that they might want scanned or examined in more detail, and the authors believe it may be convenient for readers who are interested in particular items in the Wiegman papers.

58. David Nasaw, *The Chief: The Life of William Randolph Hearst*, 246–247, citing "Memorandum for Mr. Hoover", 18 June 1920, case file 2290, record group 65, Bureau of Investigation; EH – A.F. Beach, 18 December 1915, case file 9140-4561, record group 165, Military Intelligence Division; United States Senate, 66th Congress, 1st Session, Document no. 61, Brewing and Liquor Interests and German and Bolshevik Propaganda,: Report and Hearings of the Subcommittee of the Judiciary, vol. 2, (Washington, D.C. Government Printing Office, 1919), 1590, 1951–1960; *New York American* (8 October 1916); Louis Pizzitola, *Hearst Over Hollywood*, New York: Columbia University Press, 2002), 142. The Congressional hearings mention a message from the German ambassador to the Berlin foreign office, dated December 27, 1915, which Captain G. R. Lester of the Army Intelligence Service said he could not completely connect up with German plans. It was read into the record as follows:

With reference to Decree A. N. 56 promised Hearst and *Chicago Tribune* facilities. Weigly [Edwin F. Weigle] probably already Germany. Hearst photographer Nelsons left on Ford Peace Ship. Please instruct legation. Hague facilities Edward's journey Germany." Brewing and Liquor Interests and German and Bolshevik Propaganda, Vol. 2, 1678. Von Bernstorff, Baron Zwiedenek, Austrian Chargé d'Affaires and members of the Austrian Embassy staff were photographed by Hearst-Vitagraph in February 1916. *Hearst-Vitagraph News Pictorial* no. 7 (28 January 1916). *Moving Picture World* (12 February 1916): 1010. United States, 66th Congress, 1st Session, Document no. 61, Brewing and Liquor Interests and German and Bolshevik Propaganda: Reports and Hearings of the Subcommittee and the Judiciary , vol. 2 (Washington, D.C. Government Printing Office, [1919]), 1678.

59.   Wallace's visa shows that he was already in Germany in December 1914, and that he had left Germany for Rotterdam by 15 February 1915. So Hearst News Pictorial had no cameraman in Germany at least from February 1915, which could explain why Hatrick wanted to send a new one there. Department of State, Washington, DC, Visa for A. E. Wallace, No. 43936, 11 November 1914. Private Collection; photographic scans of Wallace visa in the collection of the authors; "U. S. Passport Applications 1795–1925 record for Amel [sic] Earle Wallace"; New York Passenger Lists 1820–1957 record for Ausel [sic] E. Wallace.

60.   Hatrick to Edwards, Telegram 21 October 1915, Wiegman family papers[34b].

61.   "San Francisco Personals", *Editor & Publisher* (5 November 1915): 569.

62.   E.P. Hatrick to Louis P. Lochner, 1 December 1915. Wiegman Family papers [37b].

63.   "Joseph T. Rucker", *Moving Picture World* (18 December1915): 2194; "Universal Peace Cameraman Back", *Moving Picture World* (26 February 1916): 1273.

64.   Wiegman family papers [A34b]. Not mentioned in this poem was Mutual newsreel cameraman Lawrence Darmour who was also on board and covered the Peace Ship voyage.

65.   Francis A. Collins, *The Camera Man* (New York: The Century Co., 1919), 87–88, 109. Mitchell was to be a future boss of Edwards at Fox Newsreels. See Fielding, *The American Newsreel 1911–1967* (Norman: University of Oklahoma Press, 1972), infra.

66.   *The Argosy* (8 December 1915). Swarthmore College Peace Collection. Mary Fels, wife of Joseph Fels, was a prominent social reformer. Her husband was very important in the Single Tax movement, and she later became an ardent Zionist. The family was from Philadelphia.

67.   The German authorities imposed on the delegation a complete ban against carrying letters, opera glasses, photographs, post cards, and cameras across Germany. Louis P. Lochner, *America's Don Quixote: Henry Ford's Attempt to save Europe* (London: Kegan Paul Trench, Ltd., 1924), 104.

68.   *New York American* (2 January 1916); *Moving Picture World* (15 January 1916). The leapfrog and other footage, some of which matches the description from the 8 December photo op described supra was also featured in *Universal Animated Weekly* No. 200, released 5 January 1916, no doubt shot by Rucker. According to Francis J. Collins, Lawrence J. Darmour also photographed the leapfrog for Mutual, but the only Darmour footage of the Ford Peace Ship so far documented is *Mutual Weekly* No. 55 (20 January 1916). *Moving Picture World* (8 January 1916): 290, *Moving Picture World* (8 January 1916): 219; *Moving Picture World* (22 January 1916): 663; *Moving Picture World* (5 February 1916). Darmour returned to the United States along with Berndt G. Phillips onboard the *Kristianafjord* on 24 January 1916, along with others of the Ford Peace Party. New York Passenger Lists, 1820–1957: record for Laurence [sic] J. Darmour, http//search.ancestry.com.: Francis A. Collins, *The Camera Man*, 109; "Ford Peace Party Had Lively Trip", *Philadelphia Enquirer* (25 January 1916): 2.

69.   Baker, "Newsreel Man for 30 Years".

70.   Hans Barkhausen, *Filmpropaganda für Deutschland* (Hildesheim, Zurich, New York: Olms Verlag, 1982), 55.

71.   "International Camera Man", *Billboard* (1 July 1916): 82.

72.   "The Turk and the Teuton", *Philadelphia Record* (3 December 1916): Magazine Section, 1. J. Rickard, August von Mackensen, 1849–1945, German Field Marshal http://www.historyofwar.org/articles/ people_mackensen_august.html (7 November 2007); Martin Gilbert, *The First World War: A Complete History* (New York: Henry Holt and Company, 1994), 206.

73.   *Moving Picture World* (1 July 1916): 107; "History-Making Events in International News Pictorial", *New York American* (30 June 1916): 12. The *New York American* advertisement included a frame enlargement from the newsreel which appears to show the side entrance to the Hamidiye Mosque in Constantinople, very similar to one of the photographs in Edwards' photograph albums [76a&b]. The Sultan was probably attending the Sultan's selamlik the ceremonial on the occasion of the visit of the Sultan to one of his mosques for the Friday service. M. T. Houtsma, *First Encyclopedia of Islam*, 1913–1936. E. J. Brill and Luzak (1938), 95.

74.   "The Turk and the Teuton".

75.   Martin Gilbert, *The First World War*, 244.

76. 'The Turk and the Teuton', *Philadelphia Record*, 3 December 1916, Magazine Section, 1. See also undated newspaper clipping with caption "Edwards invention" in Wiegman family papers [A22].

77. Ibid., Magazine Section, 1.

78. Sean McMeekin, *The Berlin Baghdad Express: The Ottoman Empire and Germany's Bid for World Power* (Cambridge, Mass.: Belknap Press of Harvard University Press, 2010), 275–317.

79. "The Turk and the Teuton", 1.

80. Edwards-Messter agreement in Wiegman family papers [A57a]. Review *Hearst International News Pictorial* 48 in *Moving Picture World* (8 July 1916): 309.

81. "The Turk and the Teuton", *Moving Picture World* mentioned that Edwards photographed the Sultan, but gave the date as November 1915, which was several months before Edwards left the United States. 'The German Fleet in the North Sea', *Moving Picture World* (19 August 1916): 1268.

82. Review *Hearst International News Pictorial* 48; in *Moving Picture World* (8 July 1916): 309.

83. Actually the Darmstadt story ran in the 28 July 1916 issue, and the von Hindenburg statue story, with a dedication of the statue with Chancellor von Bethmann-Hollweg, as well as a report on the food situation in Berlin, ran on 2 August. "All over the World with Hearst International Film Pictorial", *New York American* (28 July 1916): 7. "Biggest World Events in Hearst International Film Pictorial", *New York American* (2 August 1916): 5. There is a further question on the von Hindenburg statue film. According to Anna von der Goltz, the dedication of the "monster statue" with Chancellor von Bethmann-Hollweg, which appears in the illustration in the *New York American*, was held on 4 September 1915, before Edwards got to Germany. Of course, Edwards could have gotten hold of a copy of the footage and sent it to INS. Anna von der Goltz, *Power, Myth and the Rise of the Nazis* (Oxford (England): Cambridge University Press, 2009), 31. "The German Fleet in the North Sea", *Moving Picture World* (19 August 1916): 1268.

84. *Motography* (26 August 1916): 519.

85. Ibid., 26 August 1916, 519. This issue included shots of the *Prinzregent Luitpold* in the North Sea, taken by Edwards on 16 June. "Great World Events in Hearst International Film Pictorial", *New York American* (9 August 1916, 5–6 August 1916), 519.

86. "Girdling the Globe in Hearst International Film Pictorial", *New York American* (15 August 1916): 5. See also *Moving Picture World* (2 September 1916): 1557. Bescheinigung, Presseabteilung des Admiralstabes der Marine, 15 July 1916. Wiegman family papers, [A20]. There is no evidence that newsreels or motion pictures of the submarine school were ever released.

87. "Tells How he Got Films in Shrapnel Rain", *New York American* (ca. 4 October 1916): 6. See also *Moving Picture World* (14 October 1916): 267. According to a report in the trade press, similar footage showing the German navy and the return of the *Deutschland* to Bremen was imported from Germany later that year. See *Variety* (24 November 1916): 27.

88. Lieutenant von Donat to Army General Staff Department IIIB, "Report on the Journey by a Neutral Cinematographer to Strassburg and the Vosges Front, 5–8 August 1916". Translation Ron van Dopperen. Bundesarchiv, ZfA R901/71946, 163–166.

89. *Moving Picture World* (14 October 1916): 298.

90. *Moving Picture World* (11 November 1916): 915. According to journalist Daniel Thomas Curtin, who met Edwards in Berlin, the German authorities tried to discourage him from filming women at work in the new subway because it would make the wrong impression. Daniel Thomas Curtin, *The Land of Deepening Shadow* (New York: George H. Doran Co., 1917), 230.

91. "Deutschland Filmed", *Baltimore Sun* (29 October 1916): MS4. See also *Moving Picture World* (14 October 1916): 267. According to *Motography*, the submarine story was released in *Hearst International News Pictorial* No. 79 (3 October 1916). *Motography* (21 October 1916): 952.

Chapter 5

Behind the German Lines

After the campaign in Belgium, there was something of a lull as far as the correspondents in Berlin were concerned. The photographers were back in Germany patrolling their old beat. Weigle was back in Europe, having sailed with Donald C. Thompson and publisher Robert R. McCormick of the *Tribune* to Europe on 10 February 1915, and again was staying at the Adlon in Berlin. After having been detained in Britain, Weigle and the others had finally sailed from Hull to Rotterdam on the steamer *Kirkman Abbe*. Thompson and McCormick had traveled to cover the war from the Russian side. Durborough and Ries had arrived in April and were also staying at the Adlon.

Albert K. Dawson

Albert K. Dawson was one film correspondent who had relatively little trouble getting trips out of Berlin, even to the coveted western front. He and Edward Lyell Fox were of course on the German payroll, and therefore were reliable in a way that no free agent could be. As Count von Bernstorff indicated, the German authorities in Berlin had a particularly good reason to show the American people their side of the war. Within days after the invasion of Belgium, there were rumors about German atrocities against civilians. This proved to be a serious propaganda issue which was quickly exploited by the Entente. The Germans indignantly complained about Belgian guerrilla fighters who didn't comply with the rules of regular warfare. As pointed out in Chapter 3, a lot of it came down to how one defined atrocities and whether one was inclined to admit that German soldiers could lose their heads.

From a military point of view, the German reaction to the atrocity charges may have been the appropriate reaction but it was a major blunder with regard to their public image. Stories circulating about starving Belgian civilians, as well as Chancellor von Bethmann-Hollweg's remark that Belgian neutrality was merely a scrap of paper, did not help to promote the German side of the war. Clearly there was a need to show neutrals in America what was going on in occupied Belgium and Northern France. The Germans chose Dawson.

While Dawson was waiting for his permit, the Germans had found the right colleague to join him. At the General Staff in Berlin, Dawson was introduced to Hans Theyer (1884–1955), an experienced Austrian cameraman who from 1907 had travelled around the world for Pathé as a newsreel photographer and would set up the first modern film studio in Vienna, together with Sascha Kolowrat, the founding father of the Austrian film industry. In 1912, while on an assignment for Pathé to film the American fleet, Theyer went to the Solomon Islands where he joined writer Jack London's visit to the South Sea Islands and filmed cannibals in the interior of Penduffryn. Theyer's footage was edited into *Jack London's Adventures in the South Seas.*

In January 1914 Theyer had been employed by the Messter Production Company as cinematographer. When war broke out, he was assigned by Messter to the German War Office to produce propaganda films. After their meeting Theyer teamed with Dawson. Together they would film an official documentary of the western front.[1]

Taking the midnight train from Berlin, the two cameramen prepared for a series of movie narratives. Judging from surviving film fragments now at the John E. Allen Film Archives, they decided to shoot a wide series of subjects at the frontline and in occupied Belgium. The remaining footage also shows Albert Dawson at work as an American correspondent interviewing public figures like the United States Ambassador in Berlin, James W. Gerard. The purpose of these films, as Theyer recalled, was quite clear: "I had received instructions to accompany eight American journalists and a photographer [Dawson] to the German-French front. At the request of the Central Powers, they would be given the opportunity to see for themselves that the rumors spread by the Entente about the German atrocities were false."[2]

Among these American journalists was Robert Dunn, a veteran war correspondent who worked for the *New York Post.* In his book *Five Fronts* he mentioned the two "official cinema men" and the chateau life the reporters enjoyed while wining and dining with Crown Prince Rupprecht of Bavaria and the staff of the IV Prussian Army Corps. From their hotel in Lille, the party of journalists was picked up daily. By military car they visited so many destroyed villages that Dunn established the "Ruin-Shy Club" in the back seat of the vehicle.[3] The American reporters wanted to get closer to the front and were bored by ammunition dumps and field hospitals.

On 10 January 1915 the Germans decided to take them to the Headquarters of the II Bavarian Corps at Comines, which was just across the border in France. Near the village of Houthem about two miles from the frontline, the photographers filmed German artillery operations. For the benefit of the camera, the guns started their barrage early in full daylight. Dawson and Theyer probably didn't realize that this provoked the French into a counterattack. Before they knew it, the cameramen, who had gone ahead in the direction of the trenches near the village of Hollebeke, were themselves under fire.

As Theyer recalled:

"We walked through a completely devastated area. The rain had been pouring down on us and had covered the landscape with thick layers of mud. Suddenly I saw a yellow flash in the sky, as round as a ring. I was watching this fascinating spectacle as if it were fireworks. But then I saw my colleague [Dawson] lying in the mud, and I decided to follow his example. This was when the first shell exploded. The barrage followed us quickly. I heard the shrieking sound of shrapnel going over our heads, when there was an explosion just six metres in front of us. The mud saved us at that critical moment, because instead of debris we were only covered with wet and soft lumps of earth."[4]

Theyer described how on arrival at the German battery he took about two hundred feet of film while French shells exploded nearby. It was, he admitted, a harrowing experience to crank a motion picture camera while being exposed to hostile fire. "You have to battle against fear. But there is no way you can control the twitching of your own nerves. My American colleague [Dawson] confessed to me later that the only reason why he kept on filming was that he did not want to embarrass himself in front of the German officers."[5]

In a remarkably frank interview with the *Indianapolis Star*, Dawson also told about his baptism of fire at the western front. He knew that the German battery they wanted to see was heavily shelled, but when challenged by a young Bavarian officer that he didn't dare to visit this 'hot spot', he took him on for a bet:

"The French were shelling every foot of the road out to that battery and every step I took I thought would be my last. I was scared stiff. I had cold fear, my hands and feet were literally chilled to the bone. I was so frightened that I had no more control over myself than a man in the back seat has over an automobile. But my legs kept following that officer and long before I had reached that battery I had passed all feeling and simply moved along at the lieutenant's heels like an automaton. I reached the battery, however, and took movie photographs of it in action with the shells roaring all around. But I'll never forget that afternoon as long as I live."[6]

After visiting the trenches near Arras, the publicity tour for the American journalists went to Brussels. Among Dawson's shots taken in this city are pictures of a crowded shopping street and a film scene showing him meeting a fellow correspondent.[7] Dawson recalled how on arrival in Brussels he photographed General von Bissing, the military governor of Belgium. An officer who had been detailed to accompany him had warned him not to address his Excellency until spoken to. The officer did not anticipate Dawson's bold and straightforward methods:

"General, I am an American", he began without embarrassment. "I can see that", said the General with a smile. "And I have come to take your picture", he added without wasting time. The situation was unprecedented. Every rule of military formality had been broken. The officer stood aghast. "Very well", he replied. "Go ahead. What do you want me to do?" "If you will step to the window. Now a step this way, a little farther please. No, this way", and to the horror of the attending officer the photographer laid his hand on the General's arm and arranged the pose. The picture was taken in a few seconds.

"Thank you, General", said the unabashed camera man easily. "I hope your picture turns out well", replied General von Bissing pleasantly and the interview was over. Once outside the door the officer expostulated. "How did you come to address his Excellency? It is most unprecedented. And you laid your hand on him. How could you?" "*Mein lieber freund,*" said

Fig. 45. General von Bissing, military governor of Belgium, photographed in his office in Brussels by Albert Dawson. [Courtesy Library of Congress.]

the American, "I have photographed three American Presidents and a general more or less is nothing to me".[8]

On 7 February 1915 Dawson again photographed von Bissing when he reopened the Brussels museum. Dawson's pictures show culture-minded German soldiers admiring Belgian art. In view of the enemy propaganda attacks on events like the burning of the medieval library at Louvain, such impressions must have been most welcome.[9]

Apart from scenes showing daily life in the occupied Belgian capital, Dawson secured pictures showing German soldiers ploughing fields for farmers. He also visited the docks of Antwerp (Colour Plates 2a and 2b) and the La Providence steel mills – filmed under the title "Scenes at Big Iron Works in Belgium" – which he found working at full capacity. The overall impression these films had on spectators was probably: "In Belgium it's back to business as usual". "The mines also seemed to be working", said Dawson. "I went down in the Mariemont-Bascoup Mine in Charleroi and saw the famous women miners. These women wear trousers just like men and can swing a pick or wield a shovel with equal speed. They seemed be a husky, healthy lot and perfectly able to handle a day's work."[10] There is a photograph made by Dawson of these ladies in the *New York Times Mid-Week Pictorial*.

Having gone south to the forests of the French Argonne – a relatively quiet sector of the front then – Dawson and Theyer captured pictures of the elaborate trench works built by the Germans. Well camouflaged and with ample provisions for shelter and comfort, the soldiers seemed to have constructed a new Unter den Linden. The surviving footage shows a 'human interest' scene from this frontline sector: the printing of the newspaper *Hurrah* for the men in the trenches. Lost on film, but not on photo, was a scene of a German flamethrower in action in the Argonne. Photographed by Dawson, the *New York Times* called it the first picture of this new means of warfare to reach the United States.[11]

More than just a line of trenches, Dawson called the German defenses at the western front "the catacombs of war". He compared these strongholds to the boundaries of the Roman Empire and gave a graphic account of the impregnable barbed wire: "I have seen entanglements where I know men had tried to charge through. And I have peeped through the loopholes to where grim forms hung, contorted in the entanglement where the last charge broke as a wave breaks on the shore."[12]

The underground camps that he visited showed how the Germans adapted to natural circumstances and incorporated abandoned mines and quarries into their frontline system. In the chalk hills around Soissons for instance, Dawson pictured an enormous cave where over 3,000 soldiers were encamped using the modern benefits of electric lights and a ventilating system.

In an interview later with Sigmund Henschen, a correspondent in Berlin, Dawson recalled his visit to Soissons. In January 1915 this frontline sector had been heavily fought over between the French and the German First Army that was under the command of Alexander von Kluck, the General who had commanded the right wing during the massive outflanking sweep through Belgium and Northern France, and whose army Donald Thompson had encountered at Mons.

The fighting had finally stabilized on the banks of the river Aisne, but it had taken von Kluck's soldiers a fierce battle to push the French back across the river and defend Soissons. As Dawson said, the place was still dangerous, especially for cameramen carrying tripods:

> With Dawson were four foreign photographers. None of them was a movie man, but they all had their cameras attached to long tripods. They walked down the road toward the destroyed village. They were just selecting cover from which they could make pictures of the artillery duel in front of Soissons when the French artillery cut loose.
>
> Dawson told me: 'Of course they must have seen us coming. They saw all the apparatus and probably thought we had artillery observation paraphernalia or else that we were a machinegun division. Well, they simply raked that village with fire for nearly an hour. They systematically dropped shells into every part of it. And they only stopped when they thought we were probably all dead or wounded. None of us was hit. We were hid in houses; they were only ruins. Then the walls came down with a crash and we got out. We lay our length on the streets, beside ruined walls, never moving for an entire hour. We knew they had their observers on the plane and that if they saw us moving around it was all over. So we simply had to stretch out and trust to luck.'
>
> And Dawson took a flattened shrapnel ball out of his pocket. 'This thing', he said, 'imbedded itself just in the wall over my head. I cut it out with my knife. It'll make a nice watch-charm some day.'[13]

Incorporating the A.C. Film Company

With Erzberger's financial support, Dawson's and Theyer's footage was quickly developed. Within a week about 2000 feet of negative film was ready for shipment to the United States as noted in a 1 March 1915 diplomatic dispatch from Arthur Zimmermann, Under-Secretary of State, to Ambassador von Bernstorff.

So far, the German authorities had mostly sent still pictures to America through various photographic agencies such as Underwood & Underwood. Dr. Fuehr at the German Information Service disliked this scheme, warning the Foreign Office that this did not improve the distribution of these war photographs. The Germans wanted as wide a distribution as possible and were presumably not too worried about profit. Complaints about thefts of images owned by one agency against another restricted circulation growth.[14] As a result, he advised channeling all pictures through one agency, the German Information Service.

Meanwhile in the U.S. Dr. Dernburg requested his press agent, Matthew Claussen, to draft a separate plan for the production and distribution of official war films in America. This memo, which was sent for approval to Germany on 8 March 1915, reveals all the intricacies of a secret film propaganda campaign and also describes the crucial role Dawson would play in these war movies. In his proposal Claussen emphasized the importance of moving pictures as a means of showing millions of Americans the German side of the war:

> I would respectfully suggest and recommend the following. That a small capitalized concern be started for the proper handling of this work; this concern to engage a competent moving picture operator and a director or scenario writer – a man who is familiar with staging moving pictures for the American public – that both these men be sent to Germany where they will prepare a series of six thousand feet moving picture releases, in co-operation with Mr. Albert K. Dawson, who will act the part of the American Moving Picture War Correspondent before the camera.

> In other words, the audience will see an American boy from Indiana in whom they will believe, as he travels through Germany, and by so doing will get a correct inside view of conditions as they exist today.

> In order to make a series of pictures that will make a good impression here, part of the six thousand feet should have plenty of action and should cover war scenes, while the other half can cover industrial conditions. The details of the pictures of course will be properly handled by the Director, who will act in accordance with instructions given here as to what is required, said instructions of course being subjected to the approval and review of the proper German authorities. If this proposal meets your approval the work can be started at once by having a moving picture photographer accompany Mr. Dawson and assist him in making the first set of six thousand feet of films. Mr. Dawson has already been advised as to the details in connection with his work.[15]

Several months before Claussen made this proposal, Dr. Fuehr had already worked on establishing an American company to distribute war movies using Dawson as a front man so the films would appear "neutral".

As Fuehr mentioned to his superior, Consul-General Thiel at the Foreign Office,

German war films like the newsreels by *Messter Woche* were shown to some extent in the United States. But these movies lacked "pep" and didn't appeal to the American people. Something much better was needed to communicate the German message. Too many academic books by German professors were sent to the United States for publicity purposes, Fuehr said, which had no effect whatsoever on the average American.

In order to increase the impact and circulation of German propaganda a new medium and a specific type of war film was needed, one that the American public could relate to. This was the reason that Fuehr in his diplomatic communiqués strongly recommended Dawson as a key figure in these plans, because as a professional photographer Dawson would know exactly the sort of pictures that would interest the American public.

Fuehr not only put in a good word for Dawson with Thiel, but he also recommended him as the perfect cameraman in his letters to Mumm von Schwarzenstein, chief of the ZfA. Fuehr's plan to produce war films in the "American style" was apparently picked up by Claussen. It was a smart move as far as propaganda technique went, and it also illustrated Fuehr's understanding of American culture. But when Fuehr conceived this idea he underestimated the practical implications of this revolutionary approach. Could the German authorities really work together with a bold and enterprising American news photographer like Dawson?

On 19 April 1915, Berlin wired official approval to the German Information Service establishing the proposed film company. At a meeting the next day in New York City, the American Correspondent Film Company was incorporated. This new project was financed by issuing shares for $10,000. On 30 June 1915 the invested capital grew by $12,000 when Dr. Albert advanced the sum as a one year loan without interest. There was a stipulation that if the film company was not showing a profit by June 1916, Dr. Albert would be entitled to demand liquidation of the firm. In accordance with the suggestion previously proposed by Claussen a majority interest of 51 percent was controlled by Dr. Fuehr who was appointed secretary and treasurer of the A.C. Film Company, and acted as official representative of the German government.

Claussen, as an American citizen, was put forward as a figurehead for this new company and named as president of the new film company. As a shareholder he did have a small financial interest, but as he admitted when interviewed by the Justice Department in 1917, he didn't know the rudiments of the movie business. He never took an active part in the management of the firm and was kept in the dark by the Germans on all important decisions.

Within a short time Claussen was overshadowed by vice-president and general manager Felix Malitz who had been engaged by the Germans to run the daily operations. An enterprising business man in more than one way, Malitz had started his film career as general manager for Pathé in the United States. According to his

Fig. 46. Managing the American Correspondent Film Company: Matthew B. Claussen (left) and Felix Malitz (right). Portraits reproduced from Motion Picture News *and* Motography.

own statement he was fired by his French employers in 1915 because of his German origin, although he had applied for American citizenship.

As a result, Malitz switched to the German side and started working for the American Correspondent Film Company. In return for his valuable services, he became shareholder with an interest of 33 percent in the company's revenues and he received a weekly salary of 75 dollars. Claussen clearly resented the way Malitz took over the film company and his ambitions about expanding business: "Pretty soon Mr. Malitz ran out of money and the amount of capital was raised to $140,000 and a total of $80,000 was paid in by Dr. Albert and his friends. Malitz had met Dr. Albert and they had become enthused over the rosy pictures of prospective profits portrayed by Mr. Malitz. He had by this time wound himself around Dr. Albert and his friends, and my ideas of conducting the company were entirely changed. Malitz opened offices at 220 West 42nd Street. He had a secretary Mr. Engler and another in his private office by the name of Sanders, a medium-sized, blond man, who left after a short while. I never could find Malitz in the office mornings. They always talked German at the meetings and as I could not understand it, I decided to get out."[16]

With the additional money backing from Dr. Albert, the firm of Brown & Dawson in June 1915 became a nominal shareholder and business partner of the American Correspondent Film Company. Brown & Dawson received 7 percent of all shares. Most of the money totaling 9,000 marks was paid directly by the ZfA to Dawson while he was in Germany as an advance for future photographic services. The German foreign propaganda agency decided to finance Dawson's activities because Dawson first needed to pay for raw footage and his new photographic equipment, as well as an assistant camera operator, and these bills had to be covered immediately before any film production could start. Dawson also complained about problems in communication with the German Information Service, likely a result of the British holding up mail crossing the Atlantic.[17] Meanwhile, at his firm in Stamford, Connecticut, new photographic supplies arrived for the reproduction, printing and editing of motion pictures.

By May 1915, with offices set up and a plant available for production, the American Correspondent Film Company was ready to present itself to the American movie industry. By a stroke of luck for Dawson, this also was the moment when the German and Austrian armies started a new, successful drive on the eastern front.

The Battle and Fall of Przemysl

On 28 April 1915 Dawson left Germany to cover the upcoming offensive on the eastern front by a combined Austro-German army commanded by General August von Mackensen. As a result, the Austrian province of Galicia was conquered and the Russian army began its long retreat to the east into Poland, culminating in the fall of major cities such as Przemysl, Lemberg (Lvov) and Warsaw.

Dawson's departure for the front appears to have been a great surprise to the German authorities who had no idea what he was up to. Shortly after his trip to the western front with Theyer, Dawson had found a new camera operator, John Allen Everets, a fellow American who also stayed in the Witts Hotel and was on the payroll of the ZfA until August 1916. Together with Everets, Dawson headed for Teschen and had himself attached to the k.u.k. Kriegspressequartier, the Austro-Hungarian military press office. Their work resulted in *The Battle and Fall of Przemysl,* the first feature documentary produced by the American Correspondent Film Company.

During the period after Dawson left Berlin to record these events, a memo regarding Dawson was also making an impression in the German diplomatic records, but not a particularly good one. On 27 May 1915 from the AA, Consul-General Thiel wrote to Dr. Fuehr in New York City:

> It isn't an easy job to work with that protégée of yours, Dawson. The man is endowed with a great amount of American impudence. In fact, he has been doing some very unpleasant things over here. I am not telling you this to criticize you or to get rid of him. Dawson is, I have been told, a very professional photographer. And perhaps we should accept his American insolence in order to get what we need for our propaganda in the United States. It's just that I am afraid that if we don't control him things will get out of hand. Of course you know about the natural tendency of our military authorities to keep these strange trench tourists [*fremde Schlachtenbummler*] as far away from the front as possible. Well, if we don't act Dawson may never be allowed to go anywhere!
>
> I have been told for instance that while he was at the western front Dawson acted with a most typical American insolence. One day, to make his film more interesting, he walked towards a commanding General while the camera was rolling, so that he could shake his hands as if they were best of friends. On film you can clearly see that the General isn't amused by this

effrontery and how he flinches. No doubt, these democratic Americans when they see that scene will get the idea that militarism is so strong in Germany that a General thinks himself too important to meet this photographer. Of course we will make sure this scene is cut out of the movie.

Recently Mr. Dawson was taken along to visit a number of German cities. When he discovered that another photographer was also in his group, he immediately left the company and went back to Berlin where he wrote me a very snotty letter. Then he suddenly vanished into the Carpathians. How he got permission to do so remains a mystery. I am telling you all this so that you are informed. Personally, I don't care that much and if necessary I can cope with this kind of nuisance. But there are people in this country who abhor this lack of proper manners and they can become a great problem to Mr. Dawson. When he has come back from the Carpathians I will talk to him about this and I will try to find the proper words for this conversation.[18]

The reason for the disappearance of Dawson without properly informing his German employers remains undocumented. In his letter to the ZfA, while billing the agency for his photographic expenses on trips inside Germany, he simply said he would leave the country the next day and didn't give his final destination. He probably had received his military permit by then to join the Austro-Hungarian army and just didn't care to share this information with the German authorities.

Dawson's sense of timing proved to be right because on 2 May 1915, just four days after he had left Berlin, the heaviest artillery bombardment yet seen on the eastern front started on the line between Tarnow and Gorlice. Dawson was soon there, and what he did there will be discussed in the next chapter.

Inside the German Empire

While Dawson was covering the offensive on the eastern front, the American Correspondent Film Company in May 1915 sent Edward Lyell Fox back to Europe. As on his previous trip, he was financed by the German Information Service, and paid for his expenses by drawing money from a bank account of the Hamburg-America Line. Fox's earlier reports for the Wildman Magazine and News Service had gone well with his publisher. He had also written *Behind the Scenes in Warring Germany*, a book on his experiences that was strongly pro-German.

Fox sailed and contacted the ZfA as well as Dr. Fuehr's chief, Fritz Thiel. The A.C. Film Company had hired him to collect footage showing the German home front. These educational films were produced with the assistance of the German authorities and showed a completely different approach compared to Dawson's Przemysl movie. The goal was to show on the American screen images of the strength of German culture and economy.

From the health resorts of Germany, Fox reported on the virtues of Teutonic country life in *Bad Ems* and *Baden-Baden*. He also assembled a four reel scenic, industrial feature with the appropriate title *System, The Secret of Success*. A few parts of this film contained scenes previously shot by Dawson and Theyer on the western front, such as the segment showing a German flamethrower in action in the Argonne.

Dawson himself was shown in this film while receiving his credentials in Berlin from Ambassador Gerard. This particular scene was also used in the accompanying publicity to emphasize the "neutral" character of the A.C. Film Company's productions. Most of the film consisted of images showing the "thrift, the riches and the preparedness of the great German Empire". To illustrate this message scenes were shown of the public markets at Hamburg and Dortmund, the harbor of Lübeck, the Krupp munitions factories, treasurer Karl Helfferich – "the man who handles billions for Germany" – and "the agricultural activity which converted Belgium into one great farmland".[19]

These educational films were released September 1915 by the A.C. Film Company and

Fig. 47. German flamethrower in action in the Argonne. Photo © Brown & Dawson. [Courtesy Library of Congress.]

proved to be a dismal failure. References in the American film trade press are scarce and there must have been little interest in distributing this material. The release of these films also showed a total lack of understanding by the Germans of what interested the American movie-going audience. As general manager Felix Malitz reported to his German employers, regular war films with plenty of action and interesting scenes were easily accepted by the public, but the American people aren't interested in this specific kind of *Kulturfilm*. Even when using a small amount of educational scenes in a regular war film production, he warned Berlin, the propaganda effect would be negligible. As a result, the production and distribution of educational films from wartime Germany soon ended.

While staying in Germany, Dawson also reported on the war films that were being shown in Germany. In a letter to his brother Charles in Vincennes, Indiana, published in the local press on 16 December 1915, Dawson mentioned he had visited several cinemas in Berlin. The most interesting footage from the front, he wrote, strangely enough came from the enemy:

> Probably the most important part of every program is the War Films. I should say were the most important part, for the films from the front do not begin to attract the attention they did six months ago. The reason being that the film companies are not getting any new or original stuff, just the same old subjects over and over again. Soldiers eating, soldiers washing, soldiers marching, soldiers drinking coffee. If Warsaw happens to be in the news a column of soldiers marching along is titled 'Our Victorious Troops Entering Warsaw'.

> The reason for this is twofold, a man who is able to hike around after an army carrying a camera is also able to carry a gun and most of the good operators are now at the front as soldiers. The censorship is also pretty close and does not allow any pictures of artillery in action, dead, wounded or anything which might tend to depress work or the feelings of the people. The only exception to this was a picture I saw showing the Germans burying two English aviators.

> There are three companies which put out weeklies every week of about three hundred feet, Messter, Eiko, both German, and Sascha, Austrian, of which Sascha is probably the best. A couple of other firms also put out a 'weekly' whenever they can get enough film to make up one. The two German companies seem to be very hard up for film now for I have seen stuff in their weeklies which I know for a fact was made nearly a year ago.

> But the most surprising thing is that at present one can see in the theatres all over Berlin war films of the French, Belgian, English and Italian armies. I would hardly have believed this if I had not seen it myself. They are of course made from dupe negatives but good interesting subjects. Scenes in Paris with troops around a railroad station. The French president presenting flags to new regiments. One could tell that the titles were made by a German for whenever you see the enemy's troops marching the title always reads 'French infantry retreating from the Argonne', 'English field artillery retreating', 'Belgian cavalry defeated at place', and so on. They are interesting nevertheless and are well received by the public.[20]

Dawson's letter is significant because it reflects precisely what Josef Schumacher, head of picture propaganda at the ZfA, and others complained about in German newsreels. Schumacher reported to the ZfA in 20 October 1915 that Consul Cremer in Amsterdam, who handled ZfA picture propaganda in Holland, had told him that the French had recently produced very effective shots of the theatre of war. Schumacher largely blamed excessive censorship on both official and unofficial levels.[21]

Schumacher reported that the German film industry's inability to show similar pictures to theatergoers was particularly regrettable as for instance in Holland at that time, there was a lot of interest in Russian war prisoners. Also recalling the difficulties that the leaders of the Army had gone to, Cremer added to this report "the astonishing recommendation" that it makes no difference to the filmgoer if the shot were made directly at the front or whether it was "another shot taken in a similar terrain". Leaving aside the aesthetic and ethical questions in faking shots, Schumacher is already pointing out the German newsreels were boring.[22] And it is not as if most of the shots mentioned by Dawson or Schumacher would needed to have been faked in any case. If two months after the fall of Novo Georgievsk German newsreels could not get permission to use shots of German troops hanging around a railroad station, of presentation of flags to new regiments, or of Russian prisoners in their newsreels, something must have been definitely wrong. One can wonder if in fact Dawson had talked to Schumacher about the problem.

While in Germany Dawson had been escorted on several photographic tours that were organized for neutral correspondents. These tours started in February 1915 and were led by Schumacher. Before the war he had been in charge of the German Federation of Tourist Agencies. He knew how to handle foreign journalists and was experienced in promoting Germany abroad which made him the proper man for this job.

Under Schumacher's guidance, Dawson was taken to Düsseldorf where he took pictures of the German war industry. On his next visit to Lübeck he took some interesting pictures of the local military flying school. One of his most striking war pictures shot in Germany was taken on that occasion and shows a Taube airplane in flight. Nicknamed the "Dove" because of its remarkable wings, the plane was photographed by Dawson exactly at the moment when it flew above him. The striking picture ended up on the cover of the *New York Times Mid-Week Pictorial* in January 1917.

Like the educational films by Fox, Dawson's pictures of the German prisoner of war camps, released in the United States as *Friends and Foes*, were also part of a specific publicity campaign by the German government. The first camp that he visited was at Zossen near Berlin in December 1914 together with Edward Lyell Fox. At that time the Zossen camp contained a mixed group of prisoners from various countries, but by his next visit in the spring of 1915, the Germans had converted the camp to a special purpose. It had been turned into a recruitment centre that was strictly reserved for Islam soldiers from the French colonies in North Africa. These prisoners of war received special handling: use of a mosque that had been built, lectures on the Koran and organized excursions to Berlin. Eventually over 2000 soldiers were trained at the camp for a Holy War against the Entente and sent to the Turkish front.

Dawson's report on the Zossen camp was published in the German press in May 1915. He noted how well these Arab prisoners were treated and praised their quiet and civilized behavior. His pictures seem to illustrate this statement and show a group of dignified chieftains from Moroccan tribes who had been part of the French colonial forces. Most of these Arab colonial soldiers, Dawson related, were shipped to Europe without knowing their destination and were immediately sent into the trenches by the French as mere cannon fodder without any proper training. As indicated by his report in the *Berliner Illustrierte Zeitung*, Dawson's photographic work was used by the Germans to publicize the special attention given to these Arab prisoners of war.

In contrast, there was a public outcry in Germany in 1915 against what was called "the black disgrace". The French also recruited soldiers from Senegal. The idea of a European nation sending these "primitive" African soldiers into combat against another European nation was intolerable to the German government. Within a short

Fig. 48. The giant of the Zossen camp, photographed by Albert Dawson. Reproduction from Berliner Illustrierte Zeitung, *2 May 1915.*

time, the French were accused in official reports of sending barbaric murderers into the trenches who would go out into No Man's Land at night and cut the throats of German soldiers. These black soldiers were also accused of raping women.

Dawson's report of the Senegalese soldiers, as well as his pictures, underscores this German propaganda theme. When read today it clearly is racist, but at the time many German readers must have agreed with Dawson's observations:

"The biggest man in this prisoner of war camp is a huge Negro out of the Sudan. The man is almost two meters tall and as powerful as a gorilla. I was told that the French used him as an observer, not only because of his unusual height but also because he has such a sharp eyesight compared to white men. He also knows how to climb a tree very quickly, as if he is monkey. In fact, when he was caught he was sitting on the top of a tree while he was shooting at Germans. He said he didn't wear any shoes because these hurt his feet and he had thrown them away. He feels much better walking on bare feet. In the damp German climate however he needs to have shoes, so a special pair of wooden shoes to fit his enormous size was made for him.[23]

On his return from the military campaign in Galicia, Dawson made a short visit to Thüringen where at Ohrdruf he reported on the living conditions in yet another prisoner of war camp. His pictures again were published in the German press and show French soldiers handing out books in a library that they had set up themselves, a barber shop and a well-supplied kitchen. Dawson was particularly impressed by the splendid work that was done by a relief committee for comrades who had no friends or family at home.

Meanwhile in Berlin, the Foreign Office was trying to persuade the General Staff to give a number of American photographers, including Edwin Weigle of the *Chicago*

Tribune, more allowance to film the German theatre of war. As a result, Dawson's name appeared on the application list and for a while it looked as if he would be permitted to film the military training grounds at Alten-Grabow as a replacement for Irving Guy Ries, the cameraman for Wilbur Durborough. The General Staff however soon changed its mind about Dawson, and on 25 June 1915 it was officially announced to the Foreign Office that both he and his camera operator Everets would not be permitted to go to the German front for the time being, because they had made nuisances of themselves. What exactly happened is somewhat unclear, but Dawson's reputation with the German authorities as a troublesome photographer must have been an important reason for this radical change of policy.

Dawson's career as a war photographer in Germany seemed to be coming at an unexpected end. He was invited to the Foreign Office on 12 July 1915 and told that his further stay in Germany had little purpose.[24] "The General Staff just doesn't want anything to do with him", Fritz Thiel explained in a personal letter to Dr. Fuehr. "That young man is so unmannered and rude. He makes everyone upset and angry. I also heard that he has made himself disagreeable with our Allies while he was at the front. It is my considered opinion that you would do best to get Dawson out of here as soon as possible. Fox appears to have made himself quite popular and I don't expect any problems with him. We can be of enormous assistance to Fox if we decide to make him Dawson's replacement."[25]

If the German authorities thought they could terminate Dawson's own plans they were soon in for a nasty disappointment. When told that it was futile to stay in Germany, Dawson casually remarked that he had already decided to leave for the front again. Within eight or ten days he would be joining the Austrian military forces as an accredited war photographer.

Troubles Ahead

Between his adventures in Galicia and Poland and the time Dawson arrived in Vienna to have his footage inspected by the censors, his American Correspondent Film Company released its first feature film. While this film, *The Battle and Fall of Przemysl*, may have been a commercial success in American movie theatres, the company soon experienced a sudden setback.

In May 1915 as a result of the sinking of the *Lusitania*, German propaganda in the United States had run into some serious problems. Shortly before the ship sailed, the German embassy had placed an advertisement warning all American passengers that by travelling on belligerent ships they would risk their lives because their destination was within a war zone. But when U-20 Captain Schwieger ordered the successful attack on the *Lusitania*, he not only dealt a death blow to the lives of 1,119 passengers, he also struck a lethal blow to the heart of American public opinion.

German propaganda backfired enormously because the warning made it appear that the *Lusitania* had been a target from the start of its voyage. Americans began to feel themselves the subjects of a conspiracy, and any rational arguments about the ship carrying munitions for the Entente made no lasting impression against the striking image of innocent American citizens that perished in the Irish Sea.

Dr. Dernburg tried to defend the attack in a speech prepared by the German Information Service while he was in Cleveland, Ohio, in May 1915. Bernhard Dernburg was generally in charge of press propaganda in America. He had already made speeches in America explaining that Antwerp was a German harbor, that Belgium belonged to Germany geographically and that Germany needed areas like Morocco for settlement after the war. The reaction to the Cleveland speech was so sharp that the Germans recalled Dernburg and appointed as the new head of the German Press Office in America Heinrich Albert, whose previous experience had been in the commercial sector. Albert, like Dernburg, had little or no experience in the field of propaganda.

Another result of the sinking of the *Lusitania* was President Wilson's ordering Secretary of the Treasury William Gibbs McAdoo, whose department controlled the Secret Service, to begin surveillance of the German and Austrian Embassy staffs.

On 24 July 1915 Albert got on the New York subway near his offices at 45 Broadway and like so many before and after him, he dozed off before arriving at his station. When he awoke at 50th Street, he sprang for the door when in a flash he suddenly realized he had left his briefcase on the subway. Frantically, the doctor fought his way back onto the train but he was too late; the briefcase with his papers had been taken by the U.S. Secret Service agent following him.

The subsequent publication of the Albert portfolio was another severe blow against the German Information Service. It dramatized German publicity efforts. Although nothing illegal was found in these documents, the reports on the attempts to buy up ammunition plants, to subsidize writers and speakers and to finance newspapers served to fasten the stamp of "propaganda" upon the work of Dr. Albert's collaborators. Looking back on his experiences in these eventful days, George Sylvester Viereck noted that most members of Dr. Albert's committee didn't seem to realize the full importance of what was happening. Their operations had been exposed, but the general feeling was they hadn't violated any law and were doing the same thing as the Entente.

As with arguments used to justify the sinking of the *Lusitania*, this may have been true but it showed a complete lack of understanding of public relations. Among Albert's papers was the contract signed by him to finance the American Correspondent Film Company. The document was partially reprinted in the *New York World*. When asked by journalists for a statement, Claussen admitted the loan by Dr. Albert had been advanced but he said the film company was a straightforward business proposition. Americans had become dependent upon English censors; he wanted the American people to see for themselves what was going on in Europe. "This is a news service, not a secret service", Claussen retorted.[26] Felix Malitz also made a statement emphasizing the official character of the war films and the fact that these were made by American photographers like Dawson.

Reports in the trade press indicate that the A.C. Film Company even tried to cash in on the free publicity that was generated by the news about the Albert papers. An advertisement was run saying: "Exhibitors! The Battle of Przemysl has received NATION WIDE PUBLICITY worth HUNDREDS OF THOUSAND OF DOL-LARS within the last week. This publicity was neither BOUGHT nor PAID FOR, but it has made 100,000,000 people still more desirous of seeing the GREATEST WAR PICTURE EVER MADE!"[27]

Compounding these problems, the A.C. Film Company also had to consider what to do with Dawson. Consul-General Thiel wanted him shipped out of Germany as soon as possible. In New York City, Dr. Fuehr made an abundant apology for Dawson's behavior, mentioning to his chief that a telegram had been sent to the film company ordering Dawson's immediate return to the United States.

Dawson's reputation as a tumultuous cameraman, Fuehr stated, was well-known to the staff of the A.C. Film Company, and he had previously warned Claussen and Malitz to keep a watchful eye on him:

> "They have given him a thorough brush-off, Herr Consul-General, rest assured that this has been done. I am deeply sorry about the problems Dawson has brought about. It is most regrettable that he thinks this operation of ours revolves around him personally, and that he doesn't consider the good cause that we are working for.
>
> There is no excuse for this kind of behavior. However, on the same day that I sent this telegram the management of the A.C. Film Co. also received the wireless message from you and Dr. Horstmann, which was understood to mean that you didn't insist on Dawson's immediate departure.
>
> At this stage of the war, we need our own photographers both in Poland and on the Italian front. In addition, a third camera man would be most useful, and Fox was never meant to be a replacement for Dawson, although his salary is modest.
>
> Also, sending Dawson back to America will cost us a lot of money. Therefore, I humbly suggest that you decide yourself on this matter. If that tactless fellow doubts your authority, just send us a short radio flash – something like "recall Dawson"- and he will receive his marching orders right away. Under no circumstances is he allowed to bother you any longer!"[28]

Fuehr's intervention saved Dawson because Thiel decided to wait and see if his personal behavior showed any improvement. In case he decided to have Dawson leave the country, a letter was drafted by the A.C. Film Company authorizing his departure. The letter was sent to the ZfA in Berlin and filed, to be used by the German government at the appropriate moment, although in the end it was never sent to Dawson at all, who may have had no idea of his narrow escape.

Shortly after his return from the Ivangorod campaign in September 1915, Dawson also got into problems when he was trying to finish his footage. This was an entirely different complication but no less important for the future of German film propaganda in the United States. While staying at the Witts Hotel in Berlin, Dawson received an alarming telegram from Felix Malitz warning him that he had been tricked by Austria's leading film company: "Watch, Sascha fooled you, sending dupe negative Ivangorod stuff. Want original negative urgently."[29]

The information on what had happened is sketchy, but evidently Dawson had struck a deal with the Sascha Company and agreed to share his footage in return for additional war pictures. The agreement appears to be similar to the contract that he had closed with the Austrian government in June 1915 on his Przemysl movie. This time however the Austrians seem to have profited most by keeping the original negatives and sending an inferior duplicate to Berlin. How Dawson dealt with the situation isn't known, but it must have contributed to a serious delay because his footage wasn't ready for exhibition in the United States until December 1915.

Following the Przemysl movie, the A.C. Film Company released two new feature films. One of these films, *Battles of a Nation,* premiered on 18 November 1915 at the Park Theatre in New York City. Situated at the corner of Broadway and Central Park, the theatre was considered an excellent location for exhibiting this new war film. As with the previous movie, Dawson again appears on screen as a camera correspondent while the audience watches his journey to the front. From behind the German lines, Dawson is seen visiting well-stocked food store houses and military factories. He also goes to a Zeppelin hangar and is shown the big airship as it leaves for a raid to London.

The film also has a number of human interest scenes, such as pictures of German children collecting metals for the war industry, a shot that has been retrieved in the CBS *World War I* series. The second reel shows the aftermath of the siege of Przemysl. Segments from this specific reel have reappeared in the John E. Allen Film Archives in Culpeper, Virginia. We see Dawson handing out newspapers to Austrian soldiers shortly after the capture of this city, followed by troops entering the captured fortress. The next two reels pictured the attack on Lemberg (Lvov), the Galician capital, as well as Warsaw. Dawson wasn't on the spot when these latter events took place, so these scenes must have been culled from official footage supplied by the Austrian military press office.

Research on frame enlargements of *Battles of a Nation* found at the Library of Congress has also identified a number of scenes from this movie in the BBC *Great War* series, such as a shot showing Austrian 30.5 Skoda mortars in action.[30]

Except for the first two reels, most of the footage of *Battles of a Nation* appears to have been taken by Austro-Hungarian military cameramen. Dawson's contribution to this film was probably limited although he was credited by the A.C. Film Company as cinematographer together with John Allen Everets. Reviews in the press praised the beautiful, tinted footage but on the whole the general opinion was that the film was too lengthy and lacked punch and action.

As for its political inclination, *Variety's* report on the exhibition at the Park Theatre noted: "The unities of neutrality are nicely preserved here by a slide request to the

Fig. 49. German children collecting metals for the war industry. Frame enlargement from
Battles of a Nation. *[Courtesy Library of Congress.]*

audience not to take sides audibly accompanied by a bid for riots in a regimented soprano Fräulein who sings Die Wacht Am Rhein".[31]

In order to increase circulation, *Battles of a Nation* was sponsored by the New York *Buffalo Times*. State rights were also sold by this newspaper because the A.C. Film Company didn't have its own distribution channel. The necessity of working together with an American newspaper to publicize these war pictures became increasingly important.

General manager Felix Malitz noted in his reports to Germany that without this support the public interest in any new film would prove to be a total disappointment. For this reason, he had entered into negotiations with the Hearst papers, offering to take all Hearst news pictures through the A.C. Film Company in return for a royalty, but the plan soon foundered because Hearst had his own film organization and wanted his own newsreel cameramen like A. E. Wallace and Nelson Edwards in Europe to handle these war films. Malitz therefore went to a competitor, Norman E. Mack, and through his chain of newspapers – including the *Buffalo Times* – ran advertisements promoting the A.C. Film Company productions.[32]

Sponsored by Mack's news organization, Dawson's next feature, *The Warring Millions,* opened at the Olympic Theatre in Chicago on 4 December 1915. This film contained the footage that Dawson had shot during the military drive to Ivangorod. When the movie premiered, the producers advertised it as a huge success. *Variety* reported that the police were brought in to hold back the crowds.[33]

Dawson's film actually resulted in a full-scale riot but the reason was somewhat different than that suggested by the publicity writers. The Olympic had been paid a full month in advance in order to show Dawson's film. However, because of some technical flaws in the film print, the movie had to be sent back to the studio. Trying to make some money for the rest of the period, the *Buffalo Times* wanted to sublet the theatre and show a French war film instead.

When the owners of the Olympic refused to cooperate, Mack had to employ some twenty-five policemen as well as a hundred Pinkerton detectives armed with an injunction to enter the theatre by the fire escape. This in turn triggered the Hearst competition that was showing a similar French war documentary nearby, to marshal two hundred men (further proof, if any is needed, that even though Hearst and the A.C. Film Company might be pro-German, business trumped politics). Furnished with searchlights they were instructed to buy as many tickets as possible and prepare to wreck the theatre. A confrontation with Hearst's forces was avoided at the last moment when the management decided to close the Olympic.[34]

A synopsis of this film that was used for the copyright application gives a good idea how a propaganda message was edited into *The Warring Millions*, stressing the combined strength of the German and Austrian armies. This is particularly interesting, given the fact that while filming this campaign Dawson had been given no support whatsoever by the German authorities. The work had been done on his own initiative and with the assistance of the Austrian k.u.k. Kriegspressequartier.

> "A. K. Dawson, camera correspondent attached to the Austro-Hungarian armies, leaves Berlin and proceeds to Ivangorod. On his way to the front Dawson observes intensive farming system organized in conquered Poland. At Radom soldiers' encampment is made and preparations are gone through for the assault on Ivangorod. The next day camp breaks up. A captive balloon is used to get the enemy's range. Dawson is allowed to go up on this important venture. Aviators equipped with bombs are also sent up to destroy the Russian outposts. German field gun in foremost trenches bombards the enemy's position.
>
> Terrific onslaught of the Russians compels Teutonic commander to ask for more troops, but wires are broken. A volunteer rides forth to carry the message through. In the meantime wires are repaired. Air scouts report vantage point and the big Austrian guns begin bombardment of Ivangorod. The volunteer arrives at the destination and the Austro-Hungarian commander sends reinforcements. The German commander also receives word that more infantry is needed at once, and they are sent.
>
> Reinforcements arrive in the nick of time and turn the tide of battle. Ivangorod falls. The Russian forts are a mass of ruins. Wounded are taken from field shelters to well equipped hospitals. Dawson inspects smouldering ruins and is also shown Russian system of trenches. Archduke Frederick reviews army. Pictures of Russian prisoners are made. The final scene depicts a cemetery where representatives of different faiths unite to pay homage to the dead."[35]

Reviews of Dawson's latest film from the eastern front were mixed. Kitty Kelly, describing the documentary for the *Chicago Tribune*, called the film a mistake in nomenclature. Instead of millions of fighting Teutons, the actual war scenes were so few that the producers should have called it "The Warring Hundreds". With the exception of a short scene showing the infantry storming Ivangorod, most of the film pictured the preparations for the siege:

> "There is marching and drilling of soldiers, shooting of big guns, masking of guns under cut grain, a balloon ascension, people going across a pontoon bridge and back again, many heaps of debris, and A.K. Dawson, the intrepid photographic war correspondent who spent a good deal of time in front of the camera. A messenger on horseback who is madly galloping across grassy turf and soft dirt roads, does so with much interpretive clatter of hoof beats rendered by the inspired [musical] 'effects'. Another stir up was made in the economical use of the one picture of an exploding shell from the big guns. That explosion gets to be very familiar."[36]

Miss Kelly's scorn is not really so much an indictment of the film as the inherent loss of drama in a silent war film. Despite the lively orchestra or because of it, *The Warring Millions* only had a seven days run in Chicago. During the 1915 Christmas holiday, the film was also shown at the Tech Theatre in Buffalo, New York. The exhibition rights had been bought by the *Buffalo Times* for a continuous one-week show. The newspaper, admittedly a biased source, gave the movie extensive publicity, calling attention to the realism and exhilarating scenes like the battle of a German airship and an aeroplane. "How the Central Powers crowd out a victory by the quick bringing up of reinforcements creates a fine basis for thrills."[37]

According to the *Buffalo Times*, the documentary had been shot by three American cameramen. Clearly, this doesn't fit with Dawson's own account. In a short time, he had to do all the photography on his own with only the help of an Austrian soldier.

Demise of the A.C. Film Company

According to a press report in the *Kansas City Star* on the inside operations of the A.C. Film Company, general manager Felix Malitz's hidden intention was to "milk the German cow". [38] He had set up an extremely expensive film company, and his personal contract was quite lucrative with an indemnity of a year's salary in case the company was dissolved.

Claussen's comments that Malitz had wound himself around Dr. Albert and had him invest more and more money in the film company are confirmed in this remarkable press story. In fact, with Albert's dough bag wide open, the total amount of investments in the A.C. Film Company by the end of October 1915 had gone up to $78,600. This did not deter Malitz from preparing even more grandiose plans. Among his proposals to the Germans was a plan to buy a complete chain of premiere theatres to increase the circulation of these films. The total costs amounting to $200,000 were too great for the German government to take on.

Meanwhile, Malitz must have seen the writing on the wall when he received a report from Stamford, Connecticut, on the sad condition of the actual footage that had been shipped from Europe. Out of the 20,000 feet of film that was shipped, 75 percent was considered worthless. There was only enough to make one good feature film on the siege of Przemysl; the company needed much better war film material to create another.

This is also a recurring theme in Dr. Fuehr's letters to Berlin. By the end of 1915 Fuehr was complaining directly to Freiherr von Mumm, head of the ZfA, that something should be done to compete with the increasing number of war films that were shown in the United States by the Entente. "Out of the footage that we have received so far – most of it from Austria – our general manager has made four pretty good feature films. But there is no doubt that we can do much better if our camera men get more freedom to make new films. Could you please ask the military authorities for their cooperation? These films are not just an appetizer for American sensationalism. It is of the utmost importance to the German cause that we get more war pictures."[39]

The ZfA was of some assistance to the A.C. Film Company. Arrangements were made in November 1915 for a monopoly of all German war films to be released on the American market through this firm. In addition to this, John Allen Everets was sent to join Germany's new ally, Bulgaria, in October 1915, and shot film for the German Information Service. Together with Edward Lyell Fox, he travelled to the Balkans and covered the fall of Pirot and Nish. Dawson was left behind in Berlin, presumably because the Germans preferred to send more compliant cameramen.

This clearly didn't conform to Dawson's own wishes. He frantically wired the Austrian Kriegspressequartier three times within one month asking for permission to go to the front and witness the upcoming attack by the Central Powers on Serbia. Each time he was told to wait. The Austrian authorities apparently tried to hold Dawson off but they didn't take into account his personal commitment to get the pictures that he wanted made.

Dawson decided to go to Vienna and on 28 October 1915 he appeared at the War Museum where he usually had his films censored, explaining to the officials that the Austrian War Office had already given him a permit to visit the front. Bluffing his way to the firing line, Dawson was caught in Belgrade six days later and shipped back to Vienna. His photographic equipment and films were also confiscated.[40]

Undaunted by this setback, Dawson next attempted to bypass both the German and the Austrian authorities. He resolved to cover the retreat of the Serbian army into Albania. In order to witness this historical campaign he took a wide detour to Sofia, the Bulgarian capital, dressed up as a native Bulgarian peasant and entered the Balkan front from Bulgaria with new photographic equipment.

Dawson's journey to Bulgaria started in December 1915 when he boarded a train in Vienna with Horace Green, a reporter for the *New York Evening Post*. In Budapest, they changed their Austrian money for Rumanian lei and then began their long trip through Bucharest to Sofia. For four days and three nights they never changed their clothes. On the evening of the second day, after a night sitting up in their 2nd class coach, with crackers, chocolate and schweck – the local Hungarian drink – to satisfy their inner man, they piled out at Kronstadt, the frontier station on the north side of the Hungarian-Rumanian border. Green at that moment was arrested as a spy because his papers had notes on German military regiment losses. He could have been executed on the spot for this grave mistake but the Hungarians set him free. Going into neutral Rumania the next day, Dawson and Green reached Predeal. This time Green lost all his luggage and had his passport confiscated by the Rumanian military police as well. Green and Dawson finally met again in the American Legation at Bucharest.[41]

After arranging a new set of permits and a temporary passport for Green, Dawson entered Bulgaria, Germany's recent ally. As he mentioned later in an interview back in Berlin, it was a harsh and tiresome experience:

> I reached Belgrade just two days after the Austrians had occupied the town, and it must be said in truth, that they managed and organized everything wonderfully. I was there eight days, and it rained the entire time, with the exception of three hours. I returned to Vienna and then went to Sofia, by way of Romania, that being the only route then open.

Fig. 50. Dawson, dressed as a Bulgarian peasant, holding his Kodak camera. Eastern front, 1915–1916. [Courtesy Smithsonian American Art Museum.]

> The Bulgarians were exceedingly kind to me, brought out a crack regiment to go through its exercises, so that Americans might know the kind of people they were. And then they forwarded me to Kjoestendil, whence I had to make the best of my way to Prizren. And thus I started on foot to make the journey across Serbia. To carry my baggage and cinematograph apparatus, I had a wagon which travelled along the ever winding roads, while I cut through the old tracks, always arriving long ahead of the wagon. It was a terrible hard life, as there were no places under cover fit to sleep in. The whole country was simply crawling with lice and vermin. I had to sacrifice all my underclothes. But that doesn't matter in comparison to the fact that I was able to obtain some excellent films which I have been given to understand were seen and appreciated by Czar Ferdinand.

151

> I followed the track of the Bulgarian army, and saw all the strong positions which had been taken by storm and without artillery from the Serbians. From Prizren there is a fine road to Albania, and that had been followed by the king and his army. At the end of that road, a strange and weird sight met my eyes. The road is just cut into the side of the mountains and there is a rushing mountain stream below. So, when they reached the point where the roads ceased, they just set their automobiles running at full speed, jumped off them and let them take a big leap over the side into the gorge below. There too, a pathetic sight, was the old-fashioned royal coach of King Peter, a queer ramshackle specimen of the coachman's art in bygone times. Also masses of artillery that had been destroyed as much as possible. At one point, I saw an entire train which had been burnt and which remained as just a long black patch.[42]

The Balkan campaign undoubtedly resulted in some fine footage, but these films were never released in the United States. By the time Dawson had arrived back in Germany, the A.C. Film Company was teetering on the edge of bankruptcy. The firm's financial losses were overwhelming and the authorities in Berlin couldn't cope with the problems besetting German film propaganda in the United States.

Consul-General Thiel on 30 December 1915 in a personal letter to Dr. Fuehr described these complications in rather frank terms. The ZfA, he admitted, just didn't have enough money from its own funds to finance any new major film projects for the A.C. Film Company. He also complained about the lack of cooperation by the General Staff and the strict military censorship of these war films. As a result the scenes that would have been most interesting to the American public never made it to the United States. Staging some of these scenes, he said, could be a solution but he couldn't accept this on principle because German propaganda should be based on facts and not on fiction. Besides, the American movie-going audience, Thiel firmly declared, would notice the difference anyway and criticize any sensationalist film exhibited by the Central Powers.

Thiel's remarks on the need to base all propaganda on facts, without the use of any additional footage that brought a "heart interest" to these movies, strike at the core of what had gone wrong during this covert film propaganda campaign in the United States. The idea of producing remarkable war films with correspondents like Dawson in front of the camera had been a master stroke from a propaganda perspective. However, the whole concept of reaching out to the American audience by making the films really "American" and appealing to them was never fully and effectively executed. Dawson was given his permits, his camera operators and his photographic outfit, but the German authorities never understood how they could benefit by having an American photographer like Dawson actually direct these movies.

The lack of cooperation by the German army was another major obstacle to the improvement of the film campaign in America, as Count von Bernstorff noted in his memoir. Dawson's self-centered behavior probably reinforced the General Staff's insistence that it was best to keep him away from the front as much as possible. In the end, what Dawson accomplished as a war photographer was more a result of his own initiative than that of German professional film production. Thus ended Dawson's war film career on a rather ignominious note.

Durborough

When war started in Europe in August, Durborough was eager for an assignment to cover it and the NEA was just as eager to offer the coverage for its many clients. Durborough never thought twice about a new photographic adventure and welcomed his assignment to Germany. But when he proposed expanding his war photography to include film as well as still photos, Sam Hughes resisted the additional financial risk.[43] But as with the earlier aerial photography company, they struck a deal that allowed Durborough the initiative to fund his own film enterprise. As long as it didn't interfere with providing the NEA his usual photographic material while in Europe, they would pay his usual liberal expenses; he would have to fund any additional expenses for the film project. This flexibility was attributed to the NEA benefiting from the halo of film publicity that might accrue to Durborough who was closely associated with that news service.[44]

In late 1914 Chicago had a complete complement of basic components needed for such a film project: some local businessmen interested in taking the financial risk of investing in a film opportunity presented by the expanding war, the Universal Camera Company which produced film cameras, Watterson R. Rothaker's Industrial Film Studio where one could edit and print a film, and not least important but most surprising, Durborough, an accomplished news photographer with no actual film-making experience but unlimited self-confidence and a most persuasive personality.[45] His very limited vicarious experience with film probably only consisted of observing the Pine Ridge Reservation *The Indian Wars* filming, possibly some vicarious learning from Charles A. Pryor while covering the Battle of Ojinaga and his close relationship with Weigle during his filming of *The Battle of Vera Cruz*. Durborough later described the assignment in his manuscript: "So, my job was, first, to get into Germany, and then, to try to see the war from the German side. Always an optimist, I tackled the job."[46] Clearly it was this personal confidence and optimism that enabled him to bring the components together necessary to produce his film.

War Film Syndicate

While waiting for the NEA to acquire the necessary German visa and other credentials for his assignment, Durborough managed to seek out and convince a small group of local investors to form the ad hoc War Film Syndicate to back his independent film project. Although little is known about this group that appears to have existed for about two years, Durborough held a quarter financial interest and the other local investors whom he called "a group of my friends in Chicago" held a controlling three quarters interest.[47] The only member he names in his manuscript was a "Marston", referring to local Chicago journalist Carl M. Marston.[48] Two other likely members were Siegfried T. Jacobs and John F. Cuneo Sr., both Chicago businessmen involved in the printing industry. Cuneo printed the Hearst newspapers in Chicago. Jacobs, who worked in one of Cuneo's companies, was the individual who filed the copyright for the Durborough film in December 1915. Cuneo was also an investor in the local Essanay film company which had made the 1913 *The Indian Wars* film that Durborough covered as a photographer while it was being filmed. He was probably one of the first individuals Durborough approached for financial support of his own film project, which appears to have been presented and undertaken simply as a good financial investment opportunity.[49]

Besides any personal money invested by the principals, the Syndicate raised additional funds for the project by soliciting subscriptions from newspapers around the country, many if not most from the NEA subscribers, for future local screening rights prior to Durborough's departure for Germany.[50] Many local newspapers across the country signed up believing it would enhance their local image as well as realize a net profit from film ticket sales. While there clearly was overlap in Syndicate subscribers and NEA members, some large city papers who weren't members would also sponsor the film.

After finding financial support, Durborough needed to assemble needed equipment and supplies for his trip. The two movie cameras from the Universal Camera Company of Chicago were the most mundane purchase while the most unusual was a Stutz Bearcat roadster, one of the fastest, sportiest cars the public could buy. This American-bought car wasn't the most practical transportation solution for an American photojournalist and cinematographer to cover the European war and it's doubtful any other American journalist took a car all the way to Europe and into the war zone.[51] It was bought by Durborough and certainly fit his personality. Indeed not only would it be closely identified with him but it became part of his image while in Germany. The car was as much film prop as transportation and would appear in many film segments; only Durborough himself would be present in more.

Another budget component probably proposed by Durborough as part of his original film project was the need for an assistant cameraman to help handle all the necessary film paraphernalia. Besides, if he was to satisfy his desire to appear in the film at important actions or with important personalities, he would need to bring his own camera operator; one might find someone to snap a photo with a still camera in a war zone but not likely someone to reliably crank a film camera. He may have wanted to take along Nicholas McDonald, his good friend and fellow photojournalist at the *Chicago Examiner* who had even less exposure to film cameras than his own very limited vicarious experience, but the Syndicate probably required him to choose Irving G. Ries, an experienced cameraman working at Watterson R. Rothacker's company in North Chicago.[52] Ries' film camera experience and fluency in German were two critical skills that Durborough didn't possess and were very much needed, although his cigar smoking habit was mutual.

Lastly, in preparation Durborough cultivated social contacts with key members of

Fig. 51. Durborough, in a typically jaunty mood, crossing the border into Germany. His Stutz car was as much film prop as transportation. [Courtesy Library of Congress.]

the Chicago German-American community, notably the Eitle brothers, whose thriving Bismarck Hotel and Restaurant business was an unofficial center for local German culture and had premiered Weigle's *German Side of the War*. It was at the Bismarck's New Year's Eve party that Durborough and his wife Molly greeted 1915.

Getting There

After Ries filmed their Chicago friends' goodbyes to Durborough sitting in the Stutz, they sped east to New York City. They bought 25,000 feet of fresh unexposed film stock a little before boarding the SS *Nieuw Amsterdam* and sailed for Holland on 24 March 1915.[53] They arrived in Rotterdam in early April and Durborough had to place the Stutz in storage before proceeding to Berlin as he lacked permission to bring a personal car into Germany. Although the NEA had obtained all the credentials he personally needed for entering Germany, effective 1 April Germany had abolished the use of private autos without military approval to conserve fuel so critical for war needs.[54] Carless Durborough and Ries proceeded to Berlin and booked themselves into the Adlon Hotel in Berlin with most of the other American journalists covering the war. The next immediate task was to register on 8 April with the AA for permission to film and photograph followed a week later with another request explaining why his work assignment required use of his personal car currently stored in Holland to drive around Germany.[55]

While waiting for the necessary military approvals and credentials, Durborough settled into the community of American journalists at the Adlon. As in Mexico, while they were competitive in trying to develop news sources and influential contacts, most were collegial and often shared information and advice. Being from Chicago, it's not surprising that he quickly became acquainted with Oswald F. Schuette and Raymond E. Swing, war correspondents for the *Chicago Daily News*. Unlike most other papers covering the war, the *Chicago Daily News'* owner and editor Victor F. Lawson had earlier established foreign correspondents in major European cities with small *Daily News* bureaus in London, Paris and Berlin to avoid any bias of foreign news filtered through London.[56] While most foreign correspondents worked out of their hotel rooms, Lawson wanted attractive offices in the major cities to project a professional image to the locals and also provide a welcoming refuge for visitors from home in which to relax while reading the *Daily News* and other papers subscribed to its foreign news service. For visitors from Chicago, he asked his correspondents to act as informal advisers providing visitors with friendly advice and assistance. They were often mentioned in the paper.

Schuette, appropriately described as a "passionate Germanophile" by the overworked Raymond Swing he was hired to augment, was a bachelor who networked well and enjoyed assisting Chicago visitors, especially those important enough to be news makers.[57] It was natural for Schuette to meet and interview Chicagoans Jane Addams, Alice Hamilton, as well as Aletta Jacobs from the Netherlands, on 20 May shortly after the women arrived in Berlin from the Women's International Peace Conference just concluded in The Hague. They were on a quick tour to the major European countries to present the conference resolutions to key ministers. This group managed to meet with both Chancellor von Bethmann-Hollweg and Foreign Minister Gottlieb von Jagow before leaving on 23 May for Vienna.[58] Back in Chicago, Jane Addams would credit Schuette for arranging the meetings with the German ministers on such short notice.[59] Durborough, less than two weeks in Berlin, had also arranged on short notice to film Addams and Dr. Hamilton in front of the Brandenburg Gate. Possibly Durborough's relationship with Schuette, whose assistance he later acknowledged as important to his film project's success, began with facilitating this filming opportunity.

Durborough also formed a close relationship with another American correspondent, Walter Niebuhr, who will reappear several times in this account. Born in San Francisco on 28 April 1890, Walter Niebuhr was a journalist from Illinois and the owner of the Lincoln, Illinois *Courier Herald*. In 1915 Niebuhr was invited by the *Chicago Tribune* and the Western Newspaper Union to cover the war from the German side.[60] He was a brother of the famous theologian Reinhold Niebuhr, the second of four children. His father, Gustav Niebuhr, was a missionary to German immigrants. His mother, Lydia Hosto Niebuhr, was not only a minister's wife; she was a minister's daughter as well. Walter's three siblings chose careers in the church. His sister Hulda was a religious educator who taught for many years at McCormick

Theological Seminary in Chicago. His younger brothers, Reinhold and H. (Helmut) Richard, were celebrated teachers and authors for decades.

Walter chose a different path. After graduating in 1908 from high school in Lincoln where his father was pastor of a church, Walter went to Lincoln College. One year later he transferred to Illinois Wesleyan Law School in Bloomington. While there he worked as a reporter for the local newspaper. Niebuhr became the owner and publisher of the *Lincoln* [Illinois] *Courier-Herald* in 1911, covering all aspects of small town life. In 1914 he ran for state political office and a year later Niebuhr was invited by the *Chicago Tribune* and the Western Newspaper Union to cover the First World War on the German side.

Niebuhr's adventure as a reporter began almost immediately when he wrote his first stories after his ship, the *Rijndam*, was struck by the Norwegian ship *Cuneo* on 25 May 1915 near Nantucket. First taken aboard the *Cuneo*, the *Rijndam*'s passengers were transferred to the battleship USS *South Carolina*. Sailing again from New York on the SS *Rotterdam*, Niebuhr traveled in distinguished company. On board were Dr. Jacobs of the *New York Sun*, James O'Donnell Bennett of the *Chicago Tribune* and Hendrick Willem Van Loon of the Associated Press and Arthur Ruhl of *Colliers*.

Niebuhr was ardently pro-German, attracting the attention of Ambassador Gerard in Germany as well as the Secret Service later back in America. So it was natural that he also quickly developed a close relationship with another Germanophile previously mentioned, Lewis Hart Marks.

Niebuhr, who spoke perfect German, was of great help to Durborough, who didn't speak the language. When visiting the eastern front he often traveled with Durborough in his Stutz Bearcat roadster and translated for him, greatly facilitating his navigation and filming. In Europe Walter Niebuhr witnessed a number of major battles including the fall of Warsaw, Verdun, Kemmel Ridge and the battle for the Goritzian Bridgehead. His scrapbook contains articles which bear titles like "Holland Has Dread of The War Scourge", "Berlin Shows No Suffering From Warfare", "Austria Has Strength For Supreme Test", "War Sorrow Casts Pall Over Towns", "Miracles of Surgery Save The Wounded", and "Old Argonne Forest Sees Worst Fighting", indicating he had little difficulty getting approved for the arranged tours to the fronts for neutral correspondents.

Army permission and the logistics required for foreign journalists and especially cinematographers to film training exercises were more easily arranged than getting to the active war zone, the *sine qua non* of a true war correspondent. Along with the military restrictions on private car use and fuel rationing that began before Durborough arrived in Germany, the Army also established a more controlled process for press correspondents' visits to military facilities and the war fronts, the most visible being a special uniform issued to approved members of the press. Another control was being accompanied by German officer escort from the time journalists left Berlin. These changes were probably instituted in an effort to eliminate unauthorized press access to the war zones. As mentioned elsewhere, German censorship was stringent, and it became more so. Early in the war journalists could travel unescorted to the front by train carrying their credentials. But several unauthorized individuals had often managed to get very close to the front and wander around before being noticed and apprehended. Like most countries at war, German military used control of journalists' access to military areas and individuals to shape the content of foreign news dispatches more than their censorship of all dispatches.

In late June the first Durborough photographs began appearing in American newspapers. It is likely to have taken nearly a month for the photographs to arrive by mail via a Scandinavian ship. One of the very first announced Durborough's arrival sitting in the Stutz with his German escort, Capt. Erwin Herber, and a caption noting he had already motored 2000 miles in Germany and along battle lines.[61] Among these first photos were stills of the different phases of a German Army attack,[62] an infantry mass charge,[63] machine guns in operation,[64] Red Cross staff preparations and their use of trained dogs[65] and the Entente prisoners at the Döberitz POW camp, built on one of the German Army's largest training grounds not far from Berlin.[66] All of these scenes were also included in his film. Although much of his war film was taken on the eastern front during the actual drive resulting in the capture of the Russian fort at Novo Georgievsk, some of these initial pictures, namely those non-POW scenes noted, were taken from an exposed camera position that indicates they were an army exercise well back from the front. Durborough and Ries likely filmed these scenes staged for them in June at the Alten Grabow army training ground.[67] Clearly the content of his early photographs indicate he never made it to the actual trenches at the front lines during these first trips to photograph and film the German Army at locations controlled by the military.

It was only a very short while after his first military filming trips before Durborough donned his press uniform again on 19 June 1915. This time he joined a group of other American press correspondents waiting at the Adlon Hotel to leave for the front. It was important enough for Ries to document the event in both film and photo.[68]

Edwin F. Weigle

Back in Germany, Weigle had as much trouble getting out of Berlin to photograph the war as he did on his first trip. Like Dawson, he spent his time photographing around Berlin, mostly describing the high morale of its citizens, the ample foodstuffs and ample materiel that Germany claimed it still possessed in spite of the British blockade. It was not until Weigle repeated his idea that he had used with the Belgians that he had any success. He approached the Austro-Hungarians, and suggested that if the Austro-Hungarian government would give him passports to the front, he would agree to give half the proceeds of his film to the Austro-German Crippled Soldiers' Fund. Austro-Hungarian Field Marshal von Schleyer agreed, and on 6 May Weigle got his passports for the front. It might be mentioned here that this was only four days after the opening of the Gorlice-Tarnow Offensive, which probably had a lot to

Fig. 52. American reporters at the Adlon Hotel, June 1915.
From left to right: Cyril Brown (New York Times), T.K. Meloy (Chicago Daily News), H.J. Reilly
(Chicago Tribune), Oswald Schuette (Chicago Daily News), Wilbur H. Durborough (NEA),
Dr. Lewis H. Marks, S.B. Conger (Associated Press), S.M. Bouton (Associated Press),
Carl Ackerman (United Press), Karl H. von Wiegand (New York World).
The same scene was also filmed by Irving Guy Ries and appeared in Durborough's war film.
[Photo courtesy of Richard Francis Schuette. Identifications from Editor & Publisher, 24 July 1915.]

do with the timing. Later, the Austro-Hungarians gave Weigle further warm cooperation on this trip. A report from the Kriegspressequartier describes how Weigle was escorted by Captain Gschliesser who joined him when he headed for Galicia. He also assisted Weigle for one month when he filmed in Italy at Lavarone, Folgara and the Ortler area. Under Captain Gschliesser's close supervision, Weigle's film was censored and cleared for exhibition. From the archives in Vienna, the Viennese also gave him additional footage of siege guns in action, the mobilization at the outbreak of the war and even some pictures of the Kaiser Wilhelm, probably the ones with the Kaiser in Vienna in Austrian uniform later shown in his films.[69] It might be noted that this is just what the Germans had done with Wallace, and which de Beaufort tried to make a scandal.

Weigle went to the western front, and on 6 May Weigle arrived in Charleville, Kaiser Wilhelm's Imperial Headquarters. That night a French aviator bombed the Kaiser's headquarters, and Weigle reported that the Germans later dropped 500 shells on Rheims in retaliation. Weigle also visited the 1870 battlefield of Sedan where he met his fellow *Tribune* correspondent James O'Donnell Bennett. They and a group of other newspapermen were given an excellent dinner with printed menus while sitting in the German trenches with the French positions only a few hundred feet away. On 8 May Weigle went to St. Quentin, then to Péronne. In his book, he mentions the white, chalky stone and the extremely complex series of fortifications that the

159

Germans were able to construct in it. In fact Weigle was at the Somme, which was then a very quiet sector (probably why the Germans took him there), but which on 1 July 1916 was destined to become the site of one of the bloodiest campaigns in the war, partly because of those murderous German fortifications.[70]

Weigle was with the Austrians at Przemysl, of which we shall write later, but on 23 May 1915, Italy declared war on Austria-Hungary. Weigle left Vienna for the Trentino on 13 June, so he was present in the opening rounds between the Austrians and Italians in the South Tyrol. He visited Lake Garda, which a few weeks before had been a major tourist attraction for visitors from all over the world. Now Weigle could not find any sign of life. He traveled through the Tyrolean Alps and witnessed the heavy artillery rearranging the landscape.

Weigle returned to Vienna and showed his film to the censor, who passed it, and gave Weigle a passport. It must have been some passport because when he reached Warnemünde, an exit point from Germany which was very strict, the authorities never even asked him to open his suitcase. From Germany, Weigle went to Copenhagen and sailed for New York on the *Frederik VIII*. He arrived in New York on 3 August 1915, exactly one year from the date he arrived at the war zone.[71]

In Chicago, his film *The German Side of the War* opened on 28 August 1915 and was shown both at the Studebaker Theater and at the Bismarck Gardens, a comfortable old German beer garden in the Lakeview district of the city. The best short description of Weigle's trip and the film is one that was written by Weigle himself in a theater program made for the showing. It describes the contents of the film (much of the prose seems to be directly from the intertitles), and also demonstrates Weigle's pro-German stance.[72]

Weigle showed *The German Side of the War* at the Forty-Fourth Street Theater in New York in September of 1915, where it sold out every performance. Weigle lectured between showings. Because the billboards suggested that this show would be a one-day only presentation, more than 5,000 people gathered before 11 a.m. on 20 September, the first performance. According to the *New York Times*, mainly German-Americans had assembled to see this film. Scalpers started selling fake tickets to the people in line, many of whom could not speak much English, and extra policeman were called in to keep order. The lines at times reached all the way from the theater to Broadway. Weigle's film resulted in a record number of visitors for the Forty-Fourth Street theater: 8,555 persons on a single day. That first day only the film was shown in eight runs. Receipts were $14, 972.00.[73] During its first run in New York, *The German Side of the War* generated $32,000. Sales of distribution rights brought in an extra $56,000. The reason for this substantial financial spinoff was, according to *Variety*, the *Chicago Tribune*'s intensive publicity campaign. A correspondent for *Variety* noted: "Exchange advertising between the *Chicago Tribune* and the New York papers gave the pictures a tremendous quantity of publicity. It is said the *Tribune* is particularly satisfied with the advertising it is securing; which allows

Fig. 53. Theater program for The German Side of the War *(1915).*
[Private collection Cooper C. Graham.]

F. Ziegfeld Jr. who has the war film under his direction for New York, a large margin of profits on the return."[74]

Despite its commercial success, *Variety* and the *New York Times* remained critical of the film. Not even a complete battalion of German troopers would have outdone the wild applause given to the pictures of the Kaiser, wrote the *Times* reviewer. *Variety* also noted the pro-German message, but took a more professional approach to the movie. "These war pictures are no more, no nearer 'war scenes' than any of the others that have preceded."[75] The trade paper drew attention to scenes that had apparently been reconstructed for the camera. According to the reviewer, in one scene German

161

Fig. 54. Advertisement The German Side of the War (Second Series), reproduced from Chicago Tribune, 23 July 1916.

soldiers were seen hiding from an air attack. Since the action took place in a dense forest, the pilot could have not seen them anyway; therefore it could only mean that the scene was a fake. As a movie, according to *Variety*, *The German Side of the War* was not much more than a standard newsreel. The reason that it was a hit was because it cashed in on the interest of so many German-Americans in and around Chicago in seeing their fatherland in action.

Weigle sailed in November 1915 to return to the fighting. Patterson wrote two letters of recommendation for him along with a check for $20,000.00 for the blind and crippled soldiers' fund of the Austro-Hungarian Empire, and said the *Tribune* would be able make further payments in the near future. One letter was to General Max Ritter von Hoen, head of the *Kriegspressequartier* in Teschen, Austria, the other to an unknown person whom Patterson addressed as "Your Excellency".[76] On the western front, Weigle was stationed with Prince Rupprecht's Bavarians in the Sixth Army Corps in France, where he was based in Lille. Weigle said that in the Fromelles region, he witnessed and photographed the demolition of French positions, where the Germans had been mining and had buried tons of high explosive under the French trenches for weeks. The explosion, which filled the sky with clumps of earth and body parts, left a hole thirty or forty feet deep, and Weigle had no idea how many French soldiers died: "It is not a pretty thing to see a 300 yard trench full of soldiers blown up by a mine. At the moment of course you are busy with your moving picture camera, for the chance to take such a picture does not come often. But afterwards you get to thinking about it."[77] About seventy-five surviving French came running in terror to give themselves up. The Germans allowed Weigle to keep the film of the surrendering French, but confiscated the rest of the film, telling Weigle that he could have it after the war was over. Possibly some of Weigle's footage is in the Bundesarchiv in Berlin. Weigle was in the German trenches on Christmas Eve, 1915, in a cathedral tower at Laon. He also photographed at Douai, Lens, Messines and Fromelles, so he apparently was in the Artois region, somewhat north of the Somme and south of Ypres. Although he was on the western front at the right time, he did not apparently witness any of the battle of Verdun. After Lille and the western front came a trip to Russia and the trenches near Riga. Here he saw the Russian attacks, many of them without any preliminary artillery fire and some of the charging men actually without rifles.[78] To get his war footage back to America, Weigle got 1,000 feet of scrap film to produce when the British authorities searched him, which sure enough, they confiscated. Weigle had hidden his real war film on the *Bergensfjord*, upon which he set sail and returned to the United States on 16 June 1916.

According to the advertising for the moving picture, *The German Side of the War* (Second Series) contained: anti-aircraft artillery firing on an airplane; the famous wooden statue of Hindenburg in Berlin, into which one could drive nails of gold, silver and iron, the fees being turned over to the Red Cross; a cavalry charge on a Russian village, probably the one described above; first aid hospitals at the front; the Kaiser in Austrian uniform in Vienna; an advance under smoke bombs; the hurling of hand grenades; the German training camp at Frankfurt am Main; ruined cities in France; and the firing of a 30.5 centimeter gun in action.[79] The film settled in for an extended run at the Colonial Theatre in Chicago, and Weigle once again lectured between showings as well as worked in the projection booth. This was the close of Weigle's career as a war correspondent; soon he would join the U.S. Signal Corps.

Notes

Albert K. Dawson

1. Apart from filming the western front in January 1915, Theyer also shot film for Germany's foreign propaganda agency, the ZfA. He accompanied a group of neutral correspondents who visited the Leipziger Messe in March 1915. His film about this renowned German fair presumably was meant to show that Germany's economy was still going strong.

2. Hans Theyer, "Erinnerungen eines Kameramannes", *Mein Film*, no. 168 (1929): 10. All quotes by Theyer are translated from German. Hereafter given as Hans Theyer.

3. Robert Dunn, *Five Fronts. On The Firing-Lines with English-French, Austrian, German and Russian Troops* (New York: Dodd, Mead and Company 1915), 163–172. Also present among these American war correspondents was John Reed, the famous writer of *Ten Days that Shook the World*, who later reported on the Russian Revolution and wrote a brief account on this trench tour together with Dawson and Theyer to the western front in the March 1915 issue of *The Masses*.

4. Hans Theyer: 10.

5. Ibid.

6. "War Heroes of the Camera", *Indianapolis Star* (27 January 1918): SM6.

7. "Dawson Meets another American Correspondent at Brussels", Tape IW014 at the John E. Allen Film Archives in Park Ridge. This scene is particularly interesting because it shows Dawson wearing an arm band with a "P" for photographer, indicating he was an accredited cameraman. The footage appears to have been presented under the auspices of the German *Hilfsverein für Deutsche Frauen*.

8. Francis Arnold Collins, *The Camera Man: His Adventures in Many Fields* (New York: The Century Company 1919, reprint 2010), 24–25.

9. "German War-Professors", *Literary Digest* (10 April 1915): 806.

10. Albert K. Dawson, "Economic Conditions in Germany", *Scientific American* (3 February 1917): 136.

11. *New York Times*. Picture Section (8 August 1915): 1. The photograph was copyrighted by the International Press Exchange. This photographic agency was directed by Matthew B. Claussen from about October 1915.

12. Albert K. Dawson, "Military Engineering, *Scientific American* (26 May 1917): 525.

13. Sigmund Henschen, "Taking Moving Pictures At The Front", *Omaha World Herald* (16 January 1916): 11–12.

14. Schumacher to ReichsMarineAmt (RMA), v. 20 October 1915 BA/MA RM3/v 9901, cited in Barkhausen, 24–25.

15. Bundesarchiv, R901/7265. ZfA, File America, 1915–1917. Memorandum by Matthew B. Claussen, no date given but probably written in February 1915.

16. NARA, case file Claussen. Interview by agent Benham, 2 March 1917. "Sanders" probably was Albert Sander, editor for *Deutsches Journal*. In 1916, he set up the Central Powers Films Exchange, Inc. Although the company imported a few war films it was mainly a blind for the recruitment of spies working for Germany. Sander was found guilty and convicted in 1917. In 1933, he became foreign press chief for the Nazi Reich Film Chamber.

17. Bundesarchiv, R901/72391. ZfA. File Albert K. Dawson. Finances for Dawson's photographic work appear to have been advanced by the ZfA until 28 May 1915. The Dawson file also shows that Ambassador von Bernstorff was well aware of the financial set up of the American Correspondent Film Company.

18. Bundesarchiv, R901/7265. ZfA. File America, 1915–1917. Letter Thiel to Fuehr, 27 May 1915.

19. Felix Malitz, "System, the Secret of Success", synopsis. Courtesy of the Library of Congress. See also *Motography* (11 September 1915): 516.

20. "Local Boy in Germany",*Vincennes Commercial* (16 December 1915): 5.

21. Hans Barkhausen, *Filmpropaganda für Deutschland* (Hildesheim, Zurich, New York: Olms Presse 1982) 24; see also Ulrike Oppelt, 100–108.

22. Ibid., 24.

23. Albert K. Dawson, "In Deutscher Kriegsgefangenschaft", *Berliner Illustrierte Zeitung* (2 May 1915): 235. Quote translated from German. Dawson also reported in this German newspaper on POW camps at Heidelberg and Ohrdruf. His pictures show scenes of special facilities such as a library, the camp dentist and even a tennis court for the British. See also Gerhard Hopp's book *Muslime in der Mark* (Berlin: Das Arabische Buch 1997) on the Zossen propaganda camp. Dawson's report on the German POW camps was also printed in the *Vincennes Commercial*, 28 November 1915.

24. Bundesarchiv, R901/72651. ZfA. File America, 1915–1917. Notiz über die Zulassung Amerikanische Photographen, 12 July 1915.

25. Bundesarchiv, R901/72651. ZfA. File America, 1915–1917. Letter Thiel to Fuehr, 19 July 1915.

26. "Claussen Explains", *New York Sun* (17 August 1915): 3.

27. *Battle of Przemysl* (Advertisement), *Billboard* (28 August 1915): 47.

28. Bundesarchiv, R901/72651. ZfA. File America, 1915–1917. Letter Fuehr to Thiel, 10 August 1915.

29. NARA, case file Dawson, telegram Felix Malitz, dated 29 September 1915. The FBI file on Dawson shows that at this stage of the war, despite the fact that America was still neutral, the Naval Intelligence Division was already monitoring wireless messages between Germany and the USA.

30. BBC *The Great War* (1964), episode 7 "We Await the Heavenly Manna", has two shots from *Battles of a Nation*: the 30.5 Skoda mortars in action and "the Solitary Sentinel", a guard patrolling what appears to be the ruined forts of Przemysl.

31. Review, *Battles of a Nation, Variety* (26 November 1915): 24.

32. U.S. Congress, Senate, *Investigation into Brewing and Liquor Interests and German Propaganda*, Vol. 2. (Washington, D.C/Government Printing Office 1919), 1438.

33. "Film Flashes", *Variety* (10 December 1915): 20.

34. "Detectives Storm Theatre in War over War Movies", *Chicago Tribune* (7 December 1915): 1. See also: "Enter Theatre by Fire Escape to Show Film", *Chicago Tribune* (5 December 1915): 5.

35. Synopsis *The Fighting Germans* (Mutual Film Corporation, 1916). Courtesy, Library of Congress. This film was a revamp of *The Warring Millions* and released in May 1916.

36. "Flickerings from Film Land", *Chicago Tribune* (4 December 1915): 19.

37. "The Glories of War, Its Horrors and Many Vicissitudes Viewed", *Buffalo Evening Times* (18 December 1915): 4.

38. "From Film to Smuggling", *Kansas City Star* (31 January 1919): 3. The writer of this remarkable inside story is

well-informed. He may have got his facts from Claussen who was an informant for the Justice Department after America entered the war in April 1917.

39. Bundesarchiv, R901/72651. ZfA. File America, 1915–1917. Letter Fuehr to Freiherr Mumm von Schwarzenstein, 3 December 1915.

40. Austrian State Archives. Archives *k.u.k. Kriegspressequartier*, 1914–1918. Record group no. 28 KPQ members. Record file Albert K. Dawson.

41. Horace Green, "A Trip through Rumania", *El Paso Herald*, Magazine Section (29 January 1916).

42. "Mr. Dawson's Travels in Balkans Campaign", *Stamford Daily Advocate* (24 March 1916): 1–2. Dawson apparently embellished his account on his stay in Belgrade. The city had been taken on 9 October 1915. At this stage he was still in Vienna. When he finally entered the city, the campaign against the Serbs had already moved towards the south. He also didn't mention that he had been deported from the country by the Austrians.

Wilbur H. Durborough

43. *Editor & Publisher* (16 October 1915): 470.

44. DDM1, Sec. 33, 4.

45. *Editor & Publisher* (19 February 1916): 1124.

46. Ibid., Sec. 23, 1.

47. Ibid., Sec. 33, 4.

48. Marston was employed at the *Chicago Record-Herald* as the Cable and Telegraph Editor during WWI when he joined the Syndicate. Before the war ended he would join the *Chicago Daily News* and became its Make-up Editor and Assistant Foreign Editor.

49. Graham, "The Kaiser and the Cameraman", *Film History*, Vol. 22, No.1 (2010): 36–37.

50. *Waterloo* [IA] *Times-Tribune* (20 June 1916): 4.

51. The car was bought by Durborough. It's not clear if the NEA agreed to fund this purchase as part of his basic photography contract or the Syndicate funded it as part of his independent film project. See NARA Bureau of Investigation report by Chas. P. Tighe dated 23 September 1915. However, the car only had "Newspaper Enterprise Association" painted on the back spare tire case and during his very early Durborough research the author found a short online newspaper article from the 1930s announcing the historic car used by Durborough in Germany being stored in a suburban Cleveland barn was going to be sold at auction which might indicate it most likely was funded and owned by the NEA. Author Castellan regrets not being able to relocate this article.

52. NARA Bureau of Investigation report by Chas. P. Tighe dated 22 September 1915.

53. DDM1, Sec. 28, p. 4; *New York Times* (24 March 1915): 17.

54. "Great Shoe Famine Pinching Germany", *Chicago Daily News* (1 April 1918).

55. AAPA, Wilbur Henry Durborough, letters of 8 April 1915, A12351; 15 April 1915, 13145.

56. As early as 1900 Lawson noted the Chicago readers who were natives or their descendants of continental countries like Germany, who constituted a large market segment, wanted "an accurate, if not sympathetic, presentation of the news from 'the fatherland'". See Charles H. Dennis, *Victor Lawson, His Time and His Work* (New York: Greenwood Press, 1935), 266–267.

57. Raymond Swing, *Good Evening! A Professional Memoir* (Harcourt, Brace & World, New York, 1964), p. 61.

58. *Chicago Daily News* (21/23 May 1915).

59. Jason Rogers, *Newspaper Building* (New York and London: Harper & Brothers, 1918), 152. It quotes *Chicago Daily News* publisher Victor F. Lawson on meeting with Jane Addams upon her return from Europe. While U.S. Ambassador Gerard claims credit for arranging this meeting on pages 412–413 in his book *My Four Year in Germany*, his perfunctory cover letter to von Jagow merely forwarded "without comment" Louis P. Lochner's letter requesting the meeting with no support or endorsement. See also NARA Record Group AFI Collection, 200.496, Durborough War Film, Reel 1, which features Durborough with Jane Addams, Dr. Alice Hamilton and Dr. Aletta Jacobs in front of the Brandenburg Gate. This short film scene is possibly the only film of Jacobs and the only film of Addams during her prime.

60. William G. Chrystal. "'A Master of His Craft': The Film Career of Walter Niebuhr", *Niebuhr Studies* (Empire for LLC, 2002), 119–145.

61. *Muskegon Chronicle* (24 June 1915): 6.

62. *Reno Evening Gazette* (28 June 1915): 2.

63. *Muskegon Chronicle* (24 June 1915): 6.

64. *Muskegon Chronicle* (17 July 1915): 1.

65. *Kalamazoo Gazette* (29 June 1915): 1; *Muskegon Chronicle* (3 July 1915): 7.

66. *Daily Illinois State Journal* (17 July 1915): 1.

67. Document 06518 dated 12 July 1915 of the ZfA provides insight to German Army bureaucracy required for filming at just the training grounds. It notes the various army approvals for American photographers Durborough and his cameraman Ries as well as Weigle (and the lack of approval for Albert Dawson and his cameraman Everets). On 23 April 1915 the Corps of Guard gave "consent in principle" for access to Döberitz with the War Ministry agreeing on 5 May that Döberitz, Alten Grabow, and three other army training grounds were "suitable". By 19 May Durborough, Ries and Weigle had the approval of the local commander at Alten Grabow and the Foreign Ministry to view "troops in battle" and been provided the credentials needed for filming at Alten Grabow. Only on 25 May did the Foreign Ministry agree to notify Alten Grabow to begin the actual process to schedule their visit which probably did not occur until sometime in June.

68. This was almost certainly WHD's first trip to a front. The journalists visited four days in the area of the Champagne trenches in France based on Schuette's filed dispatches. WHD probably traveled separately accompanied by his escorting officer in the Stutz somewhere in the same general area.

Edwin F. Weigle

69. "Written on the Screen", *New York Times* (26 September 1915), Section VI, 4.

70. On the Somme's general terrain and the Germans' use of it, see also C. R. M. F. Crutwell, *A History of the Great War 1914–1918* (Chicago: Academy Publishers, 2007; first published, 1934), 257.

71. Weigle also told the Secret Service that he sailed from Denmark back to the U. S. to get his film into the theaters before his competitor, Durborough. Graham, "The Kaiser and the Cameraman", 34.

72. *The German Side of the War*, Theater Program. Author Graham's private collection.

73. "Sell Soda Checks as Theatre Tickets: Speculators Swindle Aliens at Movie Exhibition of 'German Side of the War'", *New York Times* (21 September 1915): 11; Ramsaye, 686.

74. *Variety* (24 September 1915): 17.

75. "Germany on the Screen", *New York Times* (21 September 1915): 11; "The German Side of the War", *Variety* (8 October 1915).

76. Joseph Medill Patterson to General Max Hoehn [sic], 22 November 1915; Joseph Medill Patterson to unknown, 22 November 1915, Joseph Medill Patterson Collection, Donnelley Library, Lake Forest, Illinois.

77. "War Movie Man, Edwin F. Weigle, Has New Film", *Chicago Daily Tribune* (21 June 1916).

78. *Chicago Daily Tribune* (21 June 1916): 17.

79. *Chicago Daily Tribune* (26 July 1916): 2. As previously suggested, some of this film may have come from the film archives in Vienna.

Chapter 6

Filming the Central Powers' Drive across Russian Poland

I t is difficult to impress a twenty-first century audience, especially a western one, with the importance of the siege and capture of Przemysl in Poland. Even at the time in 1915, the British and the Austro-Hungarians made fun of its name. Mary Roberts Rinehart said about the fortress: "Before I went abroad I had two ambitions among others. One was to be able to pronounce Ypres; the other was to bring home and exhibit to my admiring friends the pronunciation of Przemysl. To a moderate extent I have succeeded with the first. I have discovered that the second one must be born to."[1]

The campaigns around Przemysl in 1914–1915 have given it the apt description of "The Stalingrad of World War I". Przemysl was the center of the Austro-Hungarian defense system in Poland, protecting the crossings between the marshes of the San – Dniester River line, and so protected Hungary.[2]

World War I started when the Austro-Hungarian Empire declared war on Serbia on 28 July 1914. Austria-Hungary's reluctance to declare war on Russia can be judged by the Austrians' delaying the declaration of war until 6 August, and then only under extreme German pressure. The Central Powers now had a choice. Conrad von Hötzendorff, the not very competent Austro-Hungarian head of the armed forces, first wanted to fight Serbia, and then deal with Russia later. (It was said that Conrad could only stay mad at one country at a time). Germany, threatened by the Russian Army in East Prussia, wanted Austria to concentrate on Russia and deal with the Serbians later. They also made the not insignificant point that the Serbian campaign could be kept on hold, but the far more imposing Russian Army, which had mobilized much faster than it was thought possible, could not. So from the very beginning of the World War, the Austro-Hungarians were already fighting a war on two fronts and at odds with their partner, Germany.

Conrad promised Helmuth von Moltke, Chief of the German Staff, that he would

Fig. 55. William Heath Robinson's cartoon, "The Fall of Przemysl". The press responds to the spate of Przemysl films. Published in Puck, *14 August 1915. [Library of Congress, Swann Collection.]*

make war against the Russians before taking on the Serbians. The same promise was repeated by Emperor Franz-Josef in writing to the Kaiser. But Conrad, who had advised an aggressive war against the Serbians at least 25 times in 1913 alone, ineptly tried to sneak in a campaign against the Serbians in spite of his promises. Conrad actually sent the entire Second Army to Serbia but then had to recall his troops on their trains in transit there to divert them towards Galicia. This naturally caused a complete communications and supply shambles. The Second Army was not reassembled in time for the beginning of either the first Serbian or Galician campaigns. The Austro-Hungarians were not off to a good start and the situation would worsen. In 1914 the Russians had swept across most of Galicia, much to the rage of their German allies. The Austrians and Germans counterattacked, but in October 1914 superior Russian troops forced their withdrawal across the San.

Przemysl, the fortress on the San, remained in Austro-Hungarian hands, but the Russians laid siege from January 1915 for four months. Conrad von Hötzendorff, the Austrian Chief of Staff, made a series of disastrous attempts to reinforce Przemysl from the Carpathian Mountains, some sixty miles to the southwest. When the Austro-Hungarian troops finally started for Galicia and the Carpathians, completely unequipped for such a campaign, it was the beginning of a terrible winter. This bloody struggle in the winter of 1915 became known as the Carpathian campaign. It bled Austria-Hungary white and destroyed the morale of the Austrian army. In three attempts the Austro-Hungarians never managed to break through to Przemysl. Meanwhile both the Austrian army and the civilians in Przemysl were equally unprepared for a winter campaign and siege and began to starve. With no food, fuel or medicine, in the grip of a terrible winter, the outcome of the siege was certain; on 22 March 1915 the city and garrison surrendered to the Russians. Austria-Hungary lost 800,000 troops, six times the number of the garrison troops at Przemysl that they had set out to free.[3] This was probably the time that an anonymous German general exclaimed that the Germans were chained to a corpse.

This was a terrible blow to the country's prestige. Emperor Franz-Josef wept when he heard that Przemysl had fallen. The Austrians were determined to get it back, although with the Russians already at the foothills of the Carpathians, one could question the value of recapturing the fortress on the San. Nevertheless Przemysl was as important to the Austrians as Verdun would be to the French a year later, although the casualties at Przemysl were actually higher than at Verdun or the Somme.

The Gorlice-Tarnow Offensive and the attack from East Prussia

After the disastrous winter campaign in the Carpathians in 1915, Germany saw that something had to be done to help the Austro-Hungarians. Otherwise there was a strong chance that the Russians would break through the Carpathians and enter on to the Hungarian plain. The overall German commander and head of the *Oberste Heeresleitung* (OHL), General Erich von Falkenhayn, who had his eastern headquarters at Pless, decided on a joint attack to relieve the Russian pressure on the Austro-Hungarian front in the Carpathians. On 2 May 1915 a combined German and Austro-Hungarian force under the command of August von Mackensen began the Gorlice-Tarnow offensive to drive the Russians out of Poland. At the same time on the northern front, Generals Ludendorff and von Hindenburg were commencing a massive drive against Warsaw and the fortress Novo Georgievsk. The two movements were not designed to be pincers, but under the enormous pressure of the Ninth German army in the north and von Mackensen's Austrian-German forces in the south, it was felt that the Russian Army would be driven out of Poland.

Both attacks were a pronounced success.

Once the breakthrough at Gorlice and Tarnow had achieved all its objectives, Headquarters in Pless decided on 12 May that von Mackensen and the Eleventh German Army would drive northeast to establish bridgeheads on the San River somewhat north of Przemysl and the Austrian Third Army would attack the city itself.

It was now very clear that with the extremely effective German leadership, the good weather, and especially the massive artillery, the Central Powers would soon achieve their greatest victory on the eastern front. They were eager to send neutral film correspondents to cover it and reap the propaganda value.

This chapter will deal with photographers Wilbur Henry Durborough, Frank E. Kleinschmidt, Edwin F. Weigle and Albert K. Dawson, all of whom filmed in Germany and/or Austria, and who were filming in Russian Poland in 1915 during the summer offensive, Durborough with the northern forces, the others with von Mackensen's forces at Gorlice and Tarnow. A.E. Wallace and Nelson Edwards both missed this offensive because of timing; Wallace was in Germany too early and Edwards was too late. Most of the other cameramen got their big chance to get out of Berlin and shoot film at the front because of these events on the eastern front in the summer of 1915. The declaration of war by Italy against Austria on 23 May 1915 would give Weigle and Kleinschmidt further opportunities to shoot film for the Austrians.

The overall command was in the capable hands of German General August von Mackensen. The Germans and Austrians, bolstered by total air superiority, excellent telephone communications, as well as the most effective artillery on the eastern front would simply overwhelm the Russians. The breakthrough was to originate where the Dunajec river cuts through the mountains, one of the few passes where the terrain to the east, while hilly, was not very mountainous. Moreover, this area had always been quiet and reports indicated that General Radko-Dmietrieff, head of the Russian Third Army, had removed many of his forces to support his assaults in the Carpathians. [4] Yet for four months the Russians had been quietly fortifying positions, most 400–500 meters high in those hills, which would prove to be murderous to the Germans and the Austrians. And contrary to earlier reports, the Russians had not withdrawn their forces.

So the recapture of Przemysl was far from easy. The Austrian Third and Fourth Armies had problems recapturing the city, requiring the German Eleventh Army to swing to its right and attack Przemysl from the north. The German artillery was particularly effective, inflicting massive destruction of Przemysl's defenses; Forts X and XI, reduced to empty ruined shells, would be extensively photographed by the cinematographers. By the time Przemysl fell to the Central Powers on 3 June 1915, there was very little left of the original Austro-Hungarian defenses.

It was a great victory. Von Mackensen reported to Franz-Josef that he laid Przemysl at the Emperor's feet, which somewhat irritated the Austro-Hungarians because it implied the capture of Przemysl was due to the Germans alone. The Emperor and Kaiser Wilhelm were pleased to send medals to all the major commanders.[5] The recapture of Przemysl was important to the Central Powers as the stepping stone that would ultimately lead to the conquest of the Polish salient. By the end of the summer the Russian army was in full retreat in the province of Galicia and had evacuated most of Poland.

Frank E. Kleinschmidt

Frank E. Kleinschmidt was born on 28 September 1871 in Alt Rüdnitz, Germany. He was one of many who emigrated when economic conditions worsened in Brandenburg at the end of the 19th century. He helped train and fought with the army in Chile, then left to join his large family who had already left Germany for America. But Kleinschmidt was not the type to settle; he was an adventurer. After traveling around the world as a sailor, he went to the Klondike in 1897 to prospect for gold. He fell in love with the Arctic, moved there in the early part of the century, then married and raised a family in Alaska. Kleinschmidt got deeply involved in polar exploration and collecting bears, walruses and birds. He made one film for the Andrew Carnegie Foundation and several other very famous films on the Arctic. Of all the cameramen mentioned in this book he and Merl la Voy were the only real explorers.

On 18 July 1914 together with his wife and children Kleinschmidt left America from the port of New York and arrived in Hamburg on 25 July. While he was crossing the Atlantic, political tension was building rapidly due to the assassination of the Austrian Crown Prince Franz Ferdinand at Sarajevo. Within a week of his arrival, Europe was at war. Kleinschmidt, who had planned a holiday in Europe while promoting his films, now found himself stranded in Berlin. On 2 August when war had just been declared, he applied for an emergency passport at the Embassy of the United States to get his family safely out of Germany. The family embarked on the SS *Rotterdam* and returned to America on 7 September; the next month Kleinschmidt applied for a new passport and sailed back to Germany with plans to stay for a year.

Accredited with letters from the *New York Evening Post* and the *New York American*, Kleinschmidt upon returning to Berlin sought permission from the General Staff to accompany the German army. Although his latest film on the Arctic was then being shown in Germany, his request was turned down like so many others. At the beginning of 1915, Kleinschmidt finally found the magic key to help him gain access to the front when he was invited by Crown Prince Karl at the Austrian Military Headquarters to lecture on his Arctic films before the Commander in Chief Archduke

Fig. 56. Big game hunter, explorer and cinematographer Frank E. Kleinschmidt. Alaska, c. 1905.
[Courtesy Ruth Sarrett.]

Frederick and his staff. According to Kleinschmidt, this presentation was such a resounding success that he was given some extraordinary privileges, such as the use of a car and the assistance of a driver, two military servants and a guide. More important, he said these privileges enabled him to stay at the front permanently for one and a half years with complete freedom to cover the war. As already noted previously in Chapter 1, the Austrian approach to correspondents was generous, intelligent and sensitive.

Research by the authors on Kleinschmidt's files from the k.u.k. Kriegspressequartier at Vienna has shown that Kleinschmidt was attached to the Austrian army as an official cinematographer for almost one year. He was with the Austrians from February till December 1915, far longer than most correspondents were allowed to stay at the front. In compliance with regulations, his permits to visit the front had an expiration deadline. He was usually accompanied by one soldier who assisted him with his camera work. As will be described in more detail, Kleinschmidt was under military surveillance. What made him unique was that he was the only official cinematographer from a neutral country who stayed with the Austro-Hungarian army for such a long duration. This allowed him to see the war on three different fronts.

Kleinschmidt's first recorded trip to the front was on 4 March 1915, when he travelled from Vienna to Cracow, a city that was a major target for the Russian army in the opening months of the war. By December 1914, the frontline had stabilized on the line of the rivers Dunajec and Biala, some twenty miles to the east of Cracow. Behind the lines, Kleinschmidt described his experiences in a letter to a friend in New York. He mentioned he had been in a plane flying over the frontline and was hoping to get permission to film the beleaguered forts of Przemysl from above. As there are no such scenes in his film *War on Three Fronts*, Kleinschmidt was probably too late to capture this event. The Austrian garrison of Przemysl finally surrendered to the Russians on 22 March as previously mentioned.

Kleinschmidt returned to the fighting in April 1915 just in time to film the most stunning victory of Austro-Hungary and Germany over Russia: the Gorlice-Tarnow Offensive.

The chief of staff of the German Army, Erich von Falkenhayn, firmly believed that the war would be decided on the western front, not in the east, and had little patience with the Austro-Hungarians. Nevertheless, in order to relieve pressure on them and also to protect the flank of the forces of von Hindenburg and Ludendorff which were attacking east in the general direction of Warsaw further to the north, he ordered that a strong force consisting of the German Eleventh Army and the Austrian Fourth Army break out of the Carpathians between the towns of Gorlice and Tarnow and head east, and when they had gotten behind the Russian salient in Galicia, head northeast and roll the Russian forces up.

Most but not all of his film *War on Three Fronts* is lost. But we are extremely fortunate in having a detailed description of the film and its contents in the form of a lecture, probably written by Kleinschmidt that was to accompany the showing of the film which was copyrighted in 1916.[6] The film evidently was shortened and shown quite differently when Louis J. Selznick controlled it in 1917. A far different sound version of the footage was re-rereleased in the 1930s. However, since this lecture is by far the most complete version that has been found, it will be used as the outline of the original film. Note the film and the accompanying lecture do not follow the strict chronology of the campaigns.

The first front: the Gorlice-Tarnow Offensive in Galicia

In the opening scenes of *War on Three Fronts* of reel 1, we see a close up of Kleinschmidt being introduced to Viktor Graf Dankl von Krasnik. The film depicts Kleinschmidt presenting his military credentials and proudly saluting the command-ing general of the First Austrian Army. However, he apparently spent most of the next week or so with the Austro-Hungarian Fourth Army, led by Archduke Josef Ferdinand, which, along with Mackensen's Eleventh Army, spearheaded the drive against the Russians. This appears to fit the official histories, as most of the battles Kleinschmidt mentions were very near Tarnow where the Fourth Army attacked. The Fourth Army was made up of the IX Corps under the command of Rudolf Kralicek and XIV Corps under the command of Paul Roth. It also included the four

Only Pictures Ever Made of the Dreaded U-Boats in Action.

Airplanes Surrounded by Bursting Shrapnell.

Fig. 57. The infantry engagement at the "Duck's Bill" trench. Brochure Carnegie Hall exhibition War on Three Fronts, *February 1917. [Courtesy Ruth Sarrett.]*

regiments of the Tyrolean Kaiserjäger (Imperial Chasseurs), and the 59 Infantry Division.

War on Three Fronts starts with the breakthrough at Gorlice and Tarnow on 2–5 May. Kleinschmidt ascends in an observation balloon from the hill known in German as *der Wal*, and is able to get shots eastward, probably with an air-compressed Aeroscope camera, of the Dunajec looking toward the positions at Hill 419 and other Russian strong points, already under artillery attack. As he mentions in a voice-over on his sound rerelease, Kleinschmidt's first impression of the destruction of the Great War was at the Dunajec near Tarnow. In his film Kleinschmidt showed how the Prussian Guard was transferred from the western front in only two days, how Austrian engineers built pontoons across the Dunajec in a matter of hours and how dentists and field kitchens followed the infantry – all presented as examples of Teutonic efficiency. The construction of pontoon bridges and the field kitchen footage still exists.

Even prior to the advance, Kleinschmidt recorded some outstanding action scenes. At one point his camera in the frontline trench pans across No Man's Land and clearly shows the Russian positions on an adjacent hill called the Sugar Loaf (Zuckerhut in German or Zuckerhütl in Austrian German, Glowa Cukru in Polish), located near Lichwin in Poland and part of the Tarnow Region.

For two weeks Kleinschmidt was in the trenches at a place nearby called "Duck's Bill". The Duck's Bill was a salient in the Austrian frontline which projected into the Russian position and was flanked on either side by the enemy. It may have been part of the Tuchow Salient, a bulge that projected into Russian lines at Tuchow on the

Biala River near Tarnow near the confluence of the Biala and Dunajec Rivers. The Russians were only eighty yards away and it was at this location that Kleinschmidt filmed a most striking scene mentioned in many film reviews. According to the movie description, Kleinschmidt was continually under fire. He had placed his camera in a communicating trench which drew the enemy's attention. "The next scene was taken an hour later from where the officer is now seen standing. Here you will see for the first time in moving picture history men actually being shot and dying within 20 feet of the camera. See here, for instance, in the back part of the trench, two men falling. Notice them back there! Here a soldier dies like a man, without a whimper and in silence. The Captain did not realize what kind of picture he was getting; he saw nothing of this, for his attention was riveted upon his camera."[7]

Until recently, all that remained from this remarkable scene was a frame enlargement showing a group of Austrian soldiers lined up in a trench and shooting at the enemy. On the foreground an officer is seen taking care of a wounded soldier. However research by the authors in the John E. Allen film archives found the actual footage. It is a most bizarre and eerie sequence. After a close up of a dead Austrian soldier lying on the bottom of a trench, the film shows a group of infantry men firing through a loophole in a steel plate. Expecting the enemy to go over the top, Kleinschmidt lifts the camera up but the top of the trench is so heavily riddled by bullets that he must take the camera down again. He apparently had just enough time to film a short scene of a dispatch dog running back with an urgent message from a squad of sharpshooters. The film then cuts to the inside of the Duck's Bill firing line showing a mortally wounded soldier. An officer tries to give him water but decides to pull his cap over his face – a clear sign he had just died. Meanwhile the firing continues with an Austrian infantry man getting hit within just eighteen feet of the camera. The way he falls to the bottom of the trench – like a broken doll with no theatrical gestures – is most impressive. The camera position and every detail of the filming indicate this probably is a genuine scene.[8]

Reel 2: the Dunajec front

Judging from the film lecture, Kleinschmidt was at the Dunajec front on 4 May 1915 when the 30.5 cm. Skoda mortars opened the barrage upon the Russian lines, the first time these fearsome weapons employed by the Germans at Liège were used against field fortifications. He also filmed the shelling of Tarnow, although he scrupulously mentions that he did not film the effects of this shelling in Tarnow until three weeks after the actual event. Tarnow was by all reports virtually destroyed by the German shelling.[9] He filmed the totally destroyed railroad station and the damage caused by a single hit on the Cloister of "Sacré Coeur" near Tarnow. An intertitle in the surviving footage explains: "A single shot timed to catch the Russian staff at dinner killed 130 staff officers. The shell tore its way through the roof, exploded inside and blew out a piece of the wall four feet thick." Apparently this shot was aimed to kill

Capt. F. E. Kleinschmidt
presents
"War on Three Fronts"
Controlled by Lewis J. Selznick.

Fig. 58. Austrian gunners firing the latest type of 15-centimetre artillery. D.W. Griffith used this scene for his film Hearts of the World *(1918). [Courtesy National Archives.]*

the Russian general during his lunch at the Cloister. "If the general had remained for another eighteen minutes, he wouldn't have survived."[10]

Reel 3: the second front, Serbia

By taking on Russia and Serbia at the same time at the beginning of the war and splitting its forces, Austria-Hungary's first campaign against Serbia had been as great a disaster as the Carpathian campaign. But in October of 1915, Bulgaria, predominately motivated by the wish to capture Serbian Macedonia but also impressed by the German-Austrian victory at Gorlice-Tarnow, entered the war on the side of the Central Powers. Meanwhile Turkey was worried about a Serbian attack on Constantinople and was only holding its own after recent defeats by the Russians in the Caucasus and the British in Mesopotamia in the war. The Germans themselves wanted to capture Serbia to reopen their tactically and diplomatically important Berlin-Baghdad railroad. So with Bulgarian, Turkish and German interests aligned, von Falkenhayn favored a renewed Serbian campaign soon after the conquest of Russian Poland. Military operations shifted to the Balkans giving Austria-Hungary the chance to settle accounts with its old enemy, Serbia.

Kleinschmidt was now attached to the newly formed Austrian Third Army, which was commanded by General Kövess. Together with the German Eleventh Army, the Central Powers closed in on Belgrade along a fifty mile front, this time attacking from the north. On 7 October troops crossed the rivers Danube and Sava west and east of the city. Once again Kleinschmidt appears to have been remarkably close to the offensive front line. Two days before the taking of Belgrade, he filmed the siege of the Serbian capital from an airplane. He captured scenes from about 3,000 feet over the Kalemagdan heights, the great stronghold of Belgrade: "The ground of the fortress looked to me like the face of the moon: crater upon crater made by the huge projectiles; houses with gaping holes in their roofs; magazines and big buildings with roofs blown away – all presented a grotesque appearance. Through the bottom of the aeroplane I pointed the lens of my cinematograph and took one of the most fascinating films in my life."[11] During the flight which took an hour and a half, the pilot had to change altitude several times to avoid giving gunners below the chance to determine their exact range.

Kleinschmidt also captured scenes of the War Island. From this island in the Danube, Austrian engineers built a pontoon bridge during the night, enabling the troops to storm Belgrade. On 9 October the first Austrian soldiers rushed into Belgrade. In a detailed report, Kleinschmidt described the assault: "A furious fight was waged in the streets of the city; barricades were erected and taken by storm, houses were burst open by the butts of guns, and bayonets clashed with bayonets in halls and rooms".[12] As a fitting illustration of the defeat of Serbia, Kleinschmidt filmed the interior of the Royal Palace of King Peter, whose throne was torn to shreds when a shell was dropped into the palace.

After the fall of Belgrade Kleinschmidt followed the advance south to Albania where the Serbian army was trying to find a safe haven. A report from the k.u.k. Kriegspressequartier indicates that he was in Eastern Herzegovina; he also spent some time near Cattaro on the Dalmatian Coast. Cattaro (Kotor) had been a bone of contention between the Austrians, the Serbians and Montenegrins since the first Balkan War. An important naval port controlling the Dalmatian coast, it was used as a harbor for submarines. It was probably from this port that Kleinschmidt filmed a rare scene of an Austrian submarine in action. The remaining footage of *War on Three Fronts* shows the submarine on its return, rising to the surface as filmed from a ship nearby. The intertitle noted it had just torpedoed and sunk a steamer.[13]

After the Aegean, Kleinschmidt returned to the Gorlice Tarnow area where he captured his strongest and most dramatic film. Thus the film dramatically returns to Russian Poland.

Bloodshed at Hill 419

The Eighth Infantry Division attacked in the following order of battle: the 4th k.u.k [königliche und kaiserliche] Regiment of the Tyrolean Kaiserjäger in the direction of Hill 419, towards Dunajec; the 3rd k.u.k. regiment of the Tyrolean *Kaiserjäger*

Capt. F. E. Kleinschmidt
presents
"War on Three Fronts"
Controlled by Lewis J. Selznick.

Fig. 59. Austrian submarine filmed by Kleinschmidt off the Dalmatian coast. Still War on Three Fronts.
[Courtesy National Archives.]

toward the horseshoe and Lubcza Szczepanowska; the 1st regiment of the k.u.k. *Kaiserjäger* as a reserve directed toward Hill 402; the k.u.k. Infantry Regiment no. 14 on the right.

Colonel Lercher attacked Hill 419 once again in the early morning hours of 3 May with three battalions of the k.u.k. 4th regiment of the Tyrolean *Kaiserjäger*. The sappers suffered heavy losses during the night attempting to open passages in the barbed wire. The attack was supported by three battalions and heavy artillery fire and machine gun units. In heavy defensive fire from the Russians the *Kaiserjäger* of the 8 infantry division remained pinned down in front of the shot-up barbed wire and were forced to dig in directly facing the Russian positions. An attack from the Brigade Reserve was also unsuccessful. In the area of "the Horseshoe" it was possible to fend off a Russian counterattack with machine gun fire and hand-to-hand combat. Simultaneously the Third Infantry Division was able to break into the area of the Wal, already deep into the Russian positions. The previously withdrawn Upper Austrian k.u.k. Infantry regiment no. 14 (Hessen) advanced from Hill 456 against the mountain hut 402 in order to support the Eighth Infantry Division in its breakthrough on its front and to make possible an ensuing attack in the direction of Rzuchowa. The Russians did not give way but counterattacked, pushing the 4th

Battle Hill 419.

Fig. 60. "The death of these men on Hill 419". Scene from War on Three Fronts, *reproduced from* Moving Picture World, *14 August 1915.*

Kaiserjäger Regiment back to its original positions, and in the night hours once again attacked the Horseshoe. The 4th *Kaiserjäger* regiment alone lost 186 dead, 746 wounded and 365 missing on 2 and 3 May on the heights of Dunajec.[14] The Austrian official history of the war says of Hill 419: "Its name should be kept in memory because much young blood from the Inn and from the Etsch (Ital. Adige), from the Salzach and from the Traun had to redden the earth before the Russians surrendered it".[15]

Kleinschmidt made the bloodshed at Hill 419 symbolic of the whole campaign and maybe the whole war. At the conclusion of the film Kleinschmidt's lecture notes ruminate upon the difference of a corpse in an accident and death in battle:

> "It is different upon a battlefield. The silence is full of eloquence. The rigid body still portrays the will that carried him thus far. With face towards the enemy, fists still clenched in dying grasp, the whole attitude breathes an indomitable will, set purpose, defiance of death, heroism and sacrifice, that demands instantly your highest admiration, compels you to pay tribute and do homage to a hero. There is no revolting feeling of horror or repugnance, but your heart swells with admiration, mingled with a deep pity and sadness that such heroic sacrifice had to be at all.
>
> If I should have the choice in which manner to pass out of this life, I should choose no other than the death of these men on Hill 419."[16]

Meanwhile, Edwin Weigle had left Berlin for the Austrians and an opportunity to actually film the war at the front. He most definitely succeeded. He was at Tarnow and Hill 419, followed the Austrian troops when they broke through the Russian lines on 2 May, and later joined them at the recapture of Przemysl. The best statement of what Weigle photographed appears on his theater program for *The German Side of the War*:

I was at Tarnow when the Teutons broke through the Russian lines. I was at Tarnow where Germans and Austrians machine gun batteries were strikingly offensive. Each of these machine guns had a capacity of 600 shots a minute. During the battle I stood in trenches which the Teuton troops had occupied for three to five months. At length the Germans and Austrians victorious and the Russians were forced out of Tarnow and toward Jaroslaw. The Teutons advance, taking with them their heavy 30 centimeter guns which are drawn by 200 power tractors. The guns themselves are mounted on caterpillar wheels. I accompanied the Austro-German Army on a wonderful advance of 125 miles, the distance from Tarnow to Przemysl. This area was covered in twelve days, which is nothing short of remarkable. I was with the Teuton Armies when they marched into the famous Austrian fortress Przemysl. The fortress which only a few weeks before had fallen to the Russians ... .[17]

Weigle captured pictures of the Germans building a bridge across the San River in an hour and forty-five minutes and of the artillery bombardment of Przemysl with a special telescopic lens. He also filmed the victorious Germans resting on what was left of the fortress. Some of this footage still exists in the John E. Allen Collection.

Weigle was only in Przemysl for a very short time. On 23 May 1915 Italy declared war on Austria-Hungary. While Kleinschmidt was east at the Isonzo front toward Trieste, Weigle went from Vienna to the Trentino on 13 June.

Albert K. Dawson and the *Battle and Fall of Przemysl*

As mentioned in the previous chapter, on 28 April 1915 Dawson left Germany to cover the forthcoming Gorlice-Tarnow offensive. Dawson's departure to the front was a great surprise to the German authorities who had no idea what he was up to. Together with his new camera operator, John Allen Everets, Dawson headed for Teschen and had himself attached to the k.u.k. Kriegspressequartier, the Austro-Hungarian military press office. Their work resulted in *The Battle and Fall of Przemysl*, the first feature documentary produced by the American Correspondent Film Company related earlier.

Dawson's work at Przemysl during the Gorlice-Tarnow campaign was the climax of his work in Europe both in terms of his career and cinematically. Covering the advance, Dawson used a horse-drawn wagon that carried his photographic equipment. The k.u.k. Kriegspressequartier also supplied him with a soldier as his guide, and he was filmed while visiting the frontline by military cameramen of the Austro-Hungarian army. The cooperation with the Austrian authorities proved to be most rewarding and resulted in an official contract with Dawson that was closed shortly after he had returned from the Przemysl campaign. The agreement stated that in return for paying Dawson all his expenses and 10 percent of their net receipts in the United States, the Austro-Hungarian government would get 20 percent of these films' revenues in the United States of his war film *The Battle and Fall of Przemysl*. In addition to the scenes that Dawson and Everets themselves shot, the A.C. Film Co. received a supply of 8,000 feet of negative footage from the Austro-Hungarian military press office. Many of these official shots were edited into Dawson's first feature film.[18]

180

Fig. 61. Dawson's photographic outfit during the drive in Galicia. Reproduced from Deutsch-Amerika, *6 January 1917.*

Dawson talked about his dangerous experiences during the making of his film in an interview with the *Continental Times*, published 10 June 1915:

I travelled the entire distance from the Carpathians to Przemysl with the army. It took four weeks. All fared alike; officers and men ate from the same Goulash Cannon, leading exactly the same life and, as often as not, sleeping out in the open. The same blanket did for everything. I was lent a blanket at night by the soldiers. The Russians kept on retreating and retrenching and then we would have to wait for the bringing up of the big guns, and it took several days to set them up. Just about when it was ready, the Russians would move out, break up the roads or blow a hill into them and then the whole thing would begin again. But finally, on June 3, I entered the town with the advanced guard after a 16 kilometres march.

I immediately began taking pictures of the Austrian and German troops entering the town. I also took pictures of the forts as they were after the rough treatment they had had. The damage done by the Austrian 30.5 mortars and the 42 centimetre German Krupp guns was stupendous. Wherever a shell from such guns fell, why there was a hole left large enough to build a house in. Nothing could exist within a large area around where those shells dropped.

It was a maddening, nerve-rending experience to go through and having seen and heard such a bombardment, I could easily understand what was told me, that one of the hospitals was full of Russians who had gone mad owing to the noise, excitement and strain. Especially around fort No. 10 was the damage immense. There was a wood a little to the back of it. There the Russians had sought shelter. The machine guns had been turned upon them. You could scarce take a step without coming across their remains and often in groups, lying on top of one another.'

Had the Russians rebuilt the forts?

"Yes, indeed! They had done wonders. Not only had they rebuilt them, but [they] had also mounted heavy cannon there and these remained in the hands of the Austro-German forces. I was within one and a quarter kilometres of the forts and have taken films in which are to be seen, quite distinctly, the effects of the giant shots, the fragments being thrown high into the air.

Big shots fell several times quite near me, and my assistant Everett [sic] had a narrow escape. Had any of the big splinters and stones flying about hit me, I would have no further interest in this world."[19]

Out of the footage shot and collected by Dawson the American Correspondent Film Company edited a four-reel motion picture that was ready for exhibition in the United States by the end of July 1915. On a full page in the trade paper *Variety* the movie was advertised as the ultimate sensation of all war films. The publicity also focused on the overwhelming military strength of the Central Powers on the eastern front, with the payoff "Smashing The Armies Of The Czar!"[20]

Claussen's hand as a publicity agent for the American Correspondent Film Company can be traced in many of these ads that emphasized the work done by neutral, American cameramen. Apart from Dawson other cinematographers are mentioned such as Fritz Arno Wagner, but this is not likely since he had joined the German cavalry. Edward Lyell Fox was also mentioned as a war correspondent for the new film company. Fox wrote a lecture to accompany the exhibition of this film and he was, like Dawson, on the payroll of the German Information Service, but for the Przemysl movie he did no specific camerawork.

Although most of the footage is considered lost, some fascinating segments of the Przemysl film have reappeared in the John E. Allen collection and in the archives of the Imperial War Museum in London.[21] These shots were taken by Austrian military cinematographers and show Dawson wandering through the woods around Przemysl where at Fort 10 he views the dead Russian soldiers that he mentioned.

Another clip has him inspecting the ruined forts of Przemysl with an Austrian guide. A remarkable scene showing German soldiers on top of one of the broken gun turrets of the Przemysl forts also appeared in the American press as a still picture with a Brown & Dawson copyright, indicating the arrangement by Dawson of a photo opportunity for both film and still photography.

Despite the loss of film, many Brown & Dawson photographs of the capture of Przemysl have survived making it possible, together with the descriptive lecture and a collection of film frames from the Library of Congress, to reconstruct parts of the movie as well as his photographic work during this campaign. In fact, based on this material Dawson's claim that he scooped his colleagues and was the first cameraman to enter Przemysl appears valid. His picture of a victorious General von Mackensen, taken shortly after the conquest of the Polish city, scored a news beat and appeared on the cover of the *Berliner Illustrierte Zeitung* of 20 June 1915. The Germans, despite having problems with his personal behaviour, were evidently interested in using his excellent pictures.

Opening with Archduke Frederick, Commander-in-Chief of the Austrian forces, inspecting his favorite regiment of Uhlan scouts, *The Battle and Fall of Przemysl* in the first two reels pictured the preparations for the infantry attack. A bridge at Biala that was destroyed by the Russians is blown up by dynamite and new pontoons are quickly constructed to bring the soldiers across the river. General Puhallo von Brlog, Commander of the Austrian Third Army, who led the attack on Przemysl is next shown on screen, consulting his staff while his soldiers are inoculated against cholera.

Apart from medical attention, a special meal of roast pig is served and on the eve of battle we see the Austrian soldiers around the campfire, joyfully dancing the Rumanian Kolo. Herds of cattle are also thrown on screen as well as bakeries just behind the frontline, evidently to impress on the audience how well the army takes care of its soldiers.

The Dawson film has many of these human interest scenes, like shots of children left behind in the villages and soldiers in the field shown receiving their presents from home. Close up shots of special units in their colourful uniforms, such as the Hungarian Red Devils, also added to the interest in this war picture. Lost on film but preserved as a frame is a striking scene showing two spies who had been caught while trying to signal the Russians on the position of the Austrian forces.

Despite the fact that most of Dawson's film was taken behind the front lines, it showed some amazing aspects of warfare. Austrian brigade headquarters are seen being hit by a Russian shell. A pilot takes off in his plane to locate the enemy's battery. High above Przemysl the artillery's position is marked on a map and the guns are finally destroyed. Such a clear-cut sequence is rather exceptional for a World War I film as scenes were often edited without much attention to continuity. Then in the third reel the great siege guns are put into action while a group of machine-gunners

Fig. 62. Capture of a Russian spy. Film frame from Battle and Fall of Przemysl.
[Courtesy Library of Congress.]

move forward into the fight. As a climax, soldiers are seen rushing up the heights around the river San in their attempt to storm the forts of Przemysl.

According to the descriptive report by Fox, Dawson nearly lost his life while filming this scene. Contemporary reviews in the American trade press singled out this shot as an absolute money maker. "It is so well photographed", explained *Variety*, "that one might for a minute expect it is staged for the benefit of the camera, but this is overshadowed when one sees the dying kicks of one poor devil who fell as his comrades strode into the rain of bullets. The manner in which he falls and his dying convulsions are enough to convince the most skeptical. This scene alone will repay anyone."[22]

After the action, the aftermath of the siege of Przemysl is shown in the final reel. Soldiers are decorated, including a "charming heroine", Marie von Fery-Bognar who fought as a volunteer and was promoted to corporal.

Again, we have more of these human interest scenes including some picturesque shots of troops from Bosnia and soldiers taking care of a wounded mascot dog. To mark the contrast, the film closes with a scene showing wounded Austrian soldiers in the hands of skillful surgeons while dead Russian soldiers are left behind on the battle-field.

The Battle and Fall of Przemysl was praised by the American film trade press. *Billboard* described the movie as "the most vivid and real of all war pictures". *Motion Picture News* qualified the film as "a valuable attraction".

Fig. 63. Infantry attack on Przemysl. The scene was probably staged and also appeared in Dawson's film. Reproduced from New York Times, *17 October 1915.*

Most reviews made no comment that this film had been produced with the cooperation of the Austrian authorities. Only Lynde Denig in his review for *Moving Picture World* noted that the film tended to glorify the prowess of the Teutonic Allies. "It could not be otherwise, for Cameraman A.K. Dawson was one of them during the campaign in Galicia. But an audience that is totally out of sympathy with the motives behind the armies of the Kaiser and Archduke Frederick may overlook the political significance of the operations and marvel at scenes that so graphically suggest human tragedy and military resourcefulness."[23]

Reports in the press indicate that from a commercial point of view, the movie also did well. Over a period of two months, the film could be found in theatres across the country, from Washington, DC; Baltimore, Chicago, Indianapolis and Toledo to San Antonio and Los Angeles. The film was distributed through several exchanges by the selling of state rights. The film was also shown in Dawson's hometown at the Princess Theatre.

Wilbur H. Durborough

Meanwhile, in the north the forces of von Hindenburg and Ludendorff drove from East Prussia and the Masurian Lakes toward Warsaw, accompanied by Durborough. This was an extension of the movement east that Wallace had seen first-hand at Bolimow. As previously mentioned, there could have been an enormous pincer

Durborough With Big German Drive at Russia

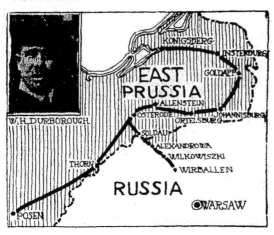

Fig. 64. The map of Durborough's first trip through East Prussia. Salt Lake Telegram, 9 August 1915.

movement between the von Hindenburg forces in the north and the German-Austrian forces in the south, essentially rolling the Russian forces up in a huge cauldron, and von Hindenburg and Ludendorff urged precisely this. But von Falkenhayn was having none of it, not wanting to open a major campaign on the eastern front resulting in a whole lot more Russian prisoners that the Germans would have to feed and house. All he wanted to do was drive the Russian forces across Poland and secure East Prussia and Austria from the Russians. Later in July as the German juggernaut was driving toward the capture of Warsaw, the German General Staff felt confident enough of success to attempt to reap its propaganda benefits. Arrangements were quickly made for neutral war correspondents to be rushed to the eastern front and General von Hindenburg even took the time to telegraph an invitation to Swedish explorer Sven Hedin, a favorite of the Kaiser, urging him to hurry if he wanted to see Warsaw fall, which it did on 5 August 1915.[24]

It is unclear exactly who was on the Stutz as it headed east, but it appears that at various times it was Schuette, Niebuhr, and Ries accompanying Durborough. They left Berlin for four days behind the eastern front, very fluid with the Austro-German army's generally steady advance, and the Russian army's equally steady retreat from what was then Russian-controlled Galicia and Poland. During this trip Durborough was able to take Ries and they stopped in Posen to film Durborough interviewing General Friedrich von Bernhardi at his headquarters. Given Durborough didn't speak German any "interview" probably consisted of little more than a short filming session.[25] Although von Bernhardi was born in Russia, he grew up in Silesia and served as a Hussar in the victorious Prussian army in the brief Franco-Prussian War of 1870–71. He retired and became a military historian and writer most famous for his 1911 book *Germany and the Next War* in which he claimed war was part of the natural law, an extension of the biological struggle for existence.[26] He had come out of retirement to serve again.

Moving east Durborough stopped at Thorn on the Vistula River to film Red Cross

186

Fig. 65. The front at Bloni. Note Durborough (top of picture) loading film while Ries was filming. The Russian sniper appears to have penetrated the perimeter and shot from the side of the wall. Film frame from Durborough's movie.

boats and troops on their way to the front. As they traveled through East Prussia getting ever closer to the front they passed through Allenstein, Pillkallen, Ortelsburg and finally Schirwindt and Goldap near the border with Lithuania, they began capturing on film not only the endless lines of German troops and supplies heading to the front but some of the massive destruction the war had wrought on the people, towns and castles.

At Warsaw Durborough filmed what appeared to be a curious citizenry, a relatively undamaged city and cathedral with a Zeppelin patrolling overhead undisturbed. Although the Warsaw that Durborough filmed appeared to be a safe, secure and open city under the Germans, it was in nearby Bloni 16 miles west of Warsaw that Ries was filming Durborough with his still camera only a few yards back of the German line the moment a Russian sniper's bullet knocked down a German infantryman. The intertitle noted: "Surprised by Russian snipers at Bloni, in which one man was wounded, and we were very nervous for a few minutes while the 'fun' lasted".

The suburb of Praga north of Warsaw would be the German Army's push off point for the film's climax, the fall of the massive Russian fort at Novo Georgievsk just a few miles farther north. James O'Donnell Bennett reported:

The German General Staff took us out over the wide Warsaw plain in a black and shining motor bus that held sixteen people uncomfortably and that from one point of view bore a sobering resemblance to an auto-hearse, while from another it recalled those reeling vehicles that hurl the hostess and the entire dinner party through the icy streets to the theatre....

All along the way out of town triple spans of horses were plunging down the river bank with the munition wagons and out to the pontoon bridge, which was fairly streaming with these wagon trains. On the masts at the entrance of this bridge the German flag and the Hungarian flag, which is broad stripes of green, white and red, and the most striking combination of national colors I ever saw, were flying, and half a mile down the yellow river the shattered spans of the enormous Alexandrowski Bridge, which is nearly 600 yards long, and which the Russians had blown up, went lurching along to Praga.[27]

The recent improvements in German artillery demonstrated its effectiveness against the massive but now obsolete Russian fort which quickly fell on 19 August. As described by O'Donnell Bennett:

Beyond the immediate environs of Warsaw the plain is marked off in potato and cabbage patches, and the present picture derives its historical interest solely from superb trenches, many of which the Russians never used, and from the grass-grown humps of forts which Napoleon would have found useful – indeed, he started the building of the fortress of Novo Georgievsk in 1807 – but did not withstand long in these days even so much as the threat of the Austrian "thirty-point fives ... ." All day long we wandered amid such scenes, and finally, what with the body's thirst and leg weariness, the mind ceased to react upon them, and men looked with a tired eye on the most stupendous evidence of destruction and woe. Besides, to most of these men, the shifting and shattering of huge blocks of concrete and the laying bare of the innards of fortresses was an old story, and the fresh survey of these things served only to confirm what they had learned at Liege and Maubeuge and Antwerp and Przemysl, and that this war brings an end to the stationary fortress and establishes the validity of the field fortress which moles and mines its way from week to week and month to month into the vitals of an enemy's position.[28]

These "superb trenches" are probably similar to the ones that Dawson filmed in such detail at Ivangorod.[29]

On returning to Warsaw, Bennett and the other correspondents learned that two of the perimeter forts had already fallen, and the rest were expected to fall soon. The Germans captured 700 guns and 90,000 Russian prisoners, including thirty generals. Being present at the event enabled Durborough to vividly capture on film the still burning mounds of munitions, the pulverized mountains of destroyed fort masonry and hundreds of abandoned Russian cannons. The most poignant part of the film documents the plight of the local peasant families who had suffered so greatly from the earlier fighting and were returning home in late summer to face the coming winter with virtually nothing left of their homes and farms.

When Ries was filming, Durborough often took the opportunity to appear in the film, sometimes holding his still camera used throughout his time in Germany to provide his NEA Editor, Sam Hughes, the photos which the Scripps newspapers and other NEA clients printed with great satisfaction. From the number of film segments with Durborough present, it appears that cameraman Irving G. Ries justly deserved

Fig. 66. The Kaiser at Novo Georgievsk. He is talking to Sven Hedin, the Swedish explorer, whom von Hindenburg invited to the Kaiser Review. Frame from Durborough's movie.

his title and was operating the camera most of the time. However the most newsworthy filming episode during their European travels occurred just after the fall of Novo Georgievsk when only Durborough held the camera.[30] Early on the morning that the Russian fort had fallen, the correspondents were awoken and driven to see the results. Filmed from the moving car, the burning piles of munitions and large number of abandoned Russian cannons make impressive film segments as well as the immense column of Russian prisoners marching away. But they happened upon and were allowed to witness a most impressive Kaiser Review ceremony as related by the *Los Angeles Times* correspondent Harry Carr:

"I never believed they intended us to see it; but we accidentally bumped into the most majestic of military ceremonies – a Kaiser review. The troops which had taken part in the battle were assembling on the battlefield when we got there. It was a splendid picture. The fortress was on fire against the sky. Down one road filed a long procession of Russian prisoners marching to the rear. Down another road trundled the big guns that had driven the Czar out of Poland. They had finished one job and were on the way to the next battle. In the middle of a great hollow square of troops stood the War Lord leaning on a little cane addressing his soldiers. Behind him were his field marshals, von Hindenburg, von B[e]seler, von Falkenh[a]yn and his sons, Prince Eitel Fritz and Prince Joachim.

"Of course this was perfectly miserable stuff for moving pictures!

"Durborough begged our officer to let him slip in between the files and shoot a picture. The worthy captain looked as though he was going to faint at the suggestion. 'Aw, just for a minute' pleaded Durborough, pathetically, but the captain had turned from him to a correspondent who had lit a cigar. 'One does not smoke at a Kaiser review', he said in a thunderous stage whisper. Which shows what kind of a thing a Kaiser review is.

"Finally the ceremony came to a close. 'Adieu, Comrades!' cried the Kaiser. 'Adieu, Majesty!' they shouted back. The ranks fell back: the square opened. The Kaiser strode back to his auto and climbed in. Spying Dr. Sven Hedin, the famous Swedish explorer, in the crowd, the Emperor beckoned him to the car. This was more than Durborough could stand. He suddenly broke away and we saw him running full tilt across the cleared space that the awe of the soldiers had left around His Majesty. Our captain was too much overcome to follow. The captain just stood waiting for an offended heaven to strike dead the impious wretch.

"To the frozen horror of the whole German army, Durborough set up his machine about thirty feet away from the Kaiser's car and began grinding away for dear life.

"The Kaiser looked up and took in the whole situation with his quick, comprehending eyes. He laughed and lit a cigarette, talking a little while longer, we believe, to give the plucky Yankee boy a chance.

"Finally the Emperor and Dr. Hedin shook hands; the chauffeur of the car threw in the hop and the Imperial auto started with a leap.

"As it went by him, Durborough took off his hat and said with honest sociability, 'Much obliged!' The Kaiser straightened up and one gauntleted hand rose to the visor of his helmet in salute to the American boy who had had the nerve to snap an Emperor without asking permission."[31]

Durborough also took other purely physical risks while making his film in Germany. Along with fast horses and roadsters, he clearly enjoyed the thrill of flying. He welcomed opportunities to fly over both eastern and western fronts and be shot at in planes much improved in the three years since his brief commercial venture back home in aerial photography.[32] His film features a segment taken while flying over Russian trench positions of "a Russian rear guard in Poland routed by the German advance, fleeing from a forest …".[33] Irving Ries also flew at the front and was awarded the Iron Cross by the German Army General Staff for his aerial photos taken of Russian fortifications while on the eastern front.[34]

On his way back to Berlin through the mountains with Ries in the roadster, Durborough wrote with emotion some thirty years later of the near loss of the auto and all their gear. They were pressing through a hard rain on slick muddy clay roads when they rounded a curve and came to an ominous, long steep grade with a sheer drop on the left that curved right at the bottom. They rigged a drag anchor by attaching a log to the rear axle with a tow rope. Ries rode the log down "digging in his heels" providing the necessary additional braking until just before the curve when the rope broke and the car surged forward in the slick clay mud. Durborough relates:

"Just when the good old Stutz with all our stuff aboard was within about five feet of the edge of the cliff, I muttered a prayer, and jumped. I had turned my back. I began to cry. My nerves were all shot. I had rigged that car up just the way I wanted it. I had traveled in it, I had brought it along all the way from Chicago, thousands of miles. It was my pal, I had grown so accustomed to its every whim, that it seemed like an old friend. I had left it once chained to a tree in a woods up in Poland. I had burned out the clutch, trying to get across a sandy stretch of country. Several weeks later, there it was, still chained to the tree, and not a thing missing. I had repaired it and we had taken to the road again. No, I couldn't bear to see it go slipping over that cliff. I sunk down on my knees in the mud, with my hands over my eyes."[35]

Fig. 67. Durborough poses with his movie camera for a publicity shot. Both he and his camera operator Ries flew above the front. Reproduced from Cine Mundial, March 1916.

When Ries caught up with him, he brought Durborough out of his daze by telling him the car remained hanging right on the edge. They found a local farmer with a team of horses who got the car back on the road and on their way. However impractical and burdensome the car was financially and logistically, it had clearly served him well not only for transportation but in attracting attention. This manuscript section written years later reveals just how emotionally attached he had become to his Stutz Bearcat roadster; just as telling is the observation his manuscript has no similarly emotional passage about any person, not even his assistant Ries.

Dealing with the German Film Censors

Back in Berlin there was little time to finish processing the exposed film, have it reviewed by the censors, pack up and leave for home. In his manuscript, Durborough accounted for his film stock and wrote about his experience with the film censors. He had purchased 25,000 feet of negative film stock in New York just prior to leaving for Europe. He entered Germany with a little over 24,000 feet, having exposed some on the trip over. In Germany he printed a little over 22,000 feet for review by the censors at a Berlin movie studio, having tossed out some and keeping 400 feet for filming on the trip home. He claims the censors initially were going to allow him to take only 6300 feet home from Germany, a pronouncement he didn't take passively.[36]

Preemptively just before he was to meet with the censors for their verdict, Durborough had organized an evening party at the Adlon Hotel to view nearly all of the film he had submitted for review. It went from 7 to midnight with a break at 9, followed by a supper and dancing from 1 a.m. into the wee hours. He invited all his German civilian and military friends and acquaintances, those he had filmed, those who had assisted him and anyone one else important or owed a favor. These included several General Staff officers and Foreign Office officials, one of whom introduced him to the audience.[37]

Prince Max of Baden, whom Durborough had met, filmed and established a friendship with during his time in Germany, attended the party. He frequented the Adlon Hotel and was in the tea garden when Durborough returned dejected and angry from his meeting with the censors. He explained the situation to Prince Max

Fig. 68. Durborough (right), received by Prince Reuss of the General Staff, Prince Max von Baden and Count von Bernstorff, son of the German Ambassador to the USA. Frame from Durborough's film.

and appealed for his help. Durborough claims Prince Max immediately left to make some calls and returned to assure him there would be another review by the censors and he would be sitting with the Board of Censors himself. He also assured him of a more favorable result. Durborough had to delay his ship departure for a few days while this second review was done. His contemporary interviews about the film back in Chicago note he returned with 16,000 feet which is consistent with his feature film length of 8,500 feet assuming a roughly 50% film editing for this type of feature and the period.[38]

Fall 1915: Returning Home

Ries was sent ahead by train to Rotterdam with the film negatives because the Stutz was fully loaded with other baggage. Durborough left Berlin a little later with Walter Niebuhr covering the last of his 10,000 miles in Europe as he drove out through the Brandenburg Tor side arch, the Tiergarten, Grunewald and Wannsee before they fastened their chin straps, pulled down their goggles, and accelerated to 75 mph.[39] When the SS *Nieuw Amsterdam* left Rotterdam on the evening of 18 September, he had been assured that his film and car, as on the trip to Europe, were not on the manifest and safely hidden to avoid problems with the British inspection near Falmouth. After a few smooth days at sea they encountered stormy weather for most of the remaining voyage before arriving in New York harbor on 30 September.[40]

Needing to deal with U.S. Customs, they spent a night in New York City at the Roosevelt Hotel. Durborough found his colleague Edwin Weigle, the *Chicago Tribune*'s war cinematographer who had returned from Germany a few weeks earlier, hosting his film *The German Side of the War* at a local theater.[41] Durborough claims that F. Ziegfeld, Jr., who was managing the New York City showing of Weigle's film, contacted him to propose a similar deal for hosting his film. Durborough informed him he could only present his proposal to the War Film Syndicate back in Chicago. Of more concern to Durborough was a phone call with his Editor Sam Hughes about a Federal Agent in Chicago urgently trying to meet him about some important matter involving Ries.[42] The matter was indeed urgent. The British newspapers had announced that a spy named Irving Guy Ries was to be executed at the Tower of London on 27 October 1915.

What had transpired was this: the Germans had obtained possession of Ries' passport in order to provide him with a visa when he was to accompany Durborough to Germany. But while it was in their possession, they must have decided that since Ries was not very well known, they could get away with copying his passport in order to provide a forged copy to one of their agents, which they promptly did. The false Ries traveled to London and then applied in London for a visa to Rotterdam. The American vice-consul in London noticed that the passport appeared to be a forgery, and notified the police. The British arrested the phony Ries as a spy. Meanwhile, the Department of Justice opened their investigation into the matter and the story was picked up in the American newspapers. In the middle of this, Durborough and the genuine Ries arrived back from Germany, totally confused about what had happened. Once they got back to Chicago, it was all eventually sorted out, and the Department of Justice dropped its investigation of Durborough and Ries.

But leaving the ludicrous part aside, the Germans appear to have destroyed a lot of the advantage they might have gained from screening the film in America. Although Germany wanted to have Americans showing the German side of the war, portraying its citizens bravely coping with the difficulties of the war both on the home front and in the field, it was revealed they were stealing the identity of Americans for espionage purposes, including those like Ries, whom they had invited themselves. In fact, the Germans forged rather a lot of passports and had even set up a special office in America to accomplish this, apparently with the connivance of Ambassador von Bernstorff.[43] It was revealed once again, shortly after the Albert briefcase incident of 24 July 1915 and before the Zimmermann telegram of 1917, that whatever Germany might say, its intentions towards America were far from friendly. And it kept getting caught.

Once Durborough satisfied Customs and the film had been express shipped to Chicago, he and Ries sped to Philadelphia for lunch with Durborough's parents at a local hotel before continuing on to spend the night at Pittsburgh. They went on to Cleveland to meet with Sam Hughes for lunch and got to Chicago the following day. Upon arriving back in Chicago, Durborough claims crowds swarmed them when he stopped to greet a friend with his Stutz now covered in European hotel decals and the signatures of many soldiers and civilians acquired while in Germany. He briefly visited his former colleagues at the *Chicago Examiner* before proceeding a few blocks north to the Syndicate's office in the Mallers Building where Carl M. Marston greeted him.[44] Marston appears to have been the active Syndicate manager and the individual Durborough worked with most closely upon his return.[45]

The announcement of the Durborough film noted the film's local connections, Chicagoans Wilbur H. Durborough and *Daily News'* own correspondent Oswald F. Schuette. Schuette advised and collaborated with Durborough in Berlin and had traveled with him during at least part of the critical filming period on the eastern front. Shortly after Durborough's return to Chicago, the paper featured an interview with him accompanied by a photo of Schuette with Durborough in the Stutz Bearcat roadster. The article covered some of his personal experiences while in Germany and also included his tribute to its Berlin office: "It is like a branch consular office to Americans ....", and to Schuette: "He is popular with all classes, official and private, and has the confidence of those in highest position. His friendship was valuable to me in my task of getting real war pictures … ."[46]

For Durborough, as he acknowledged in his praise, the key to obtaining access to the war zone was likely Schuette, who spoke fluent German, understood the German culture, and clearly had developed very good contacts in the Foreign Office. As noted earlier, Jane Addams attributed him with obtaining meetings with the Chancellor and Foreign Minister on very short notice. Later, H. L. Mencken, only recently back from the front when the U.S. broke diplomatic relations, would credit Schuette for getting approval within a day from General Ludendorff out at the front, the only one who could waive the military restriction on his leaving the country so soon with Ambassador Gerard's train.[47] As an additional tribute, Durborough inserted an intertitle with Schuette's greetings to friends back home in the Stutz repair scene of the Chicago film and a similar one in the first film showing in Milwaukee where Schuette had also worked as a newspaperman: "The American camp. Mr. Schuette, of the Chicago Daily News, is some mechanic as well as one of the best newspapermen I have ever met". No documentation has yet been found but one might also surmise Schuette was not only helpful to Durborough in getting his "real war pictures" but may have been the critical link for the *Daily News'* sponsorship of its early Chicago presentation. Yet whatever his role in facilitating Durborough's access to film in the war zone or the *Daily News'* Chicago sponsorship for the film, Lawson's announcement labeling the film as the "Durborough-Schuette pictures" greatly exaggerated Schuette's role. There is no indication he participated in any part of the actual filming or film production process; that appears to have all been done by Durborough with Ries' assistance. But while Schuette's influence behind the scenes in obtaining sponsorship back home may have been important, there is little doubt his influence in Germany was the critical difference that enabled Durborough, unlike Dawson and

Fig. 69. Advertisement Chicago Tribune, *7 December 1915.*

Weigle, to enjoy the support of the AA and the German Army for access to the front lines for filming.

Durborough's film first opened in Milwaukee on 28 November 1915 sponsored by Scripps' *Milwaukee Free Press* for an eight-day run it. It was advertised with the generic title *Durborough's German War Pictures* with only one newspaper item noting it consisted of nine reels.[48] It next started its longest city run anywhere when it opened with the title *On the Firing Line With the Germans* in Chicago's Fine Arts Theater on

Monday, 6 December 1915. Factors contributing to this record were the substantial ad campaign by initial sponsor *Chicago Daily News*, Chicago's large German-American population and the film's reputation being quickly established as the best war film to date by *Chicago Tribune*'s film critic Kitty Kelly's early enthusiastic review awarding it the "Blue Ribbon" for war films.[49] Durborough lectured at every performance during the *Chicago Daily News* sponsorship which concluded after three weeks on Christmas Day. His lectures continued during the film showings now managed by the War Film Syndicate in the LaSalle Theater from 27 December until 10 January, when the LaSalle continued showing the film with ads reverting back to using the generic title *Wilbur H. Durborough's German War Pictures*. Although the film was consistently advertised during the *Chicago Daily News* run as being eight reels and/or 8,000 feet, the War Film Syndicate sponsored run noted the length as nine reels and 8,500 feet.[50] This was likely the finished film filed for copyright on 20 December supported by nine 35mm photoprinted paper rolls[51] and later advertised as 8500 feet for countrywide distribution by the Syndicate.[52] Audience viewing time was two hours.[53]

Durborough's film played in local movie theaters around the U.S. beginning in 1916. One film showing of special interest to Durborough was sponsored by the *North American* in Philadelphia, the city where his parents and brother still lived, in February 1916. He traveled east by train to visit with his family and arranged for the Stutz roadster to arrive later on another. With his typical promotional flair, Durborough drove it up and down Chestnut Street firing a big gun before parking it in front of the Chestnut Street Opera House when he lectured at each show.[54] While he was no doubt warmly received by his family, his film was not so well received by the Pennsylvania State Board of Censors. It had a legal mandate to review and prohibit the showing of "[films, reels or views] as are sacrilegious, obscene, indecent or such as tend, in the judgment of the board, to corrupt morals. This section does not apply to announcement or advertising slides."

After reviewing the submitted film, the Board of Censors delivered its verdict requiring 75 feet of film removed just days before the scheduled opening on 7 February 1916. They censored the portraits of von Hindenburg and the Kaiser that appeared near the very end of the film fearing the large portrait views might incite demonstrations resulting in a riot in a mixed audience of German and English sympathizers. They also forbade using 2'x3' posters of these individuals' portraits for promoting the film by claiming they were false advertising since von Hindenburg and the Kaiser wouldn't actually be appearing in person (Colour Plate 3). The immediate verbal protest to the Board was ignored. Although a few weeks later it was determined the Board acted wrongly, there was insufficient time to appeal the ruling at the time; the posters were confiscated and the 75 feet of film were removed before the initial Philadelphia showing.[55]

The film bookings slowed through the second half of 1916 into 1917 until public interest in German war films quickly evaporated after diplomatic relations were severed with Germany and the country headed toward declared war on 6 April. The local newspapers that wrote articles about the film and Durborough's frequent appearances generally merely noted the fact he introduced the film and then described some film content, usually mentioning the several Kaiser family appearances, scenes from local Berlin city life, the impressive German military drive, the totally destroyed fort of Novo Georgievsk and possibly the suffering refugees. While the movie content is certainly pro-German and Durborough made the best use of his opportunity to document the story of the German side of the war and the successful eastern front offensive campaign, his motivation appears to have been that of a film reporter, not a propagandist, much like his film project investors who considered the project as a good financial investment opportunity.

However that isn't necessarily the case for another film tour he did in the fall of 1916. In 1916 Robert W. Woolley was the Publicity Chairman of the Democratic Campaign Committee (DCC) responsible for directing President Wilson's reelection publicity campaign and the one credited for the campaign slogan, "He Kept Us Out of War".[56] As Publicity Chairman, he was interested in exploiting film and the film industry for political purposes to a greater extent than any previous national campaign. Many political and film historians know President Wilson spoke before nearly 1,000 people including most of the reigning film moguls at a Motion Picture Board of Trade banquet in New York City on 27 January 1916.[57] Woolley noticed Durborough's war film and conceived and secretly paid for a fall 1916 film tour in a few selected states to hopefully tip the balance for Wilson's re-election. He approached Durborough through NEA editor Sam Hughes and commissioned Durborough to assemble a film emphasizing the horrors of war in Europe and the troubles in Mexico and to introduce each show by describing the film, giving his personal witness to the horrors of war he experienced while filming and concluding with strong support for President Wilson's position of keeping the country out of these conflicts. But to be effective, Woolley wanted the presentation to appear as though from an unbiased, independent film journalist and to keep the DCC's relationship with the project hidden.[58]

Durborough created a film titled *With Durborough on the Firing Line* composed from parts of his film taken on the eastern front, a little taken on the western front augmented with other sourced film, and some Mexican film he took when covering Pershing's Spring 1916 Punitive Expedition augmented with some Vera Cruz film almost certainly from Weigle's *Battle of Vera Cruz* and possibly other sourced material. It was presented at brief stops for a day or so in theaters bought out on short notice with payments to compensate for any losses due to prior film bookings. The shows were staged only in cities of states judged by Woolley to be closely contested between Charles Evans Hughes, the Republican Party candidate, and President Woodrow Wilson. Durborough mentions opening the tour in Portland and a few other cities in Maine, followed by Boston, New York and Ohio, with Pennsylvania skipped for political reasons. He introduced each show with his remarks concluding with an endorsement to Wilson's policy of keeping the U.S. out of the war so far.[59]

The *Daily Kennebec Journal* articles at the start of the film tour described Durborough only as "the famous war correspondent on special commission by the Scripps-McCrea league of newspapers" with no hint of any political connection. As agreed with Woolley, he was speaking out as a witness to the human toll of war:

> "This interesting man said that he felt 10 years older since going to Europe and that now there were more grey hairs in his head than in his father's. To visit the war hospitals and see the wounded is a sight to long be remembered. Along with the maimed ones there are so many who have gone totally blind. Many have gone crazy with fear, strong men all shot in pieces and human wrecks, all caused by the horrors of war. ...."[60]

In his manuscript, Durborough claimed that when NEA Editor Sam Hughes sounded him out about his views, he said he had voted for Wilson in 1912 although he and his family were traditionally Republicans and that he planned to vote for him again. His film introductory comments reported in the newspapers about the horrors of war appear consistent with what he witnessed and filmed. He may very well have been entirely truthful in his comments and endorsement of Wilson. However the fact remains that it was not made known his film and tour were sponsored by the Democratic Campaign Committee which tainted his appearance as an independent journalist.

Photographing on the eastern front was a major struggle as Weigle, Durborough and the others have given us ample witness. There were few ways to get around. Cars and trains were scarce on the eastern front; often a horse and cart and, in some cases, travel on foot were the only means of transportation. They dealt with cold, lice, rain and unsympathetic generals. Describing their photographic equipment as cumbersome is an understatement. The luggage they carried with them was so heavy that it is astonishing these film correspondents were able to do their job at all. As Albert Dawson described in a notebook that he kept during the war:

> "My baggage is a great problem in this line of work. I cut it down to the bare essentials. But even then the total weight is about 200 pounds. There are five pieces, not including the hand camera which I always wear around my shoulders. First there is my film camera that is packed in a box; second the tripod; third a packet of four reserve motion-picture films also containing toilet articles, underwear, Kodak films, flash lights, a torch light, a box of cigars and a bottle of cognac (they come in handy as a present), powder for developing the films and finally a screw driver for my camera.

> Then I carry a big piece of hard sausage, or 'salami' as the Hungarians call it; a couple of boxes of sardines, cheese, some pounds of chocolate; insecticide powder; a bunch of illustrated magazines from Germany and the United States; a red light to change the films. Attached to all this baggage, I have a big and warm travelling blanket which is made of camel hair. My biggest piece of luggage is a sack of about three feet high, made of brown sailing cloth. There are handles on both sides. In it, there is my reserve supply of motion-picture films, as well as more clothes, a blanket, extra boxes of sardines, a sweater. It is always full. And I always need

two men to carry this sack. Because there is no porter at the firing line, you better make sure you don't lose these guys out of sight."[61]

These gentlemen, whatever the difficulties of filming at the front, finding film, getting to where the battle was and struggling with censorship, provided a fine picture of major fighting on the German-Austrian eastern front in Poland in 1915. It was an amazing feat.

Notes

Frank Kleinschmidt

1. Mary Roberts Rinehart, *Kings, Queens, Pawns: An American Woman at the Front* (New York: G.H. Doran Co. [1915]), 135.

2. Graydon A. Tunstall, *Blood on the Snow: the Carpathian Winter War of 1915* (Lawrence, Kansas: University of Kansas Press, 2010), 8; Graydon A. Tunstall, *Przemysl, Verdun of the East* (Forthcoming).

3. Graydon A. Tunstall, *Blood on the Snow*, 12.

4. Richard L. DiNardo, *Breakthrough: The Gorlice – Tarnow Campaign, 1915* (Santa Barbara, Cal., Denver, Col. and Oxford, England: Praeger, 2010), 42–68. DiNardo's book is a useful recent overview of the campaign in English, and his list of primary reference sources is invaluable. Also useful to the authors were *The Story of the Great War: History of the European War from Official Sources* Vol. 3, 264–297; *Encyclopaedia Britannica*, 12th edn., s.v. "The Battles of the Dunajec-San", on line at: http://www.theodora/com/encyclopedia/d/battles_of_the_dunajecsan.html, 1–11; 'The Reconquest of Przemysl and Lemberg', *Times History of World War*, Part 56, Vol. 5, 14 September 1915 (London: Times Publishing Company, 1915), 121–160; 'Die Durchbruchsschlacht bei Gorlice', *Österreich-Ungarns Letzter Krieg 1914–1918*, Vol. 2, (Vienna: Verlag der Militärwissenschaftlichen Mitteilungen, 1931) 315–337.

5. Richard L. DiNardo, *Breakthrough: The Gorlice-Tarnow Campaign*, 1915, 82–83.

6. "With Capt. F. E. Kleinschmidt in *War on Three Fronts*", Film lecture, copyright MU759, 23 October 1916. Library of Congress, M/B/RS Division, Washington, DC.

7. Film lecture "With Capt. F. E. Kleinschmidt in *War on Three Fronts*", 6–7.

8. Footage *War on Three Fronts*. John E. Allen Collection at Park Ridge, New Jersey. Tape ID IW06, ubit 19200136, Duck's Bill scene at 43:56 minutes from screener. Tape ID IW03 has another 30 seconds from this remarkable scene.

9. DiNardo, *Breakthrough: The Gorlice-Tarnow Campaign*, 46.

10. Footage *War on Three Fronts*, part 4, 1916. Intertitle at 9:28 minutes from screener. Courtesy of UCLA film archives. The Sacré Coeur cloister is still in Tarnow, looking much as it did in 1915 but with the damage restored.

11. "The Taking of Belgrade", *Pearson's Magazine* (February 1918): 354. His files at the Austrian State Archives show that Kleinschmidt was issued a pass to travel from Belgrade to Semlin on 20 October 1915.

12. Ibid. For a silhouette photo of Kleinschmidt in Serbia observing artillery operations, see *New York Times, Picture Section* (19 December 1915).

13. Footage *War on Three Fronts*, part 4, 1916. Intertitle scene at 18:14 minutes from screener. Courtesy of UCLA film archives.

14. Erwin Fritz, "Die Gefechte bei Lubcza Szczepanowska 1915" in Kämpfe in Galizien 1915, http://militaria-fundforum.de/showthread.php?t=236974. See also http://www.it.tarnow.pl/index.php/pol/Atrakcje/REGION-TARNOWSKI/Cmentarze-wojskowe-z-czasow-I-Wojny-Swiatowej.

15. "Die Durchbruchsschlacht bei Gorlice", *Österreich-Ungarns Letzter Krieg 1914–1918*, Vol. 2, 321–322.

16. Film lecture "With Capt. F. E. Kleinschmidt in *War on Three Fronts*", 30–31.

Edwin Weigle/Albert K. Dawson

17. Edwin F. Weigle, "The German Side of the War: Story of the Films and Their Taking", Theater Program, 1915, Author Graham's private collection.

18. National Archives, Record Group 59. Papers Dr. Albert. Memorandum of Agreements with Mr. Albert K. Dawson and the Imperial Austrian Government, dated 24 June 1915. The only restriction placed by the Austrian government was that some of this footage could be used by the American war correspondent James F. J. Archibald. The AA archives show the Germans paid Archibald a financial bonus for his lectures in America. Later in the

19. "Dawson Describes Przemysl's Recapture", *Stamford Daily Advocate* (2 August 1915): 2. *The Continental Times* was published by the ZfA.

20. Advertisement, *The Battle and Fall of Przemysl*, *Variety* (15 August 1915): 21.

21. John E. Allen Collection. Unidentified World War I footage/WWI 4391. Library of Congress, MBRS Division, MAVIS number 1870314. Two clips showing Dawson at Przemysl from the collection of the Imperial War Museum are online at http://film.iwmcollections.org.uk/index.php Record numbers: 1060023359 and 1060023348. These clips have Hungarian intertitles indicating the authorities also used this footage for circulation within the Austro-Hungarian Empire. A longer version of this footage has been uploaded in 2014 on the European Film Gateway project website http://project.efg1914.eu Courtesy George Bonsall.

22. Review, *The Battle and Fall of Przemysl*, *Variety* (6 August 1915), 33; Edward L. Fox, "Descriptive Complete Report of The Battle and Fall of Przemysl" (New York: A.C. Film Co. 1915), 12–13. The scene has survived as a frame enlargement and was reprinted in Kevin Brownlow's *The War, the West and the Wilderness*. Judging from the camera position and the explosion that seems to be simulated, Brownlow suspects this scene had been staged. His analysis appears to be correct. A frame, taken from the same scene and located at the Library of Congress, shows the infantry attack from beneath the hill while shells explode nearby. Several cameramen must have worked on that scene from different positions, which indicates that it was probably staged.

23. Reviews, *Moving Picture World* (14 August 1915): 1175; *Billboard* (7 August 1915): 67; *Motion Picture News* (14 August 1915): 85.

Wilbur Durborough

24. *London Daily Mail* (29 July 1915): 5.

25. Durborough's captions and correspondence rarely if ever covered policy or analysis. See the bogus interview discussion in Chapter 4 and Professor Stein's comment in the supporting end note 14.

26. Originally published as *Deutschland und der Nächste Krieg*. See http://en.wikipedia.org/wiki/Friedrich_von_Bern-hardi (accessed 13 July 2012) and *Muskegon Chronicle* (12 August 1915): 1.

27. James O'Donnell Bennett, "East from Warsaw with the Germans", *New York Times* (13 October 1915): 3.

28. James O'Donnell Bennett, "Plain of Warsaw is all Desolation" (14 October 1915): 3.

29. Dawson, "Die Reise Nach Ivangorod", *Deutsch-Amerika* (27 January 1917): 20. After the American entry in the war, Dawson wrote a detailed report on the Russian trench line system that he had visited near Ivangorod. For more information, see: Albert K. Dawson, "Military Engineering", *Scientific American* (26 May 1917): 524–525

30. When Ries accompanied Durborough behind the western front his manuscript noted he was left behind due to army policy when Durborough proceeded with his escort to the actual front. DDM1, Sec. 13, 2. Whether Ries' absence for this event was due to army policy or for some other reason, it appears that Ries was not with him on their visit to the captured fort when they happened upon the Kaiser Review.

31. Harry C. Carr, "Capturing the Kaiser", *Photoplay*, Vol. IX, No. 4 (March 1916): 112.

32. DDM1, Sec. 21, pp. 1–6; Durborough Film Copyright Paper Roll, Reel 5, Intertitle #1: "Yours truly takes ride in an aeroplane out over the front. Aside from getting shot at several times and very much sea sick, I had a fine trip", Film Copyright Paper Rolls, Boxes 129 & 130, Paper Print Fragments Collection, Moving Images, Library of Congress.

33. *Wilkes-Barre Times* (26 October 1915): 13.

34. *Moving Picture World* (22 April 1916): 602.

35. DDM1, Sec. 22, 3–5.

36. Ibid., Sec. 28, 4–[5]; Sec. 29, 2–5.

37. Ibid., Sec. 28, 1–3.

38. Ibid., Sec. 29, pp. 1–5; *Chicago Daily Tribune* (10 December 1915): 15; *Chicago Daily News* (16 October 1915): 1.

39. DDM1, Sec. 30, 3; Sec. 32, 1.

40. Ibid., Sec 32, 4–5; Wilbur H. Durberough (sic), SS *Nieuw Amsterdam*, 30 September 1915 Arrival Date, New York Passenger Lists, NARA MF T715, Roll 2433, Line 1, p. 66 (Ancestry.com, accessed 22 May 2014).

41. See Cooper C. Graham and Ron van Dopperen, "Edwin F. Weigle, Cameraman for the Chicago Tribune" in *Film History*, Vol. 22, 389–407, especially p. 399.

42. DDM1 Sec. 33, 3–4; Graham, Cooper C., "The Kaiser and the Cameraman: W.H. Durborough on the Eastern Front, 1915", *Film History*, Vol. 22, no. 1, 2010; 33–35.

43. Reinhard R. Doerries, *Imperial Challenge: Ambassador Count Bernstorff and German American Relations, 1908–1917* (Chapel Hill: University of North Carolina Press, 1989), 144–146.

44. DDM1 Sec. 33, 1–5; Sec. 34, 1–5.

45. Chicago Press Veterans Association Application, Carl Morton Marston, MSS Collections, Chicago Historical Society; DDM1, Sec. 34, p. 6: "... and Marston here and a group of his friends helped me finance the moving pictures". If Durborough wrote more about the Syndicate, it is now among the missing parts of his manuscript. The existing parts also have nothing written about his participation in this film's editing process or his travels to speak before the film's presentations.

46. *Chicago Daily News* (16 October 1915).

47. Editors Fred Hobson, Vincent Fitzpatrick, Bradford Jacobs, *Thirty-five Years of Newspaper Work, A Memoir by H. L. Mencken* (Baltimore and London: John Hopkins University Press, 1994), 66.

48. For ad example see *Milwaukee Free Press* (1 December 1915): 9; for reel number, see *Milwaukee Free Press* (1 December 1915): 9.

49. Kitty Kelly's "Flickerings from Filmland", *Chicago Tribune* (10 December 1915): 15.

50. See e.g. *Chicago Daily News* movie ads on 6 December 1915, 17; 7 December 1915, 15; 14 December 1915, 20; *Chicago Abendpost* (4 December 1915): 8.

51. All film copyright paper rolls have "Dec. 20, 1915", "Jan. 7, 1916" and "©CLM 500" stamped on the underside of each roll. The author interprets the "December 20, 1915" stamp as the date the Register of Copyrights at the Library of Congress received the paper rolls.

52. *Moving Picture World* (15 January 1916): 481; (15 January 1916): 481.

53. *Warsaw [KY] Daily Times* (10 March 1916): 2

54. *Motion Picture News* (19 February 1916): 1068. Credit to Ron van Dopperen.

55. *Philadelphia Evening Ledger* (5 February 1916): 1; ibid. (11 February 1916): 2; ibid., (12 February 1916): 1; ibid. (27 March 1916): 1.

56. National Press Club's *Goldfish Bowl* [Newsletter], July 1938, 4. As noted, Woolley's original phrase was shortened from "With honor he has kept us out of war".

57. Max Alvarez, "Cinema as an imperialist weapon: Hollywood and World War I", https://www.wsws.org/articles/2010/aug2010/holl-a05,shtml accessed 27 March 2014.

58. See DDM1, Sec. 52, 1–5; DDM1, Sec. 53, 1–5; DDM1, Sec. 54, 1–5.

59. Ibid;.*Lewiston Evening Journal* (8 September 1916); *Portsmouth Herald* (11–13 September 1916).

60. *Daily Kennebec Journal* (7 and 8 September 1916).

61. Dawson, "Die Reise Nach Ivangorod", *Deutsch-Amerika* (6 January 1917): 6.

Chapter 7

Cameramen with the Entente

It was noted in Chapter 1 that the French, Russian and British armies did not allow foreign correspondents at the front. This remained the case throughout the war.

There was one way that correspondents could circumvent this and that was by gaining entry to the battlefront by private means. Edwin Weigle was smart enough to have figured this out in Belgium. If a journalist or cameraman could establish a relationship with a non-governmental organization, such as a private charity or the Red Cross, or alternatively, approach an individual with so much clout that he could make his own rules, the cameraman would be able to make an end run around the government. And the few individuals featured in this chapter did just that.

Ariel Varges

Varges was the major exception to the ban on non-official and foreign correspondents in Britain, which is all the more ironic as Varges started the war as a Hearst photographer. Hearst was such an anathema to the British that in 1916 all Hearst representatives were banned from any British theater of war. But it is the exception that proves the rule, because it came about in an extremely British way: by pressure from an individual too rich and prominent to ignore.

Born on 11 June 1890, Ariel Lowe Varges grew up on the north side of Chicago. His grandfather Charles was born in Germany and emigrated to the United States sometime in the 1850s. When the Civil War broke out, Charles was commissioned as first lieutenant in E Company of the 69th Illinois Infantry Regiment. The Varges family appears to have done relatively well in Chicago. Ariel's father Adolph was listed as an engineer. He also worked as a janitor at Horace Greeley High School, the same school that was attended by young Ariel.

Shortly after his graduation from high school Ariel started working as a photographer for a local Hearst newspaper, the *Chicago Examiner*. Around 1911 he moved to New York and joined the photographic staff of the International News Service. Varges' work apparently soon caught the attention of his superiors. When the Hearst

Fig. 70. Ariel Varges, removing debris from an unexploded bomb dropped by a Zeppelin. The picture was probably taken at the Salonika front. Moving Picture World, *1 July 1916.*

organization decided to join forces with film producer Colonel William N. Selig and produce the first American newsreel, Hatrick had ten Moy-Bastie motion picture cameras ordered from Britain. He also selected from his own staff a special group of press photographers who were taught how to handle these new film cameras. Among the men who learned to operate these movie cameras and graduated from America's first topical film academy was Ariel Varges. According to Academy Award winning cinematographer Victor Milner, who worked for Pathé at the time, Milner was the one who introduced Ariel Varges into newsreels.[1]

As we have already mentioned, although William Randolph Hearst's political inclinations favored Germany, he was first and foremost a businessman with a keen and a sharp eye on making his international news organization more profitable. He was always interested in pictorial news coming from all belligerent countries, as long as these stories appealed to a wide audience. In November 1914 Hearst's newsreel chief Hatrick had sent Ansel E. Wallace to Germany. Not to be outdone, Varges, also a Hearst employee and Wallace's colleague cinematographer, left the United States one month later with an assignment to cover the World War from the Entente side. It propelled Varges into a remarkable lifelong career as an ace war photographer for Hearst's newsreels that lasted almost until his retirement in 1952.

At the outbreak of the European war, Varges had just returned from Mexico where he shot film of the U.S. marines' attack at Vera Cruz and Pancho Villa's army. He was in Washington, DC, photographing statesmen when his chief Hatrick sent him an urgent telegram, telling him to join any of the Entente armies. By 21 December 1914 his passport was received and his first destination was Britain. From there he planned to cover the British forces on the western front in Belgium and France but nine days in London knocked that idea out of his head. After arriving on the RMS *Lusitania*, it soon became very clear to him that the British authorities had no intention whatsoever of allowing a film correspondent to accompany their army, let alone a foreign cameraman from the United States.

Without any letters of introduction or official credentials, Varges' assignment was in jeopardy. Then on 13 January 1915 a tremendous earthquake occurred in central Italy that resulted in 30,000 casualties. The town of Avezzano was literally toppled from the shaking and only one high-rise building survived. Practically all inhabitants were killed instantly in the worst casualty zone. Varges decided to head for Italy and film the earthquake. However, getting out of Britain with his cameras and motion picture film still remained a challenge. In a series of interviews by reporter Hayden Talbot, Varges told how he managed to slip out of the country with all of his photographic equipment:

> "That earthquake gave me a chance to get out of England and I saw that chance when the first news came out on the ticker. Of course, it wasn't exactly easy, even getting out of England – with a motion picture camera and tripod and a Kodak, not to mention a lot of movie film and plates. Everybody said I couldn't get out of England with a camera, and their deep pessimism actually got me wondering if perhaps they weren't right. So I looked around to try to find a second string to my fiddle, in case I did lose the stuff I had with me. And just then I heard about Sir Thomas Lipton and the special trip he was going to [make] in his yacht [for the Red Cross in Serbia].
>
> If I found I really couldn't get with the British or French, when I got over there, I decided I would have to try Serbia, whether I liked it or not. Through Lipton's friendship (I had known him in New York) and just plain American persuasion I finally managed to smuggle 70 per cent of the movie films and plates I had and two spare cameras aboard the Erin, in the face of a refusal by the Red Cross people. She was to go via Gibraltar and Marseille – and I had planned to get back from Italy and the earthquake in time to meet her there and either get on board or get my material off."[2]

Sir Thomas Lipton, a Scot, was the producer of Lipton's Tea and one of the richest men in Britain. He was a dedicated yachtsman and owned a fleet of yachts, spending much of his energy on trying to regain the America's Cup for Britain and visiting the

United States a fair amount of the time. During World War I, Lipton helped organizations of medical volunteers. He placed his yachts at the disposal of the Red Cross, the Scottish Women's Hospitals Committee of Dr. Elsie Inglis, the Serbian Supporting Fund, etc., for the transport of volunteer doctors and nurses and donated medical supplies. Serbia especially seized his interest. Some have commented that the Scots felt a particular empathy for Serbia, a small, mountainous nation with large and aggressive neighbors. In Serbia during the winter of late 1914 through the spring of 1915, several British hospital teams were working with Serbian military and civilian doctors and nurses. A catastrophic typhus epidemic erupted, killing thousands of civilians, soldiers, and prisoners of war; medical staff were among the first victims. At the height of the epidemic Lipton decided to visit Serbia, traveling aboard his yacht *Erin* via Sardinia, Malta, Athens, and Thessaloníki (Salonika). Once in Serbia he visited hospitals and medical missions in Belgrade, Kragujevac, Nish, Vrnjaèka Banja, and elsewhere. His modesty made him very popular among the people. He asked only for modest lodgings and requested for meals only what the common people ate under war conditions. He also liked to pose for photographs with Serbian officers and soldiers. In addition to visiting many hospitals, where he inspired doctors, nurses and soldiers, he found time to attend traditional fairs and to take part in blackberry gathering and fishing. The city of Nish even proclaimed Sir Thomas Lipton an honorary citizen.[3]

By way of Paris and Rome Varges arrived in central Italy on a military relief train. While filming a ruined cathedral a second earthquake shock surprised him and he was hit by falling debris. His films from Avezzano were edited in *Hearst-Selig News Pictorial* no. 14 that was released in America one month later on 18 February 1915.[4] Varges' next move was characteristically cheeky and unexpected. He went to Marseille, France, and presented himself before the naval harbor master as a personal courier of Sir Thomas, sent in advance to collect all his letters and radiograms. When Lipton arrived in Marseille, Varges could tell him all he needed to know about the whereabouts of his yacht and thus managed to gain his trust and confidence. When the ship finally sailed for Serbia, Varges was on board, possibly as a stowaway, together with four English reporters and another photographer.

The *Erin* was now fully equipped as a hospital ship for the Red Cross. When she arrived in Catania on the south Italian shore, Varges temporarily left the ship to film the local carnival. On the way to Piraeus, Greece, he also went ahead on a motor bike and photographed the ship as it ran through the Corinth Canal. Arriving at their final destination, Salonika, the *Erin*'s captain, who also commanded the British Red Cross operation in Serbia, decided to ditch Varges for good. The young American cinematographer was told he could not board a special train for the Red Cross to Belgrade. Varges however successfully outwitted the British captain. He sent a cablegram to the London INS office; with the help of his employer he had a train compartment reserved for him as a personal friend of Sir Thomas Lipton. According to his own statement, Varges also secured the cooperation of the British consul at Salonika to enter Serbia.

Varges was there during what is usually called the First Battle of Serbia. It was a vicious war and in this first round, the Serbs were decisively defeating the Austro-Hungarians. But win or lose, it was a war marked by epidemics and atrocities carried out by both sides against the other. Varges' first impression of wartime Serbia resembled an immense graveyard. The whole country appeared to be a succession of funerals. Thousands of Serbians were dying as a result of typhus, a disease that would kill many people near Varges and threaten his life as well. By taking a daily hot shower and rubbing his skin with kero-

Fig. 71. The Erin passing through the Corinth Canal. Photograph by Varges, reproduced from New York Times, 7 March 1915.

sene, he claimed he wasn't infected by the plague. On arriving in Belgrade he was invited to the Royal Palace by Crown Prince Alexander, who took a great interest in Varges' film equipment, a technology which the Prince had never seen before. During the course of his stay with the Serbian army Varges frequently met Prince Alexander and became his personal protégée. This personal connection was why Varges received some extraordinary privileges to accompany the Serbian army and film military operations both behind the lines and at the front. Varges had been adopted by Sir Thomas Lipton; now he was adopted by Crown Prince Alexander.

During his first visit to the Royal Palace, Belgrade was already under intense siege by the Austrian artillery. Varges soon discovered this made filming the war complicated:

> "While I was [photographing] the crown prince and Sir Thomas outside the palace, another shell dropped about 200 yards away. Sir Thomas beat it away in a wagon and the crown prince skipped in the opposite direction – to do rescue work! Perhaps this wasn't a regular bombardment, but it looked pretty regular to me. So I went back into the palace with my cine camera, hoping to get a hundred feet or so of the bursting shells, if I could get up high enough inside the palace. The shells were dropping all around but I discovered that the

Fig. 72. Varges demonstrating the latest type of Eyemo newsreel camera. [Reproduction from American Cinematographer, *March 1942.]*

explosive violence of these shells is so great they set no fire and the dust is all over in three seconds. So to get a shell bursting you've got to have your camera right on the spot where it strikes – and, of course, that's a matter of luck."[5]

On his return from the Serbian front to London in July 1915, Varges said he found this war was no photographer's war. Most of the artillery operations were accomplished from shelters deep in the ground. Batteries were hidden so carefully that one could guess the position only by the noise. But there was – in the words of Hayden Talbot – a "breezy optimism" in this young American cinematographer that accounted for his staying in Serbia long after the other British correspondents in his company had left the country. Inside an old Rumanian fortress outside Belgrade, Varges witnessed the Serbs dropping twelve-inch shells into Semlin, a strongpoint held by the Austrian forces. Semlin was in flames in twenty places and the Serbs destroyed an Austrian military river boat that was patrolling the river nearby. Due to the long distance and bad weather all Varges could film while this was happening was a destroyed Serbian artillery battery.

The next day, 21 February 1915, he left for the Serbian military headquarters at Kragujevac and proceeded to Nish. At General Headquarters Varges was given a military pass by persuading the Serbs that they needed an historical photographic record of the war, which apparently convinced the Serbian military staff. Together with Umberto Romagnoli, an Italian correspondent and motion picture operator who would later join *News of the Day*, Varges worked over sixty miles of front from Belgrade. He accompanied the Serbian infantry to Saganita Island in the middle of the Sava River, held by both the Serbian army and Austrian forces. Austrian shells were sweeping the open stretch of water continuously, Varges said, but under a hail of bullets he reached the Serbian trenches that were located only eighty yards away from the Austrian lines. He claimed the Austrians used highly mutilating dum dum bullets. While looking through a loophole Varges himself nearly got shot. "It's a beastly place", he recalled, "except where the interlaced mattings of small trees are placed on the ground, you sink into the mud up to your knees. Conditions are so bad that the men are forced to stay on the island only four hours at the time."[6]

Soon his Italian companion Romagnoli was stricken with typhus and Varges now spent most of his time attending his friend until he recovered. Many people were not so lucky. Among the plague's numerous victims were the celebrated Dr. Edward W. Ryan of the American Red Cross as well as other medical personnel and Entente soldiers who were sent to Belgrade to aid the Serbian defense. At Semendria Varges was taken by boat along the flooded districts of the Danube. On this trip Varges met the Comitages, a special battalion of Serbian guerilla fighters under the command of Major Voja Tankosic, one of the founders of the Black Hand Group. This secret terrorist organization had planned the assassination of the Austrian heir to the Habsburg throne, Franz Ferdinand, in June 1914. In fact Tankosic was one of the men who had selected Gavrilo Prinzip, the man who shot Franz Ferdinand, thus propelling Europe into the First World War. Varges mentioned he had seen Tankosic several times while he was in Belgrade and that the Serbs cheered him as a genuine war hero when they met him on the streets. A posed picture of this historical figure taken by Varges appeared in *Hearst-Selig News Pictorial* No. 51, which was shown in the American theatres on 24 July 1915.[7] Tankosic was killed in action later that year when the Serbian army retreated to Albania.

Again, Varges' adroitness paid off when he met these guerilla fighters in the Serbian mountains. One of the Comitages officers was an imposing major who had never posed for the camera before. Varges nevertheless soon found a way to convince him. "After a fine luncheon", he said, "I discovered that he carried a photograph of the two boys who assassinated the archduke [Franz Ferdinand]. That was my obvious cue and I used it. For a while he wouldn't hear of my taking his picture, but finally I showed him how bad his own Comitages would feel if anything happened to him and they didn't have his photograph. The result was he let me make a few feet of cine film of him and one Kodak picture."[8]

Varges said his relationship with the Serbs had grown so cordial and close that they didn't want him to leave the country. The crowd in Belgrade had christened him a 'first-class vagabond'. Many of the Serbian officials and officers evidently were intrigued by this curious American film correspondent, a cameraman from a faraway country most people knew little about, who carried a movie camera they had never seen before. As a joke, one of the officers in the Serbian military high command sent him an official document stating Varges had been commissioned by the Serbian government as secretary to the Admiral of the Serbian Navy. Varge's unusual naval boots that he had picked up while filming the U.S. marines in Vera Cruz in 1914 inspired this jest; apart from a couple of boats to patrol inland waterways, the Serbs had no navy.

In June 1915 Varges received a telegram from the INS office in London ordering his departure from Serbia. His arrival in Italy coincided with the Italian entry into the war on the Entente side. As his orders were to proceed to London immediately and because he was unable to buy any unexposed footage in Italy Varges shot no film of this historic event. Arriving in London he said the war had not left him untouched. When he stopped in Greece on his return, he had developed a recurrent fever and his work filming artillery had also caused hearing problems in his left ear.

Varges did not stay in London long. According to the trade paper *Moving Picture World*, he had returned to Belgrade by October 1915 when it was under severe attack by a combined Austro-German force called the Second Battle for Serbia. Frank E. Kleinschmidt was covering the same battle on the Austrian side. A review of *Hearst-Selig News Pictorial* No. 96, released in America on 2 December 1915, cites scenes shot by Varges of the Serbian retreat from their capital.[9] The Serbs in the end had to abandon Belgrade and Varges joined the army during its terrible winter march into the Balkans, a harrowing experience during which many died of cold and starvation. Meanwhile two large brigades of a combined Franco-British force landed at Salonika – modern Thessaloniki – at the request of the Greek Prime Minister. Their objective was to help the Serbs fight the Bulgarian aggression but the expedition arrived after the Serbs had been beaten. At this time while a new Entente military bridgehead was assembling in Greece, the British ordered all their civilian photographers to leave. However Varges' work so impressed the English newspapers that they requested the International News Service to provide them Varges' films and photos. As the only accredited film correspondent and official photographer Varges stayed in Salonika during 1916. He filmed scenes of the build-up of the international expeditionary force, including shots of the Greek Military Staff in conference with British officers and French General Sarrail, commander of the Entente forces in Salonika. Trade press reports mentioned he also filmed above the French and British lines in a balloon and he took aerial motion pictures above the harbor of Salonika. Several Zeppelin raids took place at Salonika while Varges was the official photographer and one of these destroyed a building across the street from his headquarters. Varges evidently filmed the burning ruins from his open window.[10]

From July 1916 his films were used by the British War Office Cinematograph Committee (W.O.C.C). A large number of films from Salonika, now in the historical collection of the Topical Film Company – at the time agents for W.O.C.C. – may be attributed to Varges. These short documentary war films were exhibited in Britain under such titles as: *Serbian Artillery*, *Mountain Guns*, *Serbian Girl Heroine* and *Stricken Serbia*. Varges by then was also mentioned in the newspapers and the trade magazines as an official cinematographer for the British forces. His work was respected in high governmental circles and on 16 June 1916 Varges' films from Salonika were exhibited in London's Scala Theatre under the auspices of the British War Office. Lord Derby introduced this show attended by Sir William Robertson, Chief of Staff.[11] Compared to his initial disappointing experiences with the British when he first landed in London, Varges had come a long way. His film career during World War I also highlights the increasing recognition the British authorities gave to the significance of film as a publicity and propaganda tool.

Fig. 73. Turkish prisoners captured at the battle of Ramadie by the British, September 1917. Photograph by Ariel Varges. [Courtesy Imperial War Museum, London.]

In March 1917 Varges was appointed to the rank of Captain in the British Military Intelligence Department. He left Salonika and accompanied most Middle East campaigns of the British forces. Although many of his films from this period are either missing or need further research, the Imperial War Museum has preserved a striking collection of his still pictures. Varges was able to cover General Maude's entry into Baghdad and reportedly was still working around Baghdad at the time of the Armistice. With little action after the British took Baghdad, Varges apparently spent his time in the city streets taking still pictures of 'types', old men, spruce merchants, coolies bent under their loads. Many of his pictures are excellent. As Jane Carmichael noted in her study of World War I pictures for the Imperial War Museum: "Possibly because of his cinematic experience the photographs have the sense, rare amongst those of the First World War, of spontaneous action only momentarily arrested".[12]

Ariel Varges returned to America on the SS *Nieuw Amsterdam* on 19 March 1919. He was officially discharged from the British army shortly afterwards.

Merl la Voy

Credited as the only civilian cameraman who filmed with the French forces at the time America entered the war, Merl la Voy's story on how he filmed World War I testifies to his remarkable personal qualities. By sheer perseverance, dodging governmental restrictions and military red tape over in Europe as well as exploiting his valuable American Relief Clearing House and especially American Red Cross contacts, la Voy managed to gain access to the battlefields of the western front, Serbia, Macedonia, Transylvania and Turkey.

211

14012-An American war photographer, Merl La Voy, ready for a motion picture flight over the Serbian front.

Fig. 74. Merl la Voy, ready for a motion picture flight over the Serbian front. Stereoscopic photograph, 1918. [Private collection Ron van Dopperen.]

Born 14 December 1885, Merl la Voy grew up in the small town of Royalton, Wisconsin. La Voy never talked much about his personal family background and in an interview with noted film historian Terry Ramsaye, he said he ran away from home with his pet dog and got his first job as a dish washer in a lumber jack camp in Oregon. He also told his friends that his parents had died when he was a teenager. His family records however show quite a different story. Merl's parents divorced when he was very young and his father Charles moved to New York where he started a new family. In 1893 his mother Luella married Arthur E. Peck, a farm laborer in nearby Tower, Minnesota. Merl also had a stepbrother, Irwin A. Peck, who was born in 1894.

Merl's youth with his stepfamily in Minnesota presumably wasn't particularly happy; around 1900 he headed west and left for Oregon, Washington, and Alaska, not to enjoy the rough company of lumber jacks – as he told Terry Ramsaye – but to stay with an uncle whose home was a log cabin in a heavily forested area. His formal schooling was erratic and of short duration. His education was acquired by reading newspapers often weeks late that sporadically reached his uncle's cabin. La Voy soon adjusted to the rugged surroundings and began exploring the Alaskan wilderness. He also found he quickly adjusted to doing hard labor and was blessed with great stamina, absolutely essential for becoming an excellent roving motion picture reporter.

A friend who knew la Voy well as a young man described him in a short obituary: "Merl was almost as much a product of the forest as was Kipling's Mowgli, but once out of his rustic environment he became adjusted to the ways of civilization with startling rapidity. His ability as a photographer was likewise a developing influence and brought him in contact with new types of minds and business interests. When he came to us in 1910, he had a camera and used it with skill, so much so, in fact, that he soon began marketing his Alaskan photographs to newspapers and magazines. In 1911 he bought a Graflex which became his most highly-prized possession. While stalking a herd of caribou with this camera, he suffered the only physical injury of his years of travel in the Alaskan wilderness. As he focused his shot, he stepped backward off a steep ledge and cut his knee to the bone. The courage and energy which he exhibited in the wilderness carried him far in his chosen profession. As a representative of Pathé Frères he girdled the earth twice and it is stated that he exposed more feet of film in World War I than any other photographer."[13]

In 1910 la Voy met mountaineer Herschel Parker when he was preparing his expedition to climb the summit of Mount McKinley, the highest mountain peak in North America. La Voy offered to join his party as the expedition's photographer. One look at him was sufficient to confirm his physical fitness, and in a few picturesque sentences La Voy outlined a background of frontier experiences that justified adding him to the expedition. Two years later in 1912, la Voy first made national newspaper headlines when he accompanied a second expedition together with Parker to conquer Mount McKinley, though bad weather forced them to turn back just 125 feet short of the summit. La Voy had by then been exploring for copper in Alaska for the Great Northern Development Company, but his fascination with photography and travel soon led him down a different road. In 1913 he accompanied Ben Boyce, publisher of a Chicago mail order journal, on his first trip around the world. Lugging a forty pound panoramic camera through the Orient, la Voy pictured many of the tourists' world wonders, such as the white marble mausoleum and jewel of Muslim art in India, Taj Mahal.

When war broke out in 1914 la Voy collected his pictures from the Orient and successfully used these beautiful panoramic photographs to obtain letters of recommendation from Josephus Daniels, Secretary of the Navy, and Lindley Garrison, Secretary of War. He also tried to get an appointment at the White House seeking an endorsement from President Wilson himself but to no avail. Armed with these impeccable official papers, la Voy was ready to cover the Great War and sailed for

Europe in March 1915. He evidently did not have any financial support for his film project and only a very vague idea on how to achieve success. His original plan, he said to a film trade paper, was to spend a few weeks in the war zone, film everything of interest, and then return to America with his footage. His plan eventually was carried out, with the exception of a "few weeks"; it took la Voy over a year to disentangle himself from the authorities before even getting to the western front.

Arriving in England, la Voy headed for 10 Downing Street in London and set up his motion picture camera to film the British members of Cabinet. La Voy found that filming British officials was not a simple matter at all. In fact the difficulties of getting war-related pictures, even on the public streets of London, were tremendous. At the beginning of the war, taking motion pictures in England was banned outright as a reaction to fear of German espionage. Later, any film coverage was intensively monitored and controlled by the police. Paul D. Hugon, manager of the British *Pathé News* office in London, related how he tried to get permission in 1915 to film British Boy Scouts and similar harmless scenes for the Pathé newsreels in Britain. His requests were all turned down:

> If the American public had a faint conception of what chances the man with the camera takes to get the various war pictures which have so far been shown on the screen they would look at the pictures with new eyes. …. Then came [in 1915] the Zeppelin scare. Thinking that possibly some of the famous buildings of London might be destroyed it was deemed advisable to fill out the library stock of such subjects. The request was made to photograph these buildings and this was also refused. One camera man was willing to take his chance and set up his motion picture camera on the banks of the Thames opposite the Parliament buildings. He was at once ordered away. Then he ordered a taxi and tried to get the picture while the cab was in motion. He had not turned the handle of his camera before he was stopped and threatened with arrest. One daring camera man got some pictures of the Trafalgar Day celebration by hiring a house on Trafalgar Square and photographing from a window. He was seen and a 'bobby' entered the house to stop him.[14]

Under such conditions it is hardly surprising that Downing Street was barred to la Voy. Within a short time, he was tailed and arrested by Scotland Yard. In an interview later with an American film trade magazine, he claimed he refused to talk until he was taken before the Chief of Scotland Yard, then won the ear of that official and told him what he was doing in London. The official reportedly saw the humor in the situation and promised to do what he could to get la Voy a permit to make pictures in Downing Street. Using both his natural charm and sheer persistence, la Voy finally succeeded in filming Prime Minister Herbert Asquith. Afterwards it was much easier for him to get the attention of other British officials resulting in his close-ups of King George, Queen Mary and Lord Kitchener.

These pictures of British war leaders taken, la Voy crossed the English Channel to Paris around April 1916 and began his campaign to interest French officials in a motion picture to be used in America to counter the various German war pictures that already had been shown there by such organizations as the American Correspondent Film Company. After having made pictures of President Poincaré, Premier

Briand, Georges Clemenceau and other leaders, he found that getting close-ups of big men was one thing but getting to the front and making action pictures in the trenches was another. The magic key that opened the door to any film coverage at the front was found by la Voy surprisingly enough not in the various departments of the French government but at an American organization in Paris, the American Relief Clearing House.

A brainchild of Myron T. Herrick, American ambassador in Paris, the American Relief Clearing House started as a joint committee set up in the opening days of the First World War by the American colony in Paris. Its initial purpose was aiding stranded American tourists in France.

Fig. 75. Getting mail in the trenches. Scene from Heroic France. *Reproduction* Motography, *16 June 1917.*

Herrick conceived the idea of a Clearing House in Paris for processing and distributing gifts and donations from the United States for French war victims. With the help of his predecessor, Robert Bacon, he formed a Committee that created the American Relief Clearing House in November 1914. Many of these notable Americans who helped create the Clearing House were also involved with similar initiatives such as the American Ambulance Corps in France and the American Red Cross activities. Their cultural and political sympathies were with France, a country where they had lived many years, a state that was an inspiring cultural centre and a symbol of what these Americans considered to be an international example of the Spirit of Lafayette, a true form of Republican democracy. These men and women enlisted on the moral side of what they considered to be the victims of German "frightfulness". As Herrick explained when asked why he did not leave Paris before the approaching German armies entered the city: "Paris belongs not only to France. It belongs to the world!"[15]

In short, these Americans in France were openly pro-Entente. Officials of the

Fig. 76. In the French trenches. Scene from Heroic France.
[Reproduction from Moving Picture World, *16 June 1917.]*

American Relief Clearing House in Paris saw the importance of showing motion pictures in the United States which might arouse interest in their work as well as that of the American Red Cross. The chief of the Clearing House – probably President H. H. Harjes – talked with la Voy and saw a unique opportunity to publicize the French cause on the American screen. He lent his support to la Voy's film plans, contacted his friends in various French governmental and military circles and obtained the necessary permission for la Voy to pack his motion picture outfit clear through to the first line French trenches. Information on his whereabouts in France is sketchy, but we know that – apart from filming in Paris and at Verdun – he was at the Somme battlefields in the fall of 1916 when he filmed one of the first tank attacks in the Great War. La Voy said:

> We were feeling our way in an early morning fog in the Somme, and as the mist lifted we noticed that the soldiers along the way were gazing ahead at some object of interest, and presently we learned that it was one of a squad of tanks going into action. It was the first I'd seen, and I made up my mind right there that I was just going to tuck away a few feet of it in my little camera. It was a magnificent sight, that great lumbering machine forging ahead thru the deep mud without any apparent effort, and a bit farther on it crossed a reserve trench – about nine feet wide, I should say. When its nose had just reached the opposite side, it just pushed ahead, and the rest crawled along like a giant caterpillar. Barbed-wire entanglements were nothing in its young life; it plodded thru them like a bear thru brambles.
>
> About this time my circulation was about as spry as it ever gets, and it was all I could do [to] keep my hands off that camera. I begged the officer in the car for permission to 'shoot' the tank, but he said 'No!' emphatically – couldn't think of taking a picture of it, even a 'still'. But I pleaded and kept at him with every argument I could think of, until he finally gave in.

'But quickly!' he commanded in French, and I didn't waste any time. I ground away until that tank was out of sight, and wanted to get some more of it farther on, but my officer wouldn't hear of it. However, I had at last filmed a tank in action, and was feeling mighty chesty about it, and didn't begin to worry; yet, how was I going to get it to America? I had the film, and that was quite enough for the present.[16]

Unfortunately la Voy, once back in Paris, cabled a group of about thirty pro-French business men in Chicago who had promised to finance his film project. His cable was intercepted by the French War Office and la Voy's priceless tank scene was cut by the censors. Some of the Chicago business men who supported la Voy were probably Red Cross members. Gerry Veeder in her study on the Red Cross films of the First World War mentions Howard Logan as part of this group. Logan later took la Voy on a Red Cross mission to Serbia. "Their underwriting of this venture", Veeder explains, "was more likely to promote support for France than simply to raise funds for relief work. Probably la Voy's affiliation with the American Relief Clearing House in France was worked out by his influential backers as a means to allow him to film the war. At a time when photographers were persona non grata on the battlefield, the green pass from the Clearing House allowed la Voy to move about freely."[17] Another important business man mentioned by the *Chicago Tribune*, who openly sponsored la Voy's war film production, was Elisha Morgan Jr., head of the Morgan Envelope Company and director of many paper manufacturing industries. Morgan's father was an active Republican who served as Presidential Elector and a member of Governor William Russell's Council in the 1890s. La Voy evidently had financial support in Chicago from some very influential business men.

After touring the French battlefields, la Voy returned to the United States in January 1917. His pictures premiered at the Strand Theatre in Chicago under the title *Heroic France – The Allies in Action* on 19 March 1917. The film was introduced by Elisha Morgan on behalf of various American war charities in France, probably the American Red Cross as well as the American Clearing House. A reviewer singled out a number of scenes showing the care that was being taken of French casualties of war, as well as human interest scenes shot by la Voy from the front that add a light touch to the film. "It is a comfort to know that sometimes the soldiers in France can snatch a few moments to play ball or dance a jig. These pictures, unlike what I expected, are not gory or revolting."[18]

While America prepared for war in April 1917, la Voy's movie was shown at Red Cross benefits throughout the country. Local exhibitions were usually sponsored by patriotic societies and Red Cross representatives. In Indianapolis for instance the film was sponsored by the local Red Cross and the American Fund for French Wounded. Special notice was given in a review to a scene showing the battle of the Somme, taken from a plane above the front. La Voy also filmed above wartime Paris and had his camera attached to a military truck to show the endless lines of transports going into Verdun. Another scene described in this review by the *Indianapolis News* bears a very close resemblance to the final shots from Donald Thompson's film *Somewhere in*

Take a Trip With Us and See

"HEROIC FRANCE"

An Eight Part Picture

of Pictures Taken on the Blood Drenched Battle Fields
of Europe Where Our Boys Are Going

Photographed by

MERL LAVOY

of the Section Cinematographs
of the French Army

Twenty Five Per Cent
of the Proceeds of the Film
Goes to the French Red
Cross

Showing action at

The Somme
The Marne
Verdun
The Aisne
Perrone
and other War Scared
parts of Heroic France

Merl LaVoy at the front making "Heroic France." Mutual eight-reel special, showing our allies in action.

In presenting this picture we do so feeling that the people of Canonsburg would appreciate a two hour trip over the world's bloodiest battlefields. The horrors of war are eliminated as far as possible in taking Front Trench Pictures, dealing more with the gigantic task that faces the American people and the unreparable destruction done by the Germans.

Star Theater, Wedneseay and Thursday December 5 and 6

Open at 10 a. m.   Matinee 10c and 15c   Night 15c and 25c

Fig. 77. Advertisement Heroic France. *La Voy was described here as a cameraman with the French army cinematographers.* Daily Notes *[Pennsylvania], 30 November 1917.*

France: "Another scene that calls for more than ordinary applause is that of a detachment of French troops capturing a number of Germans. The Germans are shown advancing from the trenches, their hands high in the air while, according to the subtitles, they are calling out the usual 'Kamarad, Kamarad!' of surrendering troops."[19]

In June 1917 when America had entered the war, the Mutual Film Corporation felt confident enough to buy la Voy's film *Heroic France* and release the picture as a six-reeler nationwide through its commercial exchanges. Meanwhile la Voy was preparing to return to Europe for a second assignment. He left the United States on the SS *Chicago* on 25 August 1917; his destination: Serbia. He

was accompanied by the previously mentioned Howard Logan from Chicago and this new film assignment clearly was an initiative by the American Red Cross. Logan went to Serbia for the American Red Cross to report on relief efforts over there, and he took la Voy along as his cameraman. When they left America the Red Cross had its own film program and was becoming an important partner for the United States government, as sole distributor of the CPI official war films. Taking la Voy along to film relief work and military activities in the Balkans evidently aligned with the course the Red Cross was already taking.

La Voy's second war film *Victorious Serbia* (1918) was released in the United States at local benefit exhibitions by the Red Cross. Not much is known about the contents of this film, although quite a number of la Voy's still pictures taken on this assignment have been preserved. A striking stereoscopic picture that was distributed by Underwood & Underwood documents he took aerial pictures, probably somewhere near Salonika, and filmed military operations by the expeditionary Entente force as well as the Serbs from above the frontlines. His cinematographic equipment was transported on a mule with the assistance of several Serbian soldiers. In June 1918 la Voy accompanied lecturer Burton Holmes for his last World War film project. The men probably had met in their hometown Chicago where Holmes was known for his long career in producing and exhibiting travelogues with scenes from numerous interesting and exotic places around the world. During the final months of the war they travelled together extensively across Eastern Europe. Films and photographs were made showing Rumanian military operations in Transylvania, daily life in Macedonia and the city of Constantinople (Istanbul) shortly after the Turkish surrender.

After the war, la Voy did not return to America, but remained overseas for the newsreels and continued his notable career Over There.

Donald Thompson

After Antwerp fell to the Germans, freelancer Donald Thompson now changed sides. He followed the Germans on their march to the coast and sat in a hotel on the Ostend waterfront when the British in return started to fire their rounds. While dining with some officers, he reported that a shell fell into the party and wounded him in the face.

The London press reported that Thompson returned from Belgium probably early 1915 completely exhausted, having been unable to sit down with comfort since his misfortune. In addition to the trauma suffered, the incident left a shrapnel scar on his face. After a couple of weeks of rest Thompson returned to Germany. His experiences there are most bizarre. As Thompson later explained in 1918, he was sent to Germany by Lord Northcliffe, owner of the *London Times*, who had arranged for a faked interview in which the American enthusiastically praised the German successes on the battlefield and spirit in the war. In this way he was able to enter Germany – not as a cameraman, but as a spy for the English government.

This story is in great need of verification. In the British trade paper *The Bioscope*, an article appeared that was filed in February 1915 by a correspondent of the *Daily Chronicle* in Berlin. His report is even more extraordinary than the story that Thompson created in 1918. As incredible as it may seem and despite the anonymity of the photographer, it does suggest that this reporter is Donald Thompson. Not only does the Berlin story dovetail with his adroitness and sense of drama, it also specifically mentions the circumstances under which Thompson was wounded in Belgium. The description of this "American photographer" is as follows:

> " ... He asked for permission to go to the front as a moving picture operator. His request was refused, but he was given 8,000 ft. of film depicting war scenes for use in America. Being a somewhat unscrupulous youth, he then calmly demanded that the Government should make a special series of pictures for him, portraying him as the victim of a British naval shell, while dining in a hotel in Ostend. Such a scene, he said, would add to the interest in the lecture with which he intended to accompany the presentation of films in America.
>
> So, he was taken to a cinema studio outside Berlin, and the incident he had suggested was 'faked up' in most realistic fashion, even to the extent of providing a young and pretty 'heroine' for the drama of which he was the hero. The climax of the film shows the photographer,

Fig. 78. Thompson with his Graflex camera. Publicity picture, reproduced from Leslie's Photographic Review of the Great War *(New York City/Leslie Judge Company 1919).*

desperately wounded, in the arms of his fair companion. Having myself seen these pictures, I can testify as to the absolute truth of the above story."[20]

Most likely, Thompson's story about the faked interview is a fiction. His reason for creating the story must have been practical: writing his story in 1918, he probably wanted to avoid being remembered as pro-German. Yet contrary to his strong anti-German stance of 1918 after the Russian Revolution, a reliable proof of Thompson's work with the Germans is to be found in a report from Chicago in January 1915. There, the photographer personally appeared in the theatres to lecture on his films. He spoke about the "camera's own neutral story". But his film commentary as quoted by *Moving Picture World* would seem to be biased enough:

"You will be shown the cheering crowds in Berlin as they massed to give the Kaiser assurance of their allegiance. You will see the Germans in battle; you will see them feeding Belgian children and refugees from the kettles at the field kitchens and ministering to the victims left behind. You will see what happened when the Russians bombarded the German front in East Prussia."[21]

The footage that Thompson brought back to the United States was later in 1915 incorporated into Weigle's documentary film *The German Side of the War*. The exclusive rights of these films were controlled by the *Chicago Tribune*. Thompson's work for this newspaper soon resulted in another assignment.

Robert R. McCormick, cousin to Joseph Patterson and co-editor of the *Chicago Tribune* decided to be a war correspondent himself, just as Joe had, but instead of going to Germany, Robert headed for Russia. Since his father Robert Sanderson McCormick had been an ambassador to Russia, his mother, Katherine Medill McCormick, had kept in close touch with the Ambassador G. Bakhmeteff. She persuaded the Russians to invite McCormick as inspector of the Russian Army:

> Mr. McCormick must arrive, not as a war correspondent, but as a distinguished foreigner personally known to the Grand Duke. This would give him an extremely prominent position which is refused to others, and at the same time it will not prevent him from sending to America correspondence, which of course will have to pass through the censor.[22]

Thus McCormick would not enter Russia as a film correspondent, which was forbidden. He would enter as the personal guest of the Grand Duke. He too was "adopted".

Together with McCormick, Thompson left for the Russian front. They visited the area around the Rawka River not far from Warsaw, shortly after Wallace had been in the same area with Generals von Morgen, von Hindenburg and the Germans. McCormick mentions Thompson three or four times in his book and indirectly compliments his nerve. At the Rawka on 11 April 1915 there was a fire fight with the Germans:

> Now Thompson has the machine up and is grinding away at a real battle scene. The Germans are firing fast, the crack of their rifles, the bluck [sic] of the bullets in the parapet, and the strange crack-whistle of those flying overhead being continuous … . Thompson wants to climb out of the trench to take the smoke puffs along the way, but meets a smiling refusal [from a Russian general standing nearby]. It would be certain death. So he has to turn his camera and take the bullet-torn trees behind to show he is at the front.[23]

Evidently Thompson had his off days as do all photographers. Ernest P. Bicknell of the American Red Cross, who one may recall as having appeared in General von Morgen's headquarters on 20 January 1915 in Western Poland, showed up in Petrograd in May of the same year. He reported:

> Colonel Robert R. McCormick, publisher of the *Chicago Tribune* is here. He succeeded in securing a permit to go to the Russian front and has been down in the Carpathians where he had unusual opportunities for seeing military operations from the Russian side. He took a photographer, Donald Thompson, with him and photographic supplies to the value of several thousands of dollars. He planned to take a great series of moving pictures of the actual war, the fighting, the life in the trenches, the troops on the march, the scenes on the battlefield. He had the cordial cooperation and help of the military authorities. He intended to start a continued story of the Russian war in the *Chicago Tribune* and the same day have the illustrating war scenes thrown upon the screens in the moving-picture theaters.
>
> Colonel McCormick came back to Petrograd with a vast quantity of these films to be developed and full of enthusiasm over the success of his unique adventure. He invited us among others to an exhibition of the pictures on Saturday evening.
>
> The evening came, the invited guests were gathered into the dark, little room where the exhibition was to take place, the signal was given, the mechanism began to whir – and only then was the crushing truth revealed. Something had gone wrong. Not twenty percent of the

Fig. 79. Advertisement With the Russians at the Front, *reproduced from* Chicago Tribune, *22 August 1915.*

films were good. Was Donald Thompson too agitated by [his] nearness to the fighting to make the exposure of his films?[24]

Actually, if twenty percent of Thompson's footage taken in uncertain weather and under combat conditions was successful, that is pretty good. What is odd is that

McCormick or Thompson had not insisted on previewing the films before showing them. This is the first lesson learned by anyone who has had to exhibit films in front of an audience and Thompson, certainly a pro, should have known that exhibiting raw footage to an audience that he wanted to impress was a decided risk. One is inclined to blame Colonel McCormick, who could be both impetuous and impatient.

The result of Colonel McCormick's and Thompson's efforts was *With the Russians at the Front*, which premiered on 21 August 1915 at the commodious Studebaker Theatre in Chicago. At a press preview McCormick told about the difficulties confronting photographers at the eastern front. "The motion picture camera is a near-sighted animal, and some of the pictures worked for hardest and under the most difficult conditions prove total failures. What we have is bona fide. There isn't a thing shown that isn't true. It will be of great value to the United States army."[25] Two reels of this film survive at the Museum of Modern Art in New York and some parts also survive at the Library of Congress.

After May 1915 Thompson no longer received permission to visit the Russian frontline because the combined Austro-German offensive through Galicia, such a windfall for Albert K. Dawson, Durborough and Kleinschmidt working from the German-Austrian lines, forced the Russians to retreat. Therefore Thompson started travelling on his own as a freelancer and he worked in Rumania, Bulgaria and on the Gallipoli front with the Turkish army. Details are sketchy about his work during these travels apart from an informative report from Serbia. On 7 July 1915 Thompson was near Belgrade. He requested permission to film the ruined frontline city and also take moving pictures from an airplane. Accompanied by the Serbian Cavalry Reserve Sgt. Subotic, Thompson first went to an airplane squadron at Banjica. The cumbersome film equipment proved too heavy to use for filming from a plane. Luck again left him a couple of days later when Thompson's camera broke down while filming a cavalry squadron and artillery operations of the Serbian Army. Sgt. Subotic's detailed report noted Thompson left with the job unfinished. He next travelled to Salonica, Greece, with only 300 feet of Serbian war pictures in his camera. He claimed he was the first American cameraman to film on Serbian soil but that scoop probably has to go to Ariel Varges.[26]

Somewhere in France

At the end of 1915 Thompson was back in the United States where he presented his film *Somewhere in France*, which was mainly made with footage from the French front.[27] *Somewhere in France* premiered on 27 December 1915 in his hometown Topeka. The photographer personally appeared for the showings. The exhibition was a commercial success mainly because the *Topeka Daily Capital* had bought the exclusive rights and gave extensive publicity to the event. Thompson's appearance – his cool, adventurous presentation – was eagerly reported by the newspaper as an item of public interest. With a sense of admiration the paper wrote: "When the film shows shells bursting near enough to the trenches to kill one man out of ten, Thompson casually explains that it is an 8-inch shell that spread death and maimed the living".[28]

Somewhere in France opened with standard shots of German captives being brought from the firing line under a French guard. Quite remarkable were the next scenes filmed at the French front near Queeneviere. This reel (no. 2) first showed some innocent pictures of French soldiers playing football and doing repair work on a damaged bridge. Then brief shots were shown of killed French infantry men, one with a bayonet sticking in his chest. The film title said: "For France They Die". The American contribution to all this was clearly screened with views of heaps of barbed wire made in the U.S.A., "said to have prolonged the war".

Despite the horror shown, Thompson's film – as far as the reviews indicate – suggested that victory would be on the Entente side. Scenes of the battle of Champagne in 1915 – a major disappointment for the French – contained some remarkable pictures of a trench engagement: French and German troops were seen firing their arms at short distance. This sequence ended with shots of prisoners taken by the French. In the last reel (no. 5) there were scenes of a German aviator being forced to land behind the enemy lines. These were followed in the end by pictures of Germans prisoners in a French POW camp.[29]

Partiality towards the European belligerent countries however wasn't a subject of interest for most of the trade papers when reviewing the film. *Moving Picture World* called attention to the unusual action scenes Thompson had managed to film: "One of the gems Thompson brought back with him is of an aero plane battle between British and German machines. The American had ascended as a photographer to do some work for the British. When he and his companion were 12,000 feet up they discovered the battle between the machines below them."[30]

Apparently not all Americans agreed with Thompson's war films. In March 1916, shortly after the screenings of *Somewhere in France*, Thompson was wounded when he was staying in Des Moines, Iowa, for a film lecture. He claimed that a highly explosive powder had been put in his tobacco pouch. When he lit his pipe, the explosion threw flames in his face and he temporarily lost vision of his left eye. Shortly before this incident Thompson had received an anonymous warning to stop showing his 'pro-Entente' films.[31]

Because of the injury Thompson changed his picture plans. He originally wanted to do a lecture tour in Australia but instead left again for the European front. This time he worked for Paramount Pictures Corporation and *Leslie's Weekly*. The young American filmed in Greece, where the Entente was attempting a counter offensive against the Bulgarian drive through Serbia. On 2 July 1916, back in France at the Somme, Thompson was struck on the back of the head by a piece of shell that left him unconscious for two hours. His wounds seemed to have been severe. The *Topeka Capital* reported: "He was bleeding so profusely that he was about to be tagged as dying".[32] After three weeks in a military hospital, he returned to America with his films and a trunk full of war relics.

War As It Really Is

The results of Thompson's eight months at the European front received the promising title *War as It Really Is*.[33] The film was first shown in installments at the Rialto Theatre in New York City. This was a remarkable privilege for the photographer, the Rialto being a major premiere theatre. The weekly exhibition of trailers from his war film resulted in much publicity.[34] On 22 October 1916, a preview was screened for the press and the film trade. As usual, Thompson was present to introduce his pictures. In the course of his remarks he said that 70 percent of the footage was still in France and would remain there until after the war. Despite the military commission he said he had received from the French, Thompson received no special favors from the censor. *Moving Picture World* was strongly impressed by Thompson's achievement: "The most impressive feature of Mr. Thompson's pictures is their authenticity. Nothing is faked. The photographer was under fire repeatedly, and scene after scene was taken at the risk of his life."[35]

The distribution rights of the film were marketed by the man who had nominated himself president of his own firm, the Donald C. Thompson Company, Inc. Most of Thompson's business partners came from *Leslie's Weekly*. Quite typical of the way the company operated was the amount of hype given to the cameraman. As stated by the publicity copy writers, the exhibition of Thompson's personal war souvenirs in the lobbies of the theatres would certainly draw a lot of customers.[36]

Did *War as It Really Is* show the European War as it really was? As with his previous film, the footage indicated that Thompson, even though he worked as a freelancer, could film only one side of the story. Beginning with our "hero of the camera" exchanging telegrams with *Leslie's Weekly*, the picture showed some remarkable aerial views of the Entente fleet at Salonika; Thompson closed in on this object by letting the plane go into an exhilarating spin. For one of the most immobile wars in human history, and one that afforded the cameraman little chance for dynamic movement or editing, the film sometimes gave a lot of attention to capturing sensational action. More importantly, the film probably served to exaggerate the image of the French at the expense of the Germans. Steve Talbot, who reviewed the film for *Motion Picture News*, called it strongly pro-Entente, and he added: "Much detail is clearly screened in the corpses and skeletons piled about deserted fortifications".[37] Only as a form of peace propaganda would the film be effective, according to Talbot.

There are good reasons to doubt any supposedly pacifist motives in Thompson's film. Margaret McDonald gave the following optimistic description of the French defense, as portrayed in the film: "What is termed 'The Steel Wall of France' consisting of 50,000 troops of French soldiers with fixed bayonets revealed before entering the

Fig. 80. "Much detail is clearly screened in the corpses and skeletons piled about deserted fortifications." Advertisement War As It Really Is. Moving Picture World, *16 December 1916.*

front lines is an impressive sight. We learn by means of these pictures that France has 20,000 aero planes ready for action."[38]

War as It Really Is gave the final message away in the last reel (no. 7) when a German surrender was shown. The survivors of a French infantry attack were seen running hands up to the enemy trenches, and crying "Kamerad! Kamerad!" The film closed with pictures of the French flag and the Star Spangled Banner.[39]

Filming the Russian Revolution

What may be called the most interesting experiences Thompson had during the war took place when he visited Russia in 1917. Not only are his experiences there remarkable from a historical standpoint, they are also unique. As Raymond Fielding explained in his book *The American Newsreel*: "The Bolshevik Revolution was simply overlooked in the worldwide chaos of the period. Even the Russians, during those first violent weeks, failed to document their revolution on film".[40]

Again Donald Thompson was one of the few cameramen to film an historic event. Together with Florence Harper, a British correspondent for *Leslie's Weekly*, he took on his next wartime assignment for that paper and left the United States for Russia. Carrying three trunks packed with photographic supplies, the American travelled on the Trans-Siberian railroads and reached Petrograd in February 1917. Only a few days later the first riots started in that city. Thompson grew convinced that the strikes were a form of political intrigue. According to him, the workers were set up by the government that wished to close the factories in order to create disturbances and sign a peace treaty with Berlin. Being strongly inclined himself towards a dramatic presentation, the photographer neglected to mention the social causes of the Revolution.

226

Although he later supported the Kerensky regime against the Bolsheviks, Thompson remained at heart a conservative. The thousands of Russians living under miserable conditions may have resented the Tsar for his autocratic behavior and incapable conduct of the war. Thompson however declared with a fine sense of pathos:

> The Russian peasant has just naturally got to sing a song to someone every night when he goes to bed. The educated classes in Russia want a republic. But the peasants need a King, just for the sentiment of it. The last time I saw Nicholas he was out in the palace garden spading up a flower bed. And on the fence all around peasants were climbing up, all over each other. Some of them had walked a hundred miles to see the Little Father.[41]

Although designed to make any Marxist grind his teeth, these words were to serve Thompson well in the U.S. After America entered into the war, his work gained a distinct propaganda value. Very soon the chief villain in terms of political intrigue was identified as German. In return Thompson received some unusual privileges to film the revolutionary events in Russia.

Thompson was present during one of the first demonstrations in Petrograd. Although he didn't understand Russian, there was nothing wrong with his intuition. He saw a crowd openly raising a Red flag, but the Cossacks refused to fire. The American was already anticipating a military revolt. As he wrote to his wife on 8 March 1917: "So far, Dot, I have guessed this war to a T. The people can say what they please, but I smell trouble. And thank God I am here to get the photographs of it!"[42]

These pictures were made with great precaution. Knowing that the Secret Police was taking pictures of demonstrators, Thompson used a small camera. This way he minimized the risk of getting attacked by a mob. The films he took were operated by an Aeroscope camera. This semi-automatic model was driven by compressed air and contained a stabilizing mechanism. The American used it to good purpose. The battery was put under his winter coat. Next, he hid the camera inside a bag with the lens at a small hole.

On 12 March the Petrograd regiments finally rebelled. It wasn't a happy day for the photographer however. Thompson was in jail during most of the time; before that, he had only been able to take some still pictures. Back in the Astoria, he had just decided to take a nap when shots were heard coming from the streets below. Suddenly he had an opportunity to film a scene of the Russian Revolution:

> "I put my camera up on the window ledge, pulled the curtains across, broke out a window pane and began to photograph the mob rushing across the square. Soldiers had advanced from all directions and were firing on the hotel. Suddenly the door opened and a Russian lady ran in screaming, telling us that the police was firing from the roof with machine-guns. That meant trouble. I warned her to keep away from the window. Instead, she pulled aside the curtain to look out. She was shot through the throat; I carried her to the bathroom, where she died about fifteen minutes later. I lost a lot of my film, thanks to this woman's damn foolishness."[43]

Thompson's petulance at the woman who spoiled his shot by getting a bullet in the throat and dying demonstrates a personality totally divorced from reality.

Fig. 81. Duma messengers protected by armed guards. Picture by Thompson from The Crime of the Twentieth Century *(New York City/Leslie Judge Company 1918).*

In less than three days, the Russian Tsar was removed from the throne. A provisional government was formed and plans were made for elections by universal male suffrage. The new regime that soon received support from the Entente also tried to continue the war against Germany. Opposing the government, the so-called 'worker councils' (Soviets) called for a quick termination of the war. Land reform, bread and peace were to be the slogans for a new Russia. As a result, the government authority was disobeyed by many civilians and soldiers. Russia was rapidly moving towards a second, more radical revolution.

Donald Thompson followed the peace activities of the Soviets with great dismay. His personal feelings turned into anger after the return of Lenin, the political leader of the Bolsheviks. As he wrote on 1 May: "Lenin might say that he is not in the pay of the Germans, but take it from me, Germany is not giving a special car to anyone to travel through Germany and back to Russia who is at war with them. The best thing for Russia to do is to kill Lenin. Every day he is gaining strength and getting the support of the lowest element in Petrograd."[44]

The cooperation that Thompson received from the Provisional Government was much better than previously. With his military pass signed by Kerensky, Thompson visited the front during the last Russian offensive in the summer of 1917. Eugene Hurd, an American doctor with the Russian army, had a dark room constructed for the photographer. On 3 July Thompson reached Galicia where he witnessed the results of the drive. This led him to entertain great expectations. According to him

Fig. 82. Dead Russian soldiers hanging on the barbed wire, photographed by Thompson. Eastern front, summer offensive, 1917. Reproduction The Crime of the Twentieth Century.

the Russian soldier had regained his former spirit and turned out to be as easily influenced by Kerensky's speeches as by German propaganda.

In Galicia Thompson filmed an extraordinary trench engagement. A writer for *Picture-Play Magazine* described how he accomplished this:

> ... One of his cameras was equipped with an electric motor which started the film to grinding at the pressing of a button. This apparatus was lifted above the trenches by means of a pole, while Thompson operated in safety from below watching the scene he was taking through a periscope. One of those trench films shows the starting of a gas attack by the Germans – not for the purpose of a charge, but to enable them to place their barbed wire. A detachment of Russians is then shown going forth to cut the wire. This fails, and the artillery is called into play. At last the Russians charge. Men are seen to fall, wounded and killed.[45]

Thompson had been much too optimistic. In two weeks' time the Russian offensive was stopped. In addition to the many desertions at the front, an armed revolt in July took the government by surprise. Immediately, the American put the blame on the Bolsheviks who were allegedly working in conjunction with German agents.

Back in Petrograd Thompson began to film the street fights. A first-hand account of his work there was written by Florence Harper. It gives a clear idea of the methods he used in order to fight himself a path with his heavy camera through the crowd:

> Thompson piled his camera into a big auto, and said: 'Come On'. The tripod of the camera sticking in a tonneau looked not unlike a new kind of gun. In fact it looked so dangerous that it gave us a clear passage up the Nevsky.

> Thompson set up the camera in the tonneau and proceeded to crank. One minute the street was a mass of people, the next they had fallen flat to escape the bullets or were running for

cover. As soon as there was a lull they gathered again. All the time Thompson cranked away. His coat was off, and stripped to his belt was an army Colt. The chauffeur showed signs of panic. Thompson drew his gun and said, 'You do as I tell you, or you'll get shot too'. He ordered him to drive around and face up the Litainie, so there would be a means of escape if they swept the place with their machine guns.[46]

Despite the precautions Thompson's chauffeur got killed. With chaos increasing now both in Petrograd and on the front, the American soon began to feel affected by the situation. As he confessed to his wife: "I am a nervous wreck from what I have gone through. On top of this I have the blues, for I see Russia going to hell as a country never went before."[47] When

Fig. 83. Thompson with his movie camera on the top of a truck with a guard of soldiers. From this position he filmed the Russian Revolution in Petrograd.
Reproduction *The Crime of the Twentieth Century.*

Thompson heard that the frontiers would be closed, he began to prepare for his departure. After developing his films, the Foreign Office gave a special permission that enabled him to leave Russia without having the footage censored. On September 1917, one month before the Bolshevik Revolution, Donald Thompson reached the United States by way of Japan.

The German Curse in Russia

The first showing of his film *The German Curse in Russia* took place in New York on 9 December 1917. National distribution was taken care of by Pathé, one of the major film exchange companies in America. The opening title of the film gives a distinct impression of the message: "Since March 1917, the world believes that Russia treacherously forsook her allies, but records from my diary and camera will show that Russia's anarchy was not willed by her people, but was caused by vile German intrigue working in the unthinking masses".[48]

Such a spectacular announcement needed proof; how did Thompson convey this message into pictures? As a fitting illustration, the film opened with a close-up of the man who appeared as the ultimate bad guy: Kaiser Wilhelm II. Two starring roles came his way in 1918: *The Kaiser – The Beast of Berlin* and *To Hell with the Kaiser.*

The titles say it all. Introduced as "Emperor of all the Huns", Thompson was explicit enough about his intentions. To increase the public feelings of resentment, the word "Germany" was spelled throughout with a small "g". Having lost the privilege of a capital letter, the Germans had gained privilege of possessing the number one screen villain.

The film continued with pictures of the Russian mobilization in 1914. Titles such as "From every part of the empire came galloping Cossacks" suggested the heroic war effort of the Russian people. Step by step the picture then led up to the main theme: overcrowded hospitals, shortage of war materials and surgical necessities. As portrayed in Thompson's film, these scenes were explained not as the result of Russian incompetence, but as a proof of sabotage and German-inspired intrigue. The demonstrations in Petrograd only seemed to confirm this somewhat shady and disturbing image. As Peter Milne wrote in his review for *Motion Picture News*:

> The streets of the city are a mess of soldiers and civilians. Propagandists of all sorts harangue on every corner. Different sects march after banners bearing different inscriptions. Disorder is in supreme command. Any definite procedure is a thing remote. As a result, the spectator gets a suggestion of the chaos that ruled in the city and which is still ruling there.[49]

This description resembled Thompson's personal view; for him all Russian revolutionary parties looked alike in that they threatened to disturb a continuance of the war. Perhaps he wanted to make this clear by cutting these scenes into frontline footage; as Louis Tenny wrote: "There are scenes of the Russian troops marching erect to face their enemy, and of the same troops, their minds poisoned by German propaganda, running away".[50] Another method Thompson probably used was typecasting. It is possible that he showed pictures of rough and obscure looking men who were presented as 'typical Bolsheviks'. These scenes were combined with pictures of fresh and youthful girls who had joined the Women's Death Battalion to keep on fighting against Germany.

The final scene from *The German Curse in Russia* contained another dramatic contrast that brought the film to a climax. As an answer to the threatening close-up of the Kaiser, there appeared on the screen an image of the American president. "Three cheers for Wilson!" a man shouted during the premiere in New York. According to *Variety*, the public went into a roar.[51]

All in all, Thompson's war film was highly effective as propaganda. Giving credence to the notion that the disappearance of Russia as a war partner was no fault of her own, the American audience could now safely enjoy the patriotic drama of what was announced as a "Blood-Stained Russia, German Intrigue, Treason and Revolt".

Together with his wife, Dorothy Marshall, Thompson visited the Pacific Coast in March 1918 to lecture on the war. He presented his war footage there in connection with campaigns for Liberty Loans, the Red Cross and the YMCA. His work for *Leslie's Weekly* was picked up later that year, when together with his wife he went to Siberia and filmed the military intervention in Russia. Dorothy volunteered as a Red Cross nurse, but also assisted her husband with his photographic work. In a letter to her parents, she wrote:

> "Don has sent here for me to have developed more than thirty-one dozen films. I had to write titles, sort and list the pictures and send them to Leslie's. He took pictures of the landings of the English, French, Japanese and American troops at Vladivostok. He was appointed official photographer for the Czechs and later for the American Red Cross in Siberia."[52]

And, as noted, Thompson got out of Russia a month before the Bolshevik Revolution. He was already back in the United States when the war ended.

Notes

Ariel Varges

1. Victor Milner, "Fade Out and Slowly Fade In", *American Cinematographer* (1924), 9, 13, 14, 18, 22, cited at http://cinesilentemexicano.wordpress.com/2011/10/25/2835.

2. Hayden Talbot, "'Making' A World War", *Fort Worth Telegram* (9 July 1915): 5; Synopsis *Hearst-Selig News Pictorial #14, Moving Picture World* (6 March 1915): 1502.

3. Sir Thomas Lipton, *Lipton's Autobiography* (New York City: Duffield and Green, 1932, Kessinger Legacy Reprints, n.d.); Bob Crampsey, *The King's Grocer: The Life of Sir Thomas Lipton* (Glasgow: Glasgow City Libraries, 1995).

4. Synopsis *Hearst-Selig News Pictorial #14, Moving Picture World* (6 March 1915): 1502.

5. Hayden Talbot, "Making a World War", *Fort Worth Telegram* (13 July 1915): 4.

6. Hayden Talbot, "Making a World War", *Fort Worth Telegram* (19 July 1915): 7.

7. Synopsis *Hearst-Selig News Pictorial*, no. 51, *Moving Picture World* (24 July 1915): 712. This newsreel also included shots taken by Varges of a Serbian field battery struggling through the mountain passes as well as an infantry engagement with the Austrians in a trench.

8. Hayden Talbot, "'Making' a World War", *Lima News* (14 July 1915): 4. Varges doesn't mention the Serbian major's name, but this may have been Tankosic.

9. Synopsis *Hearst Selig News Pictorial* no. 96, *Moving Picture World* (18 December 1915): 2238.

10. "Ariel Is Rightly Named", *New York Dramatic Mirror* (20 May 1916): 24. See also reviews of Varges' films of Salonika in *Moving Picture World* (2 September 1916): 1604 and (9 September 1916): 1754.

11. "British Peers Cheer War Films by I.F.S.", *Chicago Examiner* (17 June 1916): 13.

Merl la Voy

12. Jane Carmichael, *First World War Photographers* (London/New York: Routledge, 1989), 94–95.

13. Obituary Merl la Voy, *Alpina Americana Journal* (1954): 132.

14. "Camera Man At The Front Has To Take Many Chances", *New York Sun* (11 April 1915): 10.

15. *Reading Times*, 5 September 1936, 1.

16. "The Why of the Tankless Film", *Motion Picture Magazine* (August 1917): 60–61.

17. Gerry Veeder, "The Red Cross Bureau of Pictures, 1917–1921", *Historical Journal of Film, Radio and Television*, 1 (1990): 42.

18. "Merl la Voy Shows Allies in Action", *Chicago Tribune* (20 March 1917): 14. This article also has a reference to Elisha Morgan's support of la Voy's film *Heroic France*.

19. "Complete Arrangements for Benefit Exhibitions", *Indianapolis News* (20 March 1917): 12.

Donald Thompson

20. "Germany's Official Cinema Bureau", *The Bioscope* (18 February 1915): 603.

21. "Chicago Letter", *Moving Picture World* (6 February 1915): 812; See also a report in the *Chicago Tribune* (22 January 1915): 3.

22. Lloyd Wendt, *Chicago Tribune: the Rise of an American Newspaper*, 409; Robert R. McCormick, *With the Russian Army: Being the Experiences of a National Guardsman* (New York: Macmillan Company, 1915), viii.

23. Robert R. McCormick, *With the Russian Army*, 94–95.

24. Bicknell, *In War's Wake, 1914–1915*, 235. See also a report in the *Chicago Tribune* (22 January 1915): 3.

25.   "Crowds Watch Russ War Film", *Chicago Tribune* (22 August 1915): 3. McCormick wrote a book about his experiences, *With the Russian Army* (New York 1915).

26.   Dejan Kosanovic, "An American on the Balkan Battlefield", (unpublished manuscript in author Van Dopperen's possession), July 1991.

27.   The chronology on Thompson's whereabouts at this stage of the war shows he only spent one month in France. In order to go to Europe, he applied for a new passport around 12 October 1915. Any film work on the French side must have been for a very short while because he was back in Topeka by December 1915. This, as well as lack of any reports on the making of this film, indicates Thompson secured most of his footage for *Somewhere in France* from the French army cinematographers.

28.   "Kane-Thompson War Films Get Page in Leslie's", *Motion Picture News* (15 January 1916): 247.

29.   Review *Somewhere in France*, *Moving Picture World* (22 January 1916): 670. A large part of this film still exists at the Library of Congress.

30.   "Donald C. Thompson Home from War", *Moving Picture World* (26 December 1915): 2375.

31.   "Bomb Blinds Thompson", *Topeka Capital* (12 March 1916).

32.   "Thompson Gives Use of War Films for Charity", *Topeka Capital* (19 November 1916). Shortly before going to France in 1916, Thompson reported having received a commission as a Captain in the Nebraska National Guard when he was on a lecture tour in Lincoln. However the records of the Nebraska National Guard list no Captain Thompson on their roster. His death certificate records that he was not a veteran. California Certificate of Death, Donald C. Thompson, 8 July 1947.

33.   In 1916, Thompson also released a 23 minute short entitled *Fighting the War*. Most of the footage was taken around Verdun with scenes both of the battle and the aftermath. Also recorded are French pilots and their craft, both balloons and airplanes. The film is available on DVD through www.EarthStation.com. Segments of *War As It Really Is* can be found on the internet.

34.   "Rialto Shows War Films", *New York Times* (16 October 1916): 7.

35.   "Real Thrills in Battle Pictures", *Moving Picture World* (11 November 1916): 857.

36.   "War Trophies To Help Arouse Interest", *Motion Picture News* (23 December 1916): 4012 and (2 December 1916): 3453.

37.   Review 'War as It Really Is', *Motion Picture News* (23 December 1916): 4038.

38.   Review 'War as It Really Is', *Moving Picture World* (23 December 1916): 1814.

39.   Script 'War as It Really Is', 1916, 6. Courtesy of the National Archives, Washington, DC.

40.   Raymond Fielding, *The American Newsreel* (University Oklahoma Press 1972), 125. John Dored is another cameraman shooting the Russian revolution who should be noted here. He was born in Latvia and came to the United States where he filmed Westerns, then returned to Russia in 1914 where he set up a Military Film Department. Dored shot film with the Russian army on the Caucasus front in 1915. During the Russian Civil War he filmed with the White Army. In the 1930s he covered the Civil War in Spain as well as the Italian attack on Ethiopia for Paramount News. Dored and Robert M. Low, *I Shoot the World* (Philadelphia and New York: J.B. Lippincott, ca 1938).

41.   "Lenine Anti-American As Well As Pro-German", *New York Times Magazine* (18 November 1917): 9.

42.   Donald C. Thompson, *Donald Thompson in Russia* (New York 1918), 47.

43.   Ibid., 89–90.

44.   Ibid., 159–160.

45.   "Filming the Trail of the Serpent", *Picture-Play Magazine* (March 1918): 114–115.

46.   "Thompson Risks Life to Film Russian Revolution Scenes", *Topeka Capital* (30 September 1917). Florence Harper, *Runaway Russia* (New York 1918), 260.

47.   Donald C. Thompson, *Donald Thompson in Russia* (New York 1918), 313.

48.   "Blood-Stained Russia, German Intrigue, Treason and Revolt", *Moving Picture World* (22 December 1917): 1805.

49.   Review *The German Curse in Russia*, *Motion Picture News*, 12 January 1918, 294. Thompson contributed to the war fever in the USA by saying in newspaper interviews that all German Americans should be locked up in concentration camps for the duration of the war. See *Rochester Democrat* (21 December 1917): 19.

50.   "Filming the Trail of the Serpent", *Picture-Play Magazine* (March 1918): 113.

51.   "News of the Film World", *Variety* (21 December 1917): 49. Not everyone was as enthusiastic about Thompson's film. Paul Kulikoff was sentenced to jail for six months because he hissed at some scenes during the premiere in

New York City. This fact alone indicates the war fever that was beginning to affect the American theatres. See *Motion Picture News* (12 January 1918): 263.

52. "Goes To Russia", *Topeka Journal* (2 November 1918).

Chapter 8

Mobilizing Movies: the U.S. Signal Corps and the Committee on Public Information

The American entry into the war soon attracted increased attention by the authorities to film censorship and control. In April 1917 the U.S. Attorney General in Pittsburgh requested the Pennsylvania Board of Censorship to stop exhibiting three films, including the movies *Civilization* and *War Brides*, because these productions were considered pacifistic and so had a bad influence on public opinion. In Ohio the censors themselves took action and announced all war films would be checked intensively. Senator George Allen Davis from Buffalo, New York, proposed that the Federal Government ban all films with graphic scenes of the war because these would have a detrimental effect on recruitment.

Just a few days after the declaration of war by Congress, the Federal authorities began communicating with the film companies on ways to deal with war-related footage. Josephus Daniels, Secretary of the Navy, sent a letter to all newsreel companies asking them not to show any scenes of navy ships, naval exercises or preparations for war unless these films had been approved by his department. This complicated the production of newsreels significantly. To make matters even more difficult there were no official guidelines yet on what sort of film scenes could be recorded or regulations on securing an official permit to produce such films. Not until August 1917, four months after entry into the war, did the Committee on Public Information (CPI), the U.S. wartime propaganda and censorship agency, provide guidelines to American film producers. One of the most significant measures was the regulation that no photographers would be permitted to accompany the army abroad on active service in the war zone except official photographers in the government service (shades of the European authorities in 1914!).

Fig. 84. U.S. Signal Corps film crew with French artillery observation post. Mt des Allieux, France,
26 September 1918. [Courtesy National Archives.]

On 21 July 1917, when Secretary of War Newton Baker decided to produce a
pictorial history of America's involvement in the Great War, he gave the task to the
United States Signal Corps (Colour Plate 10). The army wanted to control photographic images using similar methods employed by the European authorities. Cameramen were to be kept away from the frontline so the army could control what sorts
of pictures were taken. Another reason to put the Signal Corps in charge was its
experience in military photography, however limited. In 1896 the U.S. Signal Corps
published its first manual on military photography. The first roll-film still cameras
were just being produced that were much more compact and suitable for outdoor
photography under difficult conditions. Two years later war with Spain broke out
and the Corps sent cameramen to Cuba who would take the first military pictures
from a balloon. There is no definite documentation of when the U.S. Signal Corps
first used a movie camera but the first reference is to moving pictures of a Wright
brothers' test flight in 1909.

In many respects the Signal Corps cinematographers got caught in a crossfire of
conflicts. They had to deal with army officers who did not appreciate the potential
for publicizing the war on the movie screen. The Photographic Division had to fight
the army bureaucracy and was constantly looking for ways to expedite the processes

for capturing footage and sending it back to the United States. The army's primary interest in motion pictures was for training and observational purposes. But as we will see infra, the CPI urged taking more footage suitable for release in the American theatres to boost public opinion on the war. As CPI officials were well aware, conditions at the front made it extremely difficult to record such scenes.

The solution to this publicity problem was found not in Europe but in the United States, where the CPI promoted its official war pictures with specially arranged publicity campaigns and premiere exhibitions. As motion picture pioneer Frank Marion, founder of the Kalem Company and CPI representative in Italy and Spain, said: "Such scenes as marching troops, construction work and artillery operations are already stale and something more substantial must be secured. This kind of material cannot be obtained by cameramen in the front lines."[1] Signal Corps soldiers were assigned to companies spread across the entire United States with most of them involved in telegraphic communications. The Signal Corps was seriously understaffed with its photography unit already dealing with lack of equipment, trained personnel and supplies. In addition to this, photography played a minor role in Signal Corps operations being chiefly considered an aid to aerial reconnaissance and artillery spotting. As the official historian Dulany Terrett noted: "Photography was limited to the indirect forms of communication, and for military purposes these were associated with minor functions or with major functions in a minor way. Publicity and record were the minor, intelligence and training the major."[2]

In 1916 when General Pershing started his expedition in Mexico to capture Pancho Villa, the Signal Corps was much smaller than during the recent war with Spain. Like most units in the American army, the Signal Corps was hardly prepared for war when it was declared in April 1917. When the first photographic laboratory was started at St. Quen near Paris in July 1917, the staff consisted of just one officer and one enlisted soldier. By the Armistice in November 1918, this photographic division had expanded to 92 officers and 489 enlisted soldiers and with great effort established its professionalism.

Under these circumstances, the expansion of the Signal Corps into film coverage of the war was slow and painful. It was almost a full year before the Signal Corps was creating documentary war films on a regular basis. While the Signal Corps planned to place a four-man photographic unit (consisting of a still photographer, a cinematographer and two assistants) with each American division, it failed to provide clear instructions on what sort of film to shoot to the first cameramen sent to Europe.

The development of these photographic field units was however seriously hindered by the Corps' initial decision to use cameramen with no photographic experience whatsoever. The general idea was these men would make better soldiers because they first were drilled and trained to conform to the military way of doing things. But there was no guarantee that under such circumstances cameramen sent to the front

Fig. 85. George Creel, chairman of the Committee on Public Information.
[Courtesy Library of Congress.]

would be the best or even good. On the contrary such an attitude probably made for the worst kind of cameramen imaginable. And this is when the CPI stepped in.

The Committee on Public Information

On 13 April 1917 President Wilson signed Executive Order no. 2594 creating the Committee on Public Information (CPI). Its primary purpose was to reorganize and channel all government information in the American media. Both censorship and publicity would be combined within one single governmental agency with two mutually antagonistic aims. This recreated the bureaucratic log jam exhibited between the German General Staff and the Auswärtiges Amt in 1915. It was a difficult, if not impossible task.

The creation of the CPI was in response to several developments. Many newspaper editors complained about insufficient reliable and useful war news released by the government. In addition pressure was rising to implement a nationwide censorship policy on both a local and state level. It wasn't until June 1917 that the Espionage Act was passed by the U.S. Congress. This Act provided the legal basis for wartime political censorship in the United States. The State Department in particular was most anxious to set up a system that would control all media publications that might benefit the enemy and harm national interests.

Wilson appointed George Creel as civilian chairman for the CPI, a journalist from Denver, Colorado, who had been extremely supportive of the Democratic administration. With abundant energy and enthusiasm, Creel began setting up the CPI as a tool for what he described as "The Greatest Adventure in Advertising". As Creel saw it, the American intervention in the war had to be communicated both within the United States and abroad as a straightforward publicity proposition, a mass media campaign on a scale unequaled in history. Creel was a firm believer in public relations; positive campaigning rather than direct governmental control of the media was his magic formula. In his apologia *How We Advertised America*, Creel summarized his personal feelings succinctly: "In no degree was the Committee an agency of censorship, a machinery of concealment or repression. Its emphasis throughout was on the open and the positive."[3]

And so, in a rather ungainly fashion, this chapter is divided between two entities, the CPI and the Signal Corps. They are of course widely divergent; the Signal Corps was a branch of the United States Army while the CPI was an entity of the Executive Branch of the civilian government formed by Woodrow Wilson. But they twisted around each other. Secretary of War Newton Baker was head of the Council of National Defense and thus worked closely with the CPI. The CPI was in a position to dictate policy to the Signal Corps, which had little interest in the production of propaganda and far more in the production of training films.

The CPI altered the Signal Corps' policy of only taking on photographers and cinematographers with no experience. Following an investigation by CPI officials Kendall Banning and Lawrence Ruble, civilian photographers with a proven record in the film business were commissioned into the Signal Corps.

As the CPI concluded, not every cameraman was suited for this kind of work. Press photographers who could work independently and had a feeling for shooting the right kind of film scene that was attractive to a wide audience were considered most suitable for recruitment into the Corps. As more of these professional cameramen joined as the Signal Corps ramped up its photographic division, keeping discipline sometimes proved to be a problem. As civilians, many of these cameramen were used to working independently which made it very difficult for the drill sergeants to make soldiers of them. One of them was George Marshall who had to drill a platoon with a number of remarkable press photographers. As he mentioned in an interview with Kevin Brownlow: "It was useless. You couldn't beat them down. I had all these characters, like those fabulous New York cameramen from Hearst News; they'd never taken orders in their life. I remember one of them coming out on parade with his shirt-tail sticking out. I said 'You can clean up the barracks this morning'. He wanted to shoot me. 'Don't tell me what to do!' he said."[4]

When Creel sought to professionalize the photographic division of the Army Signal Corps, Charles Hart of the CPI actively solicited and persuaded some American photojournalists already proven in the Great War to join the ranks. Those already met include Edwin F. Weigle and Albert K. Dawson who were among the earliest and Wilbur Henry Durborough would follow later. So in August 1917 when the Signal Corps established the photographic division, the first official announcement of the initial personnel listed Major James Barnes, Major Bert E. Underwood, Captain Charles E. Betz, First Lieutenant Edwin F. Weigle, First Lieutenant Edward J. Steichen, and First Lieutenant Albert K. Dawson.[5] Weigle and Dawson were among some extremely prominent photographers. Bert Underwood was one of the famous Underwood Brothers, who as Underwood & Underwood pioneered the marketing of stereoscopic photographs, and later the sale of photographs to newspapers and press associations. Edward J. Steichen was already a famous photographer

Fig. 86. Photographer Edward J. Steichen. Studio portrait, 17 October 1917. [Courtesy National Archives.]

who had been a major innovator of the Photo Secession movement in New York. He later changed his approach to photography to a crisper style and became, among many other things, a famous military photographer. He directed *The Fighting Lady* for the U.S. Navy in World War II.

The Signal Corps also attracted a number of cameramen who in later years became part of Hollywood film history. Victor Fleming, Josef von Sternberg and Lewis Milestone all enlisted in the Signal Corps although Milestone never went to France and served as an assistant cameraman making instructional films for the Medical Corps in Washington, DC. After enlisting, the cameramen began their training at one of three Signal Corps training schools. A school of land photography opened in January 1918 at Columbia University, aerial photography was taught in Rochester, New York, and basic training lasting five weeks was at a training ground at Fort Sill, Oklahoma. "They marched. They hiked. They swept floors. And they kitchen polished. It was a process of hardening," Earl Theissen recalled in a brief historical sketch on the Signal Corps during World War I.[6]

Despite basic training the Signal Corps photographers remained a special outfit with its own unique brand and character. Although a photographic unit was attached to each American Division stationed in France, most of the cameramen worked pretty much on their own. Apart from these units was also a mobile division of photographers attached to each American army corps. These cameramen moved around in the war zone quite freely and for most of the time recorded events according to their own judgment. Ernest Schoedsack remembered: "I had no directive, no passes. They didn't give me a gas mask or a helmet, although I did get a .45 and some ammunition."[7]

Facilities for the cameramen did improve during the war. Because it was expected that most of the films needed to be developed quickly, the Signal Corps introduced special trucks with darkrooms that were stationed in close proximity to the firing line.

This was particularly useful for the processing of aerial pictures. Most of the motion picture films were processed at the Signal Corps laboratory near Paris. From February 1918 this facility was located in the plant of Pathé in Vincennes. The screening of all footage ran according to a strict procedure. Each film reel was monitored by a Signal Corps officer for any information that could be useful to the enemy. Next a duplicate negative was made which was sent to the War College in Washington, DC. This footage was screened again by military censors and after approval the films were finally handed to the CPI for editing and distribution. Altogether the war films were closely controlled both in Europe and the United States.

Motion picture cameras were hard to find. As late as December 1917 the Corps had only five working cameras. The army bought additional Pathé cameras in France but these frequently broke down. A more reliable motion picture camera was needed that was light, sturdy and suitable for use in the trenches. So the Signal Corps ordered additional motion picture cameras of a revolutionary nature made by explorer Carl E. Akeley in his own company in New York. The "Akeley Pancake Camera" changed camera design and technology significantly. Nicknamed "Pancake" for its odd rounded shape, the camera featured a gyroscopic pan/tilt head so it could tilt straight up while the viewfinder remained in a fixed position. Akeley placed two lenses on the front of the camera – one as a viewfinder, the other as the film lens. He coupled them together in a way that allowed simultaneous focusing, something unheard of at the time. The camera also allowed the operator to change film magazines in less than 15 seconds. According to *Scientific American*, the "pancake" was introduced by the Signal Corps as its standard motion picture camera.[8]

Camera technology may have improved in 1918 but conditions at the front were essentially unchanged. Insufficient light frequently made it impossible to record actual infantry engagements that usually took place shortly before dawn. The same problems that had confronted cameramen like Wallace and Dawson when America was still neutral in the war had remained. Leon H. Caverly, a former newsreel cameraman for Universal who had become a cinematographer for the U.S. Marine Corps, reported from France that lighting conditions were so bad that it was pitch-dark by three-thirty. "Besides it rains and rains and rains with the result that we are knee deep in mud spelled with a capital letter. If 'War is Hell', as Sherman said, it should be fought in the tropics to carry out the proper idea of heat. Incidentally, lighting conditions would be greatly improved."[9]

In April 1918 the CPI sent Edward Hatrick to France as a special representative in order to report on the Signal Corps activities and any possibilities to improve motion picture coverage. As chief of photo syndication for Hearst's International News Service and the one who had set up Hearst's newsreel organization, Hatrick knew what was needed to direct such an operation on this scale. He advised placing a CPI liaison officer with the Signal Corps intelligence section permanently, so more pictures would be made that could be used specifically for publicity purposes. This

Fig. 87. First Lieutenant Edwin Weigle and explorer Carl Akeley, demonstrating the "pancake" movie camera. The picture was probably taken by Albert Dawson. [Courtesy National Archives.]

would also make it possible to give Signal Corps cinematographers directions and advance knowledge on what subjects to record and at what place. While in France, Hatrick and Lieutenant Charles Phelps Cushing, who was in charge of editing films for the CPI, were interviewed by *Picture-Play Magazine* on their experiences with the Signal Corps and the difficulties of filming at the front:

'A man with a camera seems to be a jinx', said Cushing to me, while we were talking about news photography. 'I wish we could have gotten that air battle, but whoever heard of such luck? Every time I go up to the front they show me craters and tell me what unusually fine stuff I could have had if I'd been there about daybreak – when there wasn't any light for taking pictures – or the day before, when it was raining, or some other time when I just didn't happen to be there. But whenever the sun is shining right, and the cameraman's on the job, things suddenly become peaceful. I hope the folks back home know that we're doing our best to give 'em the real stuff'.

'Of course', Hatrick went on, lighting his cigar again, 'he was exaggerating about a camera man being a jinx, as I had good reason to learn before I got through, because Hubbell and I – Hubbell was my own camera man – found things plenty warm enough for us on several occasions. We didn't seem to be jinxes. But it's true that taking war pictures is a more difficult thing than you'd imagine – that is, to get big, realistic effects when the fighting is going on. In the first place, if you take a wide range of a battle going on all you get is a lot of shells bursting. There's no way of showing hundreds of men making a charge, because they don't go forward in close formation. You're lucky if you can get a half dozen figures in the range of your camera. Then the photographers, of course, like all soldiers, have to protect themselves as much as possible. A photographer wouldn't be allowed to expose himself unnecessarily, even if he wanted to.

'The first time I went up to the very front where there was heavy fighting – it was at Château-Thierry – we landed at night. We struck a village and were stopped. A colonel came

*Fig. 88. Edward B. Hatrick (left), head of Hearst's INS photo
and newsreel service, visits the front. Sommedieu, France, 30
April 1918. He is accompanied by Sergeant Adrian Duff,
formerly of the American Press Association. Duff – here seen in
the middle – was primarily a still photographer.
[Courtesy National Archives.]*

out and demanded to know what the bang bang blazes we were doing here. Say, he was one mad colonel. He let loose a volley of heavy-artillery talk and said he didn't want any photographers or correspondents or anyone but fighting men there. He didn't want the slightest chance of our drawing the attention of a Boche observer, and then – shell fire. I didn't blame him. He was dead right. Pictures were important, but human lives even more so.'[10]

An unfortunately anonymous journalist interviewed several unfortunately anony-mous cameramen, including at least one lieutenant, for *Stars and Stripes* and seconded the reports of the difficulties of filming in France in wartime:

> There is one movie-officer at present assigned to every division in the A.E.F. – one might call him the commander of the camera battery, if one wanted to be really military about it. Under him is a squad of expert photographers – some movie men, some 'still' snappers. From the time when the sun finally decides that he might as well hobble up in the sky and do part of a day's work – which isn't often, in this region – until the time that the aged decrepit old solar luminary decides again, about the middle of the afternoon, that he's done all he's going to do while the calendar is fixed the way it is, the camera battery is up and around, taking pot-shots at everything in sight. The battery – or rather, squad – goes out on 'news tips', just as newspaper photographers and operators for the 'news weeklies' go out in the states. They may be 'covering' a review, a series of field maneuvers, a march 'up front' – or merely Blank Company's wash day at the village fountain. But always, when the sun is shining, they are at it.

> 'Light conditions here in France', says one of the divisional movie magnates, 'are worse than they are anywhere else in the world. Our working day for picture taking lasts only from about 9:30 in the morning to 3 o'clock in the afternoon. But it takes us a good deal of time to get around to the things we want to film, so our actual working day is much longer, of course. At that, even with the sunshine we do get, the only color that seemed to come out is yellow – a yellowish mud color. It's fierce!'

And the cameraman continues to eulogize the old days in Mexico:

> '… Down in good old Mexico, though – those were the battles in film! Real, rip-roaring charges and open field fighting – all this Dustin Farnum wild west horseback stuff, where you could get close-ups. Half of the engagements you try to [film] over here look just like peaceful landscape, with here and there a little smoke coming out.'[11]

Fig. 89. Capt. Wilbur H. Durborough at his desk at U.S. Signal Corps Headquarters, Washington, DC., 29 January 1919. [Courtesy National Archives.]

Things might not have looked so peaceful had he been at the Meuse-Argonne in October 1918.

Wilbur H. Durborough

In late 1917 Durborough was back home and recruited to support the CPI. After an initial two months training, Durborough accepted a First Lieutenant's commission in the U.S. Army Signal Corps Reserves in November. In Creel's 1918 budget he listed Lieutenants Durborough and Weigle as two of his five Road Camera Men, the other three being civilians. In August of 1918 Durborough was promoted to Captain and honorably discharged on 31 January 1919. Durborough would later describe his army service as "photographic propaganda".

During his time in service, he produced a short film at Ft. Lewis, Washington, to demonstrate how the troops there would defend against an attack. This clearly wasn't a training film but intended to support Creel's purpose of convincing others the U.S. Army was well prepared for war. As he did in his 1915 film, he followed a story line. Initially troops are seen relaxing and visiting with family until the alert comes via semaphore and phone, then troops are mustered and deployed, followed by escalating displays of camouflaged infantry and artillery counterattack and concluding with evacuating and treating the wounded. Durborough appears to have believed it important for war film credibility to include casualties, real or staged. When writing in his manuscript about filming the phony truck train attack he filmed in Mexico in 1916, he especially noted to Captain Hunter how real it looked by having "a few of the boys carried out on stretchers to a first aid station, bandages on their head and everything". While on the west coast in Washington, Durborough also took some Seattle area shipyard film with fellow officer Lt. Edward N. Jackson after they arrived too late and missed their assignment to film the launching of the *General Pershing*.

Albert K. Dawson

After the United States entered the war in April 1917, Dawson had quickly offered his services to the government. His firm Brown & Dawson became part of a committee of news photographic agencies that actively worked together with the CPI. Dawson's name appeared on the board of representatives of this committee, together with renowned figures such as Edward Hatrick of Hearst's INS and George C. Bain of Bain News Service. In August 1917 the U.S. Signal Corps started a Photographic Division, an organization that would make it possible to recruit enough military cameramen to record a pictorial history of the part America would play in the Great War.

Dawson received a commission as First Lieutenant. Shortly afterwards on 2 November 1917 Dawson was promoted to Captain and put in charge of the U.S. Signal Corps photographic laboratory. As supervising officer for the War College in Washington, DC. Dawson's responsibility was to direct the screening, development and editing of all war-related pictures coming from Europe.

Because of his experiences in Europe, Dawson was also assigned to train Signal Corps camera men in the art of war photography. One of his soldiers in 1942 recalled how he photographed Dawson while he took a group of military camera men to the parade grounds near the War College at Washington, DC, and arranged a remarkable mock battle:

> "As I took this picture, I am not in the group. In some way, Captain Dawson borrowed some motorcycles with sidecars and we were bundled into them with our cameras and roared up to an imaginary battle line, dashed out with our cameras and photographed an imaginary battle, under the direction of the captain.
>
> You will notice the captain with his gloved hand high in the air, presumably holding up the battle while the pictures were being made. Then we had to grab our cameras, dash back to the motorcycles and were whisked away to another point of action. This manoeuvre still gives me a laugh, particularly when I think of what we actually had to do overseas when our Division was in action."[12]

Around February 1918, Dawson also got caught up in the nationwide publicity surrounding the trial against his former employer, Felix Malitz. While producing war movies for the American Correspondent Film Company, Malitz had branched out into a completely different line of work: the illegal export of rubber to Germany.

Fig. 90. Capt. Albert K. Dawson (left) and his squad of Signal Corps cameramen, 1917.
[Photo © Brown & Dawson. Courtesy National Archives.]

Malitz succeeded in getting tons of rubber goods through the British blockade, mainly as a result of a courier system that he had set up previously to get the A.C. Film Company movies to America. Malitz had also struck a deal with the head stewards of two Norwegian liners, and they arranged for the loading and shipment of these goods to Europe. Malitz's offices were raided by the American authorities, and as a result Dawson's involvement with the American Correspondent Film Company came to light. When his name was first mentioned by the *New York Times*, the U.S. Signal Corps gave out a short statement the very same day, saying he had been accused of embezzling photographic supplies worth $60.00. Dawson was tried by General Court-Martial and dismissed on 29 March 1918. No further details were made public by the military, but the general opinion in the film trade press was that Dawson was fired on a technical charge. The true reason probably was his direct and personal involvement with the A.C. Film Company. Particularly damaging to Dawson's reputation must have been a story that was run by *Motography* which mentioned his nickname for the first time. While he was in Europe, German officials referred to him as "The Boy from Indiana". According to this trade press report, his appearances in these films even made the German authorities consider producing a propaganda film with that title.

Edwin F. Weigle

As one of three officers tasked to organize the photographic division of the U.S. Army, Weigle was first assigned to the aviation section, and then in June of 1918 was ordered to duty in France.[13] Between 28 September 1918 and 15 January 1919 Weigle was the Photographic Officer attached to the 35th Division, a National Guard unit of

Fig. 91. Weigle shows General Peter Traub, the commanding officer of the 35th Division, the mechanism of his camera. [Signal Corps photograph, courtesy National Archives.]

Kansans and Missourians formed in August 1917. Among its soldiers was a future President, Harry S. Truman, who commanded Battery D of the 129th Field Artillery. The 35th was at the Meuse-Argonne offensive and suffered 7,300 casualties due to a combination of inexperience, incompetence and having to battle superior troops of the First and Fifth Prussian Guards. The Division collapsed and was removed from the front on 1 October 1918 after five days on the line. Weigle photographed the Meuse-Argonne offensive before the 35th was transferred to the Verdun sector on 1 October. He later wrote that he filmed 14,000 feet of film which captured "a fair historical record of the 35th". This film does not capture the horror of the Division's suffering at the Meuse-Argonne. His reports also echo the other cameramen's complaints about the difficulties of filming under combat conditions:

> My personal narrative of experiences as Photo Officer of the 35th Division.
>
> With the 35th Division from September 25 to January 15th 1919, as Photographic Officer and being a motion picture photographer myself I may state that war was not made to please the camera man. In order to take interesting pictures showing real war, the camera man must rely upon good fortune; he must have good light conditions and when light conditions are favorable to enable him to photograph, he must have good fortune to guide him to the right place at the right time.
>
> He may be an expert in his line and he may be an expert in staging and directing, but war in

the reality – the most interesting scenes develop and disappear before the camera-man can take his crank-handle from his pocket and commence "grinding".

The 35th Division was one of the first divisions to go over the top on September 26th, starting the Argonne Drive and remaining in the line until relieved on October first.

As I said I joined the Division on the 28th of September and I had ample time to arrange my camera and had everything prepared to register an invaluable scene showing our troops going over the top the following morning, September 29th. I had no idea as to the exact time they were going over, but my camera was in position on the front line at Five A.M. Enemy shells were dropping everywhere, and I hoped the order for going over would not be given until daylight, but no such luck. The dough-boys went over at 5:35 A.M. and it was so dark at that moment it would not make an impression in the most sensitized film manufactured. It was a case where darkness was safe and good fortune for the dough-boy, but unfortunate for the camera man – the dough-boys gained their objective by daylight with few casualties and I stood where the doughboys left me, with a camera in perfect working order and with tears in my eyes, realizing that a scene so important for historical purposes, of which one hundred feet would be worth a million feet taken back of the lines, was gone forever because of light conditions.

The 35th Division was relieved October 1st, marched back to a rest area for five days and then ordered back into the line, taking over a quiet sector east of Verdun. Even in this quiet sector the photographer could have satisfied his craving for a thrilling picture, but most of the thrilling activities took place in the night. While in this sector we had two balloon Companies attached to our Division. A report came to Headquarters that the Boche Planes were giving our balloons much trouble so that a number of our balloons along the entire front were being shot down daily. I went out to a high point where two of our balloons were up, say about a mile apart; set up my camera and attached a magazine with a 400 foot roll of film. Then came the question which of the balloons to focus my camera on. I had to choose one of the two as I could not station my camera between the two bags, they being too far apart. So I simply had to pick one of the two and take a chance that the one on which I was focusing might be shot down. I did not have a feeling of hope that one would be shot down, but my thoughts were on pictures, and in war the unexpected sometimes happens; and if it had in this case I would be ready and able to take a record of it. I spent the whole of one day and half of the next with the camera focused on the big gas bag 1500 feet in the air and my eyes were searching the skies for Boche planes from morning until night. About noon the next day the unfortunate happened. A Boche plane came over, took a shot at the balloon, but it was the one a mile distant, and plainly visible to me, I saw the big bag catch fire, the observer glide down safely to the earth in his parachute, and the conflagration was over in 15 seconds, but I the camera man was again unfortunate – I was there at the right time, but not in the right place.

In spite of the fact that I was unfortunate in not making all my films thrilling ones, I did succeed in making 14,000 feet of film which may be a fair historical record if the 35th Division."[14]

Another soldier from the 35th Division who fell at the Meuse-Argonne was Hobart Edwards, Nelson's brother.

Weigle stayed in France until February 1919 and arrived back in Chicago as a Signal Corps Captain on 12 June 1919.[15] Unlike Albert Dawson he had no security problems despite having filmed intensively in Germany and Austria. He received nothing but glowing reports from his superiors in the Signal Corps and was responsible for 110 miles of Signal Corps film brought back from Europe after the war.

Weigle said about 15,000 feet of the film had been devoted to General Pershing, "much to the General's disgust".[16]

Joseph Hubbell

Hubbell is a less prominent cameraman than others, but as a veteran Pathé cameraman and favorite of Hearst and Hatrick, he deserves mention. He was sent to France in 1918 by the CPI. Joseph Hubbell, Hatrick and others were ordered first to Neufchâteau and then elsewhere in France to photograph material for *The Official War Review*. Hubbell freely admits that there was some fakery in making newsreels:

> 'Our idea was to make up propaganda films to show what we were doing. On one occasion they had hospital trains near us that could run up to the front and bring back the wounded. We took a company of men, bandaged them up and laid them out in the sun on stretchers and loaded the train. I was bought up on charges that I was faking it. Well, that wasn't a good word. I was representing an occasion that you wouldn't take the chance with a lot of wounded men. And it looked just the same.'[17]

Troubles at the CPI

Under the guidance of its first director, Louis W. Mack, the CPI Film Division set up twelve offices across the country to make war documentary films available to schools, State Councils of National Defense, patriotic societies and the like. Through these promotional channels the CPI released war-related documentaries with titles such as *The 1917 Recruit* and *Labor's Part in Democracy's War* but circulation of these films remained limited. A fundamental change of policy occurred when Charles S. Hart, former advertising manager of *Hearst's Magazine,* succeeded Mack in March 1918. The CPI now managed both film production and distribution which resulted in significantly increased film exhibitions. Despite having no motion picture experience, Hart greatly expanded the CPI film program in the United States and by the end of the war his agency had become a key player in the American film business. The CPI became sole producer of a new weekly newsreel that contained the most interesting scenes taken by the American military cinematographers in France: *The Official War Review*. This weekly newsreel contained scenes taken by the U.S. Signal Corps as well as military cinematographers from France and Britain.

War films from the Entente powers were marketed differently within each country. French films were sold to all companies at a flat rate of one dollar per foot. The British war films were simply sold to the highest bidder. For the American market, the CPI initially offered *The Official War Review,* assembled with difficulty from various sources, to all newsreel companies on equal conditions and the same price. This offer did not meet the film industry's expectations with newsreel companies wanting exclusive scenes to stay a step ahead of the competition. When no company was willing to purchase at the original offer, the CPI next offered a package arrangement. The Signal Corps films would be edited in several versions and newsreel companies were free to buy according to their preferences. To finance the investments that were necessary for editing, titling and printing, all companies were requested to pay $5,000

The sort of enemy we are fighting

you may see him as he is in

OFFICIAL WAR REVIEW #10

Upon a German officer captured during the latest drive by the Allies in France, was discovered an order commanding the Hun armies to 'destroy everything.' In Official War Review #10 is shown how thoroughly this damnable order was followed. Scenes of wanton destruction and murder are shown that would shame a tribe of head-hunters.

Official war pictures of the British, French, Italian and American Governments, issued one reel a week.

Committee on Public Information
George Creel, Chairman
Division of Films
Chas. S. Hart, Director
Distributed by

PATHÉ

Fig. 92. Advertisement Moving Picture World,
14 September 1918.

in advance. This package proposal had distinct advantages to the newsreel company offering the highest bid to buy the best collection of war scenes. Not surprisingly, *Pathé News* made the best financial offer and purchased *The Official War Review* as its sole distributor. Its terms gave 80 percent of all proceeds to the CPI. Films not used by Pathé were sold to other newsreel companies at a flat rate of one dollar per foot. Perhaps not incidentally, *Pathé News* was Hearst's newsreel distributor at the time.

The first issue of *The Official War Review* was released on 1 July 1918. Pathé supported its distribution with an extensive publicity campaign. Advertisements in the trade press became increasingly sensational and lurid. A good example is found in *Moving Picture World* that previewed no. 10: "The sort of enemy we are fighting. You may see him as he is in *Official War Review* no. 10. Upon a German officer captured during the latest drive by the Allies in France, was discovered an order commanding the Hun armies to 'destroy everything'. In *Official War Review* no. 10 is shown how thoroughly this damnable order was followed. Scenes of wanton destruction and murder are shown that would shame a tribe of headhunters."[18]

In his book Creel, head of all divisions of the CPI, also noted that from the start it was obvious the motion picture was as important as the written and spoken word. This may well have been Creel's personal intention, but CPI films as a publicity tool came remarkably late. It took five months before the CPI created the film division on 25 September 1917. It took another six months before the CPI began producing, distributing and exhibiting war films for the American film industry. Apart from the complexities involved in creating an extensive governmental agency like the CPI including building a staff, a comprehensive program and the financial resources, motion pictures came relatively late because they conflicted with existing commercial interests in the American film industry. The idea of sending out free publicity worked well for print media; editors and newspaper journalists were used to receiving press releases on a daily basis. But trying to release free films to American exhibitors was something completely different. Free movies – regardless of their contents – had no market value whatsoever; there was no money to be made by producers, distributors or exhibitors. As Creel learned the hard way, the only successful way to show the official CPI war films on screen was through existing commercial channels. This meant adapting to the American film industry's interests as well as recognizing that films represented merchandise and had to be promoted and sold in a manner that provided a reasonable profit.

In May 1917, several months before the CPI began a film program, William Brady, chairman of the National Association of Motion Picture Industry (NAMPI), rallied the American film companies in its first unified support of the Liberty Loan campaign. With free footage from the Eastman Kodak company, a promotional trailer was produced and exhibited in American theatres. This joint effort apparently impressed the Administration and increased awareness of the value of motion pictures to influence public opinion and build morale on the home front. In June 1917 President Wilson himself sent a letter to Brady asking him to collaborate with the CPI. "The film", Wilson wrote, "has come to rank as the very high medium for the dissemination of public intelligence, and since it speaks a universal language it lends itself importantly to the presentation of America's plans and purposes".[19]

On 6 July 1917 Creel visited Brady's office where they agreed that the delegates from NAMPI's war cooperation committee would contact all government departments and agencies such as the Food Conservation Board to coordinate with them. Creel also requested Brady to name three new members to this committee as representatives of the newsreel companies. Initial contacts between the film industry and the United States government were made.

However, when the committee discussed the subject of film distribution it soon became clear there were a number of substantial disagreements. The CPI proposed all films be given to the American Red Cross, which already had its own film distribution agency. These movies were to be shown to schools, churches, patriotic societies and other nonprofit groups under the auspices of the Red Cross. The CPI obviously overlooked the fact that regular film exhibitors would be unable to profit from films being shown for free. As *Motion Picture News* wryly noted: "For patriotic purposes it is essential that pictures be propaganda. Yet it is essential that the pictures be valuable enough to the exhibitor that he will willingly pay a price for them".[20]

Brady nonetheless forged ahead and in July 1917 he announced that the American film industry had set up war cooperation committees with most governmental departments and agencies. The CPI was not among them. Wishing to avoid conflict with commercial film companies, Creel ignored the film industry altogether; the Red Cross would be the sole distributor of official war films from Europe that had been screened by the CPI. If the newsreel companies wished to have any war films the Red

Cross would supply the footage but there should be no preferential treatment of any commercial film company.

The Red Cross involvement may have given an impartial and patriotic aspect to the CPI film distribution plan but it was soon obvious from a propaganda perspective this approach was a failure. To reach a wide audience the only way was to release these films through the regular film exchanges and exhibitors. Initially the CPI did not deal with this problem because Creel was focused on recent developments in Europe. The Russian Revolution had just started and it looked like the Bolsheviks in power might seek peace with Germany. On top of this, the French army in 1917 was crippled by mutinies and discontent among civilians about the war was rising in Entente countries. For these reasons, spreading the American "lessons of democracy" abroad had top priority over the CPI's "open and positive" approach communicating with the American public. "I made the distinct statement", Creel wrote on 1 October 1917, "that I could not and would not consider the American situation at this time, since it was all important that we concentrate upon operations in France, Italy and Russia".[21]

The offspring of this change in focus was the American Cinema Commission, a foreign film service that Brady's NAMPI developed at Creel's request, and preparations for a film campaign in Europe to distribute educational films donated by American companies such as Ford, Edison and General Electric. While the CPI was getting more deeply involved with this foreign film campaign the American film trade press became increasingly annoyed with the CPI's distribution of documentary war films released in the United States. In an editorial *Moving Picture World* openly complained about the way the American Red Cross handled the Signal Corps pictures: there was no professional film exchange, negatives were not archived properly, films when ordered for exhibition frequently arrived too late to be shown. The trade paper published a long list of complaints including its criticism of the contents of the Signal Corps films. "Audiences get tired of marching troops and dreary landscapes. Give them the thrilling fact-story instead!"[22]

And there was an additional reason why the motion picture industry may have not liked the setup that Creel envisioned. Louis Pizzitola points out that the CPI was under the thumb of William Randolph Hearst. Creel had enjoyed a close relationship with Hearst for years. He had been a humor writer for Hearst's *Evening Journal* in the 1890s, published articles in Hearst's *Cosmopolitan* and his book *Children in Bondage* was published by Hearst's International Library in 1914. He was still free-lancing for Hearst as late as 1916. Hart was even closer to Hearst than Creel was. He had been the advertising manager for *Hearst's Magazine*. When it became obvious that the CPI needed new blood, CPI's associate editor Carl Byoir and associate Edgar Sisson urged Creel to nominate Hart to lead a totally restructured film unit. Byoir had been previously employed as the circulation manager and Sisson as editor of Hearst's *Cosmopolitan* Magazine.

All this may not have been fair criticism – after all, how could you be a newspaper writer or in motion pictures then without bumping into Hearst? Half the photographers and cinematographers in this book were affiliated at some point with Hearst. Many were trained by his organization. But it went further than that.

On 23 June 1918, a sign went up outside New York's Broadway Theater warning late arrivals that a film called *The Yanks are Coming* would not be coming. In bold yellow letters the makeshift poster ordered by a furious film producer declared that the showing had been "STOPPED BY THE CREEL-HEARST COMMITTEE".[23]

What had happened was that Universal Studios had prepared a short film on production at an aircraft plant which had been rejected by the CPI on the grounds that it contained secret information. However a week earlier Hearst-Pathé had run essentially the same story duly approved by the CPI. The executives at Universal claimed foul, and that the Creel Committee was making sure that Hearst got more than favorable treatment from the CPI. Subsequently George Creel claimed that the Universal story never got the necessary permit while Carl Byoir, Creel's associate director, claimed that it had.

The most significant aspect in this dispute was the deep distrust that the industry displayed toward the government's interference in the motion picture business. At the time it must have seemed tantamount to socialism, a problem which might go dormant at times but would never disappear until the Armistice.

Walter Niebuhr and the CPI[24]

Shortly after the United States declared war on Germany on 6 April 1917, Niebuhr was working as a civilian in Washington, DC, on a motion picture publicity campaign for "national service", otherwise known as the draft. However he soon volunteered his services to Creel's CPI.[25]

The CPI, as envisioned by Creel, was an agency "that would not only reach deep into every American community, clearing away confusions, but at the same time [would] seek the friendship of neutral nations and break through the barrage of lies that kept the Germans in darkness and delusion". In other words, the CPI was to be a massive public affairs organization. And the infant medium of motion pictures was tasked with a role in this campaign for the hearts and minds of neutrals and Americans alike.[26]

Niebuhr was named the Associate Director of the CPI's Division of Film[27] with responsibility to produce America's first war films. And Niebuhr responded with the United States' earliest war documentaries with films titled *The Bridge of Ships*, *Heroic France*, *Fire Fighters* (a film about flame throwers), and *Soldiers of the Sea*, showing Marines in training.[28] These short features were designed to accompany full length motion pictures in local theaters.

Niebuhr claimed to have been responsible for launching the Committee's first feature, *Pershing's Crusaders*. Officially presented in twenty-four cities, it earned

Fig. 93. Signal Corps photographer demonstrating his Graflex camera. This type was specially designed for aerial photography. [Courtesy National Archives.]

$181,742 for the Committee through its many bookings, second only to *America's Answer*, a later CPI offering. In the words of one of its publicists, the film broke new ground. It was the "first official American War film".

> Our boys in Khaki are pictured in the very front firing line. You see Americans taking over the fighting trenches. You see Secretary of War Baker and General Pershing inspecting our preparations in France. You see the first German prisoners captured by our brave boys – two dozen disheartened, defeated Boches … You also see what Uncle Sam's countless civilian army is doing "over here".[29]

Pershing's Crusaders begins with a shot of a mounted crusader in armor (Niebuhr's work), holding a flag in one hand and a shield in the other, a shield on which a Christian cross appears (Colour Plate 7). On either side of the crusader, a doughboy in uniform marches as the following text appears on the screen:

> The world conflict takes upon itself the nature of a Crusade. The Crusades were the efforts of a new world striving after a better ideal than that of piracy and fraternal bloodshed. We go forth in the same spirit in which the knights of old went forth to do battle with the Saracen. Notwithstanding the sacrifice, we shall gain from it a nobler manhood and a deeper sense of America's mission in the world. Thousands of parents are asking "Why are we giving up our boys?" It is most essential that they see and know. The young men of America are going out to rescue Civilization. They are going to fight for one definite thing, to save Democracy from death. They are marching on to give America's freedom to the oppressed multitudes of the

earth. This mighty exodus of America's manhood to the plains of Europe may well be called "The Eighth Crusade".[30]

The next scene contains a powerful piece of cinematography. The narration reads, "The mailed fist of the 'Rule by Might' lies heavily upon Europe. To it no contract is binding, no obligation is worthy of fulfillment, no word of honor sacred."

A point of light appears on the center of the screen, moving outward, as though a drop of acid was spilled on the film, burning it from the center to its edges at a more or less equal rate. As the entire frame lightens, the viewer sees sand, nothing but sand, sand like that found in the Sahara or Mohave deserts.

Suddenly, an arm emerges from the sand, wearing chain mail. In the throes of an unnamed agony, the arm stretches and contracts, before falling back, into the sand. Symbolically, the mailed fist, "Rule by Might", is defeated. It lies heavily upon the sandy wasteland, an apt visual metaphor for the defeat of Germany.[31]

As previously discussed, Ambassador Gerard and the Secret Service believed Niebuhr, who was at the Adlon in Berlin and accompanied Durborough on his trip east, was a German spy. Like Albert K. Dawson, Niebuhr was soon accused of being a German sympathizer and forced to resign from his position with the CPI. He quickly landed a post as a motion picture counselor to the New York State Council of Defense, probably with George Creel's help.[32]

Thanks to Niebuhr, the CPI had expanded its film program of newsreels to include feature documentaries which would soon grow to three titles: *Pershing's Crusaders*, *America's Answer* and *Under Four Flags*. The CPI handled these war films similarly. To draw public attention to these films the CPI arranged previews in all major metropolitan areas in the United States and sent ahead a publicity campaigner to place advertisements and poster the streets, hotel lobbies, shops and the like. These official screenings were promoted by enlisting the support of local patriotic societies and business communities. The CPI campaigner also made sure movie critics and local dignitaries attended these premiere exhibitions. After these prereleases the CPI war films were exhibited throughout America by channeling them through commercial exchanges.

The first war feature in this trilogy, *Pershing's Crusaders*, premiered in Cincinnati, Ohio, on 29 April 1918. Howard Herrick, who had handled publicity for D.W. Griffith's *Intolerance*, was sent ahead to promote this CPI production in Cincinnati. To distribute this movie the CPI contracted with eight full-service road companies, each with its own business, sales and advertising staffs, a large orchestra that played the music accompanying the film and a technical staff that handled all theatrical effects during the movie. George Bowles, who had organized Griffith's *Birth of a Nation* in 1915, managed this nationwide tour across the United States. Evidently, the CPI under Hart's dynamic leadership was ready to use any opportunity to promote *Pershing's Crusaders* and hired the best professionals in the country to assure this feature was viewed by as many people as possible.

In July 1918, after the national tour for *Pershing's Crusaders* concluded, First National Exchange distributed it in a deal paying 70 percent of all receipts to the CPI. Nationwide distribution was promoted also by *Moving Picture World* that ran a contest: the exchange office that closed the highest percentage of contracts would be the winner of a bronze trophy. The contest was finally won by the Denver exchange, which closed the highest percentage of state bookings. *Pershing's Crusaders* was seen in 49.6% of all theatres in Colorado. The areas around New York City and Chicago ended in sixth and seventh positions in this contest, presumably because of the density of cinemas in these areas.

America's Answer, the CPI's second feature production, followed closely; it premiered in New York City on 29 July 1918 (Colour Plate 8). This exhibition was handled by S.L. Rothapfel, a well-known theatre manager who owned the Strand. George Creel was present during this premiere and commented on this film, saying: "We are carrying the message and meaning of democracy to all peoples, preaching to them the justice of our cause, the certainty of our victory, and the great truth that this victory contains no benefit for us that may not be enjoyed by the whole world".[33] As previously mentioned, Hatrick, Joseph Hubbell and a group of photographers were sent first to Neufchâteau and then elsewhere to photograph material for the *Official War Review*. However, a good deal of the footage that they shot ended up in *America's Answer*. According to Louis Pizzitola:

> … *America's Answer* purported to be patriotic propaganda, but it also presented a more subtle message that war itself might be more horrible than the Hun. Many of the scenes lacked the expected rabble-raising, focusing instead on more mundane aspects of the war effort: the clearing of land for roads and the like. One of the more striking sequences is quite bleak: it features a young, lost-looking soldier nearly shrouded by a huge pair of army boots.[34]

The official character of this war documentary was emphasized by using spacious public buildings, not a regular commercial theatre, for the prerelease run. Tickets were sold at a relatively cheap price, between 25–50 cents, in order to make it possible for many people to attend the exhibitions. Promotion also focused on attracting employers of companies nearby, which facilitated selling tickets for special 'industrial shows'. This arrangement boosted the exhibition of *America's Answer* substantially. For instance in Brooklyn, New York, out of seven exhibitions five were reserved for specially selected companies and firms.

America's Answer may have indeed been a dreary film. But the solution, as so often in America, was the marketing. And here we meet Mr. Samuel F. Rothapfel and his Strand Theatre. On 11 April 1914 the Strand Theatre in New York City first opened its doors for an immense movie-going audience of over 3500 people. This event heralded the coming of age of the motion picture industry in America. In the middle of Broadway, the scene of traditional theatre and variety, a cinema was built that challenged all previous forms of entertainment. As *Variety* commented: "It was a signal proof of the prestige that motion pictures have won during the last year".[35] Upon entering the lobby of the Strand, the audience saw palm trees, crystal chande-

Fig. 94. Samuel L. Rothapfel. Under his artistic guidance the CPI war films were turned into an impressive spectacle. [Courtesy Library of Congress.]

liers and ornate mirrors. The American film industry had gained a new image; the era of the Nickelodeon motion picture shows was definitely ending.

The Strand Theatre was one of the first top-class motion picture palaces that started business in the United States. Most of the other cinemas in this exclusive category, such as the Vitagraph Theatre, were owned by film producers and were intended as straightforward publicity instruments for the film studios. The Strand however was quite a different story. Its owner, Samuel L. Rothapfel, wished to make a shining example out of this theatre, an inspirational source for all his fellow American film exhibitors. Rothapfel introduced a style of exhibiting motion pictures that reminded the audience of exclusive variety and opera shows. More than just a regular film show, his presentations were a combination of the different theater arts. Specially arranged music and theatrical effects were combined to create a new movie viewing experience.

Rothapfel's showmanship and style didn't just attract the attention of a wide film-going audience. The American film industry also closely watched his business practices and regularly published articles in the trade press on the way he presented motion pictures. In fact, the premiere cinemas that he ran in New York City – the Strand, Rialto and Rivoli – became role models for numerous ambitious exhibitors. Questions on daily film business printed in the trade press frequently were answered by the line: "Ask Rothapfel. He knows".[36] By the time America entered World War I, Rothapfel's influence on the motion picture trade had expanded to include working closely with the film campaign by the Committee on Public Information. From 1918 the CPI war films taken by the U.S. Signal Corps were distributed by commercial exchanges and publicity methods. But Rothapfel's remarkable way of showing movies proved to be invaluable in giving these war films a genuine dramatic and promotional impact. Under his personal guidance these films were turned into spectacles.

In 1917 even before the United States declared war on Germany, Rothapfel was already exhibiting patriotic subjects on the movie screen. These scenes were assembled in the *Rialto Animated Magazine*, a newsreel that was produced for one of his personal theatres. The films were edited from regular newsreels and stock footage. What made these films stand out was the musical score that was especially created for them. Rothapfel did not just rely on music that had already been scored; he had music composed that closely matched the look and feel of his films. More than regular music, the compositions also included sound effects that added a dramatic impact to the film exhibition. For example, here is how Rothapfel presented scenes of American pilots while training to fly: "There wasn't any music at all with this, only the effect of the whirring motors and the splash as the planes hit the water. The audience sat spellbound through this part of the picture and then burst into applause."[37]

Scenes of military exercises were common at the time in American newsreels and documentary films, and they usually did not attract much public interest. Adding musical effects combined with creative intertitles could make a striking difference. Rothapfel mixed these elements into a potent cinematic cocktail, thus producing a cinematic presentation that made the audience respond to a particular scene with a laugh or cheer. In another example, in a war related scene of his *Rialto Animated Magazine* he showed as an introduction the title "Sherman Was Right" followed by the orchestra playing "Marching through Georgia". General Sherman's famous dictum that war is hell – which gave him the opportunity to ravage Georgia during the Civil War – in this way was given a new impact by both watching and listening during the newsreel.

Playing appropriate music to a particular scene sometimes triggered the audience in a most remarkable way. Here's a description from *Motion Picture News* of the German submarine warfare in the Atlantic, as arranged for his theatre by Rothapfel: "First were shown pictures of the martyr ship SS *Tuscania,* leaving New York – there was a touch of the *Finlandia* Overture, the solemnly played music that caused everyone to pay a silent tribute. This was turned into the terror scene as pictures of the German U-Boat were shown and then came the big punch: America's answer, showing a number of war ships. 'American Festival' was played here and there was wild applause and shouts all over the house, many people standing up and crying out."[38]

Impressive as these effects may have been, such movie scenes were not strictly speaking "documentary" and there was little actual news to be seen on screen. This did not matter much to the average American film exhibitor. Rothapfel's special arrangement indicated a new method of film exhibition that opened a way to add public interest to factual film, a genre that compared to drama productions usually attracted few customers in American theatres. In Rothapfel's Strand Theatre, the presentation of a specific "newsreel scene" sometimes was followed by a theatrical act that was played on stage by actors to accompany the film. As an example, in June 1918 Rothapfel showed a scene of soldiers of the U.S. Marine Corps while preparing for war, followed by the title "We Are Coming, Uncle Sam, 75,000 Strong". Next the ceiling of the interior inside the cinema changed colors and spotlights revealed the Star Spangled Banner while the orchestra played "Over There". This was the cue for the curtains to be raised and the audience now saw real American soldiers marching through the streets of Paris, ready to liberate France from the German occupation.

The Official War Review, the CPI newsreel, was also presented by Rothapfel as well as many of his colleagues in a manner that underlined drama, not just plain facts or regular news events about the war in Europe. A recurring theme in many issues of this CPI newsreel was the overwhelming superiority of the Entente forces that would ultimately be the reason Germany was going to be defeated. *Official War Review* #18 has a scene illustrating this publicity message: "When Sir John French took command of the British forces in 1914 the Germans called it England's contemptible little army. The enemy later saw the tables turned. Polish regiments are raised in France to fight the enemy. German prisoners from Lorraine are given French uniforms and sent back to fight their erstwhile comrades."[39]

The American mobilization for war was screened in this newsreel in a similar, optimistic way. While these films were being shown, the American government ran into substantial problems converting companies to wartime production in spite of prior optimistic claims about the power of American industry. There were shortages of ammunition and war supplies. The shipbuilding program had serious delays. American soldiers were armed with French artillery, and American aviators were given French airplanes. Yet hardly surprising, the image conveyed by the CPI official war newsreel was much different. In these films the industrial mobilization was pictured in an impressive way, showing scenes such as the construction of enormous military warehouses by American military engineers in the record time of one day (*Official War Review* # 9).

After the American entry in the war, the CPI contacted Rothapfel and asked for his cooperation. He was requested in July 1918 to arrange the showings of all official war films that were shown in the state of New York. As with his previous work, Rothapfel's theatrical style of exhibiting films was picked up by the American motion picture industry as an inspiring example to follow. In a series of articles for the trade paper *Motion Picture News*, he explained how he arranged these CPI film productions and made these films more interesting to the audience as well as more profitable to the film exhibitor. He said two basic principles were important in presenting these official war films. Editing had to be fast-paced, with enough continuity to watch the film as a recognizable screen story. Equally important was every film should begin with a poignant scene and climax to an equally dramatic "punch" at the end.

As another example of how the *Official War Review* was dramatized by Rothapfel, the trade press describes his use of Cecil B. DeMille's 1917 film *Joan the Woman*, a picture on the life of Jeanne d'Arc in the 15th century. At the end of the newsreel, the frontline around Rheims is pictured. A title explains: "In Spite of *Kultur* the

259

Rheims Cathedral Still Stands". At this point a scene from DeMille's film showed the Maid of Orleans mobilizing her army to defend France. Accompanying this scene, Rothapfel's orchestra played the French national anthem, the *Marseillaise*. The response by the audience was instantaneous – as if electrified many customers jumped to their feet and applauded the movie. The same special effect – a combination of a powerful drama scene and appropriate music – had been used before by Rothapfel when he exhibited the French film *Mothers of France* (1917). The CPI documentary film productions employed similar techniques.

It has been claimed Rothapfel's artistic influence can also be found in the opening scene of the CPI's first war feature, *Pershing's Crusaders,* which opened with an animated shot, not a regular film scene. As previously noted when discussing Walter Niebuhr, the film starts with a very ambitious (and rather symbolist) opening, somewhat in the style of Griffith's *Intolerance.* Whether this represents Rothapfel's influence is not known.

Some reviewers noted the titles in *Pershing's Crusaders* lacked a certain sense of dignity, which when watched today seems to be an understatement. German aviators were described as "vultures" and when the first German prisoners of war appear on screen the accompanying title states: "Zowie! Here's the first German prisoners captured by our boys. Twenty one men and two disgusted officers."[40] The movie ended with an appropriate answer to German brutality as portrayed in the opening scene. On an animated frontline map the American flag is seen, a clear symbol of victory for the Entente side and the defeat of the German Iron Fist that had terrorized Europe for four years.

Rothapfel personally arranged the New York City premiere of the CPI's second feature film, *America's Answer.* For this special arrangement, he combined all the theatrical techniques he had used before to produce a breath-taking presentation. Before the opening reel started, the curtains were raised and on stage a vocal group of one hundred sailors sang the national anthem. Next the stage changed to show on screen an American eagle and the emblem of the Committee on Public Information. Another curtain was pulled to present a tableau vivant – spotlights focused on a group of American soldiers posed as living statues while about to go over the top, with an image of the Statue of Liberty on the background. The music that accompanied this theatrical overture was *Over There* along with sound effects of an artillery barrage. Next *America's Answer* opened with close-ups of General Pershing and President Wilson. Most of the film pictured the American industrial mobilization, the first soldiers arriving in France and the building up of an American Expeditionary Force that was ready to go into the line.

As noted before by Kevin Brownlow, the titles in this film – written by Kenneth Benton – were composed as a separate story with the film title lines usually not supporting the visuals. Most of the scenes were no different from standard newsreel shots of the war that had been exhibited in the American cinemas before 1917 and showed inspections, training activities and scenes from behind the lines. Action scenes were rare, although there is a brief glimpse of the first infantry offensive by the American Expeditionary Force at Château-Thierry in July 1918 taken from afar and showing the impact of the artillery barrage on the German lines. "American soldiers supported by French tanks start on their way", the title says. "The big guns carry on to make the going easier. Forward! While the barrage screams overhead!" To convey the message of America's massive military power, the film ended with a scene that pictured hundreds of sailors posed together to form the concluding sentence, *America's Answer*.

America's Answer was distributed nationwide by the World Film Corporation in 34 cities. Because of the Spanish influenza epidemic the film wasn't released through these channels until November 1918. Nonetheless, the income from this movie grossed $185,144, which made it the most successful war documentary that was released by the CPI. An important reason for this success was the distribution contract that was signed between the CPI and the World Film Corporation. Under regular conditions, exchange contracts arranged for the use of one major theatre in metropolitan areas, so costs on producing prints could be kept low and customers were directed to a specific theatre. From a business point of view, this was sound policy. The CPI, however, wished to release this film in as many theatres as possible. Therefore *America's Answer* was shown via a different distribution plan which benefited smaller theatres. The cinemas also profited because the CPI war films were exempt from any war taxes.

The CPI boosted the publicity campaign for *America's Answer*. The film division by then had set up a special Community Section which organized a direct mailing to all important schools, churches and societies in the area around a theatre that would be showing the film. Through this mailing people in the local community were urged to attend the exhibition. They were also asked to spread the message and help the CPI by giving them names of influential people who might be of assistance in promoting the film.

Under Four Flags, the CPI's last war film, premiered after the Armistice in December 1918. By then the CPI had established a professional campaign machine that was promoting the war feature series. As with the previous movies, the publicity emphasized the local interest in these films. Exhibitors reading *Variety* saw an advertisement showing four Entente soldiers with the caption "New York Goes Over!" In the accompanying publicity the *New York Evening Mail* was quoted: "*Under Four Flags* went over the top with a characteristic American bang!"[41] Trade papers now were publishing complete publicity toolkits that included ad talks, catch lines and suggestions for promoting the film on location.

Rothapfel's showmanship made a huge difference. Granted that the local theater could not afford a chorus of 200 or special effects and lighting, anyone glancing at the trade journals for this period cannot deny the increasing importance of pageantry

Fig. 95. Advertisement Moving Picture World,
28 December 1918.

in film showmanship. And the actions of the theater owners had an influence on the photographers: all scenes must be hard-hitting. Joseph Hubbell's comments about "stretching the truth", as he put it, in his shots of the wounded should be read in the light of Rothapfel's comments that you had to make each scene count. It was a lesson that the American film industry would remember.

When the Committee on Public Information ended its operations in February 1919, the Film Division had grossed an impressive amount of money, more than $850,000.00. This was mainly because the CPI had adopted commercial ways of distributing and showing these war films, which included professional methods of promotion. The American film industry, however, was quick to terminate the cooperation with the CPI. A few weeks after the Armistice the National Association of Motion Picture Industry (NAMPI) passed a resolution at their national convention in Atlantic City. NAMPI urged the CPI to immediately stop all film activities. Because of the cooperation by the film industry, the CPI movies had been released successfully, although distributors had to return most of their income to the government. Now that the war was over, the film industry was quick to conclude the movie trade had done its part to support the war and it was time to bring an end to the United States government interfering with the commercial film business, which it now considered unfair competition.

But the film industry, the United States Government and the military had learned valuable lessons that would be applied in World War II. The country produced some execrable propaganda during World War I, propaganda that makes Nazi propaganda appear tame by comparison, but none who watch these films can doubt that America had put the message across.

Notes

1. "Frank Marion Returns to United States", *Moving Picture World* (22 June 1918): 1692.

2. Dulany Terrett, *The Signal Corps: The Emergency* (Washington, DC: Government Printing Office, 1956), 79.

3. George Creel, *How We Advertised America* (New York/London, 1920), 117.

4. Kevin Brownlow, *The War, the West and the Wilderness* (New York: Alfred Knopf, 1979), 127.

5. Larry Lane Ward, *The Motion Picture Goes to War* (Ann Arbor: UMI Research Press, 1985), 96–97; *Photographic Journal of America* 54 (Philadelphia: Edward L. Wilson Company, Inc, 1917), 486; Charles J. Columbus, "Photography Will Win the War", *Photographers Association News*, 4, no. 9 (October 1917): 272–274; Ron van Dopperen, "Shooting the Great War: Albert Dawson and the American Correspondent Film Company, 1914–1918", *Film History* 4 (1990): 123–129.

6. Earl Theissen, "The Photographer in the World War", *International Photographer* (November 1933): 5.

7. Kevin Brownlow, *The War, the West and the Wilderness*, 125.

8. "Motion Picture Camera That Is Different", *Scientific American* (2 March 1918): 194.

9. "Cameraman Writes From War Front", *Motion Picture News* (12 January 1918): 264.

10. Charles Gatchell, "Filming the Fighting Front", *Picture-Play Magazine* (January 1919): 22.

11. "Army Movie Men are the Bradys of 1918", *Stars and Stripes* (15 February 1918).

12. "Action! Lights! Camera", *American Legion Magazine* (June 1942): 33.

13. "Chicagoans Who Are Serving Country in Washington", *Chicago Daily Tribune* (24 June 1918): 6.

14. Edwin F. Weigle, "My personal narrative of experiences as Photo Officer of the 35th Division", courtesy members of the Weigle family.

15. "Day's Arrivals of Chicagoans from Overseas", *Chicago Daily Tribune* (13 June 1919): 10.

16. "Weigle Brings 110 Miles Film War History", *Chicago Daily Tribune* (13 June 1919): 2; "107 Mi. of A.E.F. Official Films Land in New York", *Sunday Republican* (Mitchell, South Dakota) (22 June 1919): Section 2, 1.

17. Joseph Hubbell, memoirs, cited in Pizzitola, 151.

18. Advertisement "Official War Review no. 10", *Moving Picture World* (14 September 1918): 163.

19. "President Wilson Appoints Brady To Mobilize Industry", *Motion Picture News* (14 July 1917): 221.

20. Creel Confers With NAMPI For Giant Film Drive", *Motion Picture News* (21 July 1917): 371.

21. George Creel, *How We Advertised America* (New York/London, 1920), 119.

22. Henry McMahon, "Uplifters Boss War Films", *Moving Picture World* (26 January 1918): 482.

23. Pizzitola, *Hearst over Hollywood*, 148.

24. All material in this book dealing with Walter Niebuhr is here largely owing to the scholarship of William G. Chrystal, who has been extremely generous. Niebuhr does not even merit an acknowledgment in the AFI catalogue.

25. William G. Chrystal, "'A Master of His Craft': The Film Career of Walter Niebuhr", *Niebuhr Studies* (Reno: Empire for Liberty, 2012), 126.

26. George Creel, *Rebel At Large: Recollections of Fifty Crowded Years* (New York: Putnam, 1947), 158.

27. George Creel, *How We Advertised America* (New York: Harper, 1920), 119. Creel explains that early motion picture work of the Committee on Public Information "was turned over to Mr. Louis B. Mack, a Chicago lawyer, and Mr. Walter Niebuhr, both volunteers".

28. Niebuhr's scrapbook lists the films he worked on during this time. The scrapbook is now in the possession of Rusty Buchanan, grandson of Walter Niebuhr.

29. Promotional brochure for *Pershing's Crusaders*, Document 105, in Richard Wood, *Film and Propaganda in America, A Documentary History*, Volume 1, World War I (New York: Greenwood, 1990), 252.

30. William G. Chrystal, "'A Master of His Craft': The Film Career of Walter Niebuhr", "American without any 'if' and 'buts': Reinhold Niebuhr, His Brothers, and the First World War", in William G. Chrystal, *Niebuhr Studies* (Reno: Empire for Liberty, 2012), 101–102.

31. *Pershing's Crusaders*, National Archives, Motion Picture, Sound and Video Branch, College Park, MD. Only three reels of the film are available.

32. William G. Chrystal, "American without any 'if' and 'buts': Reinhold Niebuhr, His Brothers, and the First World War", *Niebuhr Studies*, 107.

33. *New York Times* (30 July 1918): 9.

34. Pizzitola, 151.

35. "Crowds Flock To Strand Opening", *Variety* (25 April 1914): 18.

36. *Billboard* (16 December 1916): 49.

37. "Seeing The Rialto With Rothapfel", *Motion Picture News* (20 October 1917): 2714.

38. "Seeing The Rialto With Rothapfel", *Motion Picture News* (23 February 1918): 1138.

39. Title Sheet, *Official War Review* no. 18, 1. Courtesy National Archives, Washington, DC. See also review in *Moving Picture World* (9 November 1918): 692.

40. Ibid., 9–11.

41. Advertisement "Under Four Flags", *Variety* (27 December 1918): 147. *See also Motion Picture News* (30 November 1918): 3269.

Chapter 9

Aftermath

The impact of the First World War cannot be fully comprehended by reading statistics about the millions of casualties. These are in the end only figures. Some images tell a far more striking story. After four years of fighting, when on 11 November 1918 the guns fell silent, the frontline area between the English Channel and the Swiss border had changed into a completely devastated landscape. Treeless, scarred by mine craters and endless trenches zigzagging through muddy fields and ruined villages – these relics from the Great War as seen from a bird's eye view resembled an horrendous scene from Dante's *Inferno* that would stick in the minds of numerous soldiers who were fortunate enough to return home.

Many books have been written on the way this tremendous war was remembered in literature and poetry. Statesmen and generals wrote their autobiographies. Military regiments all had their official histories compiled. Political movements originated in the trenches, notably fascism which propagated the belief that life was a continuing struggle in which only the fittest should survive. In many respects the Great War was internalized and continued to be very much alive, if only in the minds of the men and women who had experienced it. The war provided invaluable ammunition for the Nazis as a propaganda issue and to take revenge on old enemies. On the other side of the political spectrum, the war also was a powerful motive for politicians like the British Prime Minister Neville Chamberlain to avoid a repetition of events, search for appeasement with Germany and "peace in our time". It is one of the great tragedies of the 20th century that it had to take a second global conflict before the long-term effects of the Great War were completely annihilated.

As a lasting legacy, World War I has also produced an historical film record that was used in various ways by military cinematographers, newsreel companies and newspapers such as the *Chicago Tribune*. It is safe to state that many of these contemporary war films have been lost over the years. In contrast to drama films, documentaries or newsreels did not represent valuable merchandise. Thus soon after the war ended many of these films were either destroyed or the nitrate stock slowly deteriorated in a dusty corner of an archive or private film collection. Film historian Jay Leyda wrote a short book, *Films Beget Films*, and lists the huge number of compilation films that were recycling World War I footage by the 1920s, if not earlier. He laments the destruction of this film heritage, reporting: "Within the next years [mid-1920s] it

Fig. 96. Example of a recycled World War I film: scene from Albert Dawson's Battles of a Nation, *retrieved by the authors in the BBC* Great War *series (1964).*

was common to see regular ads in *The Film Daily* offering 'over 5,000,000 feet of negatives and positives – scenes of every conceivable description', or more simply 'A MILLION FEET OF EVERYTHING'. One sales line with implications was 'We buy Junk Film, guarantee no piracy'.[1] This happened in the United States as well as Europe. The fact that nitrate films are highly flammable also didn't help to preserve these historical World War I movies.

On the other hand, this recycling has helped preserve the World War I film that is left. The documentary film preserved usually has been the result of television productions such as the classic BBC *The Great War* series (1964). Since 1918, footage from film libraries and stock collections has been edited and recycled for these purposes in a way that represents a giant jigsaw puzzle. The authors have been fortunate enough to reconstruct some of these impressive scenes and identify the original war films these motion pictures came from. However, because many films are not properly inventoried research on original World War I films continues to be a complicated if highly exciting challenge. A full preservation of a contemporary war film, as it was seen in the American theatres, is now possible because of research done by the authors on Wilbur H. Durborough's *On the Firing Line With the Germans*. Based on the original copyright data and intertitles from 1915, the content of all reels has been identified and virtually all film segments have been located by the authors;

it only needs to be reconstructed. It is hoped the Library of Congress will act on this unique opportunity to preserve the original Durborough film for future generations. The film is an historical testimony on the Great War that has been recognized by both film historians and international peace organizations.

Most of the cameramen discussed in this book did not remain cameramen. Documentary cinematography was hard, dangerous work even in peacetime and so was a young man's game. After the war the activities of these men continued although most stepped back into the shadows and were no longer mentioned in the film trade press or newspapers. The Adlon Hotel itself was certainly one of the major players in this saga and it survived the war, inflation, the Third Reich and World War II. In the twenties, it became the host for the rich and famous, movie and stage celebrities such as Marlene Dietrich, Charlie Chaplin, Josephine Baker, Ernst Lubitsch and many others and was considered to be the model for the MGM film Grand Hotel. Percy Adlon, the great grandson of Lorenz Adlon, paid it a nostalgic film tribute, *The Glamorous World of the Adlon Hotel* (*In der glanzvollen Welt des Hotel Adlon*). The Adlon performed exactly the same function in the thirties before World War II as it did in World War I. Most of the prominent columnists such as Guido Enderis, William L. Shirer, Sigrid Schultz and Dorothy Thompson covering the Nazis stayed there or at least made it their unofficial headquarters, and Fritz, the famous bartender, was still there after twenty years.[2] It survived the bombings pretty much unscathed until May 1945 when a couple of Russian soldiers got drunk and burned it down. Now it survives as the Adlon Kempinski, a luxury hotel still nestled next to the Brandenburg Gate, but not much of the Wilhelmine pomp remains.

Wilbur H. Durborough

Upon leaving the army, Captain Durborough didn't continue his prior career in film or photojournalism. A promotional opportunity for a newly organized company presented itself to parlay his command experience into a corporate position that would employ his natural talents in promotion and publicity. In 1919 the Savold Tire Company was organized in New York City based on a newly patented process for recapping worn tires much less expensively than previous methods. It was structured to license the patent to local state or regional independent Savold operating companies that would actually rebuild the tires. The company negotiated with Durborough to join as the general field manager and conduct the first serious public test by driving the Stutz Bearcat roadster he took to Germany on tires rebuilt in Savold's Chicago factory on a long promotional tour. It consisted of driving some 3500 miles from Chicago to New York City including an initial 2200 in Michigan, Ohio and Canada. The Chicago Auto Club president certified the test by placing seals on the tires at the early July start and checking them again at the finish. Except for one tire being "cemented to keep down lacerations from a ten-foot plunge into a ditch to avoid collision near Detroit", the original tires with the same air arrived 1

August in New York. Durborough, a ticketed speeder, appears to have given the tires a substantial test.[3]

After this initial publicity stunt, Durborough relocated his family to New York City and continued working as publicity and public relations director for Savold. But this position, like many earlier ones, was very brief. In post war 1919 the stock market began a frothy rise toward the Great Crash of 1929. One of the first major stock manipulation schemes of this period involved the Savold Tire Company.[4] A large number of financial press stories touting the investment opportunities in the many local operating companies' shares caused their value to soar. The few insiders who had bribed financial journalists for these favorable articles reaped quick fortunes before an equally rapid stock collapse in 1921 when the company suspended operations.[5] Durborough appears to have been an unwitting participant and might have initially believed his efforts had contributed to the rapid rise in the company's fortunes.

A decade after leaving Philadelphia, Durborough now returned there to work as photography manager and art director of the *Evening Bulletin* from 1921 to 1926.[6] But his entrepreneurial spirit moved him to strike out on his own once again in 1927 when he established the Philadelphia Pictorial News Company.[7] This new business venture disintegrated with the Great Crash of 1929 and the growing Depression. He had spent his money as fast as he earned it, never saving for or worrying much about the future. But he found for the first time that with the Depression he faced a situation that sorely tested even his optimistic outlook and persuasive personality. By mid-1930 he was struggling as a medicine salesman[8] and his home in the Philadelphia suburbs went to sheriff's sale in December 1931.[9] As he struggled through the middle of the Depression as an independent businessman pitching creative advertising for radio, the financial strain finally reached a breaking point in 1936. His wife Molly moved west with their young son Robert to live with her family.[10]

Durborough continued to struggle through the onset of World War II until America's entry into the war brought an expanding war economy with increased employment opportunities. In the summer of 1942 he moved to Utah to reconcile with his family in Ogden and obtain a civilian personnel position at the Hill Field Army Air Base. He quickly found he couldn't adjust to living at the high altitude which made him physically ill and in the summer of 1943 he managed to transfer to a position at the San Bernardino Army Air Base in California. In 1945 he left this position to work for the independent air base Civilian Employees' Association and also do some advertising and promotion consulting for local businesses. But again and for the last time this career move was cut short when he died suddenly in San Bernardino on 4 April 1946 at the age of 63.[11]

Prior to his death, Durborough started a writing project intended to be a memoir of his earlier life which he never finished. Initially it appears he drafted short sections about an important episode or part of an episode during his career consisting of 4 to

7 typewritten pages. He wrote them as contemporary conversational dialogs, streams of thought or reflection, likely modified consciously or subconsciously to enhance his role. It appears he wasn't attempting to write it as carefully documented history and it doesn't appear he was working from personal contemporary diaries. Rather he was writing to tell the story of his exciting life and experiences as a photojournalist and cinematographer.[12]

Although his manuscript now residing in the Manuscript Collection of the Library of Congress often only uses last names with misspellings and many vague date references, typos and two section 13s, all the major historical events described and most named participants can be documented with research. This material adds historical substance to Durborough's life and reveals new insights such as the Democratic Campaign Committee's secret funding for his fall 1916 film tour.

At some point, it appears he decided to change course and write a more interesting novel featuring his alter ego "Bill Randall" as protagonist. He had only drafted 75 mostly handwritten pages of this fictionalized version of his early experience as a young man working on the SS *Minnesota* before he died. But most of Bill Randall's early life appears directly based on Durborough's personal life experiences. In this section, he invented a visit with a fortune teller in Philadelphia shortly before Randall knew of the opportunity to crew on the SS *Manatawa (SS Minnesota)* that foretold in as simple a summary of Wilbur H. Durborough's real life as might be written:

> "You go many places very far away. You go in much danger. No harm come to you. You will be old man. You go more and more places all over the many seas and many countries. You marry girl long way off. You have two children, one girl, one boy. You have happy life, then unhappy life, then in end happy again."[13]

Donald C. Thompson

Thompson's post-war career kept taking him around the world. In 1920 he went to the Orient where he made a pictorial record of practically all countries for the magazine *Asia*. He accompanied the still photographer Gertrude Emerson, who handled the still photographs, while Thompson was to make short films on daily life and customs, "with special reference to native handicrafts and religious festivals. He will also make photographic studies for exclusive reproduction in *Asia*. He has prepared a complete field laboratory equipped with most modern devices for making pictures in all climates and under all conditions."[14]

In 1923 he was in trouble with the law once again for assuming the identities of United States government officers. This time he had assumed the identity of Theodore Roosevelt, Jr. and Lt. Commander Wainright of the U.S. Navy in Washington, Kansas City and elsewhere. With these assumed identities, he had ordered books, paid with a check for more than the amount, and had taken the change. Whether he served more time is not known.[15]

In 1926 Thompson moved to California where he had met his new wife Maria who was born in Chico. Travelogues and war films remained his trade. Evidently he did

Fig. 97. Donald C. Thompson. Picture taken in the 1920s. [Private collection Cooper C. Graham.]

some work for Ernest Newman and Traveltalks. He claimed to have been in Ethiopia to film the Italian invasion, but no record survives of his having been there. He was in Italy to photograph Mussolini. He was in Austria shortly before the German invasion and even claimed to have been with Engelbert Dollfuss on the day he was assassinated. And until the end of his career, Thompson remained what he was at heart: an independent freelance cameraman. At the age of 52, his feet were still itchy and he said he was eager to cover the military conflict that was expected then between Russia and Japan.

This unrelenting drive together with his talent to find a way through military regulations and red tape marked Donald C. Thompson as one of the most memorable American photographers of the Great War. He was, as he confessed himself, a man with a simple philosophy: "I live only to make good pictures and enjoy life".[16] Donald Thompson died at the Rancho Los Amigos Rehabilitation Centre in Los Angeles on 8 July 1947.

Wallace, Count de Beaufort and Dr. Marks

Scott Fitzgerald famously quipped that there are no second acts in American lives. This seems to have been true for Ansel Wallace, at least as far as movies were concerned. With his brother Harry, his father, and with the help of their wives, he worked for the rest of his life in Wallace and Sons Photography store in Evansville, Indiana. About 1920 he married Virginia M. Cobb, but there were no children. The Wallace enterprise kept totally out of the news except for a photograph of the store three feet deep in water in the terrible Ohio River flood of January 1937. He does not seem to have talked much about the war in Evansville or given any interviews to the local newspapers. The local Willard Library, an excellent source for research in local history, has only a couple of obituaries in the Wallace file. A. E. Wallace died at Deaconess Hospital in Evansville, Indiana, on 20 December 1941.[17] He and the rest of his family repose in Oak Hill Cemetery.

Not much is known about Count de Beaufort's later years. After he was thrown out of Germany and arrived in Britain, he soon got into trouble. In February 1916 he was arrested for entering the town of Chester, an area prohibited to aliens, without a passport. Why Chester had particular significance to him is unknown. He told the arresting authorities that he was a captain in the Belgian army, and then admitted he was a Dutch citizen and had deserted from the Dutch army. Later he ran up a series of bad debts and was asked to leave Britain. He returned to the United States on 17 April 1917 and petitioned for naturalization on 20 June 1917 as 'Jack de Beaufort'. Later in 1917 he was lecturing on vaudeville circuits, and then became a great hit on the tonier Chautauqua lecture circuit in wartime America. He was personable, well-spoken and no doubt convincing before an audience. He was hired by the Affiliated Lyceum Bureaus of America to speak all over the United States for the 1918–19 lecture season with great success. He lectured about his war experiences, his interview with von Hindenburg and his service as an artillery captain in the Belgian army, among others. As might be expected, much of his message was designed to inspire a war mood and to get Americans to try harder. If most of what he said was a complete fabrication, nobody seemed to mind.

On 7 September 1917 he married Helen Reiman, age 18, of Terre Haute, Indiana. At this point, de Beaufort told the *New York Times* that he was taking his new wife east, as he had been ordered to report to Governor's Island, New York, to be commissioned as a military attaché and interpreter, with rank of Captain in a contingent of American troops in France. When de Beaufort's prospective father-in-law was congratulated, he replied, "Congratulations, hell".[18] Later he got a job at the *Los Angeles Times* as a 'special writer'. He died on 15 October 1967.[19]

Dr. Lewis H. Marks returned to the United States in 1917. Military Intelligence as well as the Department of Justice continued to investigate him very thoroughly, including tapping his telephone conversations. The authorities were especially concerned about his continuing relationship with Walter Niebuhr.[20] In spite of Ambassador Gerard's cries for Marks' head, the Bureau of Investigation and the Military Intelligence Division concluded there was not much of a case against him. The Bureau of Investigation complained of political pressure by prominent friends of Marks, including U.S. Senator Robert F. Broussard of Louisiana. Nevertheless Marks was rejected for a commission in the U.S. Medical Corps on the basis of his past record.

He seems to have had a successful commercial career after World War I. He gave up espionage, certainly not his forte, and also the practice of medicine. After Marks' return to the USA in 1917 he incorporated the Markleed Chemical Company at Camden, NJ, together with his old business partner from the Mulford Co., Charles E. Vanderkleed, which was declared bankrupt on 7 June 1918.[21] Later he made quite a bit of money in various ventures. For a while he was an executive at Consolidated Distilleries, and came up with a scheme to make whiskey that tasted good without much aging, no doubt profitable after the end of prohibition. He was also Vice President of Publicker Industries in Philadelphia, manufacturers of industrial alcohol, and President of Bigler Chemical Corporation. During World War II he was area executive for the War Production Board in connection with industrial alcohol. He settled in Paoli, Pennsylvania, and raised cocker spaniels.

But Marks was in trouble again, partly due to his German dealings. To conceal German ownership of a patents company and thus evade taxes on patent royalties sent to Germany, he and his attorney, Nelson Littell, created a holding company, the American Hyasol Corporation, in 1932. The German-owned corporation held patents belonging to Henkel and Cie, Deutsche Hydrierwerke A.G. and Boehme Fettchemie G.m.b.H. Licenses were issued to several American companies including Proctor and Gamble, Du Pont and the Richards Chemical Company. Marks posed as the sole owner of the company. The payments of royalties to Germany were disguised as payments on a fictional debt of $2,000,000 which were sent to a Swiss bank. Perhaps most brilliant of all was that the contractors predicted a war which would last from 1939 to 1945 and made provisions to secure a $300,000 interest payment on the fictional debt to cover the war period.

In 1943 the assets of the American Hyasol Company were seized by the Alien Property Custodian, a government entity established to control assets belonging to enemy countries during the war. Most ironic is that the conspiracy was not discovered until Marks and Littell filed suit to recover the assets of American Hyasol after the war. Then the American government, which was closely investigating assets in occupied Germany, discovered the scam and issued an indictment against Marks and Littell. They were both convicted. Littell got a sentence of a year and a day in prison. Marks' same sentence was suspended because of a heart ailment.[22] Dr. Lewis Marks died at his home in Paoli, Pennsylvania, on 10 March 1958.

Nelson E. Edwards

Edwards got his old job back with INS and was assigned to Philadelphia. It appears that he may have found the usual routine of a newsreel cameraman boring after covering the war. He displayed a growing ambition to direct the course that the newsreel was taking. Edwards had shot the story of the opening of the Penn Highway that was released on 7 November 1916 in *Hearst International News Pictorial* no. 89.[23] About the same time he wrote a letter to R. Eugene Boyd of the INS, suggesting that it cover more substantial stories for the newsreel, such as the arrival of the explorer Ernest Shackleton at New Orleans and soldiers voting on the Mexican border. If Edwards was suffering from restlessness, international events soon provided a cure when the United States declared war against Germany and Austria in April 1917.

Even in that era, when young men went to war without much soul-searching, the response of the Edwards family can only be called remarkable; all five of the Edwards' sons joined the army. It is unclear why Nelson Edwards did not get a commission as a photographer in the Signal Corps because documents in the family papers suggest there was a slot waiting for him as cinematographer in the Signal Corps. Instead Edwards enlisted. He served in the U.S. Army from 7 December 1917 with the 152nd Depot Brigade at Camp Upton on Long Island, New York, until 21 January 1919 when he was discharged as a sergeant in Headquarters Company of the 4th Battalion.[24]

On 14 January 1919, Hatrick wrote Edwards a letter offering him his old job with INS in New York after his discharge. He stated that he was discharged from the army expressly to accompany the Armenian Relief Expedition headed by Dr. George E. White. The 250-person expedition left New York on the *Leviathan* on 17 February 1919, but Edwards had missed the sailing by five hours.[25] So Edwards proceeded to work for INS for about ten months after he was released. Back in New York he found that Cornelia Fisk had changed appreciably, as girls do between twelve and eighteen. They married in 1918 or 1919, probably in New Jersey or New York.

Edwards had always been interested in flying. He had made his first air camera pictures for Glenn Curtiss in 1911.[26] In the post-war period he started doing a lot of aerial camera work. Edwards covered the launching on 16 May 1919 of the United States Navy's epic flight across the Atlantic Ocean by three NC (Navy/Curtiss seaplanes, nicknamed 'Nancies') from Trepassey Bay, Newfoundland.[27] Forgotten since the Lindbergh flight of 1927, the 1919 navy transatlantic flight was a big story. Edwards spent some time in Newfoundland photographing the big flying boats and some of the footage survives. In 1945 Universal News shot one of those 'history of flight' stories that incorporated footage of the 1919 transatlantic flight which still exists in the Universal Newsreel collection at the National Archives. The *Memphis Commercial Appeal* also ran a series of photographs of these airplanes entitled: 'Scenes from International News No. 18 released by Universal Film Manufacturing Co.'.[28]

He photographed many American cities from the air when aerial views were still a novelty. Immediately upon leaving Trepassey Bay, he flew with the navy anti-sub-marine flotilla. The Navy sent an anti-submarine flotilla up the Mississippi stopping at all the major cities to give the Navy some publicity in this landlocked part of the world. Edwards joined this flotilla at Memphis and took photographs there: "With the ship piloted by Ensign R. W. Arthur, Edwards, perched in the machine gunners cockpit, 'filmed' from the Chisca hotel to Court Square, where he was forced to stop on account of a faulty engine. The plane was compelled to land after 80 feet of film had been taken from a height of 1200 feet."[29] Edwards resigned from INS in 1919 and helped organize the newly established Fox newsreel becoming its New York bureau manager (Colour Plate 6). "Fox News came on like thunder, the product of great energy, considerable imagination and an initial investment of five million dollars."[30] The Fox news department was headed by Pell Mitchell, and the first director of the operation was Herbert Ernest Hancock. The first issue of *Fox News* was premiered on 11 October 1919. Edwards was chief cameraman and he maintained a hectic pace. But in 1920 being continually away from his wife began to strain his marriage, so Edwards quit being a regular newsreel cameraman.[31] About spring of 1920 Edwards left Fox with the last Edwards story in the Fox archive appearing at the end of March.[32]

The Edwards moved to Baltimore in 1921 but retained some relationship with INS as he still had an INS press card in 1925 and was still corresponding with them in 1926. But by 1923 Edwards had joined forces with Milton Stark to establish a photography studio at 903 Pennsylvania Avenue, Baltimore.[33] Next year they moved into the more fashionable business and shopping district in Baltimore at 329 N. Charles Street with their business card listing them as Stark and Edwards, 'The Movie Men'.

But there was still some action. Edwards photographed the landings of the early trans-Atlantic flights, and was one of the 320 newsmen and photographers that covered Charles Lindbergh's return from Paris.[34] In 1933, Edwards covered the George Armwood lynching in Salisbury Maryland:

> After leaving a set of plates at the landing field [at Hebron Airport in Salisbury] at 11: AM, he – John Stadler and Nelson Edwards, a newsreel man, drove to Salisbury together. … They parked about two blocks from the armory and set out through the crowd of more or less subdued rioters to make their way to the building. Shouts arose on all sides. 'Here come some of those photographers! Get their cameras! Bust them up!' they were all yelling.' Stadler related last night. 'Edwards was shoving his way through the crowd while I locked the doors to the car, and then I hid my camera under my topcoat and put four plate holders inside my belt inside my vest and headed out for the armory. They kept pushing me from all sides and I could see Edwards' camera bobbing up and down. One of the Salisbury men, whom I know came over to me and told me to be careful, as he couldn't tell what might happen … .'[35]

In World War II Edwards was heartbroken when his son, Robert Edwards, was killed. Robert Hobart Edwards, a graduate of Polytechnic High School in Baltimore and the University of Maryland, evidently wanted to continue the motion picture tradition in the family. He was trained as a combat photographer at Lowry Field, Denver, and received a commission in the Signal Corps. He was ordered to the Eighth Air Force, the celebrated unit that conducted heavy bombing raids over Europe from England which suffered extremely high casualties. Although his orders were not to go on missions, but to train and organize the new photography personnel arriving in

Fig. 98. Four Edwards brothers, all newsreel cameramen, around 1948.
E.K. (Chuck), Curry, Nelson and Roy. [Courtesy Wiegman family.]

the theater, he volunteered to fly missions over Europe. On 9 September 1943 he was killed over the English Channel.[36]

Edwards told a reporter in 1944 that after World War I, his life was 'by and large a pleasant and exciting round of murders and strikes, ball games and bathing beauties, dog shows and diplomats, and always celebrities.' Even as a stringer, life was not dull for Edwards. He reminisced that he photographed the Duke of Windsor and Wallis Warfield Simpson when he was still the Prince of Wales accompanying her return to Baltimore, and he believed that he was the only man to photograph Theodore Roosevelt in a men's room. He was a member of the White House Press Photographers Association, covered every inauguration including 1912, and photographed Roosevelt and Harry Truman regularly. During World War II, Edwards probably got as much of the smoke of battle as he wanted when he visited Edgewood Arsenal near Baltimore to film some new weapons being tested that included the infamous white phosphorus and some new flame throwers which nearly burned him to a crisp.

Nelson Edwards was not the only Edwards brother to choose the newsreel business. Evidently attracted by his example, his brothers went into newsreels as well. E. K. 'Chuck' Edwards became a cameraman for Paramount in Denver for 23 years. In the 1950s he formed a company with his son specializing in films about horses. Roy Donald Edwards, who became a cameraman for Universal Newsreel in New York, took the famous films of Bruno Hauptmann on the witness stand during the Lindbergh trial in New Jersey.[37] Later on he became a cameraman for *News of the*

Day, a television news company, and was killed in October 1958 in a helicopter crash while filming a story. Curry Edwards also became a cameraman for Universal in Denver. Edwards helped his son-in-law David J. Wiegman become a newsreel photographer by sharing his tricks of the trade and advising on the many problems involved in joining the union.

Newsreel pioneer and World War I cameraman Nelson Edwards died at his home at 6 Dover Road near Reisterstown, Maryland on 17 October 1954 at the age of 66.[38] He is buried at the Arlington National Cemetery. Like his brothers, his son and his son-in-law, he wrote American history in motion pictures.

Walter Niebuhr[39]

After World War I and his employment with the CPI writing scripts, the movie-struck Niebuhr started the American Cinema Corporation (ACC). There is no information about how the Corporation came into being after the First World War, save a brief note in Niebuhr's papers, which says, "In February 1919, Mr. Niebuhr founded the American Cinema Corporation with the financial backing of Newbold Leroy Edgar, Judge Warren McConighe, J.J. Murphy and others. This Company produced independently for three seasons but suspended production during the depression in the fall of 1921 when several distributing firms, especially United Theaters, went to the wall owing American Cinema large sums of money."[40]

According to Niebuhr's note, ACC not only released the five features which are listed in the American Film Institute Catalog (*His Brother's Keeper, The Inner Voice, Stolen Moments, What Women Want*, and *Women Men Forget*), it was also responsible for two others: *The Immigrant* and *Her Majesty*. In addition, the ACC produced "six domestic comedies with Mrs. Sidney Drew".[41]

Niebuhr employed an array of talented people. Directors John M. Stahl, George Archainbaud and Roy Neill each sported an extensive filmography, working well into the 1940s. Niebuhr also hired well-known actors and actresses. Richard Barthelmess, Mollie King, E.K. Lincoln, Agnes Ayres and Riley Hatch all worked in Niebuhr's films. Yet of all those who worked on ACC productions, Rudolph Valentino was certainly the most famous.[42]

After the collapse of ACC, Niebuhr went to Europe and worked on several films. He directed *The Money Habit* in England and *Die Stadt der Versuchung* (City of Temptation) and *Venezianische Liebesabenteuer* (Venetian Lovers) in Germany. *Die Stadt der Versuchung*, filmed in Berlin, was the vehicle that made a star of actress Olga Tschechowa.[43]

In the 1930s back in America, Niebuhr tried his hand at documentary production and worked for two governmental agencies, the Tennessee Valley Authority and Civilian Conservation Corps. He also did independent film work for the Alfred P. Sloan Foundation and other clients. As such, he helped to edit the Academy Award-winning documentary *Kukan*.

During the Second World War, Niebuhr worked for the Signal Corps. From 1942–44 he was Chief Librarian of the Astoria Studios in Astoria, New York. In addition to editing raw footage, his duties included helping organizations locate and select Signal Corps footage for various film projects. In 1944 he again tried his hand at business, launching HVN Film Associates.

Niebuhr died suddenly in August of 1946. His daughter, Carol, believed that the scenes of death he witnessed daily in the Signal Corps footage he edited and stored contributed to Walter's fatal heart attack.[44]

Edwin F. Weigle

Back from the wars, Edwin Weigle married Florence (Marshall) Johnson on 4 May 1920. She was the daughter of John Erwin Marshall of Highland Park, Illinois, one of the founders of the Middleby Marshall Oven Company. Weigle moved to Deerfield, an affluent suburb on the North Shore, where he became the secretary and treasurer for the company.[45] Florence had seen Weigle in Minneapolis in January 1917 where he was lecturing with his film on Germany.[46] Previously married, she had a daughter named Lorraine, who was part of the Weigle household until at least 1930. Judging from a picture by Weigle, Florence had piercing dark eyes and a determined chin. She was a talented writer.

Together, the Weigles came up with the idea of traveling to Ireland and making *Ireland in Revolt*, a film about the troubles, and once again the trip was underwritten by the *Chicago Tribune*. To exploit the previous Weigle films, Patterson and the *Tribune* had set up corporations, such as The International Motion Picture Company for *On Belgian Battlefields*, and Indian Film Company for *The German Side of the War*. In this case an informal agreement was reached whereby three *Tribune* executives, Samuel Emory Thomason, William H. Field and Max Annenberg, would get ten percent each of the profits from the film, if any, and the *Tribune* would get the rest.[47]

Florence M. Weigle wrote the script and later wrote *Ireland as It Is Today*, a book based on the script describing their trip and the making of the film. The copy of the book at the Library of Congress contains her original handwritten dedication to President Wilson, "Trusting this may be of some interest to our President, Respectfully, Florence M. Weigle".

The film and Mrs. Weigle's book are pro-Sinn Fein, and while the book acknowledges that Britain was caught in a tough spot between Ulster and Ireland, there is very little doubt that the film and the book are decidedly against the British position in Ireland, in particular the British use of the thuggish Black and Tans and the Irish Royal Constabulary. The Weigles interviewed in glowing terms Arthur Griffith and Desmond Fitzgerald, chief of propaganda for the Sinn Fein, who gave the Weigles all the help he could.

The film was far from a honeymoon voyage. Weigle found himself in some spots as tough as any he had experienced earlier in Europe and several times was lucky to get away from confrontations with his film and his skin. One particularly hot spot they visited was Ballymacarret, an eastern district in Belfast where it had been reported that Protestants were killing the Catholics and burning them out:

> As Ed took his place behind the camera ready to turn the crank, a portion of the mob began to gather around him bristling with distrust: 'What are you doing here?' 'What is your religion?' they shouted. He tried to evade the question as the ever swelling mob pressed closer to him, screaming that they would smash him and his camera to a thousand bits if he did not answer them. He tried to temporize, 'Well I guess I have no set religion. I am just an American', for by that time he was realizing that if he answered he was a Protestant and those nearest him in the mob were of Catholic persuasion, that they would quickly dispose of him, or that if he professed Catholicism for reasons of possible safety the surrounding mob might be Protestant and act in accordance with their customs and if there were equal numbers of both sets surrounding him, then he was a goner for sure.
>
> In this case Weigle chose discretion over valor, grabbed his camera and returned to his car, followed by cries of "Go back to America and take Dr. Mannix with you".[48]

Weigle later got a few feet of footage in Ballymacarret, and then filmed in an equally troubled area called the Marrowbone in Belfast, also called the "Mustard Pot" because things often became very fiery in the vicinity.

After the Weigles returned to Chicago, the film opened at the Randolph Theater on 15 December 1920, and subsequently played in cities where there was a large Irish population. Perhaps predictably, when the film was shown to the Chicago Board of Censors, who loved it, other enthusiastic spectators were the newly appointed Chief of Police Charles C. Fitzmorris and Michael J. Faherty, former president of the Irish Fellowship Club.[49] *Variety* also gave it a highly favorable review, the only Weigle film it ever really praised.[50]

After his return from Ireland, It becomes more difficult to find traces of Edwin F. Weigle. His stepdaughter Lorraine married Hubert N. Kelley, newspaperman, author and religious writer as well as being the manager of the Middleby Marshall Company.[51] Weigle and Kelley were both prominent in Saint Gregory's Episcopal Church in Deerfield, Illinois, and instrumental in founding it. And so Weigle dropped out of cinematography and into the world of commerce and suburbia.

The immediate reason for Weigle's change in direction was a disastrous trip the Weigles undertook for Robert R. McCormick of the *Tribune*, who traveled with Donald Thompson in Russia (Chapter 8). Colonel McCormick had been buying tracts of lumber in Canada to assure the *Tribune*'s paper supply. According to letters from Florence to her mother and daughter, he commissioned the Weigles to make a film about the lumber drive in Quebec province in the spring of 1921. It was a disaster. Weigle fell through the ice, lost a camera and all his film, and evidently the Weigles quit in disgust at the appalling conditions and difficulties in filming. Thus ended Weigles' career with the *Tribune*.

One can easily imagine other reasons for Weigle's change in direction. One may have been that there seemed little place for film correspondents after World War I. *The Chicago Tribune* had done some splendid business with Weigle's films. On top of his war features the company had also produced a number of other news films. This line of production ended in 1916 when Robert R. McCormick began to look for a new journalistic approach.[52] This led him to contract with the film producer William N. Selig in December 1915. The result was the *Selig-Tribune*, a bi-weekly news reel described in its publicity as: "... a REEL NEWSPAPER which will reach the movie fans while the news on the reel is real news". According to the hype, it was to feature hundreds of cameramen under the supervision of Weigle.[53] The *Selig-Tribune* was not the success the producers had hoped and after one year the production *Selig-Tribune* stopped. But if newsreels were the coming thing, in a cinematic sense a form of mass production, where did people like Weigle and Donald Thompson fit in?

Joseph Medill Patterson

In 1919 Patterson founded the *New York News*. In 1925 he left the management of the *Tribune* to his cousin "Bertie", Colonel Robert R. McCormick, moved to New York and made a great success of his new newspaper. For a while the *News* was somewhat progressive but then the paper changed. While Patterson was still maverick enough to support Franklin Delano Roosevelt in his first two terms, he turned against Roosevelt when Roosevelt's policies toward Japan and Nazi Germany became increasingly interventionist. Patterson had never lost his isolationist tendencies, and he and his sister, Eleanor Patterson, as well as Bertie McCormick all became increasingly anti-New Deal and isolationist to the point of obsession. After a long and successful career, Patterson died on 26 May 1946.

Considering the close personal and professional relationship that Weigle had enjoyed with Joseph Patterson, it seems odd Patterson did not take him along when he moved to New York, even if only as a photographer. But then Patterson was more than well served at the *News* by his celebrated photographer Edward N. Jackson. There does not even seem to be an obituary for Weigle who died on 1 August 1973.

Ariel Varges

The war for Varges had been a magnificent stepping stone. Just a few months after returning home in May 1919, he left again for a 250,000 mile tour around the world that took four years. Varges filmed the signing of the Treaty of Versailles, then proceeded to Germany where he took motion pictures from a Zeppelin traveling between Berlin and Friedrichshaven. He returned to Berlin in time to cover the Kapp putsch by right-wing militias against the new Republican government. In Russia Varges became the first American cinematographer to film Trotsky. But it was in Germany that Varges probably scored his most impressive news beat when he bought a spectacular collection of wartime footage of the *Moewe*, a German raider, while at sea sinking Entente merchant and navy ships. Scenes from this film have been edited in numerous documentaries of the First World War.

"OKAY BOYS, YOU CAN START THE WAR NOW!"

The World's Ace Newsreel Man is on the job

Hearst Metrotone News' One and Only—

VARGES is in ETHIOPIA!

That's News! Captain Ariel Varges has moved in from the battle-fields of China. He's probably moved into Haile Selassie's guest room because he's the pal of Abyssinia's Emperor. Varges, the most famous camera-man alive, has covered practically every modern war. He works in the front-line trenches and his inside-stuff appears in HEARST METRO-TONE NEWS. *There's a new Lion of Judah—LEO of M-G-M!*

Fig. 99. Ariel Varges, back on the job filming war in Ethiopia for News of the Day. *Advertisement* Film Daily *magazine, 1935.*

Post war, Ariel Varges' name and reputation became a synonym in American newspapers for the exemplary globe-trotting war photographer. In the 1920s and 1930s he continued to film revolutions and wars in China and Ethiopia for Hearst's

News of The Day. At retirement Varges still was working for the Hearst organization as chief of the photographic laboratory in New York City for *News of the Day*. After he ceased working abroad he married Jessica Pendleton in New York City in 1945. The couple lived quietly on a farm just outside Norwich, Connecticut.

Ariel Lowe Varges died on 27 December 1972 at the age of 82 and was buried at Preston City Cemetery. Like most of his American colleagues who had filmed World War I his name by then was merely an insignificant footnote in history books.

Merl la Voy

After the war Merl la Voy remained active as a cinematographer for the Red Cross. He was commissioned as a Captain in 1919, although he had never served in the army before. A tireless traveler seeking the exotic and adventure, la Voy filmed his way through Italy, the Balkans, Turkey and North Africa. He maintained his adventurous image by posing for pictures in his Captain's uniform with a Bedouin camel in Africa and more formally with Queen Marie in Rumania. His still photographs, which seem to duplicate many scenes from his films, confirm he was an excellent photographer with an eye for good composition and exposure. He also claimed he was the first man to film the Turkish Sultan's personal harem. Although he described the ladies as fat and ill-groomed, this exploit was probably among la Voy's most prized accomplishments.

La Voy and his camera lens traveled the four corners of the world for much of his life, earning him the well-deserved title of "The Modern Marco Polo". He was probably best remembered by moviegoers for his South Seas Islands documentaries and photographic studies of the Inuit. In 1927 Pathé News appointed him globe-trotting cameraman and in this capacity he indeed travelled around the world. When President-elect Herbert Hoover went to South America on a good-will tour in 1928–29, la Voy was on board the USS *Maryland* to cover the journey. During the 1920s he also visited Australia, the Solomon Islands, the Philippines and China where he nearly got shot by a firing squad. Many of his pictures in China were taken in Nanking during the Kuomintang rule of Chiang Kai-shek.

Merl la Voy died unexpectedly on 7 December 1953 as a result of a heart attack while staying in Johannesburg, South Africa, and his body was cremated at Braamfontein Crematorium. According to his last wishes, his ashes were shipped to his stepbrother Irwin in Seattle, Washington, and scattered across the wilderness around Oregon that he loved so much.

Albert K. Dawson

Albert Dawson escaped relatively unscathed from the war. He changed the name of his firm to the "Publisher's Photo Service" and kept his hand in photography until 1922. As a camera reporter, Dawson covered the visit of Prince of Wales, later Edward VIII, to Canada in August 1919. In 1922 while on a cruise to the Mediterranean, Dawson also scooped his colleagues when he got the chance to do an exclusive interview with Fuad I, the first King of Egypt, after the country had become independent from Great Britain. Said Dawson:

> "There is nothing about the new King's appearance to prevent him from wandering about the city unguarded. He wears a simple frock coat with fez that is common to all Egyptians. We met at a coffee house table and chatted for an hour. He expressed the hope that Egypt will enter upon a period of great prosperity as an independent state."[54]

Shortly after his return from Egypt, Dawson married Clara Hawkey, daughter of a piano dealer, in Poughkeepsie, New York. They had a son Robert (1925–1980), who shared his father's interest in technology and became an electrical engineer. Upon marriage, Albert Dawson moved to New York City and worked for Thomas Cooke as a tour guide on many cruises to the Mediterranean, the Caribbean and Latin America.

In the 1930s Dawson worked for the American Express Company as manager of their new Russian travel division organizing tours to the Soviet Union for Americans despite political tensions. He was interviewed on this groundbreaking work by his friend, radio broadcaster and newsreel reporter Lowell Thomas, who also had been a cameraman in the First World War. In collaboration with the *Washington Post*, Dawson also did a series of popular lectures on his travels to exotic locations abroad. In October 1934 his presentation of films and colored slides on the "Romance of the West Indies" at the Masonic Auditorium attracted over 1,000 people. During World War II Dawson went to Chile, where he directed several summer schools for students in South America.

Until late in life he remained what he had been from his early years as a camera reporter: an energetic globetrotter. Albert K. Dawson died in Queens, New York City, on 1 February 1967 never having shared his remarkable experiences during World War I with his relatives in Vincennes.

Frank E. Kleinschmidt

Kleinschmidt's story during World War I ends in a most ironic way. He got caught up between the k.u.k. Kriegspressequartier and the American authorities and was suspected by both parties of espionage. On 15 December 1915, two days before his assignment at the Isonzo front would end, the k.u.k. Kriegspressequartier started a full investigation. The Austrians became suspicious when Kleinschmidt told them he was a Captain from the United States army. After checking with the American embassy in Vienna, they soon discovered he wasn't listed in the officers' register. The record shows that he was in fact suspected of espionage:

> "Since February 1915, a certain Franz E. Kleinschmidt is attached to the Kriegspressequartier. The purpose of his presence is to make films which promote the Austro-Hungarian army in America. Because of his humble manners, he has been able to gain the trust and sympathy of officers. As a result of this, he was invited to the front many times and could stay with several command posts for a long time. According to professionals in the trade, he has demonstrated little experience in taking motion pictures. Until now, he has shot many scenes of pilots and airplanes, as well as submarines, and was often seen talking with officers from the air force

and navy in a lively manner. A photographer of the Kriegspressequartier has observed him, and noticed that he took many pictures of our heavy artillery from several positions. When he was seen learning French, Kleinschmidt stated he wanted to go to the French army."[55]

On the very same day, an order was sent to military headquarters in Trieste to confiscate all his photos and films before Kleinschmidt could return to Vienna. Special attention was paid to pictures showing airplanes and artillery that would perhaps be hidden from the censor. Kleinschmidt's papers also had to be searched for any sensitive information on military positions at the Isonzo front. The next day, his travel permits were taken from him, and Kleinschmidt's photographic equipment was packed and sealed in a box. Escorted by a military police officer, Kleinschmidt was put on a train to Vienna on 18 December 1915, where all his films were thoroughly searched.

After a careful examination, the Austrian army decided to give most of his films back. As is shown in the extant footage, a surprising number of close-up shots of the Skoda mortars and heavy artillery in action were passed by the censor.[56] He sailed from Copenhagen on the SS *Frederik VIII* and arrived in New York City on 23 February 1916. His return to America did not mean that he picked up his daily routine. Far from it, it soon became apparent that he could not adjust to his pre-war family life. Shortly after his homecoming, Kleinschmidt and his wife divorced. He lived in hotels for most of the following two years, trying to sell his film and telling the movie-going audience about his experiences in the trenches. In July 1916, Kleinschmidt went to San Francisco where he exhibited *War on Three Fronts* at the Portola Theatre for a week. Public opinion regarding the war on the West Coast was clearly more open to pro-German sentiments than in New York, and Kleinschmidt may have found it more expedient for this reason to show his movie over there. In a postcard to the family, written on 25 July, Kleinschmidt mentioned that he had just been to Los Angeles promoting his film. Business was looking good, and he expected to close a deal the next day. *War on Three Fronts* had a three week engagement in Los Angeles at Clune's Auditorium, the prestigious showplace where *Birth of a Nation* had its memorable premiere. The film presentation must have been worthwhile, because state rights for California, Nevada and Arizona were also sold to the owner of this theatre, W.H. Clune.[57] He probably benefitted most from his movie in his hometown Seattle. Lecturing at Seattle's leading theatre the Moore, Kleinschmidt showed his film for eight days. Eugene Levy, manager of the local Strand, was so impressed by *War on Three Fronts* and its potential as a money maker that he paid the Captain $25,000 in cash for the Northwest state rights.[58]

On 11 December 1916 Kleinschmidt lectured at the Brown Hotel in Denver, Colorado, where he made a most vigorous speech against the Wilson administration which clearly shows his feelings on the war. The President, he said, may have won the recent election with his promise to keep the country out of the war. But in reality the government is financially tied up with the Entente from head to toe, as a result of the war loans and export of munitions. Any protests against the German submarine warfare were nothing less than hypocritical: "We talk about the 'inhumanity' of sinking the *Lusitania* and the few hundred Americans whose lives have been lost. Well, weren't there 70,000 cases of ammunition on board? Our government will do nothing to stop this war. England is the big customer these days, and commerce with us is everything. England is the enemy of this country. England always has been our enemy. But we are for the dollar. And England started this war. England fomented it. It was an English scheme. But here we are selling Christ every day for thirty pieces of silver."[59]

The American intervention in the war changed Kleinschmidt's life dramatically. When he first presented *War on Three Fronts* to the trade in New York, exhibitors were anxious to recognize its commercial value. But by the time Selznick released his film for a nationwide release in April 1917, the political situation had evolved considerably. *Moving Picture World* was now openly warning the film trade they would be buying a riot and called the exhibition of the movie a sign of extremely bad taste. *Variety* even suggested banning the film: "America is not the place and this is not the time for the exploitation on the screen of the doctrine of German 'frightfulness' of which this group of pictures is a shining and shocking example".[60] Even more damaging to Kleinschmidt, he was shadowed by special agents of the Justice Department, Bureau of Investigation. This investigation would finally build up to his arrest, although the story on his surveillance also gives a revealing insight into the war fever and the fear of German espionage that was affecting the minds of the American people. Ironically, as with the Austrian authorities, the fact that he called himself a "Captain" also led Kleinschmidt into some serious complications.

It all began with a report on 26 February 1917 by special agent Petrovitsky from Seattle, Washington, to Chief Bruce Bielaski of the Bureau of Investigation. In this report, he called attention to a Captain Carl Klienschmitt [sic] who had exhibited war pictures in Seattle the year before, and was supposed to be a German or an Austrian officer, according to his own statements. An informant had said the Captain was very wealthy and that he had tried to finance a party of traders for an expedition to the islands of Puget Sound. "That bunch of Germans will need watching", he warned.[61] Kleinschmidt's case probably would have been closed, if he had stopped promoting *War on Three Fronts* the way he did when America was still neutral. Instead, he showed the film at the Edison Plant in West Orange, New Jersey, during a Liberty Loan Drive and explicitly mentioned the efficiency of the German army. A reporter from the *New York Times* was on the spot and wrote a critical story on the Captain's untimely remarks.[62] On 1 August while staying at the Astor Hotel in New York City, Kleinschmidt made another vital mistake when he sent the following telegram to the Curtiss Aviation Field at Buffalo, New York: "Are you accepting pupils for a course in flying? Private tuition. State terms and earliest date. Answer paid. Hotel Astor."[63] His telegram was intercepted by a special agent and the surveillance on Kleinschmidt was increased.

Kleinschmidt had been playing with the idea of learning to fly, ever since he had been at the front. With the money that he had earned from his war film, he now had the opportunity to do so. He was accepted at the Curtiss Aviation Field a week later, not knowing that he was shadowed. A report, filed on 30 August 1917, shows that he spoke very openly about his experiences as a war photographer with the Austrian army, much to the distrust of the airfield staff. Kleinschmidt meanwhile had created so many disturbances that he was ejected from the Curtiss airfield in Buffalo. He was handed over to the Atlantic Coast Aeronautical Station at Newport News, Virginia, with the cunning advice to give him so much flying in a very short time that Kleinschmidt would run out of money and leave school. Either the advice wasn't heeded, or his tutors underestimated Kleinschmidt's tenacity. The record shows that he was still under surveillance in September 1917, and there are reports by agent Taylor at this airfield warning his superiors that although he could find no conclusive evidence against Kleinschmidt his removal was called for.[64] By this time Chief Bielaski was also put under pressure by the army to get Kleinschmidt. On 30 October 1917 he received the following strongly worded letter:[65]

> Mr. A.B. Bielaski
> Chief, Bureau of Investigation
> Department of Justice, Washington
>
> My dear Bielaski:
>
> With reference to a report of Wm. M. Taylor, Norfolk, Va., for September 18, 1917, in re F.K. [sic] Kleinschmidt, is not this man a fit subject for internment?
>
> It appears that he is now a student of flying at the Curtiss Company's aviation fields, Newport News, Va.; that he is a native born German, a naturalized citizen of the United States, and that he accepted a commission from the German [sic] Government in recognition of his services as an aerial photographer. This acceptance would forfeit his American citizenship, as we understand the law.
>
> The Curtiss people believe he is at Newport News for some other reason than learning to fly and Colonel Arnold of the Signal Corps recommends his removal from the airfield.
>
> Very sincerely,
>
> s/ R.H. van Deman
> Lt. Col., General Staff
> Chief, Military Intelligence Section

Chief Bielaski upon receiving this letter immediately jumped into action and instructed his department to interview Kleinschmidt on the exact status of his citizenship in order to find out if he had taken a military oath of allegiance to Germany or Austria-Hungary. The question whether he was still technically an American citizen was never answered. By the time an agent had gone to interview Kleinschmidt, he was back in New York. Meanwhile, at the request of either the military or the naval intelligence service, strings were pulled and local detectives of Inspector Tunney's

Fig. 100. Kleinschmidt in an Austrian fighter plane, 1915. His passion for flying got him into serious problems when he returned to the United States. [Courtesy Wichita State University Libraries.]

squad in New York started their own investigation. They didn't need as much time as the Justice Department. On 24 November 1917, while staying at his hotel, Kleinschmidt was arrested. Evidently, the army wasn't interested in any legal subtleties. Tunney's men caught him on a technical charge, the possession of a loaded revolver and formally a violation of the Sullivan act. Reporters were present shortly after his arrest. "Now, don't make any mistake. Don't have me pro-German. I am not!", Kleinschmidt told the press. On the following morning, the news of his arrest and his film work with the Central Powers was splashed on the pages of all major American newspapers.[66]

Although Kleinschmidt paid 500 dollars and was released on bail, the news of his arrest meant that he was put out of business with *War on Three Fronts*. His film surprisingly enough had been endorsed in July 1917 by the Committee on Public Information, America's wartime propaganda agency. The Selznick Corporation had even been given permission by the CPI to use the official endorsement in the film, but with the war fever running high and the news of Kleinschmidt's arrest this all changed. In December 1917, at the request of the National Board of Review, all twelve copies of *War on Three Fronts* then circulating in the country were withdrawn from exhibition.[67] Since then, there is no further mention of Kleinschmidt's film being shown on the screen during World War I. Even though there wasn't an official ban, his movie was simply considered too dangerous to handle.[68]

After the war, Kleinschmidt stayed in New York City. His days of living in hotels were by then over. Around 1918, he married Esther Theresa Fillian. She was born in Ramey, Pennsylvania, and her father was a railroad trainman.[69] Together with his second wife, Kleinschmidt worked on a new series of movie projects. On a former submarine chaser, the couple sailed from Seattle in May 1922 and produced *Adventures in the Far North*. He was probably most successful with a short film released in 1925, picturing Santa Claus in his workshop while he visits his Eskimo neighbours and tends his reindeer. Until the beginning of the Second World War, Kleinschmidt toured many American cities promoting this film. The movie had a commercial tie-in with local exhibitors and shop keepers who benefitted from the film presentation to children around Christmas time. To promote this film, the Captain hired an airplane and flew to the North Pole, reporting on the whereabouts of Santa Claus. Flying remained one his greatest passions.[70]

Around 1932 Kleinschmidt and his wife moved to Hollywood, California, and lived at 6019 Carlos Avenue. There are a number of letters in the family collection, showing that he had a hard time financially. The income from his movies had dried up and he had to borrow money on his life insurance to pay the rent. "I have lost all pep and ambition, can't make a dollar, in fact I haven't for over two years. I don't know what is going to become of us", Kleinschmidt complained.[71] A few years later at the age of 70, Kleinschmidt was still desperately looking for a job. By then, most people had forgotten about Kleinschmidt, his adventures in the Arctic and his remarkable film *War on Three Fronts* - a cinematic gem from the past. Frank Kleinschmidt died at Good Samaritan Hospital in Los Angeles on 25 March 1949. He was buried at Forest Lawn Memorial Park in Glendale, California.

The Films

If many of these film makers disappeared from sight, so did most of their films. So far, there is no trace of *The Battle of Vera Cruz, Heroic France, On Belgian Battlefields*, or *Ireland in Revolt*. The prospect is brighter for Weigle's *The German Side of the War*. The Library of Congress has the last several hundred feet of the film[72] and the John E. Allen Archives has part of this film as well as many others. Whether enough of any of his films survives to make a restoration is an open question. Also much of the film that Weigle shot for the Signal Corps still survives. Since Weigle was the Photographic Officer for the 35th Division between 28 September 1918 and 15 January 1919, he either personally photographed or was responsible for these films deposited at the National Archives in Washington. Most notable are the *Meuse-Argonne Offensive, 26 Sep – 11 Nov 1918, 35th Division*; *Antiaircraft Activities in the AEF*; and a fifteen-reel film entitled *35th Division*. Footage of the 35th Division from this period is included in the compilation films *Flashes of Action: Shots of the World War* and several films on post-armistice training.[73] One hopes that other films of Weigle will resurface as well as more about Weigle himself. Some of Donald Thompson's films survive both at the Museum of Modern Art, the National Archives and the Library of Congress

(Chapter 7). Some of Albert K. Dawson's films or at least scraps of them have been located at the Imperial War Museum in London and the Library of Congress. There also may be copies or at least parts of them at the Austrian Film Archives in Vienna. Part of Kleinschmidt's *War on Three Fronts* is at the UCLA Archive, and in 1933, it was re-released under the title *War Debts* in a three-reel version running thirty minutes. Narrated by Wilfred Lucas, about twenty minutes of this sound version are at the Library of Congress and in the John E. Allen Collection. Kleinschmidt used this revamped film to advocate the collection of war debts by the U.S. government in order to stop the armaments race in Europe.[74] And amazingly all parts of the complete nine reels of the Durborough film *On the Firing Line with the Germans,* also known as *With Von Hindenburg's Army at the Front,* are at the Library of Congress and National Archives. So there is always hope for the resurrection of some of these remarkable World War I films.

Notes

1. Jay Leyda, *Films Beget Films: A Study of the Compilation Film* (London: George Allen and Unwin Ltd., 1964; New York: Hill and Wang, 1971), 32–33. Citation to the Hill and Wang edition.

2. Carl Flik-Steger, "The Adlon Bar Gang", *Shanghai* (Shanghai: XX Century Publishing Co., [n.d.], 399–407; Hedda Adlon, *Hotel Adlon* (Munich: Kindler, 1961 © 1955).

Wilbur H. Durborough

3. *Chicago Tribune* (20 December 1916): 21; (6 July 1919): E11; (20 July 1919): E6; *Philadelphia Inquirer* (3 August 1919): 16; *New York Tribune* (8 August 1919): 15.

4. 1920 US Census, NY, NY, ED 1462, Sheet 16A; Wilbur Henry Durborough, Civil Service Application CSA 15 June 1942, Hill Field (USAAF Base), Ogden, UT, National Personnel Records Center, Civilian Personnel Records, St. Louis, MO (hereafter cited as WHD CSA 1942).

5. Behind the honest publicity and promotions was a secret syndicate bribing newspapermen in the financial press with company shares to promote the many local Savold operating companies. Within a year the insiders had extracted their fortunes. See Robert Sobel, AMEX: *The History of the American Stock Exchange 1921–1971*, (Washington, DC: Beard Books, 2000), 84–85.

6. WHD CSA 1942.

7. Philadelphia Directories 1927–1930.

8. 1930 US Census, NARA T626 Reel 2034, ED 170, 13A, ll. 33–37.

9. Delaware Co., PA, Deed Book 925, 490, recorded 7 December 1931.

10. WHD CSA 1942; Mrs. Robert M. (Bea) Durborough, interview (n.d.) with Castellan.

11. WHD CSA 1942; Social Security Death Index; Mrs. Robert M. (Bea) Durborough, interview (n.d.) with Castellan.

12. For a more complete biography and discussion of his 1915 film: see James W. Castellan, "Wilber H. Durborough, His Life and His Film", unpublished manuscript.

13. Durborough Draft Mss., Part 2, p. 17, now in the Manuscripts Division, Library of Congress.

Donald Thompson

14. "Asia's Expedition to the Orient", *Asia: the American Magazine on the Orient*. Vol. XX No. 8 (September 1920): 754–755.

15. "Held for Posing as Naval Official", *New York Evening Post* (5 June 1923): 1; "War Photographer Held as Swindler", *New York Times* (6 June 1923): 23.

16. "War Correspondent And Photographer Sees Mongolia Fight", *Wichita Eagle* (17 May 1936).

Marks, De Beaufort and Wallace

17. *New York Times* (21 December 1941): 40; Bennett & Co.'s Evansville Directory 1902 (Evansville Indiana: Bennett and Co., 1902), 680.

18. "Count de Beaufort Marries Girl of 18", *New York Times* (8 September 1917): 9.

19. California, Death Index, 1940–1997, Ancestry.com; Jacksonville Courier, 17 October 1967, 28. De Beaufort claimed to have been an artillery captain in the Belgian Army in 1917, but there has never been any substantiation of this and neither has there been for his interview of von Hindenburg.

20. M1194, File 9140-363 (Walter F. Niebuhr) National Archives, College Park, MD.

21. "U. S. Court Names Receiver: Chemical Concern's Stockholders Say it is Insolvent", *Philadelphia Evening Ledger* (27 June 1918): 7.

22. "$500,000 Tax Plot is Laid to 2 Here", *New York Times* (6 May 1948): 18; "2 Sentenced Here for a Wartime Plot", *New York Times* (1 April 1950): 32. For more on the investigation of these companies in Germany, see "Records of the External Assets Investigation Section of the Property Division, OMGUS [Office of the Military Government of the United States], 1945–1949". NARA M1922, National Archives.

Nelson Edwards

23. *Motography* (25 November 1916): 1209.

24. "Three Months of Plattsburg Justifies America's Military Experiment", *New York Tribune* (12 August 1917): 8.

25. "Movie Operator Here in Extensive Trips; Photographed Kaiser", *Commercial Appeal* (8 June 1919): 17; "Near East Relief Expedition Leaves", *New York Times* (17 February 1919): 6.

26. Ibid. (8 June 1919): 17.

27. "Hundreds Inspect Anti-Sub Flotilla", *Commercial Appeal* (6 June 1919): 8; "Movie Operator Here in Extensive Trips; Photographed Kaiser", *Commercial Appeal* (8 June 1919): 17.

28. *Commercial Appeal* (4 May 1919): 1; see also *Polar Flight* (1926) and *Transatlantic Flight* (1919), National Archives, ARC Identifier 89108. The Archives specifically lists the contributor of the 1919 material as the International Newsreel Corporation, 1919. See also Fielding, *The American Newsreel 1911–1967* (Norman: University of Oklahoma Press, 1972), 88, 106. Very few of the early Hearst News Pictorials survive. One of the saddest things in Louis Pizzitola's book on Hearst is the description of the fate of most of them: "Once they were screened, news films were essentially up for grabs at the International Film Service Office. Morrill Goddard's son Dewitt remembers his father, who was treasurer of IFS at the time, bringing footage home to their apartment on Riverside Drive, where the youngster spliced out the fashion sequences but left in the war-related scenes to entertain his friend on a miniature motion-picture projector." Louis Pizzitola, *Hearst over Hollywood*, 170.

29. "Movie Operator Here in Extensive Trip", *Commercial Appeal* (8 June 1919): 17.

30. Raymond Fielding, *The American Newsreel 1911–1967* (Norman: University of Oklahoma Press, 1972), 60.

31. "Finds More Thrills Turning Reel Than Plowing In Kansas", *Hutchinson Kansas News* (25 July 1935): 10.

32. Fox News: MVTN 5207: NYC Clouds; MVTN A-461: Bulletproof Glass; MVTN 2455: Lord and Lady Decies; MVTN 1923: Railroad Station Wrecked by Explosion; MVTN-A-1621: Launching of the USS "S-16" (SS-121); MVTN 392: Adirondacks Trapper; MVTN 1890: New York State Assembly; MVTN 1518: Monument to Battle of the Marne; MTVN 293:James E. Fraser, Sculptor; Fox News Collection, Columbia, South Carolina: University of South Carolina, http://libcat.csd.sc.edu; 'Special Fox News Bulletin no. 46: Important Corrections of Changes in Staff Given in Bulletin No. 44', Wiegman Family papers [A29].

33. *Educational Screen*, Vol. 19 (1940): 236.

34. "Finds More Thrills Turning Reel Than Plowing In Kansas", *Hutchinson Kansas News* (25 July 1935): 10.

35. "Pictures of Combat Smuggled Through Mob by Photographer", *Baltimore Sun* (29 November 1933): 2. Whether Edwards was working for Paramount that day is not clear. The chief photographer for Paramount in Salisbury was Harry Tugander. When the mob threw his sound truck and equipment worth 25,000 depression dollars into the Wicomico River, Tugander fled from Salisbury for Easton, Maryland. Paramount then sent newsreel photographer Urban Santone by air as backup from New York. Santone got his film and, pursued by a mob looking for any photographer it could find, drove a truck lent by a friendly farmer to the nearest airport and got himself and his film out of Maryland as fast as he could. John Beecroft, 'The Salisbury Riots', *The International Photographer* 6 (January 1934): 20–21, 28.

36. Ibid.

37. "Ace Cameramen Reunite", *Hutchinson News Herald* (4 January 1948): 1; 'Hauptman Testifies, Millions Wait'. Universal Newsreel, 1935/01/30. Once again, the footage survives and is readily available on the internet. Most of the Universal Newsreels survive at the National Archive in College Park, and the Bruno Hauptmann testimony is available on youtube.com.

38. "N. E. Edwards Funeral Set", *Baltimore Sun* (19 October 1954): 15.

Walter Niebuhr

39. All information on Niebuhr is due entirely and with many thanks to William G. Chrystal. The story of Walter Niebuhr's difficulties is also documented at length in William G. Chrystal, "An American without any 'If and

'Buts': Reinhold Niebuhr, His Brothers and the First World War", *Niebuhr Studies* (Reno: Empire for Liberty, 2012), 89–111

40. A Master of his Craft: The Film Career of Walter Niebuhr, "William G. Chrystal, *Niebuhr Studies*, 128. In an interview with *Filmfreund* Vol. 27, no. 4, Niebuhr indicates he started ACC with Lucius Henderson. Henderson was an American actor and director whose film credits include the 1923 film, *Toilers of the Sea*, on which Niebuhr worked.

41. Ibid., 128–129, Citing the American Institute Online Film Catalog.

42. Ibid., 12–130.

43. Ibid., 132–138.

Edwin F. Weigle/Albert K. Dawson

44. Ibid., 140–145.

45. http://ancestry.com , U. S. World War II Draft Registration Cards, 1942 [database on line], Provo, Utah, USA; 2007; Faith J. Hasler, granddaughter of Edwin F. Weigle, telephone conversation, 4 June 2010; *Who's Who in Chicago and Vicinity* (enlarged to include the State of Illinois) (Chicago: A. N. Marquis Company, 1941), 881.

46. "War Romance: Battle Line Photographer Wins Highland Park Girl", *Chicago Daily Tribune* (16 September 1919): 6.

47. Joseph Medill Patterson, letter of understanding, 19 July 1920, Joseph Medill Patterson Collection, Donnelley Library.

48. Mrs. Edwin F. Weigle [Florence M. Weigle], *Ireland as It Is Today*, (1920) 30. Irish-born Daniel Mannix was the Archbishop of Melbourne, Australia, who by 1920 was admired by Irish Catholics and despised by Protestants. Among other things, he had advocated that Australia stay out of England's fight in World War I. Ballymacarret remains a hot spot in Belfast and was the site of some vicious fighting in the 1970s.

49. "Tribune Film on Ireland Thrills Censor Board", *Chicago Daily Tribune* (15 December 1920): 16.

50. "Ireland in Revolt", *Variety* (14 January 1921).

51. Kenan Heise, Obituary of Hubert N. Kelley, *Chicago Tribune* (6 December 1991): 17.

52. Lloyd Wendt, *Chicago Tribune* (Chicago: Rand McNally, 1979), 419.

53. *Chicago Sunday Tribune* (26 December 1915): VII, 3; *Chicago Daily Tribune* (3 January 1916): 17.

54. *New York Evening Telegram* (15 April 1922): 8.

Frank E. Kleinschmidt

55. Oesterreichisches Staatsarchiv. *Kriegsarchiv, Armeeoberkommando 1914–1918, Kriegspressequartier. Akten Franz E. Kleinschmidt.* File 20561 – Message to Military High Command, 15 December 1915. Quote translated from German.

56. Footage *War on Three Fronts*, part 4, 1916.

57. *Moving Picture World* (2 September 1916): 1527; *Los Angeles Times* (12 August 1916): II3; *Riverside Enterprise* (15 September 1916): 2; Postcard Frank Kleinschmidt to Hattie Kaufmann, sent from San Francisco on 25 July 1916: "Have been to Los Angeles and back".

58. "Buys Rights on Kleinschmidt Films", *Moving Picture World* (23 December 1916): 1844. The local exhibition in Seattle, Washington, was accompanied by much publicity. See: Advertisement "War on Three Fronts – Story of a Big Deal", *Seattle Daily Times* (26 November 1916): 5.

59. "U.S. Betrays Christ for Gain in Ignoring War", *Denver Post* (11 December 1916): 5. Kleinschmidt's critical remarks on the *Lusitania* were justified. The ship was stacked with ammunition, all of it contraband. Apart from loaded shrapnel shells, it carried over 4 million rounds of .303 Remington bullets, representing more than 10 tons of explosives. See: Colin Simpson, *Lusitania* (London: Penguin Books 1983), 104–109.

60. Review "War on Three Fronts", *Moving Picture World* (21 April 1917): 448. Review "The War on Three Fronts", *Variety* (6 April 1917): 24. See also *Motography* (28 April 1917): 903. Only the trade paper *Billboard* in its review on 14 April 1917 took a positive approach and called the movie not pro-German and merely an exposition of military tactics.

61. NARA, case file Kleinschmidt, report agent Petrovitsky, 26 February 1917.

62. "Praises Germans in Edison's Plant", *New York Times* (13 June 1917): 8.

63. NARA, case file Kleinschmidt, telegram quoted in report by agent Berkey, 15 August 1917.

64. NARA, Military Intelligence Division, case file 10080-750. F.E. Kleinschmidt. Reports by agent Taylor, 4 September 1917 and 16 November 1917.

65. NARA, case file Kleinschmidt, letter Lt. Colonel Van Deman to Chief Bielaski, 30 October 1917. See also Colonel

Arnold's note to Van Deman, dated 24 October 1917, in Kleinschmidt's case file from the Military Intelligence records. Van Deman was instrumental in setting up a professional military intelligence department, modelled on the example of the British. Colonel Arnold was Henry "HAP" Arnold, first man in his class at West Point to make this rank. In 1942, he was promoted to Commanding General of the U.S. Army Air Force. Under his personal supervision Arnold's B-29s bombed Hiroshima and Nagasaki.

66.   "Austrian Arrested and Weapons Found", *New York Times* (25 November 1917): 7. The news on Kleinschmidt's arrest was wired by the Associated Press on the night of 24 November. Reports in the regular newspapers and in the film trade press clearly state that he was arrested on a technical charge. A letter by Division Superintendent Offley to Chief Bielaski, dated 28 November 1917, states Kleinschmidt was under surveillance at the request of either the Military or the Naval Intelligence Service as a German suspect. The Kleinschmidt files demonstrate that U.S. government agencies were not always working together on the same line in these surveillance tasks. This is also evident from the case file on Kleinschmidt by the U.S. Military Intelligence. At the request of the State Department, the Military Intelligence Division in January 1918 reported on Kleinschmidt's arrest. They could only find a file on another German-American suspect, Karl R. Klienschmidt, who was arrested on the same charge of having a gun in his possession. Chief Van Deman concluded that the two men probably were confused by the informant. But Tunney's men may also have arrested the wrong Kleinschmidt on that fateful day. The news story by the Associated Press in the Military Intelligence files has a disturbing handwritten note: "Apparently confused with Karl R.".

67.   NARA, Military Intelligence Division, case file 10080-750, F.E. Kleinschmidt. Letter National Board of Review Motion Pictures on *War on Three Fronts* to Military Chief of Staff, 29 December 1917.

68.   D.W. Griffith when working on *Hearts of the World* was offered a print of Kleinschmidt's film by W.H. Clune who had exhibited the movie in Los Angeles. Griffith's attorney advised him not to pay for it, because Clune did not control any film rights. He also asked Griffith to consider the negative publicity that might occur as a result of using Kleinschmidt's war picture. A letter by the Captain to Griffith, written on 26 December 1918, shows that Griffith only used a couple of shots from *War on Three Fronts*. Kleinschmidt was clearly disappointed Griffith hadn't used more.

69.   Information on Esther Fillian, supplied by Holly Scott on 4 August 2011. California Death Certificate Extract #5376 on Frank Emil Kleinschmidt, supplied by the Margaret Herrick Library to the authors on 5 November 2011.

70.   In the family papers collected by Ruth Sarrett is an interesting list of films, dated 16 December 1939, mentioning all movies produced by Frank Kleinschmidt. This document shows that he made more movies than are mentioned in the catalogue of the American Film Institute.

71.   Letter from Frank Kleinschmidt to his niece Minnie Louise Bismarck, 16 December 1939. Family papers Ruth Sarrett.

72.   *Newsclips from Various Newsreels, no. 9*, AFI/Rubin Collection, FEB1156. Library of Congress, Motion Picture, Broadcasting and Recorded Sound Division, Washington DC.

73.   Philip W. Stewart, *Battlefilm: U. S. Army Signal Corps Motion Pictures of the Great War* (2nd edn) (Crestview, Florida: PMS Press, 2010).

74.   *Bakersfield Californian*, 12 January 1933, 10; *Film Daily* (20 March 1934): 10; *Film Daily* (6 May 1933): 4.

Colour plates

Fig. 1. Uncle Sam filming world leaders. An injured Dove of Peace looks on. Poster © 1914,
New Electro Corporation.
[Courtesy Library of Congress.]

Fig. 2a. Picture postcard sent by Albert Dawson to a friend in Vincennes. His handwritten note says: "Antwerp last week. Through Belgium in a military auto." Dawson is in the back seat at the right. Dated Berlin, 24 February 1915.
[Private collection of the authors.]

Fig. 2b. Reverse side of Dawson's picture postcard, February 1915.

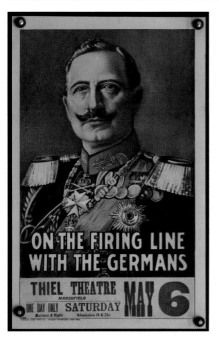

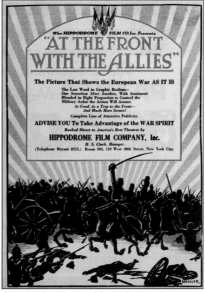

Fig. 4. The Charge of the Light Brigades, 1916.
Some American movie companies advertised their
war films in a highly misleading way.
Reproduction Motion Picture News, 25
March 1916.

Fig. 3. On the Firing Line with the Germans poster. The
Thiel Theatre in Marshfield, Wisconsin, only opened in
April of 1916. In 1890, two-thirds of the townspeople were
of German ancestry and one of the two local newspapers,
Die Demokrat, was published in German. There was
much pro-German feeling during the World War.
[Courtesy Hershenson-Allen Archive (eMoviePoster.com).]

Fig. 6. Press card Nelson E. Edwards for Fox News,
1918–1919. [Courtesy Wiegman family.]

Fig. 5. The Hearst newsreel organization promotes their
cameramen. Moving Picture World, 17 June 1916.

295

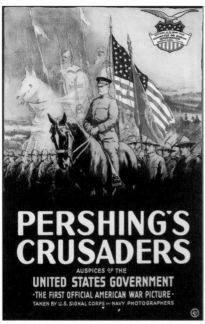

Fig. 7. Poster for America's first official war feature film, Pershing's Crusaders *(1918). [Courtesy Library of Congress.]*

Fig. 8. Official poster for CPI's second war feature film, America's Answer. *[Courtesy Library of Congress.]*

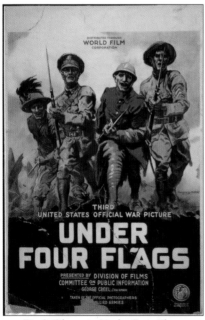

Fig. 9. Film poster Under Four Flags. *[Courtesy Library of Congress.]*

Fig. 10. Lobby poster for official war pictures by the Committee on Public Information, 1917–1918. [Courtesy Library of Congress.]

Acknowledgements

Albert Dawson

The story on Albert Dawson is the result of input by many people over many years. Kevin Brownlow lit the first spark in 1979 with his magnificent book *The War, the West and The Wilderness*. His chapter on the American cameramen of World War I revealed to us the unsearched wealth of material on this subject both in the United States and in Europe. Armin Loacker of the Austrian Film Archives sent invaluable information on cameraman Hans Theyer. The Austrian State Archives made available the Dawson file at the k.u.k. Kriegspressequartier. Further details on Dawson's photographic work in Germany were revealed at the Federal and Foreign Office Archives in Berlin in the autumn of 2012. Special thanks also to: Doug Carroll, Richard Day and Norbert Brown (Vincennes), Brian Spangle at the Knox County Public Library, Richard King at Vincennes University Library, the New York Public Library, the German Society of Pennsylvania, Anton Holzer and Sema Colpan (Vienna), George Bonsall, Niels Lange and Alex Klomp (Utrecht), David Wiener, Lloyd Billingsley, the Buffalo and Erie County Library, the Margaret Herrick Library in Los Angeles, the National Archives, the Prints and Photographs Division of the Library of Congress, and George Willeman and Rosemary Hanes at the Library of Congress in Culpeper, Virginia and Washington, DC, respectively. Last but not least, this book wouldn't have been possible without the support by the Dawson family: his grandchildren, his late nephew August Schultheis, his late niece Lida Joice, his relatives Jacqueline Reed Bever Balogh and Brian Reed, Rose Ann Walter's children – Ben Walter and particularly Martin Walter who shared with us his impressive knowledge and research records on the Dawson family background.

Wilbur Durborough

First and foremost, we would like to thank the Durborough family for sharing photos and information, especially the late Bea Durborough, who trusted Jim Castellan with Durborough's manuscript; Brian Durborough, who with family support generously donated Durborough's manuscript to the Library of Congress; William Durborough and granddaughter Mary Herbert. Next are the many archivists and reference librarians without whose help and advice we could never have learned so much about Wilbur H. Durborough and his life, especially the staffs at the Library of Congress (with special thanks for Dave Reese assisting Jim's inspection and transcription of the copyright paper rolls in the Moving Images Section and George Willeman at the NAVCC in Culpeper for assistance with obtaining frame images), the National Archives and Records Administration, the Newberry Library (with special note of those who organize and support its comprehensive Chicago newspaper and journalist manuscript collections) and the Chicago History Museum Research Center. Dr. Gerhard Keiper at the Auswärtiges

Amt Politisches Archiv in Berlin was very helpful in locating Durborough and other material held there and in other German collections. Thanks to Florian Bielefeld, whose research assistance and translations were indispensable for making Jim's brief visit in Germany so productive, and Concept2, Morrisville, VT, for partially funding this trip. Dale Zacher provided insights about the Scripps organization and the NEA and provided comments on an early draft. Ron van Dopperen also reviewed and constructively commented on an earlier draft. We thank Phoebe Isales helped by her husband Ramon and daughter Lydia Isales for providing Spanish translations and Tom and Bonnie Bethea for timely Chicago newspaper research. Lastly, Jim thanks his family and friends, especially Cornelia Haselberger, for encouragement and support over the years for his many research trips, extending warm hospitality during his travels with special note of John & Anne Tkacik, R.I.P.; Jamie & Mollie Tkacik and Joan Castellan for innumerable and always pleasant visits; Ron wants to thank Luis Anaya for his great Spanish translations, and we all want to thank William G. Chrystal who provided us with his unpublished manuscript on Niebuhr's film career, as well as a great photograph of Durborough and the Stutz Bearcat filled with correspondents.

Nelson Edwards

The authors would like to thank, as always, the Library of Congress, in particular the Periodicals Division; Robin Cookson of the National Archive II at College Park, MD, for his efforts to find several needles in the haystack; the New York Public Library; the Swarthmore College Peace Collection, Swarthmore, PA.; The Maryland Room of the Enoch Pratt Library in Baltimore, Maryland; William H. Fisk III of Easton, Pa.; Kia Afra for information on Hearst-Selig Newsreel papers; the Fox Newsreel Collection at the University of South Carolina. Although not visited specifically for this article, the hospitality of this latter archive in several past visits has borne fruit. The authors would also like especially to thank Patricia Wiegman, Nelson Edwards' daughter, her husband David J. Wiegman and their son Nelson. Nelson Edwards and the Wiegmans never threw anything away; their boxes of photographs and records as well as their hospitality and helpfulness have been invaluable.

Walter Niebuhr

We want to thank first and last William G. Chrystal, Niebuhr scholar, for his great help in and granting us access to his research. We and he both feel that there is a book on Walter Niebuhr waiting to be written.

Donald Thompson

Donald Thompson has been a source of fascination for the writers ever since one noticed his *Somewhere in France* at the Library of Congress and his name first appeared in Kevin Brownlow's *The War, the West and the Wilderness*. Thompson later received attention from David Mould who wrote an article on him for the Kansas State Historical Society (1982). Since then new information on Thompson's life and work has come to light, both from the film trade press, the film archives as well as two trips to Topeka in 2013, which merits an updated analysis. We would like to thank Kevin Brownlow, David Mould and Gerry Veeder for introducing Donald Thompson to the public. We are also greatly indebted to the Kansas Historical Museum and the Topeka and Shawnee County Public

Library, both in Topeka, Kansas, as well as the National Archives, Kansas City, Central Plains Division.

Ansel Wallace

We thank Don and Kathy Koepp, for their information on the Wallace family; Sandra Burkhart Mutchler; Alenka Satler for her translation of an article on Wallace and Eddie Hatrick which made its way to Slovenia; the Library of Congress, M/B/RS Division, P&P Division, Serials Division; National Archives, Washington, DC, and College Park, MD,; Indiana Historical Society, Indianapolis, IN; University of Southern Indiana Archive & Special Collections, Evansville, IN; John E. Allen Collection; Boston Public Library, Microtext Reference Division; Kevin Wadzinski of the St. Joseph County Public Library, South Bend, IN; the Willard Library, Evansville, IN; the Bundesarchiv in Berlin and Annegret Wilke of the Auswärtiges Amt, Politisches Archiv, also in Berlin.

Frank Kleinschmidt

We would like to thank Kevin Brownlow for sharing his research notes on the Captain; David Shepard; Ron Kerber at John E. Allen for his background information on the footage of *War on Three Fronts*; the staff of the Austrian State Archives at Vienna; the National Archives in Washington, D.C.; Zoran Sinobad, reference librarian in the M/B/RS Division and the Geography and Map division at the Library of Congress; Wichita State University Libraries; the Margaret Herrick Library in Los Angeles, California; the Army Intelligence Library at Fort Huachuca, Arizona; the University Library in Amsterdam and Holly Scott. The writers would like especially to thank Ruth Sarrett, great granddaughter of Captain Kleinschmidt's sister Wilhelmina, for providing us with some impressive research documents on her ancestors.

Edwin F. Weigle

We want to express our deep thanks to Kim Tomadjoglou, Rosemary Hanes, Zoran Sinobad, George Willeman, and Josie Walters-Johnson in the M/B/RS Division, the Prints and Photographs Division and the Photo Duplication Section of the Library of Congress; The Austrian State Archives in Vienna; The National Archives; Arthur Miller at the Donnelly Library, Lake Forest, Illinois; The Military History Institute, Carlisle, Pennsylvania; Alderman Library, University of Virginia; The Newberry Library in Chicago; The Chicago Historical Society; St. Gregory's Episcopal Church in Deerfield, Illinois; Faith K. Hasler, Stratford Dick, and the rest of the family of Edwin F. Weigle; and Margaret Graham, ace IT person in the Graham family.

* * *

All the authors would like to thank Patrick Loughney, formerly of the Library of Congress, who broached the whole subject of this book with the Cineteca and made it a reality.

We all would like to heartily thank our long-suffering families, who have seen us go into countless trances at the dinner table or at the computer, completely oblivious to everything, and have taken trips not to Hawaii or the Canary Islands, but to dusty archives in strange cities. God bless you all.

Suggestions for further reading

Most books and articles published on contemporary First World War films released in the United States focus attention on drama productions, not documentary film. This may very well have been because films such as Charlie Chaplin's *Shoulder Arms* (1918) were extremely popular at the time and received wide attention in the trade papers and popular magazines. We are therefore listing a few publications for readers who would like to know more on World War I and documentary films from this period.

There are in fact very few core books on this subject. The fisherman is in uncharted waters. Most histories, especially the one-volume histories, are too broad and vague to be of much help in tracing the ins and outs of obscure campaigns, or the cinematographer's place in them. One is better off with the *Times* (London or New York) as well as contemporary periodicals, or contemporary histories of campaigns. A series we found very useful several times was *The Story of the Great War*, published by *Collier's*, a multi-volume history of the war from 1914–1916. It was particularly good on the campaigns on the eastern front, which tend to get ignored in later books. The *Encyclopedia Britannica* (12th edition, 1922) was also extremely useful.

Here is a list of sources to which we found ourselves continually returning:

American Film Institute Catalog: Feature Films, 1911–1920. Berkeley, Los Angeles, London: University of California Press, 1988.

> In the case of these WWI documentary films, there are a fair amount of inaccuracies in the catalogue due the arbitrary way that distributors and producers changed titles when the films were released, but still an invaluable source for World War I films and the period in general.

Brownlow, Kevin. *The War, the West and the Wilderness*, London/New York: Alfred A. Knopf 1979.

> Brownlow's study is a must-read for anyone interested in the history of factual films in the silent era. Extremely well illustrated and documented, this magnificent book also draws on many interviews with actors, producers and cinematographers.

Campbell, Craig W. *Reel America and World War I*, Jefferson, N.C./London: McFarland & Company 1985.

> Basically a filmography, *Reel America* documents numerous contemporary war films that

were shown in America between 1914 and 1918 with a brief synopsis and notes on production. The information on documentary films is scant and mostly based on research in the trade papers.

Carmichael, Jane, *First World War Photographers.* London/New York: Routledge 1989.

Carmichael's book examines still photographers from Britain and has a wonderful collection of photographs from the Imperial War Museum in London. There is a short segment on Ariel Varges in this study.

DeBauche, Leslie Midkiff, *Reel Patriotism. The Movies and World War I.* Madison: The University of Wisconsin Press 1997.

Mixing film history with social history, *Reel Patriotism* examines the role played by the American film industry during World War I. Practically all films described in this book are drama feature productions.

Dopperen, Ron van and Cooper C. Graham, *Shooting the Great War: Albert Dawson and the American Correspondent Film Company, 1914–1918.* Charleston, SC: CreateSpace 2013.

Based on previous articles in *Film History* journal and additional research in the German archives, the authors describe Dawson's adventures as a war photographer at the front, as well as how his pictures were used for propaganda in the United States.

Fielding, Raymond, *The American Newsreel, 1911–1967.* Norman: University of Oklahoma Press 1972.

Professor Fielding's book still is the standard-setting study on this subject. An extended edition appeared in 2006.

Mould, David, "Donald Thompson: Photographer at War", *Kansas History. A Journal of the Central Plain* 5, Autumn 1982: 154–167.

Mould's description of Thompson's life and work draws heavily on newspaper reports which sometimes lack credibility because of Thompson's natural tendency for self-promotion. The article, as well as Mould's thesis on contemporary American news films, is one of the few studies on this particular subject.

Spears, Jack. *Hollywood: The Golden Era.* Cranbury, NJ: A.S. Barnes & Co. 1971.

Based on a series of articles for *Films in Review*, Spears in one chapter describes and reviews many contemporary World War I films that were shown on the American screen.

Ward, Larry Wayne. *The Motion Picture Goes to War: The U.S. Government Film Effort during World War I.* Ann Arbor: UMI Research Press, 1985)

A well-researched examination of the film program by the Committee on Public Information in 1917–1918

A group of books that are not about film *per se*, but are extremely useful on giving background on the Great War, the life of war correspondents, journalism during the period, and some of the various theaters, especially on the little-covered eastern front.

De Beaufort, J.M. *Behind the German Veil: The Record of a Journalistic War Pilgrimage.* London: Hutchinson and Co., 1917.

The British version is preferable to the American one because of its reference to A. E. Wallace. De Beaufort's book is far from totally accurate, but he did not lie about everything and in many ways, his book is well-written and informative.

Fox, Edward Lyell, *Behind the Scenes in Warring Germany*. New York: McBride, Nast and Company 1915.

Gerard, James W., *My Four Years in Germany*. London, New York: Hodder and Stoughton, 1917.

Knightley, Phillip, *The First Casualty*, Revised Edition. London and Baltimore: Johns Hopkins University Press, 1975, Revised Edition 2000.

Powell, E. Alexander, *Fighting in Flanders*. New York, Charles Scribner's sons, 1914.

Pizzitola, Louis, *Hearst over Hollywood: Power, Passion and Propaganda in the Movies*. New York: Columbia University Press, 2002.

Shepherd, William G., *Confessions of a War Correspondent*. New York and London: Harper and Brothers, 1916.

Stone, Norman, *The Eastern Front*. London: Penguin Global, 1974.

Tunstall, Graydon A., *Blood on the Snow*. Lawrence (Kansas): University Press of Kansas, c2010.

Wendt, Lloyd, *The Chicago Tribune: the Rise of a Great American Newspaper*. Chicago: Rand McNally, 1979.

Here is also a group of books or manuscripts that were written by the cinematographers themselves.

Dawson, Albert K., "Die Reise Nach Ivangorod", *Deutsch-Amerika*, January–February 1917. [Fragments from Dawson's war diary, translated into German, on his film work at the eastern front, July–August 1915].

Durborough, Wilbur F., "Durborough Draft Manuscript I"(DDM1). Library of Congress, Manuscripts Division. Washington, DC.

Durborough, Wilbur F., "Durborough Draft Manuscript II"(DDM2). Library of Congress, Manuscripts Division. Washington, DC.

Thompson, Donald C., *Bloodstained Russia*. New York: Leslie-Judge Company, 1918.

Thompson, Donald C., *Donald Thompson in Russia*. New York: The Century Company, 1918.

Thompson, Donald C., *From Czar to Kaiser*. Garden City (New York) Doubleday, Page and Company, 1918.

Weigle, Edwin F., *My Experiences on the Belgian Battlefields*. Chicago: Hamming Publishing Company, 1914.

Weigle, Edwin F., *On Four Battle Fronts with the German Army*. [Chicago: Chicago Tribune, 1915].

Weigle, Edwin F., "The German Side of the War". Theater Program. Author Graham's private collection.

Weigle. Florence M. (Mrs. Edwin F. Weigle), *Ireland as It Is Today*. [no publishing data], 1920. Available at the Library of Congress, Washington, DC.

And always the film trade papers:

Moving Picture World

Motion Picture News

Index